Enterprise Java™ Development on a Budget: Leveraging Java Open Source Technologies

BRIAN SAM-BODDEN AND CHRISTOPHER JUDD

Apress™

Enterprise Java™ Development on a Budget: Leveraging Java Open Source Technologies
Copyright © 2004 by Brian Sam-Bodden and Christopher Judd

ISBN-13 (paperback): 978-1-59059-125-3
ISBN-13 (electronic): 978-1-4302-0682-8

Printed and bound in the United States of America (POD)

Trademarked names may appear in this book. Rather than use a trademark symbol with every occurrence of a trademarked name, we use the names only in an editorial fashion and to the benefit of the trademark owner, with no intention of infringement of the trademark.

Java™ and all Java-based marks are trademarks or registered trademarks of Sun Microsystems, Inc., in the United States and other countries. Apress, Inc., is not affiliated with Sun Microsystems, Inc., and this book was written without endorsement from Sun Microsystems, Inc.

Technical Reviewer: Jeff Linwood

Editorial Board: Steve Anglin, Dan Appleman, Gary Cornell, James Cox, Tony Davis, Chris Mills, Dominic Shakeshaft, Jim Sumser, Karen Watterson, John Zukowski

Project Manager: Sofia Marchant

Copy Manager: Nicole LeClerc

Copy Editor: Mark Nigara

Production Manager: Kari Brooks

Production Editor: Janet Vail

Compositor: Susan Glinert

Proofreader: Linda Seifert

Indexer: Rebecca Plunkett

Artist: Kinetic Publishing Services, LLC

Cover Designer: Kurt Krames

Manufacturing Manager: Tom Debolski

Distributed to the book trade in the United States by Springer-Verlag New York, Inc., 233 Spring Street, 6th floor, New York, NY 10013 and outside the United States by Springer-Verlag GmbH & Co. KG, Tiergartenstr. 17, 69112 Heidelberg, Germany.

In the United States: phone 1-800-SPRINGER, e-mail orders@springer-ny.com, or visit http://www.springer-ny.com. Outside the United States: fax +49 6221 345229, e-mail orders@springer.de, or visit http://www.springer.de.

For information on translations, please contact Apress directly at 2855 Telegraph Avenue, Suite 600, Berkeley, CA 94705. Phone 510-549-5930, fax 510-549-5939, e-mail info@apress.com, or visit http://www.apress.com.

The source code for this book is available to readers at http://www.apress.com in the Downloads section.

To the memory of my father Gilberto,
To the courage of my mother Arlene,
To the love of my sisters Karen and Krystel,
To my "Tia" Donna,
To my wife and best friend Anne,
And to my baby boy Michael.
—Brian

To my supportive wife and best friend Sue,
To all the individuals and organizations who have contributed
their time, talents, and treasures to Open Source,
And to my Heavenly Father for all the blessings
he has bestowed upon me.
—Chris

Contents at a Glance

Contents

Foreword

J2EE DEVELOPMENT IS HARD. I've been developing with Java for the past six years, and there are areas of the enormous API that I haven't touched. J2EE covers security, distributed transactions, persistence, messaging, web services, interoperability, and much, much more. Enterprise Java development doesn't mean coding only with this API, but rather involves the entire suite of Java editions. J2EE layers on top of the standard edition (J2SE). And to make your head spin even further, J2ME entered the rapidly growing mobile world.

To exacerbate matters, our industry still reels from the great .com shakeout. Like many of you, I experienced the joy of being dot bombed…*twice*. We rise from the ashes to contend with more complexity and fewer resources than ever. Our teams are smaller and budgets are tighter. Failure is not an option. Do not despair, however.

In fact, times have never been better! Smaller teams allow us to act and react more quickly. Attention to fiscal responsibility means that we focus on client satisfaction and quality workmanship. From our need to simplify, the agile methodologies speak to us at an instinctive level. "The hard and stiff will be broken. The soft and supple will prevail."[1] We create *soft*ware. As such, it is malleable. Refactoring keeps code clean as requirements change. As code evolves, keeping top-notch quality demands that we test. Testing addresses complexity, partly. We can focus on a single unit at a time, test it thoroughly, and build upon it with confidence.

Kent Beck said, "Any program feature without an automated test simply doesn't exist," which speaks to the importance of confidence and another facet, automation.[2] Repetitive tasks are vital, such as a heart beating. Such repetitive tasks, though, should be effortless. The failure of such tasks elicits grave concern. Effortless, yet unmistakably vital—otherwise the complexity would overwhelm us and suffocate our projects.

Open Source factors into both the testing and automation realms of Java development. JUnit and Ant are the de facto standards, and are built into all modern development environments. These projects, and the others discussed in this book such as Struts, Hibernate, and XDoclet represent more than just free software to use. Communities are thriving around these projects, and you benefit from the collective contributions of individuals around the world. Besides addressing the problems of a limited budget, Open Source addresses the complexity and quality

---

1. *Tao Te Ching.*
2. Beck, Kent. *Extreme Programming Explained: Embrace Change* (Addison-Wesley, 1999) p. 57.

issues from several angles. Common problems generally have open source alternatives; avoid the reinvention of the wheel and concentrate on adding business value, not plumbing. Many Open Source projects have comprehensive test suites, thereby relieving you of reliability concerns. And when the inevitable bug appears in an Open Source library, or a need for enhancement, robust test suites make opening the hood a real joy. Tune in to the mailing lists, and other avenues of collaboration including wikis and blogs, of the Open Source projects you leverage. It's commonplace that questions are answered within minutes, putting to shame most commercial support contracts.

All of this philosophizing leaves us wondering what to do next. We have real work to do, and real deadlines to meet. Deriving from a Greek word meaning "to do," *pragmatic* is what we must be. As pragmatic programmers, books are a fundamental part of our craft. The book you're holding contains many gems of wisdom gleaned from hard work. There's no substitute for experience, but it would be foolish not to learn from the experiences of others. I prefer practical examples and the voice of experience on technical topics, and this book provides both. Chris and Brian have made one of life's greatest sacrifices, the authoring of a book. I commend them for their effort, and applaud them for the quality.

—Erik Hatcher
Coauthor of *Java Development with Ant* (Manning 2003) and *Lucene in Action* (forthcoming from Manning 2004)
Member, Apache Software Foundation
Committer, Ant, XDoclet, Lucene, and Tapestry

About the Authors

Brian Sam-Bodden has been working with object technologies for the last nine years with a strong emphasis on the Java platform. He holds dual bachelor degrees from Ohio Wesleyan University in computer science and physics. He currently serves as president and chief software architect for Integrallis Software, LLC (http://www.integrallis.com). He has worked as an architect, developer, mentor, and trainer for several Fortune 500 companies in industries such as taxes, insurance, retail sciences, telecommunications, distribution, banking, finance, aviation, and scientific data management. As an independent consultant, Brian has promoted the use of Open Source in the industry by educating his clients on the cost benefit and productivity gains achieved by it. He is a Sun Certified Java programmer, developer, and architect. Brian is a frequent speaker at Java user groups and at conferences throughout the country. You can contact him at bsbodden@integrallis.com.

Christopher Judd is the president and primary consultant for Judd Solutions, LLC (http://www.juddsolutions.com), and is an international speaker, Open Source evangelist, Central Ohio Java Users Group (http://www.cojug.org) board member and JBuilder-certified developer and instructor. He has spent the last nine years developing software in the insurance, retail, government, manufacturing, service, and transportation industries. His current focus is consulting, mentoring, and training with Java, J2EE, J2ME, web services, and related technologies. He also holds a bachelor's degree from Ashland University in computer information systems with minors in accounting and finance. You can contact Chris at cjudd@juddsolutions.com.

About the Technical Reviewer

Jeff Linwood is a software developer and consultant for the Gossamer Group, LLC in Austin, TX. As a consultant, he has designed and developed J2EE content management solutions for several Fortune 500 companies. Jeff is the coauthor of the book *Professional Struts Applications: Building Web Sites with Struts, Object-Relational Bridge, Lucene, and Velocity* (Apress 2003), and has written articles for JavaWorld (http://www.javaworld.com/) and *Dr. Dobb's Journal.*

Acknowledgments

THIS BOOK HAS BEEN a long time coming and, like an Open Source project, is the labor of many. It would not be in your hands without the kind help of many people.

We wish to extend our gratitude to the hardworking folks at Apress, including Jason Gilmore for getting us started down the path of authorship, our editors John Zukowski, Craig Berry, and Steve Anglin, all of whom contributed to shape the big picture of what this book was to become. A million thanks to the team that molded our technology ramblings into a coherent body of work: our tireless and forgiving project manager Sofia Marchant, our copy editor Mark Nigara, our production editor Janet Vail, and our copy manager Nicole LeClerc. Thanks also to Bobby Harris and Rob Warner, the authors of *The Definitive Guide to SWT and JFace* (forthcoming from Apress 2004), for their help.

As consultants we're engaged in an endless cycle of learning and teaching and without the input and opinions of numerous colleagues who have reviewed and engaged in dialogue with us this work would not be what it is. We wish to thank Jeff Linwood, our technical reviewer for sticking with us for what must have seemed like an eternity. We also wish to thank some of the informal reviewers who took time out of their busy lives to comb through our work, including Erik Hatcher, Craig Asplund, Chris Asplund, David Vu, Bret McGee, Matt Arnett, and Tim Hatfield.

While writing this book, we experienced one of the aspects of Open Source that you would never get from a commercial vendor: free help unencumbered from the greed of profit. We wish to thank many of the members of the Open Source community for their assistance, including Per Nyfelt, Leo Mekenkamp, Thomas Mahler, Robert Muir Coup, Armin Waibel, Thomas Dudziak, Klaus Wuestefeld, Michael Glogl, and Aleksey Aristov.

Finally, we want to thank you the reader, for without you this book would be a pointless exercise.

Preface

TODAY THE JAVA 2 PLATFORM, Enterprise Edition (J2EE) is the most complete and effective platform for enterprise development. J2EE unifies and embodies the knowledge gained from building up-to-date, multitier applications, and provides this knowledge as a standardized set of modular components and services. We believe that J2EE simplifies many aspects of enterprise computing, but it is by no means a simple technology to master. The technology choices, techniques, APIs, and patterns can be overwhelming.

Open Source has had a profound effect on the Java community. As consultants, we know that every new assignment brings new challenges. During our day-to-day work we've found Open Source to be invaluable for simplifying the work of our teams and helping us to concentrate on what really matters.

Enterprise Java Development on a Budget: Leveraging Java Open Source Technologies is a book for Java professionals who look beyond the tools placed in their hands by their employers. It's a book for those trailblazers who time and again tell their colleagues, "I've been playing with this tool…and I think this could really make our lives easier." This book compiles the experiences of two seasoned Java developers and gives the reader a roadmap of best practices and Open Source tools that will support those practices. Open Source is more than just free software; it's a force that's shaping the way we think about software and how software is made. Open Source and Java are a perfect combination to tackle the challenges of enterprise development with an open, extensible, nonproprietary arsenal that reflects the best that the industry has to offer.

What This Book Is About

This book is about Open Source in the world of J2EE development and how it can give you choices to replace or enhance what is commercially available. The book covers tools and projects that encompass many aspects of building an enterprise application, from development and testing to deployment. We focused on delivering real code for real programmers, but wanted to give you a sound foundation on the topics covered as well.

What This Book Is Not

This book isn't another rehash of online documentation and it doesn't cover every esoteric feature of the tools used. Instead it's an example of how to use Open Source tools in synergy while developing a real application. Only relevant features are covered and whenever there's a topic or feature that we don't cover, we attempt to point you in the right direction so that you can expand your knowledge.

Who Should Read This Book

This book is aimed at moderately experienced Java developers who have an intermediate knowledge of J2EE, and who are looking to learn how to maximize their productivity. Additionally, this book offers readers a guide to explore some of the roads less traveled when it comes to enterprise Java development.

Guide for Readers

Like the software covered in this book, the book itself was written in an agile fashion, with many rounds of refactoring involved. One of the consequences of agile development and XP is that software is no longer built in a linear or waterfall fashion, yet books have to be clearly divided into chapters. We attempted to divide the book into chapters so that each chapter deals with an aspect of the design and development of the application as it relates to a specific tool or the specific framework being used. In areas of the application where there may be implementation choices in terms of which Open Source project to use, we'll show one or more possible paths and explain why, in the context of the application, we chose one tool vs. a similar one. The book is composed of ten chapters.

- **Chapter 1:** This chapter begins by briefly talking about Open Source and Java and then moves to explain the case study system that you'll be constructing throughout the rest of the book.

- **Chapter 2:** This chapter covers the UML design tool ArgoUML and introduces some of the techniques used to produce the design of the case study application.

- **Chapter 3:** This chapter sets out to create a solid Ant-based build system that will be used in the rest of the book. This chapter offers "best practices" and a collection of Ant-based tools that can improve your builds.

- **Chapter 4:** This chapter offers a concise look at testing in J2EE by introducing JUnit, Cactus, and DBUnit testing.

- **Chapter 5:** This chapter sets out to build the business tier of the case study application using EJBs on JBoss. This chapter sets the stage for subsequent chapters by showing alternative ways to tackle different tiers of the application.

- **Chapter 6:** This chapter covers the different choices available to store enterprise data in J2EE. From relational databases to object-oriented databases, in this chapter you'll learn how to integrate and work with data storage technologies.

- **Chapter 7:** This chapter covers object-relational mapping tools with OJB and Hibernate and gives you an introduction to the sometimes frustrating task of mapping objects to relational databases.

- **Chapter 8:** This chapter shows how to use the Struts and Tiles frameworks to create the web tier of the case study application.

- **Chapter 9:** This chapter delves into web services and how you can produce and consume them in a J2EE application. A J2ME mobile client is also created to show how you can integrate different channels into a J2EE application.

- **Chapter 10:** This chapter deals with the creation of a management utility application for the case study application using the SWT/JFace user interface frameworks.

Enterprise Java developers are usually grouped into myriad categories, including architects, presentation tier developers, server-side developers, and data developers to name a few of the commonly used monikers. If you're in management or the tools that you use depend on somebody in management we strongly suggest you read Chapter 1. If you're an architect or a designer, Chapter 2 might give you some techniques that you might not have encountered before. For anybody dealing with the creation or maintenance of a build system, Chapter 3 is a must. For the server-side developer, Chapters 4 and 5 will provide a good foundation. For those involved with data, Chapters 6 and 7 deal with many of the issues you'll encounter. For those wanting to learn about presentation technologies, Chapter 8 provides a good introduction to the Struts framework. For those wanting to explore the world of Web Services as they relate to J2EE, Chapter 9 gives a good introduction to the Axis web services framework. For those looking to build a great-looking administration interface or rich UI clients, Chapter 10 provides an alternative to Swing and AWT.

Companion Website and Contact Information

The official companion website where you can get software, updates, errata, and other materials is http://www.ejdoab.com. We realize that tools evolve rapidly, especially in the Open Source arena, so we'll strive to give you tips and suggestions on this site that will keep you abreast of the major changes in any of the tools used in this book.

We also invite you to inquiry, debate, and discuss your opinions about this and any other topic at the Apress Forums located at http://forums.apress.com/.

CHAPTER 1

The Open Source
and Java Synergy

"We'll outsmart Open Source."

—Microsoft's Steve Ballmer in an interview with ZDNet[1]

DEFINING OPEN SOURCE is in the eye of the beholder; for some it means a way to develop software, but for others it means a twist on traditional business models. On a larger scale, it can be seen as a social movement. Open Source has its roots in the same spirit of cooperation that has driven computer science advances since the end of the Second World War. Projects like the Linux operating system and the Apache web server are prime examples of shared innovation and the freedom of choice that Open Source brings to the table.

Separating the hype from reality isn't easy when it comes to Open Source. Not only has it become the technological buzzword du jour, but it has also become the epicenter of a great deal of controversy: from copyright laws and intellectual property debates to freedom of speech and arguments about free-market competition. Steve Ballmer's comment only reiterates the impact that the Open Source movement has had on the business of software as a whole. When the best funded, 400-pound gorilla of proprietary software acknowledges the need to "outsmart" a "ragtag band of software geeks" (as Open Source collaborators are sometimes referred to) there is no need to emphasize that Open Source is making inroads socially, technologically, and economically.

This book is primarily about tapping into the large set of Open Source resources available to you, the developer. Particularly when it comes to the J2EE platform, Open Source is leading the pack and going beyond the confines of the specifications by providing technical innovations not seen in commercial products as well as a solid and stable infrastructure for enterprise-level applications.

The J2EE market has evolved swiftly, first by going through a phase of consolidation and now by entering a phase of commoditization. This second phase has been driven largely by the fact that in order to show value, application server vendors can no longer rely on their core application server. This has created a market of value-added offerings, particularly in the area of development tools and development

---

1. See http://zdnet.com.com/2100-1104-959112.html.

productivity. Many of the Open Source tools and frameworks showcased in this book are in this category.

Open Source is also changing the way programming is being studied in universities around the world; new generations of programmers leaving academia and entering the workplace have either used or contributed to Open Source. Students nowadays can learn by examining enterprise-level software that displays contributions from a great many sources from around the world.

At corporate IT departments worldwide, programmers are rallying behind Open Source projects like Ant, JUnit, Tomcat, and JBoss. Though the battle for the acceptance of Open Source has been largely fought at the level of the programmer and middle management, upper management, given the recent impact of Linux on corporations, is beginning to see the many advantages of Open Source, especially in the area of enterprise Java. Organizations seeking to reduce software development expenses have found that Open Source software (OSS) provides a lower cost of ownership when compared to commercial offerings, primarily because Open Source software is free, both in price and restrictions.

Official Open Source Definition

The universally accepted definition of Open Source is promoted by OSI, a non-profit corporation originally created by Bruce Perens and Eric Raymond with the sole purpose of guarding and promoting the Open Source Definition. OSI also provides a certification mark that is awarded (on request) to projects under an OSI-accepted license.

The Open Source Definition (version 1.9) defines Open Source software as software that adheres to the following list of criteria:

- **Free redistribution:** The software can be freely redistributed without requiring any royalty payments to the original authors.

- **Source code:** The software's source code should be easily obtainable in order to allow the code to evolve.

- **Derived works:** The software can be modified and the modifications must be redistributed under the same terms as the original.

- **Integrity of the author's source code:** The software's license might require that modifications are distributed as patches to some well-known base distribution. This ensures that users know the origin of the software they're using.

- **Discrimination against persons or groups:** The software license must not discriminate on the bases of national origin, race, religion, and so on. Because many countries, including the United States have export restrictions on cryptographic software, the license can warn or advise the licensees of the legal ramifications of their actions but it cannot directly enforce said restrictions.

- **Discrimination against fields of endeavor:** This prevents the license from preventing the usage of the software based on the field that it's being used in such as insurance, banking, and so on.

- **Distribution of license:** The license applies to whoever the software is distributed to without the need of any additional licenses or clauses. This prevents the software rights, as granted by the license, from being overridden by an additional license or usage clause.

- **License must not be specific to a product:** The rights granted cannot depend on the software being part of a particular distribution or configuration.

- **License must not restrict other software:** The license can't place restrictions on other software that might be distributed together.

- **License must be technology-neutral:** Acceptance of the license should not depend on specific technological means of distribution. This prevents "click wrap" in which a user must agree to the terms of a license before using or obtaining the software. This is another area of controversy, for example, the Uniform Computer Information Transactions Act (UCITA) legalizes click-wrap licenses.

 NOTE   For more information on the Open Source Definition and the Open Source Initiative visit http://www.opensource.org.

Open Source Licenses

The Open Source Definition sets guidelines for the characteristics of an Open Source licenses. There are over 37 licenses that meet the requirements for certification. Not all OSI-certified licenses apply to Java development. See Table 1-1 for a comparison of the most common Java Open Source project licenses and the JDK/JRE license.

Table 1-1. Comparison of Open Source and the JDK/JRE License

License	OSI Certified	Free	Available Source	Distributable Source
Java JDK/JRE	N	Y	Y	N
Apache Software	Y	Y	Y	Y
GNU General Public (GPL)	Y	Y	Y	Y
GNU Lesser General Public (LGPL)	Y	Y	Y	Y
BSD	Y	Y	Y	Y
Artistic	Y	Y	Y	Y
Sun Public (SPL)	Y	Y	Y	Y
IBM Public	Y	Y	Y	Y

Distributable Binary	Modifiable	URL	Projects
N	N	http://java.sun.com/j2se/1.4.1/j2sdk-1_4_1_01-license.html	JDK 1.4.1, JRE 1.4.1
Y	Y	http://www.opensource.org/licenses/apachepl.php	Ant, Tomcat, Log4j
Y	Y	http://www.fsf.org/licenses/gpl.html	jEdit, Jext
Y	Y	http://www.fsf.org/licenses/lgpl.html	JBoss
Y	Y	http://www.opensource.org/licenses/bsd-licensc.php	Castor, HSQL database
Y	Y	http://www.opensource.org/licenses/artistic-license.php	Jetty
Y	Y	http://www.opensource.org/licenses/sunpublic.php	NetBeans
Y	Y	http://www.opensource.org/licenses/ibmpl.php	Eclipse

Organizations desiring to use, embed, or distribute Open Source projects and frameworks will find most of the common Open Source license restrictions and requirements acceptable. Like commercial products, they all contain a warranty disclaimer protecting them against any liability expressed or otherwise. They also require the inclusion of the license agreement and copyright in either the documentation or an appropriate place in the running applications, such as an about box. Most of the applications also require that the source of the Open Source portion be made available when it's distributed.

The two exceptions to the acceptability of the license agreements are the GNU General Public (GPL) and the GNU Lesser General Public (LGPL). The dependency or embedding on a project or framework with a GPL license automatically relinquishes intellectual property rights by forcing the dependent code or module to also be distributed under the GPL license. This includes making the source code available. Therefore, this license wouldn't be appropriate for commercial vendors. The LGPL was developed in an effort to offer some of the rights and freedoms of the GPL yet allow commercial products to use common libraries. In the case of Java, the LGPL would allow commercial products to use JARs with the LGPL license without giving up intellectual property rights. However, if the JAR was to be incorporated into an executable (library didn't remain a separate entity) intellectual rights would be lost, the source file would be forced to be made available, and the product would have to fall under the LGPL.

Software licensing is a complicated issue. Lawyers should be consulted before using, embedding, and distributing Open Source or commercial software. Although these licenses are similar, you should make sure to read and understand the license details before incorporating the licenses into any corporate or enterprise application. Fortunately, these licenses encompass many bodies of work and should only need to be approved once. This can reduce time and expense.

Advantages and Disadvantages of Open Source

Many organizations are using Open Source projects to varying degrees in daily development. Some organizations allow Open Source to be used only during the development phases so that it doesn't affect any production environment. These organizations might use Open Source for building, unit testing, or integrated development environments (IDE). Organizations may also use Open Source libraries as a form of reuse for activities such as logging and XML parsing. Open Source application servers, web containers, and Common Object Request Broker Architecture (CORBA) servers can be used to provide the infrastructure. Organizations using Open Source are discovering there are some compelling reasons for using Open Source besides the financial benefits. Unfortunately, these organizations are also discovering that there are some disadvantages as well.

Advantages

The most obvious and compelling reason to use Open Source is the initial lower cost of ownership. Organizations are free to copy and distribute software to multiple developers and users. Consider an application with an installed base of 100 users and a 10-person development team using a $500 licensed commercial product. This would total $55,000 in expenses. Now consider the use of a competing Open Source product. The organization could immediately eliminate the large expense and increase the install base without incurring additional expenses. Other financial benefits can be realized as well. Because Open Source is free to copy, the expense of license management isn't incurred. In addition, legal departments only have to review and approve an Open Source license once for all projects using that license rather than each time for each commercial product license. Using popular Open Source projects can reduce training expenses by providing a larger resource pool. Developers can be hired from outside the company with existing knowledge of Open Source frameworks or projects. It's often difficult to hire developers that have knowledge of a proprietary commercial framework.

Industry support is another reason to consider Open Source. Many major companies such as IBM, Sun, Oracle, BEA, and Borland are using Open Source projects. These organizations have a vested interest in the project's success because their products rely on it. Contributors to the Java Open Source projects aren't necessarily the independent programmers writing code in their spare time anymore. Many of these large companies have departments dedicated to Open Source. In addition, many of the Open Source projects such as Eclipse, NetBeans, and Tomcat were initially donated by large corporate backers. Consider the use of Open Source as a means of expanding your development team to include some of the best resources from all around the world. Access to the source is an important advantage of Open Source. The source code is the only 100 percent–accurate documentation. JavaDocs, marketing material, architectural diagrams, and instructions often aren't kept up to date.

Open Source projects are more agile than commercial products in their evolution. Often Open Source projects have shorter release cycles than their commercial counterparts, if for no other reason than the fact that most projects provide nightly snapshots or direct access to the source code repository. In addition, organizations don't have to wait for a vendor's next release to get a bug fixed. Having the source code provides a means for the organization to fix the bug itself. Organizations willing to contribute to Open Source projects can also have influence on the future direction of the project. Unlike proprietary development, Open Source has the advantage of being reviewed and tested by potentially hundreds or thousands of users.

Unit and regression testing is an important part of software quality. Some Open Source projects such as the Jakarta Commons project require that JUnit tests be available and passed before version releases. Having access to JUnit tests can reduce risks by providing a means of testing new releases against the unit tests of the currently utilized release. The results of the tests can be used as a risk management tool to determine the impact of an upgrade on a project.

Open Source can contribute to an individual's career development. Developers can use the source code to learn new techniques or APIs. Open Source can also lower the barriers of entry by allowing for more economical means of evaluating new technologies. For inexperienced Java developers, contributing to an Open Source project may be a way of demonstrating knowledge to an employer or potential employer. It's common for developers to evaluate a technology and prototype proof-of-concept applications using an Open Source project as a development environment while deploying on a commercial platform for production use.

Disadvantages

Historically, Open Source projects have been documented poorly. In addition, Open Source software usually doesn't have a recognized company behind it to provide support, whether it's free or paid for. These disadvantages are changing though. A new market has grown up around Open Source to provide quality documentation and support—for a price. In addition, many of the projects have active newsgroups or forums that can be effectively used to troubleshoot an Open Source application.

Open Source projects can also be plagued with backward-compatibility problems. Open Source projects don't seem to take backward compatibility into consideration as much as commercial organizations. Yet, at the same time open source projects tend to be more daring when it comes to innovation and trying radically different ways to approach a problem.

The biggest disadvantage of Open Source is lack of marketing dollars. Often, organizations aren't aware of the existence of an Open Source project or how it might apply. Open Source projects don't have conference booths, magazine advertisements, or salespeople explaining the problems they can solve. Open Source projects also depend on the enthusiasm and number of collaborators as well as the areas that their efforts are focused on. For example, lack of documentation and administrative tools is a common complaint with regards to Open Source projects. This brings to mind the successful emergence of Open Source projects with heavy commercial backers such as the Eclipse project, which is backed by IBM and thus has very good documentation given the resources available, namely, IBM staff technical writers and editors.

Contributing to Open Source

Contributors to Open Source projects can typically be divided into particular roles. Each project refers to these roles differently. The most commonly found roles are as follows:

- **User:** Contributes defects and feature requests

- **Developer:** Contributes source code or document patches

- **Contributor:** Also called a committer, is a proven developer with direct write access to the source code repository

- **Committee member:** Determines the direction and focus of the project

- **Project manager:** Determine and organize release schedules

Getting involved in an Open Source project usually requires subscribing to a mailing list or newsgroup to stay current with the rapid changes. It also requires you to read documents that refer to contributing and coding conventions. In addition, the project requires access to the source code. Most Open Source projects use Concurrent Versions System (CVS) as a source-code management system.

 NOTE Appendix B provides an introduction to CVS primer to learn how to learn how to access a project maintained in a CVS repository.

Strategic Uses of Open Source

Depending on an organization's acceptable level of risk and the needs of a particular project, you may decide to incorporate Open Source into some aspects of the development life cycle. Open Source may be incorporated as early in a project's life cycle as in the technology evaluation and training stages or as late as the production stage.

Evaluation Technologies

Evaluating technologies is a great time to use Open Source. Organizations can implement an entire prototype or application using a technology without getting locked into a particular vendor's product. Many organizations have a tendency to make a platform or vendor selection based on marketing before they determine their technology needs. Fortunately, many of the Java APIs are based on standard interfaces that allow multiple vendors or Open Source projects to implement the technology. Using Open Source as a means of evaluating the technology allows an organization to make an informed decision. Part of an application can be written and evaluated using Open Source and then tested on different vendor products.

Training Technologies

A popular and economical means of providing training is through the use of computer-based training (CBT). Unfortunately, CBT doesn't provide an effective means of applying the knowledge. Using a commercial product may not provide the best method of application because of the expense or number of licensed copies. Open Source can fill the gap by allowing students to build real applications on a shoestring budget.

Development

Organizations concerned about using Open Source in a situation where it could affect the runtime behavior of an application can still reap the benefits during the development process. Many of the Open Source projects are development tools written by developers for developers. The Open Source projects can increase developer productivity without affecting an application's runtime behavior.

Production

Some Open Source projects have been proven to be of "production" quality. Organizations are incorporating them into mission-critical applications. Incorporating Open Source frameworks or libraries in an application can improve productivity and quality. Using an Open Source framework or library is basically a form of reuse. An investment of time and money isn't required to reinvent the wheel. Likewise, there can be an increase in quality because the framework and and libraries have already been thoroughly tested and debugged by many developers and users.

Useful Open Source-Related Resources

There are many sites on the Internet dedicated to managing Open Source projects and providing news concerning Open Source.

- `http://jakarta.apache.org`: The Jakarta project (jakarta.apache.org) is a collection of Java projects, referred to as subprojects. Many of the projects are frameworks that can be incorporated into applications. For example, regular expressions are covered by the Jakarta Commons project. Other subprojects are intended for web development and some are development tools. As projects mature and become mainstream, they might be promoted to "top-level" projects such as Ant, which you can find at `http://ant.apache.org`.

- `http://xml.apache.org`: The XML projects are a collection of subprojects for parsing and transforming XML documents.

- `http://sourceforge.net`: SourceForge.net is the world's largest repository of Open Source projects. Many but not all the projects are Java-based. Many of the hosted projects are stable, production-quality projects, but even more of them are still in the planning or early development stage.

- `http://www.exolab.org`: ExoLab hosts Java and XML enterprise projects.

- `http://www.tigris.org`: A mid-sized Open Source community focused on building better tools for collaborative software development.

- `http://gjt.org`: Giant Java Tree is a collection of unrelated Java packages.

- `http://www.objectweb.org`: ObjectWeb.org hosts Open Source middleware projects and adaptable components.

- `http://www.codehaus.org`: An up-and-coming Open Source community that caters to projects that aren't under the GPL or other business-hostile licenses. Projects such as Middlegen and XDoclet2 are making codehaus their home.

- `http://www.newsforge.com`: NewsForge is an online newspaper reporting the news about Linux and Open Source.

Case Study

One of the reasons the Open Source community is so productive is the fact that for all but the most trivial of applications, software is difficult and expensive to produce. The complexity of building software systems is a direct consequence of the nature of real-world business problems. Business problems are driven by changing requirements, rapidly evolving technologies, multiple data sources, service-level agreements, interoperability, time to market, return on investment, and many other factors. The inability to cope and balance all these forces results in projects that go over budget, over schedule and don't deliver in functionality. These projects quickly spiral out of control due to their inability to cope with complexity and change.

Even if such systems deliver in a specific area of business functionality, their overall business value is diminished by their maintenance costs. These horror stories aren't rare, on the contrary, they're the norm; 84 percent[2] of all enterprise software systems are considered failures. This failure rate is a characteristic signature of the "software crisis" that's plaguing the industry. Projects fail due to a combination of poor engineering and management choices. A 2002 study by the Carnegie Mellon Software Engineering Institute (SEI) lists the following top ten reasons why software projects fail:

- Inexperienced staff

- Lack of team cohesion and experience

- Lack of emphasis in using modern software-engineering practices

- Lack of a process or incorrect emphasis in the application of a process

- Inadequate project management methodology

- Unclear, misunderstood, and undiscovered requirements

- Size; the larger the projects the more likely they are to fail

- Lack of planning and estimating

---

2. According to a Standish Group survey, which studied about 8,000 software projects in the U.S. in 1995.

- System-specific and technology-related issues are considered too late in the process.

- New technologies and unforeseen problems.

The IT industry has championed several approaches for dealing with the inherent complexity of designing, building, and maintaining software-intensive enterprise systems. Object-oriented, component-based, distributed systems represent state-of-the-art in enterprise-level systems technology. This book deals with some of the issues of building enterprise applications at a practical level when the "silver bullet" that has been handed to the information technologist is Java, specifically J2EE. J2EE poses some dangers to the inexperienced because it makes a perfect technological silver bullet due to its countless APIs. The real-world experiences are far from software utopia, as a recent study by the Seybold Group suggests that there is a gap in management between the expectations of adopting J2EE and the achieved results. One of the reasons for this is the lack of tools that cover the many aspects of J2EE development. Open Source enterprise Java tools and frameworks are emerging to help bridge this gap.

Learning how to build enterprise applications with a combination of Open Source frameworks and tools provides a low-cost, low-risk, ideal prototyping environment in which to master distributed computing technologies. Open Source lowers the entry barrier into the Java and J2EE worlds by providing choices besides the traditional proprietary offerings.

The rest of this chapter introduces a real-world example that puts the application of J2EE technologies into clearer perspective. It introduces a realistic business problem to be used as the backdrop for the learning process of designing, building, and deploying an enterprise Java system using Open Source technologies. The rest of this chapter serves as a vision document and a high-level architectural blueprint, which provides a conceptual analysis and highlights the requirements for the system.

Technology Conference Management System Case Study Background

The TCMS case study presented in this chapter is a collection of systems and utilities used to advertise, prepare, and support a technology conference. A technology conference is an event that spans a predetermined period of time and consists of one or more sessions (presentations, keynotes, and so on).

NOTE The technology conference chosen here is especially well suited for the purposes of this book. The main stakeholders, that is, the people who have a vested interest in the system, are technologists, just like the authors and readers, which make it easier to relate to the needs of the user, and consequently, make the gathering of requirements, analysis, and design processes clearer.

Technically, a technology conference presents some unique challenges in the fields of distributed computing and enterprise development due to the dynamic nature of the information requirements and the logistics involved in running such an event.

Defining the Stakeholders

To understand the dynamics of such a system it's important to determine who the stakeholders of the system are and how their individual information needs change over time. The main stakeholders to be considered in the context of a technology conference are as follows:

- **Attendees:** Individuals attending the conference

- **Presenters:** Individuals presenting one or more sessions at a conference

- **Sponsors:** Organizations sponsoring and promoting the conference

- **Administrators:** The person or persons organizing and running the conference

To create a clear picture of the changing needs of the stakeholders it's useful to view the conference as three separate periods of time: the preconference, the conference, and the postconference periods.

Preconference

During the preconference period, data is collected, evaluated, and created. Collected data includes documents such as calls for papers, abstracts, and outlines for the different presentations. From the collected documents, content must be created and also maintained as the source documents change. Aside from the document management needs, facilities must be provided for attendees to register and manage the schedule of events they plan to attend. At this time it's also crucial to provide information in a timely manner to make the process of registering and getting to the conference easier. Among the experience-enhancing utilities are items that allow you to obtain driving directions or information about special conference rates for travel and hotel accommodations.

Conference

The information needs at conference time are crucial to the success of the conference. Satisfied attendees are more likely to return the following year. Being able to cut through the noise, pinpoint areas of interest, and choose sessions to attend are factors of great importance to maximizing an attendee's experience. Providing interactivity and constant feedback ensures that attendees are always in tune with the heartbeat of the conference. At the beginning of the conference, attendees need to be checked in and given conference badges. Changes or updates to any sessions or presentations need to be communicated effectively in order for attendees to manage their schedules.

Postconference

Once the conference has closed its doors, a large amount of work remains to be performed. Attendees are now alumni and as such they're a prime target audience for future conferences. Providing a sense of continuity is important to alumni and future attendees of a technology conference. There should be a bridge from the topics and content of previous conferences to ongoing and future conferences.

In the realm of document management, these requirements translate to the management of the transition of dynamic documents into static documents or archives. The numerous documents such as presentation slides, notes, follow-up discussions, and supporting materials related to different presentations or sessions must now be made available to the conference alumni and possibly to the general public. For the organizers of the conference, information such as the number of attendees, the popularity of topics for courses, and other statistical information is a crucial business indicator that will determine the future changes and enhancements made to the conference.

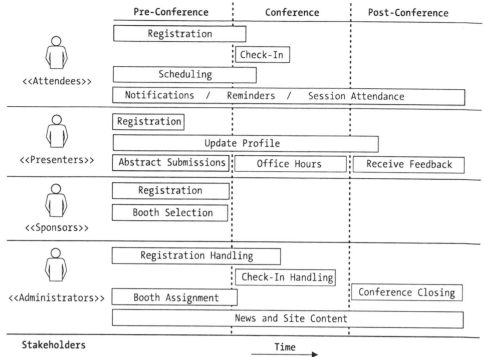

Figure 1-1. Stakeholders' requirements timeline

The Business Problem

To manage the information needs of a technology conference, a software system is needed that will provide an interactive information channel to manage the needs of the different stakeholders. There is a business drive mandating that the systems that will be developed serve as the basis for a new line of products tailored to the organization, execution, and maintenance of technology conferences. These products are to be sold as a collection of components or subsystems that can be adapted to the particular needs of a customer.

The separation of roles and functionality needs to be clear in order to have a system that can be easily customized and enhanced. It's important for the system to account for the fact that attendees and presenters are geographically dispersed. There should be no need (or as little need as possible) for users to install or configure any software.

General Application Requirements

This section outlines the general business requirements that the system must meet. Based on the general software distribution and configuration requirements, the primary medium chosen for the application is the Internet, in particular the Web. The Web provides the advantage of nearly zero cost for distribution and configuration. As the design process gets underway, refinements based on real-world constraints will be factored in. The following requirements have been organized on a per-stakeholder basis to facilitate the separation of functionality at the design stages.

Attendees

Attendees are the primary focus of the system and as such, greater priority is placed on the functionality that affects them. The requirements of attendees encompass the majority of the functionality of the system.

- **General information:** Prospective attendees (the general public) need an easy and intuitive way to learn about the details of the conference. A web-based application should provide an intuitive way for users to learn about the conference details. The application must be easy to navigate and the addition of common website functionality such as news and printable views of content must be easily accomplished.

- **Registration:** Attendees should be able to securely register for the conference and receive confirmation via email. The system should accommodate both individual and group registrations.

- **Session browsing and selection:** The system should provide intuitive and powerful searching capabilities to assist users in the selection of sessions to attend.

- **Session evaluations:** Presenters should be able to review session evaluations online.

- **Scheduling:** The system should provide users with the ability to easily view and manage their schedules. The schedule data should be available in a variety of formats that target different mediums and devices (for example, the Web, PDAs, emails on demand).

- **Notification and reminders:** The system should provide users with the ability to subscribe to a conference notification service. These notices can include mailing lists, schedule-related reminders, and session-related news.

- **Accommodation assistance:** The system should provide a way for attendees to find area maps, venue maps, hotel directions, locations of interest, restaurants, and other information to enhance their experience at the conference.

Presenters

Properly assisting and serving presenters will result in a higher quality of content for the conference. This in turn, benefits the primary stakeholders, that is, the conference attendees.

- **Registration:** Presenters should be able to securely register for the conference and receive confirmation via email.

- **Profile information:** Presenters should be able to enter contact information and biographical information, upload a picture, and provide other information of interest.

- **Call for papers:** Potential presenters should be able to submit abstracts for a session. The system should allow the presenter to select the target audience, the session track (session category), and the room requirements for a session.

- **Speaker availability:** Presenters should be able to schedule the office hours during which they can be available to assist presentation attendees with questions or problems related to a session.

- **Books by a presenter:** Presenters who are published authors can select one or more books from a list of their published books, and associate them with a session. The list of books will be presented as part of the session information. The list of books and the detailed information for each book is obtained from an external provider at runtime.

Sponsors

Sponsors make a financial investment in a conference. Their interest is based on the rewards of public exposure and an improved industry image. It gives them an opportunity to connect with the community and provides them with a forum to present their products and services. The presence of high-profile industry players as sponsors legitimizes a technology conference. Ensuring that it's easy for sponsors to participate in the conference is of the utmost importance to the success of the event.

- **Registration:** The system should allow sponsors to register and select a level of sponsorship.

- **Booth selection:** The system should allow sponsors to select a conference booth. Booths are allocated based on sponsorship level.

Administrators

Managing the complex interactions of a conference is a challenging process. One of the goals of the system is to ease the tasks of management and reduce the amount of personnel needed.

- **Check-in and registration:** Administrators need to check in attendees as they arrive at the conference and provide them with badges and other materials.

- **Speaker evaluations:** The system should provide administrators with the ability to create and view the results of speaker evaluations.

- **News:** Administrators should have an easy interface to update conference-related news.

- **Booth assignment:** Administrators should have the ability to select a booth for a sponsor based on sponsorship level and physical requirements.

- **Conference closing:** An interface must be provided for conference administrators to easily transition the selected content into a static site. Specific data now becomes legacy data and must be relocated or archived appropriately.

- **Dashboard:** Utilities must be provided for conference administrators to gather statistics and performance indicators for the conference. These tools should be able to provide a snapshot view of the overall health and success indicators of the conference.

Architectural Requirements

Architectural requirements refer to the infrastructure needs that must be present for the system to achieve the desired business goal. A multitude of factors are involved in determining these requirements, such as experience with similar systems, operational constraints, existing physical infrastructure, and application services needed across multiple systems (cross-cutting concerns). These requirements are useful in performing a gap analysis of infrastructure features when selecting a product or set of products on which to build enterprise applications. It's the architect's job to then determine the build vs. buy decisions.

A set of general architectural requirements can be listed from the general application requirements previously outlined and the experience gained while building similar systems.

- **Data management and persistence:** Data must be easy to store, retrieve, search, and modify. Data integrity shouldn't be compromised in the face of multiple sources that are attempting to modify the same data.

- **Maintainability and extensibility:** The system must be easy to maintain and extend. Pieces of functionality should be easily added or removed, or turned on or off, depending on the operational characteristics applicable to a specific deployment.

- **Security:** Data must be stored and retrieved in a secure and efficient fashion. Users of the system must have access to functionality according to their roles or security levels.

- **Scalability and reliability:** Multiple users should be able to interact with the system. The performance characteristics of the system shouldn't change dramatically with an increase in the concurrent user base.

- **Personalization and customization:** The user-interfacing elements of the system should have a customizable look and feel, allowing for branding and dynamic changes based on the identity of the interacting user.

- **Document and content management:** The system should provide facilities to manage the variety of documents used and also allow for the manipulation, classification, editing, and transformation of document-based information.

- **Administration:** The system should provide a framework to easily add management capabilities to individual components. Administrative functions should be relatively easy to create and customize.

- **Messaging:** Asynchronous communication facilities are expected to be required between certain subsystems. The architecture must provide a messaging framework or the ability to seamlessly integrate one.

- **Integration with legacy and external resources:** The system should facilitate the acquisition of data from external and legacy sources, as well as the ability to publish data to external entities in an industry-standard fashion.

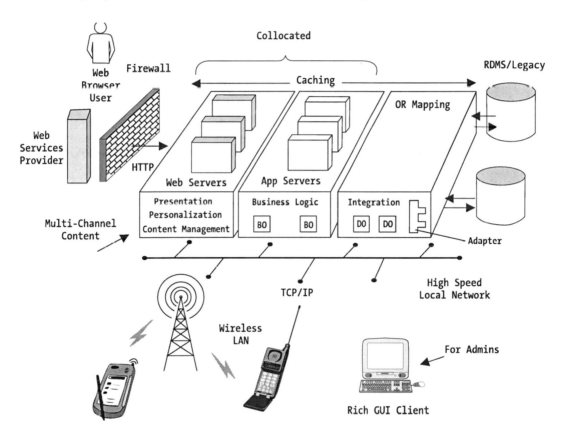

Figure 1-2. Architectural requirements diagram

A Word on Architecture

Architecture is by far one of the most misunderstood and misused terms in the field of software engineering. The role of the software architect and the products necessary for the process of architecting a software system aren't consistent from one organization to another.

The role of the software architect can be defined as the bridge between the stakeholders' needs and the builders of a software system. The architect is a client advocate who possesses and owns the vision of a soon-to-be-built system, and at a high level he understands the risks involved in the construction process. An architect knows and understands the client's language and concerns and is the one responsible for balancing the multitude of forces involved in the process of planning, constructing, and maintaining a system.

In this book software architecture represents the highest level of abstraction of a system. It entails the definition of the largest identifiable parts and the interfaces or contracts needed among those parts in order to satisfy the requirements of the stakeholders. As a whole, a system's architecture should enable you to analyze and predict the major forces that will impact the design and implementation decisions with an acceptable degree of confidence. More rigorous ways of specifying a system's architecture exist; for example, there are approaches based on the use of an architecture description language (ADL).

An example of one such formal approach for modeling and documenting a system's architecture is the Reference Model for Open Distributed Processing (RM-ODP), which is quickly evolving as an internationally acceptable object-based architecture standard for use in architecting distributed systems. RM-ODP provides a consistent way to generate a well-formed architectural specification. More information about RM-ODP can be found in Janis Putman's *Architecting with RM-ODP*.[3]

Based on the architectural requirements outlined in the previous section, you should begin to see a clearer architectural vision for the system. The system's architecture should accommodate both the functional (business and application requirements) and nonfunctional requirements (architectural requirements). The architecture diagram for the TCMS is divided into tiers of functionality, which can represent a logical or physical partitioning of the system.

The architecture consists of the following tiers (following the well-known partitioning of the J2EE platform):

---

3. Janis Putman, *Architecting with RM-ODP* (San Francisco: Prentice Hall PTR, 2001).

- **Client tier:** Represents client-facing portions of the system

- **Presentation tier:** Represents subsystems responsible for the generation of the user interface presentation-handling logic

- **Business tier:** Represents subsystems responsible for the handling of business logic

- **Integration tier:** Represents subsystems responsible for integrating external sources and destinations of information, including any legacy systems

Figure 1-3 shows the application tiers and how messages are exchanged between them.

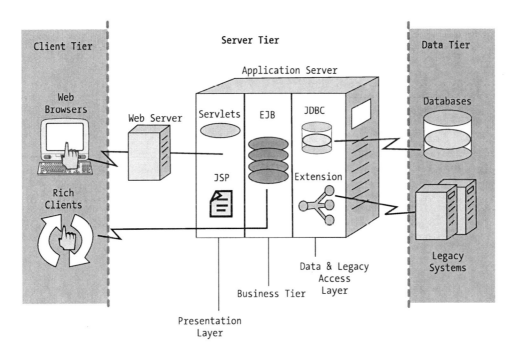

Figure 1-3. Architectural tiers

Open Issues and Assumptions

The dynamic nature of enterprise development forces you to make assumptions based on previous experiences and to delay dealing with certain aspects of the system until later in the development stages.

Assumptions

Some of the assumptions made are the result of implied requirements gathered from stakeholders' meetings and projections about the future usage of the system. Some of these assumptions include the following:

- Concurrency requirements are expected to increase over time.

- A large percentage of attendees are technologically savvy.

- Applications will be accessed remotely via the Internet using a browser-based interface.

- The conference internal network will be protected with an HTTP firewall.

- A large percentage of attendees carry network-ready personal digital assistants (PDAs) or other mobile computing devices.

Open Issues

It's expected that as the system is designed and developed your understanding about the dynamics governing its behavior will coalesce. New relationships and interfaces will be discovered and previously unidentified usage scenarios will appear. Preparing for such discoveries by infusing flexibility in your designs is key for any system that will evolve in a controlled fashion. Some of expected open issues are as follows:

- Unidentified stakeholders.

- With multiple channels being serviced by the application, you need to find a way to produce channel-specific content.

- You need to create several system-level systems for authentication, registration, and the handling of payments.

- Large number of implementation choices available.

- Unidentified alternate usage scenarios.

- Unidentified requirements.

Summary

Java has emerged as the number one language and environment for enterprise computing, and it has also become one of the most widely used languages in the Open Source community. At the time of this writing there are upward of 10,000 Java Open Source projects on SourceForge—second only to C++. Though not every Java Open Source project is applicable to the creation of enterprise applications, you'll nevertheless find a largely untapped set of resources for the J2EE platform. This chapter also introduced the Technology Conference Management System, which presents a fairly complex and representative problem that encompasses several areas of enterprise development.

The rest of the book will guide you through the process of designing and developing the applications to fulfill some of the requirements of the case study system. The case study weaves together the knowledge gained in the individual chapters. By tackling the software development process one layer at a time in an incremental and iterative fashion, this book will provide you with insight about the planning involved at various stages of the software-development life cycle. By using open-sourced J2EE offerings and supporting tools you'll be able to build a basic, yet representative enterprise system. Each subsequent chapter is devoted to a tier of the application and to one or more stages (or activities) of the software development process. Wherever necessary, multiple solutions to a particular problem will be demonstrated to provide the reader with some insight into the typical decisions encountered while developing an enterprise Java application.

Design with ArgoUML

"Luck is the residue of design."

—Branch Rickey

JAVA HAS FOUND a niche in the server side of contemporary distributed computing, in which the most prevalent service model is the browser-based application or web application. The rise of the Internet as a global network for business has given enterprise computing its greatest weapon and also its greatest challenge. More power and possibilities mean more challenges and complexity.

Software engineers have realized that without a solid architecture and some semblance of a process that emphasizes analysis and design, a project's failure is all but imminent. Keeping with the demands of the evolving "connected" enterprise is no easy task; applications not only need to work well, but have to work well together. Interoperability, maintainability, scalability, and performance are now implied characteristics when one speaks about an enterprise system. When designs, in the form of models reflecting an architectural vision, are the driving force behind implementations, systems evolve in a controlled fashion. The opposite scenario, implementation-driven systems that grow in an organic fashion, are destined to head down a certain path of "architectural drift" in which an application moves further away from its intended goal of servicing the needs of stakeholders with each development iteration.

This chapter aims to be a brief overview of the practical application of object-oriented analysis and design (OOAD) concepts and the Unified Modeling Language (UML). OOAD techniques are used to provide a solution to the problems presented in the case study. You'll tackle the initial design of the Technology Conference Management System (TCMS) system using ArgoUML, a freely available Open Source modeling tool. Object modeling tools have historically been fairly high priced. Open Source offerings such as ArgoUML diminish the high entry cost for adopting a modeling tool.

The initial analysis and design of the system is performed in this chapter by elaborating and expanding upon the knowledge gained about the TCMS case study system introduced in Chapter 1. In the interest of an iterative and incremental development process, subsequent chapters introduce, elaborate, or re-factor the design of a specific subsystem, feature, or component.

Object-Oriented Analysis and Design Overview

OOAD is a combination of problem solving mechanisms that facilitates the two following primordial tasks of software engineering:

- Understanding and describing a particular problem and its domain

- Formulating a conceptual solution to a problem

The results of OOAD are expressed in the language of objects. These results should be independent of the process or methodology used. Yet OOAD doesn't work in a vacuum, for the principles and guidelines it promotes are meant to be used in the larger context of a software development process. Always keep in mind that the models produced by analysis and design are used both to understand the problems and to formulate a design that must eventually become code. The final product is in the trade code; without code there is no measurable level of completion. That said, it's important to remember that technologies come and go and that many times the same problem gets solved over and over during the life of a company. Code isn't the best artifact to carry knowledge and problem-solving lessons into the future—models are.

The case-study application introduced in this book is a tad more complex that the typical trade book example, yet it's still simple enough to be understood in its entirety by one individual. This is far from the norm; rarely do you start with a manageable set of requirements, and only in rare cases is it possible for one individual to have a complete understanding of every detail of a system. You'll use models for managing the complexity of systems, which further your understanding of the systems as artifacts of knowledge continuity.

Understanding the Problem with Object-Oriented Analysis

Object-oriented analysis (OOA) is concerned with developing requirements and specifications expressed in terms of objects that accurately represent a particular problem domain. OOA helps determine what is to be built rather than how to build it. Analysis aims at capturing the essence of a problem without introducing implementation-specific artifacts that can taint future design decisions. The process of analysis can be further qualified into requirements gathering and object analysis.

During the requirements-gathering phase you should be concerned with the discovery and understanding of the requirements. Use-case modeling is the primary technique used in this book to gather, evolve, and manage requirements. Although use-case modeling isn't specifically an object-oriented activity, it has proven extremely beneficial when used in conjunction with OOAD techniques.

In the real world, requirements aren't set in stone and the discovery of new requirements goes on for as long as or even longer than the lifetime of most software systems. Most methodologies have come to accept this fact and acknowledge changing requirements as a primary driving force in the software development life cycle. In iterative development an iteration involves the management of requirements. The number of requirements discovered and the changes to existing requirements are expected to diminish as the system evolves iteratively.

During object analysis, the focus shifts to the discovery of the domain entities at the conceptual level, with an "emphasis on defining software objects and how they collaborate to fulfill the requirements."[1] The products of this activity are conceptual object models that provide a visual organization of the concepts needed to create a coherent design.

Solving the Problem with Object-Oriented Design

Abstraction, encapsulation, information hiding, and generalization play a primary role in design. Software design hinges on the ability to disregard inessential details and focus on the essential. The goal of OOD is to arrive at a system as simple as possible that meets the stakeholders' requirements while allowing a certain amount of flexibility. OOD entails the modeling of a system's structure and behavior in terms of objects and interactions among objects. OOD tackles the development of object models that represent a solution to a problem in a specific problem domain. These object models represent a solution to a problem in the solution domain (technology-specific, less abstract, geared toward being implemented in code) while maintaining conceptual consistency with the problem domain.

OOD builds on the products developed during analysis by refining and mapping these into an object-oriented programming language (OOPL). Analysis, design, and coding are closer to each other in the world of objects than in other paradigms. For this reason, the notations used during analysis and the early stages of design are very similar. However, in OOD, technology-specific concepts that were nonexistent in analysis need to be specified, such as the datatypes of the attributes of a class, or the business logic in a class's methods. Knowing when analysis ends and design begins is usually hard for those new to modeling. Some would argue that it's more of an art than a science.

---

1. Craig Larman, *Applying UML and Patterns* (Prentice Hall PTR, 2001).

TIP   When in doubt about whether a piece of information belongs in the analysis or design model, ask yourself the following questions: If removed, will it diminish the understanding of the problem? Will it prevent a developer from correctly implementing a feature?

Models and Modeling

The main artifacts of OOAD models are visual representations of a system's components and the interactions between those components. Edward Tufte, a pioneer in the field of information design tells you that "graphics reveal data."[2] This statement is particularly truthful when applied to software models. Models can reveal hidden characteristics of a system. They can help you see a system at different resolutions, and different angles. A model can focus on structure, behavior, or both. Simply speaking, a model is a visual abstraction for the purpose of understanding something before it is to be built.

The power of models lies both in their visual expressiveness and their ability to focus on a particular view or concern of a system at a time. Textual descriptions are great to enhance or clarify the description of an entity or process, but as with any representation based on natural language, ambiguities are easily introduced. Visual models reduce the ambiguity of textual descriptions by infusing objectivity through a constrained but extensible set of syntactical and semantical rules.

Models are vital tools in understanding and conveying problems and their solutions. They provide structure and a measurement of feasibility that isn't easily captured in textual descriptions alone. A model can help pinpoint areas of risk in a soon-to-be-developed system and it can determine what components or subsystems might need to be prototyped in advance before making an implementation, technology, or vendor decision. Models encourage experimentation and enable the evaluation of different ways of solving a problem without incurring the expenses of building an actual system.

Models also help focus the level of concern and detail. They can give you the 50,000-foot view or a detailed view of a system, subsystem, component, or process. Used properly, a model is a formidable weapon in coping with the inherent complexity of software-intensive systems.

Software modeling refers to the practice of visually creating and documenting the results of the analysis and design processes using suitable object models.

---

2.   Edward R. Tufte, *The Visual Display of Quantitative Information* (Cheshire, CT: Graphics Press, 1983).

Model-driven development has proven effective in reducing time-to-market, decreasing development costs, and managing the risk of software projects.

 TIP   The goal of OOAD is to simplify the understanding of a problem and its solution. Overly complex models go against this very principle. Therefore, it's important to keep your models as simple as possible. Whenever possible we try to follow George A. Miller's heuristic for the human capacity to assimilate, retain, and process information.[3] Models with around seven elements (give or take two) convey enough information without overwhelming your senses.

The Unified Modeling Language

The UML is a general-purpose visual modeling language used in the analysis, design, and maintenance of software-intensive systems. It's a refinement of several modeling notations used by the most prevalent object methodologies. The core concepts are derived primarily from Grady Booch's OOAD, James Rumbaugh's object modeling technique (OMT), and Ivar Jacobson's object-oriented software engineering (OOSE). In the late 1990s the Object Management Group (OMG) embraced and promoted the UML as a standard modeling language for object-oriented systems. The OMG is a nonprofit consortium of nearly 800 members that includes major industry players, developers, and users of object technologies worldwide.

The UML plays an extremely important role in OOAD; it standardizes the visual vocabulary of software architects, designers, and developers by providing software-modeling artifacts born out of best practices and notations that have successfully been used to model complex business problems throughout the years. The OMG defines the UML as follows: "[A] graphical language for visualizing, specifying, constructing, and documenting the artifacts of a software-intensive system. The UML offers a standard way to write a system's blueprints, including conceptual things such as business processes and system functions as well as concrete things such as programming language statements, database schemas, and reusable software components."[4]

The UML represents the de facto standard and lingua franca for visually documenting the processes of OOAD in a methodology- and process-independent.

---

3.   G.A. Miller, "The magical number seven, plus or minus two: Some limits on our capacity for processing information" (*The Psychological Review*, vol. 63, 1956) pp. 81–97.

4.   Object Management Group, "OMG Unified Modeling Language Specification," Version 1.5 (March 2003), p. 1–1.

It's relatively easy to learn, semantically rich, and it addresses several contemporary development issues such as scalability, distribution, and concurrency.

It also represents a natural evolution of the software-engineering industry toward standardization. If you make an analogy to the construction industry, it's easy to see the benefit and need for the UML. In the construction industry, an architect designs a building. The result of the design process is a set of blueprints that the builders use to construct the building. Different blueprints are tailored to different tasks. For example, structure builders need to know about load-bearing walls, plumbers need to know about waterlines, and electricians are concerned with the electrical layouts. In construction, models specify the level of detail and areas of concern for specific construction tasks. The more complex the building, the more crucial it is for the information embodied in the blueprints to be easily understood by the builders.

The UML is the unifying force behind making blueprints in the software trade as commonplace as they are in the construction trade. The rewards of the UML are many, including standardization, globalization, and the emergence of a modeling-tool marketplace that has increased the acceptance of modeling as a standard practice of software engineering.

The semantics of the UML align well with the semantics of object-oriented languages; after all, it was the object-oriented paradigm that triggered the events that eventually led to the creation of the UML. The UML doesn't present a very steep learning curve for Java developers accustomed to "thinking in objects." For a comprehensive introduction to the UML in the context of a methodology (such as Unified Process), we recommend Craig Larman's *Applying UML and Patterns*.[5]

As implementations rapidly develop in complexity, the design decisions and lessons learned are quickly lost in the noise of the construction details. The UML fosters an industrywide memory by providing a vehicle in which designs (both good and bad) in the form or patterns and antipatterns, can outlive implementations and provide value in the present as well as the future. The debates about notation don't exist nowadays. Thanks to the wide adoption of the UML, the debate centers on methodologies and processes.

Java and the UML

The Java community has benefited enormously from the revolution in modeling that the UML has created. Among the many benefits that the UML has brought are the following:

---

5. Craig Larman, *Applying UML and Patterns* (Prentice Hall PTR, 2001).

- Java's open, accessible core enables developers to take advantage of the now extensive UML tool market support for reverse engineering as a technique for understanding the APIs.

- In general terms, the UML has elevated the communication level between stakeholders, business analysts, architects, and developers.

- Industrial-strength automation via source-code generation from predefined UML design templates is commonly achieved with many UML tools.

- Templates for well-known design patterns are available along with facilities that turn generic models into J2EE components.

- The lost art of documentation has been given a new breath of life; most tools support the creation of comprehensive documentation suites from models and source code. Most Java tools support the creation of JavaDoc documentation enhanced with UML.

UML Diagrams Used in This Book

In its current incarnation (version 2.0), the UML has a set of 13 diagrams that can be classified in three categories: behavior, interaction, and structure. The original 9 diagrams (pre-UML 2.0) are the class, component, deployment, object, package, sequence, state machine, and use case diagrams. The new additions to the specification include the communication, composite structure, interaction overview, and timing diagrams.

There are also three-model management diagrams tailored to the modeling of different aspects or views of a system at different levels of detail. Stand-alone UML diagrams in isolation lack cohesion without a higher level of organization. They become disconnected pieces of a puzzle. The UML model management constructs bring a set of diagrams together in a coherent way, thereby imparting a higher level of understanding by grouping and further classifying individual diagrams in a model. The model management elements include packages, model, and subsystems and will be used throughout this book when needed in conjunction with some of the core UML diagrams. Table 2-1 shows a list of the different diagrams used throughout the book for the design and development of the TCMS system and a short description of their intended usage.

Table 2-1. UML Diagrams Used in the Analysis and Design of the TCMS System

Diagram	Type	Used for Modeling
Use case	Requirements/ High-Level Behavior	Relationships of actors and use cases within a system
Class	Static Structure	Class structure and relationships among classes
Sequence	Interaction	Message exchanges (time perspective)
Component	Implementation	Organization and dependencies of components

These four diagrams provide a comprehensive coverage of a system's structure and behavior from multiple perspectives. The core concepts of the UML enable these perspectives to be used together to build a self-consistent system. These diagrams represent the primary artifacts used in the analysis and design of the system. Knowing which diagrams to use and when to use them is one of lessons that you'll eventually learn. The basic approach is to find a combination of diagrams that both reflect the static structure of the domain you're trying to model as well as the interaction and behavior of the system entities. Throughout this chapter and the rest of the book you'll learn the diagrams shown in Table 2-1 in greater detail in the context of the TCMS case study.

UML Stereotypes

An important quality of the UML is its extensibility, which gives the UML the ability to grow in a controlled fashion to meet future demands while remaining true to the object-oriented paradigm. At the core of the UML, you'll find the meta-model that defines the basic abstractions from which all modeling elements are defined. The UML extensions exist to enable the enhancement of the UML expressiveness without affecting or changing its core, that is, the metamodel.

Of these extension mechanisms UML stereotypes are by far the most powerful and popular extension mechanism to date. They characterize UML components that are imparting specialized semantics. In other words, UML stereotypes are used to further qualify an element of a UML diagram. The simplest way to explain a stereotype is as a label or tag that can be attached to a model element in order to enhance its meaning in the context of a given diagram. Stereotypes can be used with most elements of an UML diagram, including classes, components, operations, and associations.

Many methodologies use stereotypes to add extra levels of expressiveness to UML diagrams. UML stereotypes allow the semantics of the UML to be extended in a way that models become more expressive. Stereotypes "brand" other model elements by imparting a set of values, constraints, and optionally, a different representation. Stereotypes have many possible representations, with the most commonly used being a string enclosed in guillemets (that is, << >>). You make extensive use of stereotypes when modeling components in the J2EE environment and in general by adopting Peter Coad's modeling-in-color technique and the domain-neutral component (DNC), which are techniques used to produce better object models and enterprise components.

Model-Driven Architecture and the UML

Where is the UML headed? How will it affect enterprise Java development in the future? These are questions that many developers think about. Field experience tells you that the UML currently has an impact on the initial stages of analysis and design of a J2EE system, but its usage sharply dies off after this stage. The OMG is strongly promoting the concept of a Model-Driven Architecture (MDA) in which applications (with the help of the UML) are defined in a completely technology-independent fashion and are then realized in an given platform such as CORBA, .Net, or J2EE.

The MDA is the next step in the evolution of the software-engineering practice and places the model as the centerpiece of your trade. In essence the MDA concerns itself with specifying a system independently of a platform, specifying platforms, and then transforming a system's specification into an implementation given a chosen platform. Its primary goals are portability, interoperability, and reusability.

Open Source MDA tools are beginning to emerge, such as AndroMDA, which generates Enterprise JavaBeans (EJB) components from a properly annotated (using stereotypes) component model file in eXtensible Metadata Interchange (XMI) format.

Future of the UML and Java

As with any committee-driven initiative, it's expected that the OO languages that the UML is meant to support will evolve at a faster pace than the UML. Emerging component architectures like EJB and new service-oriented paradigms like web services are currently partially supported via some of the extension mechanisms previously mentioned in this chapter. Using a UML profile such as the one proposed by JSR 26 (UML/EJB Mapping Specification) will standardize the extensions used and enable tool interoperability.

 NOTE JSR 26, the UML profile for EJB, defines extensions that will enable tool vendors to standardize on a set of UML extensions used to annotate models in a way that they can be used to generate EJB components. Also the extension will enable the reverse engineering of a system composed of EJBs into a UML model. The EJB-JAR format is targeted as a possible carrier for a "UML Descriptor for EJB," which is an XML file that "identifies UML models stored in the same EJB-JAR and their relationship to EJBs in the EJB-JAR".[6] Enterprise tools could then use these store descriptors for automation and reflection.

But you could argue that if UML profiles proliferate at too high a rate, the UML will become a fragmented beast representative of the problems it was created to solve in the first place. A delicate balance must be achieved by the OMG between adding new concepts to the core of the UML and the liberal use of the extension mechanisms.

Like any general-purpose technology in the rapidly changing landscape of today's technology, the UML is still a work in progress and it will probably remain that way for the foreseeable future.

Expect Java development to further benefit and extend from the new enhancements to the UML. Problems such as the impedance mismatch between objects and relational databases are being addressed at a conceptual level within the UML. Tool interoperability is slowly becoming a reality with XMI, which goes to show how XML is slowly finding a place within the UML. The ability of business rules to be expressed in the context of an object model is gaining ground with the usage of the Object Constraint Language (OCL).

The notion of executable UML models is rapidly gaining followers in the world of embedded and real-time systems. Executable UML models are an attempt to once again raise the level of abstraction at which humans deal with problems and their solutions. Several efforts are underway to make executable UML a reality, and it's expected that yet another breed of tools will emerge and that the lessons learned will trickle down into the UML specifications. The OMG and their MDA envisions the complete specification of systems using models. These models are built on a Platform-Independent Model (PIM) that models a solution without any ties to a specific implementation technology. In the fall of 2001, the OMG extended the

---

6. Jack Greenfield (Rational Software Corporation), "UML Profile For EJB" [JSR-000026 UML/EJB(TM) Mapping Specification 1.0 Public Review Draft] (2001), p. 8.

semantics of the UML with a very complete set of semantics for actions defined at a very high level of abstraction. UML models will rely on these actions to accurately translate models into executable systems. Executable UML is more that just mere forward engineering; it's a move upwards to a higher level of abstraction that makes code a rarely seen low-level entity as obscure as CPU registers are to a Java developer.

Code Generation and Round-Trip Engineering

Many of the OOAD CASE tools available nowadays feature both code generation and forward and reverse (round-trip) engineering of models to code and vice versa. Knowing when to use those features is a judgment call that must be based mostly on the capabilities of a given tool.

In the Java world, round-trip engineering is gaining new ground as tool vendors experiment with the concepts of MDA, Metadata (see Java Metadata Interface (JMI) specification, JSR 40) and the previously mentioned UML profile for EJB. Tools like AndroMDA are paving the way for the creation of J2EE components from a UML model.

In iterative development, reverse engineering can help in the discovery of potential areas of code reuse, in the application of design patterns, and with possible structural problems such as high coupling and low cohesion. Possible encapsulation and the discovery of component interfaces are activities that can also benefit from a process of reverse engineering. Also, in the case for which there is an existing code base—which is a typical case in the industry because unfortunately most projects seem to go through more than one attempt—reverse engineering can help you determine what code can be reused and what needs to be thrown away. In the absence of documentation, some of the lessons learned in any previous attempts might be revealed for the benefit of the current effort.

In combination with forward engineering, CASE tools can help a system remain true to its architectural vision by providing near-instant feedback on the results of an iteration, and allowing for corrective and preventive measures to be taken.

That said, it's important to point out that code generation and round-trip engineering are in their infancy and you must take care not to get caught in a cycle of manually correcting poor, skeletal code.

Methodologies, Processes, and the UML

Most modern methodologies have adopted the UML as the foundation for their notations. That said, it's important to note that the UML doesn't impose a specific methodology or process, yet it enables a model-driven, architecture-centric, iterative and incremental process especially suited to work with distributed, object-oriented, component-based systems. The UML is therefore an enabling force that encourages the application of methodologies in the form of processes.

There are a variety of methodologies and processes, and an equally large set of reasons why one might be a better fit for a particular development effort. Factors such as the personality makeup of a development team, the size and scope of a system, and the target architecture all weigh heavily in deciding what methodology to follow. Experience shows that no methodology is a perfect fit for every organization and for every system. But most experts in the industry seem to agree that any semblance of a process is better than no process at all. Of course, devotion to process for the sake of process leads to what Steve McConnell refers to as "cargo cult organizations"[7] in which there is the perception that the production of process-related documentation guarantees a project's success. But the reality is that the combination of a committed team and the right amount of process are key to a project's success.

Most successful contemporary methodologies share one common trait: None are linear. Iterations, with discovery, assessment, and enhancement cycles, are the norm. Waterfall or "big-bang" development has proven ineffective and inflexible when dealing with the dynamic nature of contemporary applications. Incremental development with small, well-defined models and test-driven deliverables are winning the race and delivering on-time and on-budget quality software systems.

In the neverending debate over methodologies, contrasting lines have been drawn between the so-called heavyweight methodologies and their counterparts: the lightweight or agile methodologies. Describing and comparing both methodologies and process types is rather difficult. No proponent of a methodology refers to it as a heavyweight methodology; the term has been coined in a negative context to mean that a methodology focuses excessively on the actual process and documentation and not on the results. Agile methodologies have risen out of the frustrations caused by negative experiences in trying to follow rigid and predictive methodologies. By adapting rather than predicting, agile methodologies acknowledge that a map is hard to follow when the landscape is constantly changing. Agile methodologies focus on people first by accommodating the way programmers work and viewing coding not as a construction-only phase but also in large part as a design-refinement phase. This notion is a notable departure from the usual analogies to the construction trade, in which design is thought of as a creative process and construction is a repetitive, manual process. Agile methodologies view coding as an extension of the design as well as an equally creative process. Because creative processes are quite hard to predict, as agile proponents claim, it's very hard to control such a process with a methodology that's rigidly designed to control predictable processes.

---

7. Steve McConnell, "From the Editor," (*IEEE Software*, March/April 2000). Available online at http://www.stevemcconnell.com/CargoCultSe.pdf.

NOTE   It bears mentioning that proponents of methodologies considered heavyweight or formal are quick to show that their methodology can be implemented as a light or agile process. One common example is the Rational Unified Process (RUP) for which there are several references in the literature on how to implement an "RUP instance" in an agile fashion.

In this book you'll draw ideas and best practices from several of the most prevalent methodologies. You'll use ideas from the Unified Process (UP)[8], Feature-Driven Development (FDD),[9] and Extreme Programming (XP).[10] As a guide for newcomers to the modeling world, the OMG suggests that you first select a methodology and then find a UML modeling tool that best supports it. Your approach will be simpler and much more cost effective, when possible, and for the sake of continuity you'll use a tool that will enable you to evolve your models as your system development gets under way. Current tools aren't as flexible as you'll want them to be and aren't conducive to collaborative work in the way that a simple whiteboard and a set of markers are. Therefore, if the tool is getting in the way of progress put it aside and go the low-tech way!

Methodology Lessons Learned

We've listed a brief set of best practices or general guiding principles from the methodologies previously outlined. These methodologies share many common traits that can be used by anyone to improve the quality of software.

A development model is needed to guide, document, and provide feedback to the customer, stakeholder, or client. In the race to deliver quality software on time and on budget, several methodologies have evolved to mitigate the often drastic trade-off between quality, time, and cost of construction. Most contemporary methodologies acknowledge the following:

- Feedback to the customer in the form of working software, as opposed to reports or mockups, is of the utmost importance for a project to remain alive.

- Any processes need to strive to minimize the overhead of applying the process. Programming is a creative endeavor and an overly constrained process is a quick way to kill creativity.

---

8. Jacobson et al, *The Unified Software Development Process* (Addison-Wesley, 1999).

9. Coad et al, *Java Modeling In Color With UML: Enterprise Components and Process* (Prentice Hall PTR, 1999).

10. Kent Beck, *Extreme Programming Explained* (Addison-Wesley, 1999).

- Models are only good if they guide the development of a system. A model is nearly useless in practice if the resulting code base isn't a reflection of the models.

- No methodology is a one-size-fits-all solution. Some work better with different team personalities, different project domains, and different levels of project complexity and different team sizes. If a model-driven methodology is selected hastily, it's never too late to switch into a more appropriate methodology. The UML can make this transition smoother by enabling models to be universally usable by any methodology or process.

- If at all possible, reinforce a methodology by selecting a CASE tool that enforces the values and practices of said methodology. But if no available CASE tool fits your team's work methodology you can always rely on low-tech approaches to successfully mitigate the task of modeling.

We encourage teams to borrow practices from different methodologies. After all, only the application of a practice can help you discern those based purely on theory from those based solely on practice. For example, we usually borrow ideas from Jeff Sutherland's SCRUM project's management methodology, which includes daily SCRUM meetings in which we ask ourselves what has been accomplished since our last meeting, what roadblocks we've encountered, and what we plan on doing between now and the next meeting. Other practices we subscribe to include the minimization of static modeling and active on-the-job knowledge transfer.

NOTE SCRUM is a lightweight, agile way to manage a project that shares many of its ideals with XP. Like XP, it's centered on the concept of an iteration as a period of planning and execution that results in a perceivable and measurable value. In SCRUM, a daily iteration is called a "scrum" though the external iteration is termed a "sprint," which is a manageable "scrum" collection that makes up a milestone (usually not more than 30 days).

Design Roadmap

To tackle the ongoing design process of the TCMS system, you should follow a simple design roadmap that will guide the reader through the creation of the models and the consequent production of the code that will materialize those models into a working software system. The roadmap consists of several steps or activities, many of which can be accomplished in parallel as follows:

- **Creation of an analysis object model (domain model):** An understanding of the domain is documented in the form of a static model (class model) that will serve as guidance during the requirements analysis and creation of the design models. This step gives a high-level foundation from which it's easier to see subsystems of related objects and components emerge. A domain model also serves as a way to validate any assumptions or preconceived notions about the domain and solidifies and centralizes the knowledge about the problem domain.

- **Requirement analysis:** Actors are defined from the analysis and architectural documents. User use cases (a use case that fulfills a specific feature) are created for high-level interactions of the primary actors with the system. User use cases are then decomposed into system-level use cases if necessary. System-level use cases depict actions taken by specific components in the system to accomplish a task needed for the fulfillment of a user use case. Quick assessment of the reuse of system-level use cases is performed. High-priority use cases are written in detail to curtail major risks (detail doesn't mean implementation-specific details). Analysis of requirements continues iteratively for as long as the project or product is alive.

- **Iteration planning:** Iterations are planned based on a group of use cases. Integration planning is performed to determine points of integration and modifications, or enhancements to the overall automation of the integration process are made. In this book each chapter is set as an iteration that sets out to fulfill a certain number of use cases.

- **Iteration execution:** Detail is added to use cases, both user and system use cases. Tests are written for each feature, and integration code or scripts are created or enhanced. Detailed dynamic models are created (detailed enough to be implemented and detailed enough to utilize any forward-engineering features of the CASE tools available to the maximum). Class diagrams for any subsystems created are defined and the overall model diagram is updated to reflect the results of the iteration. Whenever necessary, component diagrams and subsystem diagrams are created, thereby displaying the component interfaces and their relationships to the object models.

The activities described provide a baseline for the development plan. As the system evolves, the choices of the models and diagrams created have a high impact on how a specific problem is solved. Experience is the best guide as to how to pick the number and types of diagrams needed. Again, always remember that the code is the final product and no amount of diagrams will make a customer happy. Figure 2-1 shows a diagram depicting the activities followed for the TCMS system.

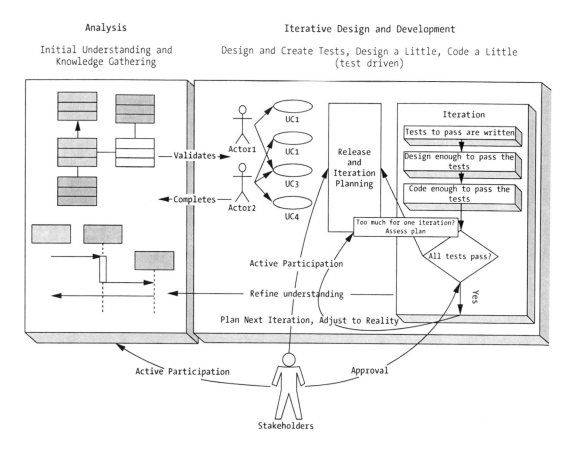

Figure 2-1. TCMS system-design roadmap

ArgoUML

The OMG, in its introduction to the UML, recommends that when getting started with OOAD and modeling you should first select a methodology or process and then select a modeling tool that properly supports the chosen methodology. The reality is that it's hard to judge what methodology will be a better fit for a certain project. It's only after working with the same team on a similar system that you can say with confidence whether a methodology is a good fit or not. Consequently, choosing an OOAD, UML-compliant CASE tool is also no easy task and the high price tags associated with the leading CASE tools could make a bad decision in this area have a negative impact on the bottom line, especially for mid-sized and small businesses.

NOTE   Although a set of models as depicted in this book might give you the impression that the design was done in a "big design up front" (BDUP) fashion as Scott Ambler of agile modeling fame refers to it. [11] The reality is that the models depicted in this chapter are the result of an evolutionary process that took a nontrivial amount of time and involved throwing away many intermediate models. The result of this process is displayed in this chapter, and then we will concentrate on development-centric issues in the rest of the book.

It's important to understand that many times a modeling tool just gets in the way of modeling. Many times a whiteboard, some markers, and a couple of Post-it notes are all you need to successfully model a system.

 TIP   A common practice is to bring a digital camera and take snapshots of a model on a whiteboard as the modeling process progresses. CASE tools haven't yet matched the level of collaboration that sharing a marker with a colleague achieves.

To fill the void for a low-cost CASE tool, the Open Source community has ArgoUML. ArgoUML is a 100-percent Java, Open Source (under the Berkeley Software Design License, or BSD) UML-based CASE tool. Jason Robbins and David Redmiles (Robbins's advisor) started the ArgoUML Open Source project as part of Robbins doctoral work on cognitive issues in software design at the University of California, Irvine in the late 1990s. ArgoUML is quickly evolving as the Open Source alternative in the CASE tool world and its rapid adoption has had a compounding effect on the quality of the tool.

ArgoUML, although feature-rich, still lacks some of the features of high-end commercial tools. The good news is that it's built on pluggable modules that allow it to grow in a controlled fashion. ArgoUML is part of the Tigris.org Open Source project, a mid-sized Open Source community focused on collaborative development tools (http://www.tigris.org). ArgoUML is the most prominent and active project on the Tigris.org site.

---

11. Scott Ambler et al, *Agile Modeling* (John Wiley & Sons, 2002). For more information on agile modeling also visit http://www.agilemodeling.com/.

ArgoUML is a very active project and the tool is rapidly evolving. Bugs and instabilities are being fixed at a fairly fast pace. It's built on a solid foundation that uses other high-profile and stable Open Source projects like Ant (Another Neat Tool) for building and ANTLER (ANother Tool for Language Recognition).

ArgoUML is currently compliant with version 1.3 of the UML standard. ArgoUML modular architecture employs a pluggable metamodel library that enables fast adoption of new versions of the UML standard. It also supports other standards like the XMI format (version 1.0) for the exchange of models with other tools (XMI is the standard mechanism used by ArgoUML to save models.) ArgoUML also has full support for OCL syntax and type checking as well as limited support for code generation via the ANTLR project.

Jason Robbins initially built ArgoUML as a test bed for ideas in cognitive psychology and their applications to software design. These features are unique to ArgoUML and include design critics, corrective automations, to-do lists, usage-based tool adaptation and design checklists among others. Several of these features help you keep the task of modeling focused on results rather than on the process that aligns well with the philosophy of XP. As Scott Ambler of agile modeling fame explains, a model is agile when it's sufficiently understandable, accurate, consistent, and detailed (the emphasis being in the word "sufficiently").[12] In XP terms a model should be as simple as possible but not simpler.

Obtaining and Installing ArgoUML

It's recommended that the Java Web Start (JWS) enabled version of ArgoUML is used given the simplicity and power that the JWS launching platform provides. With the JWS version of ArgoUML, installation and upgrades are automatic. To find out how to obtain and install the JWS-enabled version of ArgoUML or the stand-alone version, see http://argouml.tigris.org/servlets/ProjectDocumentList.

 NOTE   For more information on Java Web Start see http://java.sun.com/products/javawebstart/.

User Interface Overview

ArgoUML is a 100 percent swing-based Single Document Interface (SDI) application. The main application window consists primarily of four main panes, a menu bar, toolbar and status bar as shown in Figure 2-2.

---

12. Ambler et al, *Agile Modeling*.

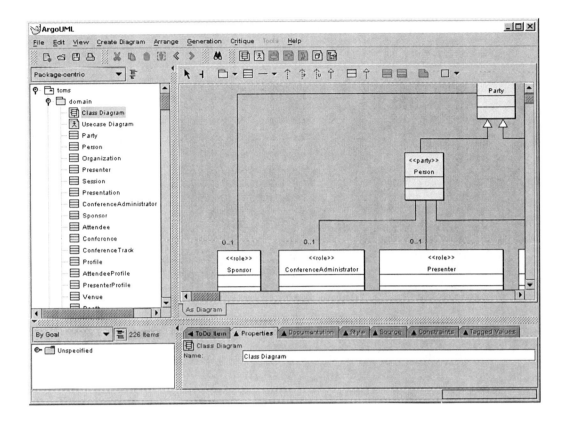

Figure 2-2. The ArgoUML UI

Now would be a good time to launch ArgoUML and begin exploring the user interface. There are many panes and controls available, and you'll need to remember a few of them in order to effectively work in ArgoUML. ArgoUML comes packaged with an array of sample models for you to explore in the www/models directory, under the installation directory.

The Navigator Pane

The Navigator pane provides a tree-based view of the model elements that can be dynamically changed based on the desired view and working model of the designer. The Navigator pane is the main navigational mechanism. The tree view allows you to expand and collapse nodes, thereby revealing or hiding model elements as needed. It allows the tree view to be structured using several options. The Package-centric and Diagram-centric views will cover most of your needs. Table 2-2 shows the different model views available in the Navigator pane.

Table 2-2. ArgoUML Navigator Pane Model Views

Navigator View	Description
Package-centric	The default view, it provides a hierarchical view of all packages, diagrams, and contained modeling elements.
Class-centric	Shows classes in their package hierarchy as well as datatypes and use case diagram elements. Similar to the Package-centric view but it doesn't show connecting or associating elements.
Diagram-centric	A rootless view showing only diagrams as top-level elements.
Inheritance-centric	Shows a hierarchy of modeling elements based on inheritance. This view is relevant mostly when dealing with a hierarchy of class elements.
Class Associations	Shows a hierarchy of classes and their associations (circular associations will be expanded ad infinitum!). It also shows all diagrams at the top level.
Navigable Associations	Supposed to show associations among classes (not working as of version vPRE-0.14.a1).
State-centric	This view shows relationships between elements of a state diagram.
Transitions-centric	Shows all transitions between elements of a state diagram at the top level with their elements connected by the transition as children. It also shows the state diagrams in the model at the top level.
Transitions paths	This view shows all transition paths between elements of a state diagram in a tree hierarchy. Circular paths can also be expanded ad infinitum.
Collaboration-centric	A rootless tree showing all collaboration diagrams in the model and their elements.
Dependency-centric	This view shows a hierarchy of dependencies between diagram elements (currently not working).

Package-centric is the default view, and it shows a hierarchy of objects for which the root is the model. Child nodes can include packages, diagrams, and any top-level but independent elements of any diagram (such as actors for a top-level use case diagram). The Diagram-centric view provides a rootless organization, which shows only diagrams at the top level and all other elements as children of the diagrams they're used in.

The Editing Pane

The Editing pane is the designer's main work area, where UML diagrams are displayed and edited. A diagram-specific toolbar shows common operations and elements that can be added to the active diagram. You'll learn about the operations and elements relevant to the creation of the models for the TCMS system throughout the rest of the chapter.

The Details Pane

The Details pane shows specific properties for the diagram or a selected model element. It's presented as a tab pane with tabs for the following:

- **To-Do Items:** Shows outstanding critic-generated and user-generated items for the selected model object. This pane allows the user to add new to-do items, resolve a to-do item (wizards guide you through the process), snooze the critic (temporarily ignore the item), or email a human expert for advice on how to resolve a critic-generated to-do item (partially implemented).

- **Properties:** Displays the main, model-related properties of a model object such as name, stereotype, namespace, visibility, and association.

- **Documentation:** Allows the designer to enter\JavaDoc tags for items such as author, version, or whether an item is deprecated.

- **Style:** Controls the appearance of the model object. Characteristics such as line and fill colors as well as size and shadow depth can be controlled from this pane.

- **Source:** Displays the equivalent Java or UML definition of the selected item.

- **Constraints:** Contains the UML Constraints Editor. UML constraints are invariants written (preferably) using the OCL.

- **Tagged Values:** Contains the Tagged Values Editor. Tagged values are name-value pairs that can be associated with a model's element. A property that has been tagged with a given name will be assigned the value associated with the tagged value. There are several predefined UML tags provided that can be used in a model.

- **Checklist:** Will eventually provide a "user-level" to-do list. In the current release of ArgoUML this tab is currently grayed out.

The most important tab, and the one you'll use the most is the Properties tab, which displays and enables you to edit any major features of the selected model element.

The To-Do Pane

The To-Do pane displays all to-do items (see the "Design Critics" section later in this chapter) in a tree-based view that can be dynamically sorted and grouped by priority, decision, goal, offender, poster, or knowledge type. To-do items can be of high, medium, or low priority. To-do items are categorized by design issue according to 16 predefined decision categories including Class Selection, Design Patterns, Code Generation, and others.

As you'll learn later in this chapter, the To-Do pane also holds the output of the design critics. The grouping options By Decision, By Goal, By Offender, By Poster, and By Knowledge Type are intimately related to the work of the design critics.

The Menu Bar and Toolbar

The menu bar or main menu is organized around the following categories, and the toolbar offers shortcuts to commonly used menu items.

- **File:** From here you can manage your ArgoUML projects and import source code to be reverse engineered into UML class diagrams. You'll also find other utility functions like printing, saving a graphic of a given diagram, and others.

- **Edit:** Provides the typical edit functions applied to the selected artifact(s) of the active diagram.

- **View:** This menu provides navigation features like tab pane navigation, and enables you to switch to a given diagram. It also provides the more familiar view controls like zooming and diagram grid management. There is also an option to toggle notations between UML 1.3 and Java.

- **Create Diagram:** From this menu you can create class, use case, state, activity, collaboration, deployment, and sequence diagrams.

- **Arrange:** Provides functions for the alignment, distribution, z-order, and fine positional adjustments of diagram artifacts.

- **Generation:** From this menu you can generate code for a class or all classes in a diagram.

- **Critique:** From this menu you can control ArgoUML's unique Design Critics feature as explained later in the chapter.

- **Tools:** Currently unavailable, it will eventually provide a plug-in point for external tools.

- **Help:** System information and the About screen. ArgoUML doesn't ship with a program-accessible documentation set or a context-driven help system.

Initial State

Once started, ArgoUML will create a brand new project or open the last saved project automatically, as long as you configure it to do so by choosing Edit ➤ Settings and selecting Reload Last Saved Project on Startup.

Cognitive Features in ArgoUML

ArgoUML provides some powerful features not found in any other UML CASE tools. Many of these features stem from the field of cognitive psychology and attempt to make the software adapt to the working habits of the designer and in many areas it assists by making predictions on what the designer might do next.

The cognitive features of ArgoUML can be categorized as follows:

- **Reflection in action:** Acknowledges that complex systems evolve and designers heavily reflect on their designs. To support reflection in action ArgoUML contains features like Design Critics, Corrective Automations, To-Do Lists, Checklists, and the partially implemented User Model.

- **Opportunistic design:** Is based on the concept that designers follow a path of the least "cognitive cost"[13] rather than a structured, hierarchical path. To support opportunistic design ArgoUML features To-Do Lists and Checklists and in the near future, a feature called Work Breakdown Structure. These tools help designers' natural tendency to evolve their designs via a path of least resistance.

- **Comprehension and problem solving:** ArgoUML includes multiple views or perspectives of the working model in order to help designers rapidly gain an understanding of a model and help them discern new connections between model elements. Features of ArgoUML supporting this theory include the navigational perspectives as shown in the Navigator and To-Do panes as well as many wizards.

Design Critics

Design Critics are an automated user interface feature that provides assistance to a designer. Design Critics are a process that works in the background as the design process is being carried out by the designer. Using a series of heuristics, Design Critics provide feedback on the decision-making process. You can think of them as a set of rules that are applied by a rule engine to the state of a model, which produces a set of actions in a form that the user can choose to ignore. It's a very unobtrusive feature. Feedback from the Design Critics is called critiques and appears as to-do items in the To-Do pane.

Design critics act as a guide and automated mentor. It's expected that as the designer gains more experience the number of critiques will diminish. Design Critics can flag perceived anomalies in a model and automatically correct them at the user's request. Critics can also integrate with other expert human designers via email. This feature is currently partially implemented and it will default to sending an email to the discussion list for users of ArgoUML.

Each critic monitors a specific design criterion and the result of its work is called a critique, which is a recommendation or statement about an aspect of a model that doesn't appear to follow good design practices.

ArgoUML Design Critics are configured via the Critique menu item. By default the option is turned on, but you can turn it off by selecting Critique ➤ Toggle Auto-Critique. The Critique menu also contains the following options that you'll need to configure:

---

13. ArgoUML online user manual, Chapter 8.

- **Design issues:** Design issues have different categories and priorities assigned to them. In this particular window a list of the decision types with priorities ranging from zero to five (zero being off and five being the highest priority) is shown. The setting here is applied globally to all critics. Setting all decision priorities to zero will effectively deactivate the critics. The decision types available include Class Selection, Naming, Storage, Planned Extensions, State Machines, Design Patterns, Relationships, Instantiation, Modularity, Expected Usage, Methods, Code Generation, Stereotypes, Inheritance, and Containment.

- **Design goals:** Higher-level guidance for the application of critiques. The same priority system used for the design issues applies to the goals of a critic. The setting on this window applies globally to all design goals. Currently there is only one design goal category: Unspecified. Setting the priority of this category to zero will effectively deactivate all critics.

ArgoUML also provides an option for browsing the existing critics by selecting Critique ➤ Browse Critics. In this window you can modify certain properties of a critic such as headline (name), priority, and long description. You can also turn a critic on or off ("snoozing" a critic in ArgoUML terms).

Critics also manifest themselves graphically on certain modeling elements. For example, in the case of a class element, a yellow note symbol will appear in the upper-left corner of the class when there are critiques associated with the class.

For example, on a newly added class, a critique telling you to name the class will appear.. To view the critique you can right-click the class and select Critiques ➤ Choose a Name. This will select the critique in the To-Do pane.

There are 85 built-in critics in ArgoUML. Some of them watch over the naming of model elements as well as the aesthetic aspects of the model—for example, in preventing overlapping graphical elements. Other critics watch for places in a model where a pattern like the singleton can be applied or decide whether two or more classes should be combined. Still other critics check more fundamental flaws and the correctness features of a model, such as, for example, circular composition, illegal generalization, nonpublic interface operations, and interfaces with attributes.

Drawing Diagrams in ArgoUML

The ArgoUML interface should be familiar to anyone who has used a drawing tool or another UML CASE tool. Diagrams are drawn using the tools available on the Editing pane toolbar, by selecting an artifact and clicking the diagram to place it at the desired position. Most model artifacts are meant to be associated with other artifacts in a diagram. In ArgoUML you have access to the most used association for a given element right from the element itself. By selecting a model artifact or hovering with the mouse over an already selected model artifact, you'll see squares appear on the artifact's periphery that hint at the possible associations available. To use them, simply click and hold the desired association hint (square) and drag it to another artifact in the diagram. Figure 2-3 shows the association hints for a class artifact.

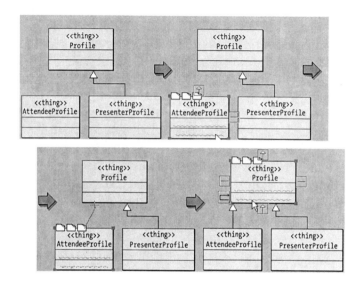

Figure 2-3. Association hints

Besides UML artifacts, the toolbar also provides general drawing tools to create rectangles, circles, lines, polygons, curves, and free-flowing text. These can be used to complement and supplement the expressiveness of a given diagram.

One of the features unique to ArgoUML is the Broom Alignment tool, which supplements the usual array of positioning- and alignment-related commands. This tool enables you to sweep several diagram elements horizontally or vertically, thereby aligning them. The Broom tool is the rotated T-shaped button (second from the left on the toolbar). The Broom's orientation is determined by the initial mouse gesture. After you select the direction, you can move the mouse and sweep elements against the edge of the broom. Moving the mouse perpendicularly in the direction of the broom increases the size of the broom's edge, thereby allowing you to cover a larger area with possibly more elements.

Case Study: Modeling the TCMS with ArgoUML

The next step is to create an analysis object model, also known as a domain model, based on the design roadmap. The choice of whether to model structure or behavior first is a hotly debated topic in object-oriented circles. In cases where the domain is well understood it's beneficial to start by consolidating the domain knowledge into a domain model. Well-chosen abstractions that are a true reflection of the business domain will naturally fall into the right roles when modeling behavior.

In ArgoUML, select File ➤ New Project (or press Ctrl-N). A new project will be created with a root element model that contains two children nodes, a class diagram, and a use case diagram, as shown in Figure 2-4.

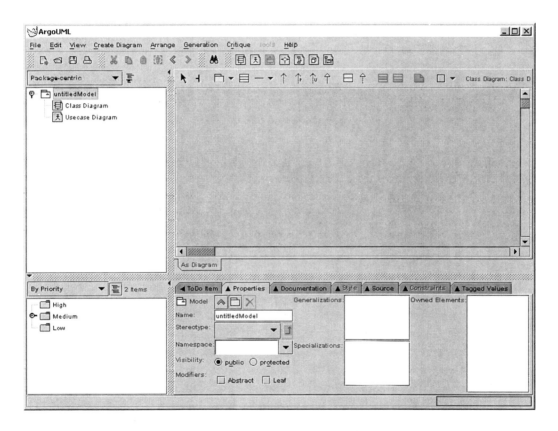

Figure 2-4. New project

Next you can rename the model root element by selecting it on the Navigator pane and then selecting the Properties tab in the Details pane. Alternatively, you can right-click the Navigator node and select Properties. In the Name field on the Properties tab, enter **Tcms**. Notice that the To-Do pane (lower left-hand corner) has changed to the By Goal view for critiques or to-do items, and Unspecified is the root node of the tree view. Expanding the Unspecified node will reveal the following two subitems:

- Revise Package Name Tcms

- Add Elements to Package Name Tcms

Select the Revise critique and the text will appear on the To-Do tab of the Details pane, explaining the critique, as shown in Figure 2-5.

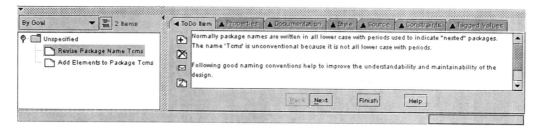

Figure 2-5. Critique details

The design critic tells you that it's a good practice for package names to be written in lowercase. To automatically fix the package name, select the Next button, which will show the suggested new package name as "tcms". You can now select the Finish button and the change will be automatically applied. Remember that the critiques are suggestions, which you can choose to ignore. Also you can choose to manually rename the model as stated in the critique explanation.

Under the tcms package you'll want to create two packages. One package will contain all diagrams for the domain analysis and the other will keep all the solution-space design diagrams. To create a package, right-click the tcms package and select Add package. A new package will appear with the name "(anon Package)". Select the new package on the tree view and, using the Properties tab, change the name to "domain". Repeat this operation and create another package under the tcms named "solution". You'll also want to remove the current default diagrams and create new diagrams under the newly created packages. To remove a diagram you can right-click it and select Delete from Model. Notice that you can only delete one of the diagrams. For a model to be valid, ArgoUML requires at least one diagram to be present. Before you remove the remaining diagram in the model, you need to create a diagram under the domain package.

To add a class diagram select the domain package on the Explorer and from the menu select Create Diagram ➤ Class Diagram. Rename the new class diagram "Class Diagram". Now you can proceed to remove the remaining diagram at the root of the project. The resulting project should look like the one depicted on Figure 2-6.

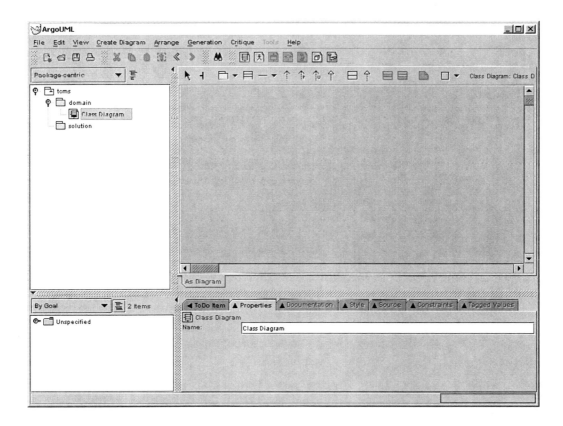

Figure 2-6. TCMS ArgoUML project

Finding and Refining Candidate Domain Model Elements

Based on the TCMS vision documents and high-level architectural blueprints introduced earlier, you can compile a list of candidate domain models. For this one you could use Class-Responsibility-Collaboration (CRC) cards or simply (as performed here) create a list of nouns and verbs by manually scanning the source documents. This process isn't merely a manual process, because it entails analyzing the understanding of the system and eliminating and discovering new candidate classes and new operations that weren't present in the source documents. This newly discovered domain knowledge can then be added to the source documents to ensure that it isn't lost.

The resulting filtered list of nouns is obtained by collapsing synonyms and eliminating nonentities (candidates that might be properties or modifiers, or may represent a state of an object). After analysis the resulting list shrinks in size. Now, the structural relationships between the candidate objects can be modeled. This process will further refine the candidate objects and will resolve many ambiguities about the understanding of the problem domain that you haven't previously encountered. The list of Nouns representing candidate entities is show in Table 2-3.

Table 2-3. TCMS Candidate Entities (Nouns)

Noun	Description
Sponsor	A sponsor is an individual or company that is "sponsoring" a conference.
Conference administrator	An administrator is an individual that has privileged access to conference-related functions.
Presenter	A presenter is an individual that presents one or more sessions.
Attendee	An attendee is a registered user who is attending a conference.
Organization	A nonindividual legal entity.
Conference	An event that consists of one or more sessions.
Conference Track	A high-level classification of the topics covered in a conference.
Presentation	A collection of materials and information to be conveyed to an audience in a predetermined amount of time.
Session	An event that embodies the act of "presenting" a presentation.
Schedule	A list of events that an attendee or a presenter will attend during a conference.
Venue	A physical location where a conference takes place.

Table 2-3. TCMS Candidate Entities (Nouns) (Continued)

Noun	Description
Booth	A temporary structure where sponsors can showcase their products during a conference.
Room	A room that is part of a venue.
Abstract	A document that explains the intent of a given presentation in compressed form.

Following Peter Coad's domain neutral component, you start the modeling of the actions embodied in the verbs (action phrases) gathered as objects in your domain model. Based on research into parallel object-oriented programming languages conducted at Stanford University[14] it was concluded that real-time tasks such as making a reservation or purchasing an airplane ticket should be modeled as objects that encapsulate (facade) the complexity of the task and simplify the associations between participating objects.

The question of whether to model the structure or behavior first is one that many beginning and intermediate modelers deal with during every new project. We recommend doing both simultaneously because modeling behavior validates the structural integrity of the model, and well-defined entities that reflect a domain naturally fall into place when modeling behavior.

 TIP Don't overanalyze with the noun and verb exploration. Concentrate on finding the principal candidates; others will emerge as you refine the analysis and design.

With this preliminary list of nouns you'll begin to construct a static model and the behavioral part of the domain model will begin to emerge. We emphasize that this is an iterative process and that the models produced will evolve as the system is constructed. In addition, certain assumptions made are validated while others are refuted. Remember, the analysis of the system helps you gain a deeper understanding of it, but doesn't prevent you from deducing knowledge that might be erroneous and based on naive, preconceived notions.

---

14. R. Chandra, A. Gupta, and J. L. Hennessy, "Integrating Concurrency and Data Abstraction in the Cool Parallel Programming Language" (*IEEE Computer,* February 1994).

Object Modeling Using Archetypes and Color in UML

An insightful and useful technique that hasn't received the level of recognition it deserves is the use of color, as proposed by Peter Coad in his book *Java Modeling in Color with UML: Enterprise Components and Process* (Prentice Hall PTR). The color in UML technique hinges on the notion of an archetype, which is a concept similar to the concept of a stereotype in UML with the difference being in the rigidity of the definition and its effect on the target class. An archetype is a way to tag a class as something that more or less adheres to a certain set of characteristics. (This is a looser definition than inheritance for example.) Coad started using 3M Post-it Notes, which come in four colors, pink, yellow, blue, and green, to label model elements. Coad assigns a color to each one of the archetypes or class categories. The addition of color gives you a sense of spatial layering that enables designers to quickly capture both structure and behavior and helps you to see dynamism in an otherwise static class diagram. Coad defined the following four main archetypes and associated them with four colors:

- **Moment-Interval (pink):** The moment-interval archetype represents an activity that can be tracked in time, something that occurs at a moment in time or over an interval of time. Registering for the conference, submitting payment, and browsing sessions are all examples of Moment-Intervals.

- **Role (yellow):** The role archetype represents the way something participates in a moment-interval, for example, a person can participate in a conference while playing the role of attendee.

- **Description (blue):** The catalog-entry description archetype represents a value or set of values that can be used to label a set of things. The easiest way to think of the description archetype is to think of information that classifies an entity but that doesn't define its identity. For example, nationality and immigration status can be considered descriptions for a person while a passport number or green card number will be a part of that person's identity information.

- **Party, place, or thing (green):** The party, place, or thing archetype, PPT for short, represents the things that can play a role in the different activities of the system.

The four basic archetypes are interconnected in a way that repeats over and over in models. This pattern in its simplest form entails a PPT playing a role in a moment-interval, which might affect other PPTs. PPT also might have descriptions associated with them. In this pattern physical entities such as PPT never interact directly but instead are participants (as role players) in an activity.

For example, in the conference attendee example a person (party) is an attendee (role) in the context of a conference (moment-interval). The temporal relationship between the conference and the person is fulfilled by the attended role. This basic pattern is depicted in Figure 2-7.

 NOTE In this book the colors for the Coad Archetypes are represented as shades of gray. Visually the power of the technique hinges on the use of color. To see the images in color visit http://www.ejdoab.com.

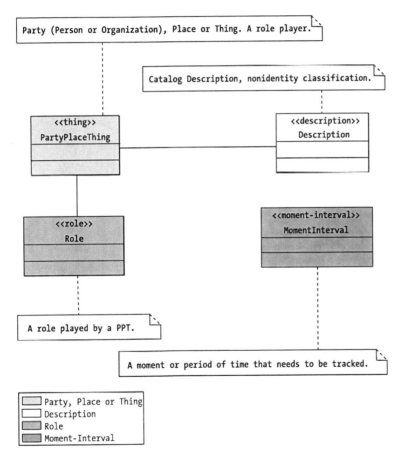

Figure 2-7. Basic relationships between the Coad archetypes

As you'll see later in more detail the main formula is to find an activity (moment-interval), find the participants in that activity (roles), and find who or what is playing that role (party, place, or things). You begin by making a list of possible m-i classes that are central to the system in question. Eventually you'll arrive at a model for which all classes belong to one of the four archetypes. Table 2-4 shows your initial list of m-i candidates. As you can see you started at the highest level and moved toward moments-intervals of finer and finer detail. For example, at the highest level you have the conference as the top m-i class. Conference is an m-i class because it's something that happens over a period of time and can be tracked for legal and business reasons. You can also see that your four main stake-holders are roles played by either a person or an organization of some kind.

NOTE   In their book *Java Modeling in Color with UML: Enterprise Components and Process*, Coad et al use an archetype called a moment-interval detail, which is also colored pink and labeled with the stereotype mi-detail. Moment-interval details are classes that hold information about a moment-interval class. They are usually associated with a moment-interval via aggregation. In this book we don't use m-i details for the sake of simplicity.

Table 2-4. TCMS Candidate Moment-Interval Classes

Moment-Interval	Participants (Roles)	Role Player
Conference	Sponsors, Administrator, Presenter, Attendee	Person/Organization
Conference Registration	Attendee, Presenter	Person
Conference Track	Attendee, Presenter	Person
Schedule	Attendee, Presenter	Person
Session	Attendee, Presenter	Person
Session Evaluation	Attendee	Person
Call for Papers	Presenter	Person

The Domain-Neutral Component

A more encompassing set of interconnections between the four basic archetypes is the domain-neutral component (DNC), which is a template built upon the four archetypes based on roles being played by the three different entitylike elements (PPTs): party, place, and thing. This results in a template model with three legs or branches: the party branch, the place branch, and the thing branch. The DNC, as originally introduced by Coad, is shown in Figure 2-8.

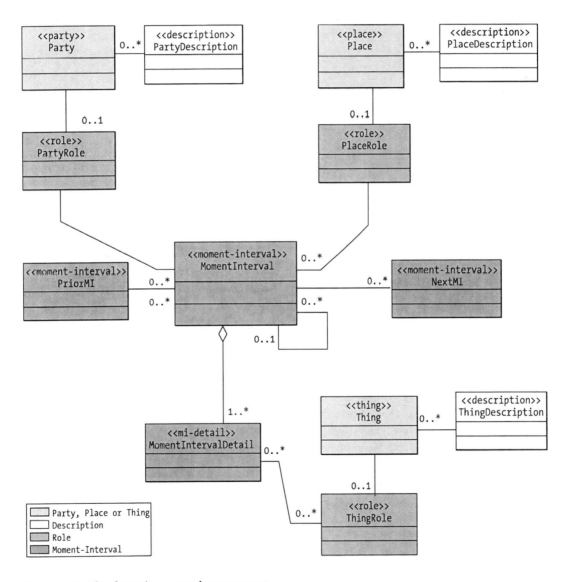

Figure 2-8. The domain-neutral component

The result is a flexible, semantic-based class diagram template that you can use to build any kind of model. The best part is that it's remarkably simple to use. You don't have to fit your model into the DNC, rather, the DNC will guide you to make your model more complete. The trick about using the DNC is an understanding that archetypes are very flexible definitions, and that elements of the DNC template can be dropped out to simplify the model. Basically you start with a very complete model and progressively collapse or drop archetypes as you go along.

This takes a bit of effort in the beginning because programmers tend to model interactions or temporal relationships between elements as a method in one of the participating elements. The DNC and the four archetypes hinge on the notion of representing these relationships as elements themselves.

You might be asking yourself where we're going with all this color stuff. The truth is that it takes a bit of time and a couple of models to begin to grasp the power of the technique. But once it sinks in it will help you produce better, more accurate, and complete models. To an extent it's a completeness theorem of sorts, especially when it comes to modeling. That's the main goal of the technique—to make you a better modeler.

Adding Modeling Elements to the Class Diagram

The next step is to graphically construct the model. Renowned object technologist Martin Fowler defines a domain model as "an object model of the domain that incorporates both behavior and data."[15]

A domain model creates a web of interconnected objects, where each object represents some meaningful entity, whether it's as large as a corporation or as small as a single entry in a user's schedule. This seemingly static model is represented with a class diagram that shows the basic relationships between the candidate elements. A class diagram models structure and contents using design elements such as classes, packages, and objects. It also displays relationships such as containment, inheritance, associations, and others.

The slight difference in this approach from the traditional static domain entity model is that you'll be adding relationships between entity classes in the form of moment-interval classes, and you'll be identifying any other classes as belonging to one of the four Coad archetypes.

Let's start with a small section of the domain, focusing on the session m-i candidate as shown in Table 2-3. Your basic strategy is to identify some m-i classes and plug other archetypes around them using the DNC as guide.

To add a new class to the diagram, follow these simple steps:

---

15. Martin Fowler, *Patterns of Enterprise Application Architecture* (Addison-Wesley, 2002).

- Select the diagram on the Navigator pane (entitled "Class Diagram").

- Click the class icon in the toolbar (yellow square with three compartments).

- Click anywhere on the Editor pane.

The new unnamed class element should appear on the Editor pane at the location of the last mouse click as well as in the Explorer. Select the Properties tab on the Details pane and in the Name field enter **person.** Repeat these steps for the following classes: Presenter, Attendee, Session, SessionLocation, ContentToBePresented, Room, and Presentation. The class diagram should now resemble Figure 2-9.

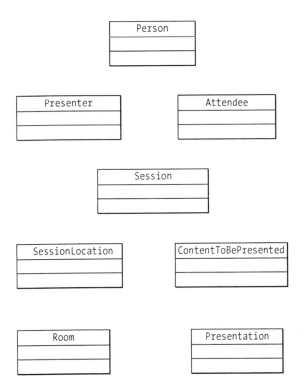

Figure 2-9. Newly created classes

The next step is to associate the created classes with one of the four archetypes. To date the only tool that includes built-in support for the Color in UML techniques, the four basic archetypes, and the DNC is Borland's Together line of products, formerly TogetherSoft's TogetherJ. ArgoUML enables the creation of custom stereotypes and also enables a class color to be selected. Although at this point it isn't possible to associate a specific stereotype with a class color or any other attribute. Therefore, for each class you need to manually assign a color. This is a small price to pay for the extra expressiveness that color brings into the process.

Creating a Custom Stereotype

Adding a new stereotype to ArgoUML is a little trickier than it needs to be (we expect the procedure to be simplified in future versions):

- Select any class in the class diagram.

- On the Details pane choose the Property tab and select any stereotype from the stereotype drop-down list.

- Click the button next to the drop-down list. The button is unlabeled with a graphic of an arrow with a 90-degree bend. This should take you to the stereotype Property tab.

- Click the New Stereotype button (the one adorned with guillemets).

- Enter the name of the new stereotype, in this case enter **party.**

Repeat the last two steps shown previously for the following stereotypes: place, thing, role, moment-interval, and description.

NOTE   The ArgoUML manual cautions about a known bug. Apparently, in certain versions of ArgoUML the newly created stereotypes will not appear in the class property stereotype drop-down list until the entire model is saved and then reloaded.

Assigning Archetypes and Creating Associations

Now that the Coad archetypes have been added to the model, you can proceed to label your classes with the appropriate archetypes and create meaningful associations between the classes following the guidelines of the DNC.

To assign an archetype, simply select a class in the diagram and change its stereotype value to the appropriate archetype name on the Stereotype drop-down list. For the classes currently in your class diagram you should use the values shown in Table 2-5.

Table 2-5. Archetype Selection

Class	Archetype	Explanation
Session	Moment-Interval	A session is something you want to track for business purposes.
Person	Party	People are role players in the context of a session.
Presenter	Role	A person presenting a session plays the role of a presenter.
Attendee	Role	A person attending a session plays the role of an attendee.
Room	Place	A room is a place that plays a role in the context of a session.
Session Location	Role	Is the role played by a room in the context of a session.
ContentToBePresented	Role	Is the role played by the material and content in the context of a session.
Presentation	Thing	The material being presented.

Now that you've defined the archetypes that your classes fall into, you can add color to your classes by using the Style tab and selecting the appropriate color for each of the archetypes using the Fill drop-down list. Table 2-6 shows a quick summary of the archetypes, their color, and the position of the color in the Fill drop-down list in the version of ArgoUML that you're using.

Table 2-6. Coad Archetypes and Their Corresponding Colors

Archetype Name	Color	Position in Drop-Down List
Party-Place-Thing	Green	11th
Role	Yellow	7th
Moment-Interval	Pink	8th
Description	Blue	10th

After choosing the Archetypes and corresponding colors you can make simple connections in your model following the basic archetypes relationship, which tells you that a PPT plays a role in the context of an m-i. This forms chains of PPT-role-m-i in your model. In the current case you have the following:

- Person-Presenter-Session

- Person-Attendee-Session

- Room-SessionLocation-Session

- Presentation-ContentToBePresented-Session

It's now easy to see the pattern. In the case of the presenter role you can read the pattern as follows: "A person plays the role of a presenter in the context of a session." Now proceed to associate the classes by clicking the Association icon in the toolbar, and then click one class and drag the cursor to the other class in the desired association. If you select an association you can change the name of the association as well as assign a stereotype to the association. All associations are one-to-one associations by default. To change the cardinality of either end of an association, right-click the association line closer to the end you want to affect, and select one of the options under the Multiplicity submenu. You can also change the nature of the association to be a composite or aggregate from the Aggregate submenu. Association directionality can also be changed from the same context menu by using the Navigability submenu.

 TIP Don't worry too much about getting all multiplicity and cardinalities of the relationships in the domain model right the first time or even in there at all. This can lead to analysis paralysis.

The resulting class diagram should resemble Figure 2-10.

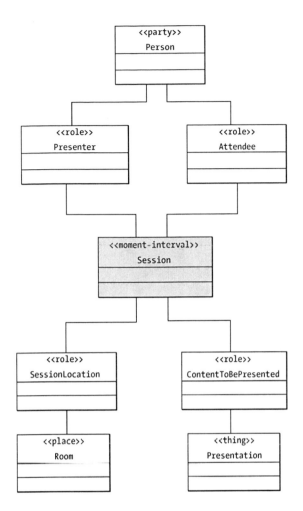

Figure 2-10. Archetypes, color, and the DNC applied to the partial model

At this point you can further simplify the model by correlating the model with the structural information and with the needs of the system in order to maintain certain information. For example, in the case of the Room-SessionLocation-Session and the Presentation-ContentToBePresented-Session legs of the diagram, you can drop both the SessionLocation and the ContentToBePresented roles because you don't need that level of detail or flexibility in the model. Therefore, you can directly connect the Green and the Pink elements in both legs of the diagram. The resulting simplified diagram is shown in Figure 2-11.

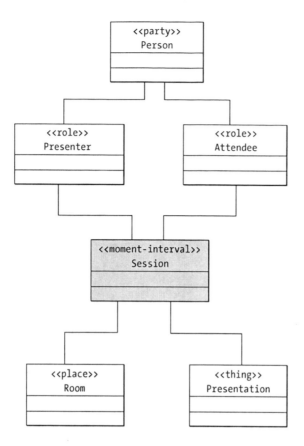

Figure 2-11. Simplified class diagram

After repeating this discovery and refinement process to the other moment-intervals identified, you'll see the domain model shown in Figure 2-12. As you can see the strategy boils down to finding the pink, then yellow, then blue and green archetypes. Then for each leg of the model you should remove any classes where complexity outweighs the flexibility provided by the class. In the case of an analysis model, remove the class only if the meaning and understanding of the model is unaffected by the removal of the class. For a design model determine if the class can be collapsed onto one of the associated classes or if it can be removed altogether without affecting the functionality of the system or component.

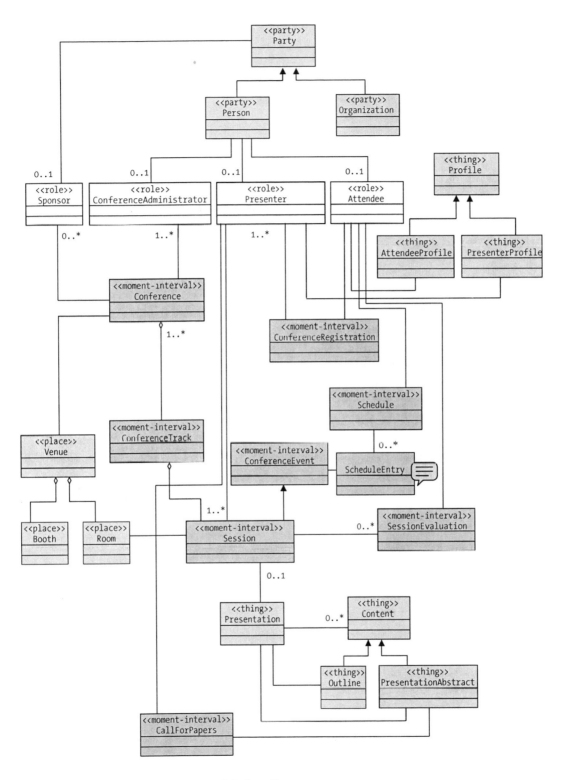

Figure 2-12. The TCMS domain model class diagram

The beauty of the DNC, archetypes, and color technique is that they all greatly enhance the expressiveness of a model, imparting a level or dynamism to an otherwise static class diagram.

Use Case Modeling

The main goal of use case modeling is to understand user needs and to enable you to view a system from the customer's point of view. Use cases describe how actors interact with the system in order to achieve some business purpose. They are procedural descriptions of the process of functional decomposition.

Even though use cases aren't object-oriented in nature, this doesn't mean that use cases have no value in OOAD, on the contrary, they are good vehicles for the understanding of user requirements and for the planning of deliverable milestones in a system.

That said, it's important to use caution when modeling with use cases because they could lead to the definition of procedures without a proper understanding of the problem domain. This can lead to the creation of many "artificial" classes to support a specific use case that taints and distorts the essence of the domain being modeled. As long as you understand this you should have no problem with use cases.

In our experience use cases are of great value to the implementation of test cases and they promote a test-driven (test-first approach) process. In this sense the completion of a use case becomes a tangible deliverable that can provide instant feedback to the system's stakeholders. With the current emphasis on service-driven architectures, use cases are a good vehicle to define the goals of services and are useful in the definition of service-oriented components (like session facades, as you'll see in Chapter 5).

Use Cases and the Domain-Neutral Component

Applying the DNC makes for a great preamble to modeling use cases because it helps prevent one of the cardinal sins of use case modeling: uses cases dictating an object-model's structure. When use cases drive a model's shape the model effectively becomes a slave of the current functionality being addressed and no longer is a true representation of the business. This means that although a use case might give you a clear understanding of a single interaction between an actor(s) and the system, it doesn't give you an understanding of the problem domain (as the domain model does), which can lead to "design tunnel vision."

To an extent, you can equate the Moment-Interval classes with either a use case, part of a use case, or an encapsulation of one or more use cases. Use cases are typically documented as short but concise textual descriptions or scenarios— a concept similar to XP's User Stories, which represents a "story" about how a system solves a particular problem.

Use Cases Overview

Use cases are primarily delivered as documents. There are many "templates" floating around in the industry that do a good job of explaining use cases, from flowing textual descriptions to enumerated bullet point step-by-step descriptions. These descriptions are usually structured around a normal flow of events, which are often referred to as a success scenario. These scenarios differ from the normal flow of events, which are documented as extensions or variations. For a sample template see Alistair Cockburn's website (http://www.usecases.org/).

In use case modeling the concept of an actor plays a central role. An actor is a role that some entity plays while the system is being analyzed or designed. Typically, actors are classified as primary and secondary actors. Primary actors are those that are deriving business value from an interaction with the system, while secondary actors are those that the system interacts with in order to fulfill the needs of a primary actor. In the case of the TCMS system, your defined stakeholders map directly to primary actors in your use cases.

At a higher level, a use case diagram can show the associations among use cases and the primary and secondary actors involved. In the case of the TCMS system you started with a high-level use case diagram to get a birds-eye view of the functionality that the system must satisfy. Like class diagrams, use case diagrams provide display associations between the use cases in the system. A use case diagram helps you organize the functionality of a system. A use case diagram is the primary artifact used in defining the services and the components that fulfill them.

Use case diagrams consist of actors (usually represented by a stick figure), use cases (represented as an ellipse), and optionally, a rectangle enclosing the use cases, which denotes a system boundary or simply groups the use case model. There are three relations between use cases: extend, include, and generalization.

- **Extend:** Represents an extension on behavior and not in structure. It signifies that the extending use case contains added behavior, not alternatives or exceptions. The new use case doesn't alter the behavior produced by the base use case. Extension points are used to determine when the extended case applies inside the base case.

- **Include:** Represents containment of behavior. Think of it as a use case that "invokes" the behavior of another use case at a specific point in a use case.

- **Generalization:** Implies an "is like" relationship between use cases. Generalization is used whenever a use case is conceptually similar to another use case.

Creating a Use Case Diagram in ArgoUML

To create a use case diagram in ArgoUML you follow steps similar to those used to create a class diagram:

1. Select the use case diagram. In the Explorer, under the tcms model, expand the domain package under the model and select Usecase Diagram. The toolbar should now change to the use case diagram controls.

2. Add actors. Using the toolbar controls, you can add different elements to the diagram including actors. Add four actors: attendee, presenter, administrator, and sponsor. This is similar to working with classes. If you select an actor on the diagram its properties (such as the name) can be changed in the Details pane on the Property tab.

3. Add use cases. Using the toolbar controls, you select the use case (white ellipse) and click anywhere on the diagram. Next, rename the use case to Browse Schedule. Repeat this step for a use case named Add Schedule Reminder.

4. Add associations. Using the Association drop-down list on the toolbar, select the directed association (on first row, right-most element in the drop-down list, which is an arrow pointing to the right). Connect the attendee actor to the Browse Schedule use case. Next, using the extend association in the toolbar (the upward-pointing segmented arrow with an "E" on the left) connect the Add Schedule Reminder use case to the Browse Schedule use case.

The use case diagram should now resemble Figure 2-13.

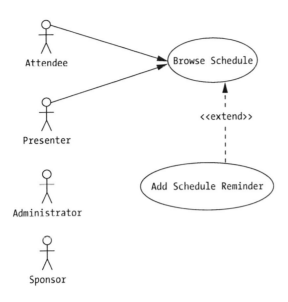

Figure 2-13. Partial use case diagram

If you feel adventurous you can complete the use case diagram using the list of use cases shown in Table 2-7. A use case diagram consisting of the collection of all actors and all use cases. It's referred to as the use case model.

Table 2-7. TCMS Preliminary List of Use Cases

Use Case ID	Name	Actors	Extends	Includes
UC-1	Browse Schedule	Attendee, Presenter	N/A	N/A
UC-2	Add Schedule Reminder	Attendee, Presenter	UC-1	N/A
UC-3	Remove Schedule Entry	Attendee, Presenter	UC-1	N/A
UC-4	Mail Schedule	Attendee, Presenter	UC-1	N/A
UC-5	Browse Sessions	Attendee, Presenter	N/A	N/A
UC-6	Add Session To Schedule	Attendee, Presenter	UC-5	N/A
UC-7	Browse Presenter Session	Presenter	N/A	N/A

Table 2-7. TCMS Preliminary List of Use Cases (Continued)

Use Case ID	Name	Actors	Extends	Includes
UC-8	Log In	Attendee, Presenter	N/A	N/A
UC-9	Register	Attendee, Presenter	N/A	N/A
UC-10	View Profile	Attendee, Presenter	N/A	N/A
UC-11	Edit Profile	Attendee, Presenter	UC-10	N/A
UC-12	Submit Abstract	Presenter	N/A	N/A
UC-13	Browse Abstracts		Presenter	N/A
UC-14	Edit Abstract	Presenter	UC-13	N/A
UC-15	Evaluate Abstract	Administrator	N/A	UC-15
UC-16	View News	Anyone	N/A	N/A
UC-17	Edit News	Administrator	UC-16	N/A
UC-18	Process Registration at Venue	Administrator	N/A	N/A
UC-19	View Statistics	Administrator	N/A	N/A
UC-20	Process Booth Request	Administrator	N/A	N/A
UC-21	Browse Booths	Sponsor	N/A	N/A
UC-22	Request Booth	Sponsor	UC-21	N/A

The resulting use case diagram—the TCMS use case model—is shown in Figure 2-14.

Technology Conference Management System (TCMS)

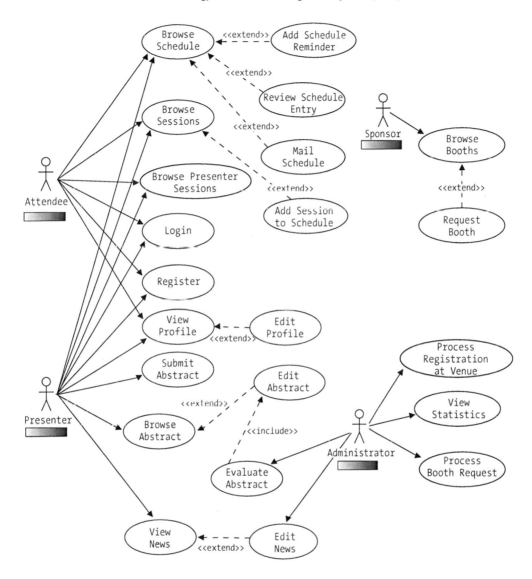

Figure 2-14. The TCMS use case diagram

Refining Use Cases with Sequence Diagrams

The UML sequence diagram models the dynamic behavior of a system by depicting object interactions over time. These interactions are expressed as a series of messages between objects. UML sequence diagrams are ideal for elaborating a use case execution in terms of objects from your domain model. One sequence diagram is typically used to represent a single use case scenario or flow of events. The message flow of a sequence diagram matches the narrative of the corresponding use case.

Sequence diagrams are an excellent way to document use case scenarios and refine and synchronize a use case diagram with respect to a domain model. A sequence diagram typically shows a user or actor and the object and components they interact with in the context of a use case execution.

NOTE   Sequence diagrams aren't working in ArgoUML as of the release of version v0.14. As an alternative, we suggest using the community edition of Poseidon UML, which is a commercial offering based on ArgoUML. We expect sequence diagrams to be available in the near future (hopefully by the time you read this!).

Whenever necessary use-sequence diagrams are used in the book to refine and validate a use case against the application's domain model.

TIP   Don't assign operations to a class without first refining complex use cases with sequence or interaction diagrams. By refining what capabilities a given class should have, you avoid the eventual generation of unneeded code. This practice aligns well with test-driven development and XP's You-Ain't-Gonna-Need-It (YAGNI).

Best Practices

Model-driven development is a practice that takes time to master, but the results are well worth the effort. We've compiled a list of best practices taken from the literature and from our own experiences to help you get started.

- Keep models simple: Don't over-model.

- Use color in your models. As seen in this chapter color greatly enhances your ability to quickly grasp the both the static and dynamic elements of a model.

- Choose model element names carefully. A model name can greatly influence the person that has to turn it into code.

- Avoid design or implementation-specific constructs in the analysis model.

- Keep models and source code synchronized: incremental changes are easier to incorporate.

- In modeling, no single view is sufficient. Approach a complex system with a small set of independent views.

- The best models are connected to reality and reality is all about trade-offs. Flexibility and performance are sometimes at odds when modeling a system.

- There will be a point in a model's life when the level of detail can only be expressed directly in code. Make sure that you don't waste valuable time trying to overmodel something graphically that can be explained with a code sample or an annotation. UML notes are a great way to address some of these issues at the model level.

Summary

As you prepare for a journey into the J2EE world it's important to remember that sound design practices—not technology—should drive the development of enterprise applications. Although at specific points you might have to make an implementation decision that's driven by the shortcomings of a particular technology, you should always keep in mind the greater picture of a solid design based on the problem space rather than the solution space.

In this era of agile methodologies and techniques, many are quick to dismiss software modeling. But as Scott Ambler (http://www.agilemodeling.com) and others have demonstrated, software modeling can be just another weapon in your arsenal of agile methods.

In this chapter you've learned a solid set of techniques and with the help of Open Source modeling tools you can make your models more robust and resilient to requirements and technology changes.

CHAPTER 3

Development and Build System with Ant

Our "Age of Anxiety" is, in great part, the result of trying to do today's job with yesterday's tools—with yesterday's concepts.

—Marshall McLuhan[1]

SOFTWARE DEVELOPMENT is a creative, fluid endeavor. In order to develop good software, developers need tools that will enable them to work effectively as individuals and as part of a team. Software development is all about people; people building tools for other people. One emerging realization of most modern methodologies is that people are the most important factor, regardless of methodology, and that every developer works differently but all of them have the same goal in mind: to create working software that satisfies a need.

In Chapter 2 we emphasized that methodologies are independent of tools, yet a tool that supports your chosen methodology will likely increase your team's productivity. Very few developers like to have a process or methodology imposed on them. By making the processes and practices supporting a given methodology transparent and mostly automatic, a team of developers can work as an orchestra against the backdrop of a supporting set of best practices.

The contributions of the Open Source community have greatly enhanced the way Java developers perform their daily work. Nowadays, for most aspects of the development process there seems to be an offering from the Open Source community, which is ready to take on the task of simplifying the job of developers worldwide. The rapid evolution of the Open Source tool market has been driven by many factors, whether it's to commoditize a market segment dominated by a commercial offering, to promote and research new ideas, or to embrace a new business model based partly on Open Source.

Development tools is probably the area you would most likely explore first when trying to incorporate Open Source in the enterprise. In this chapter you'll learn about some of the tools that are available from the Java Open Source community and explore how they can help you create high-quality software in a predictable

---

1. Marshall McLuhan and Quentin Fiore, *The Medium Is the Massage: An Inventory of Effects* (HardWired Books, 1996).

and reproducible fashion. The highlighted tools cover most of the critical areas of the software construction process and show how Open Source can support and enhance the productivity of a development team. With agility as your guiding principle, you'll explore tools that can foster a productive, cost-effective environment to help enterprise developers excel at what they do.

The Build Process

The traditional definition of a build process entails converting source code into an executable deliverable. In the world of enterprise Java development this definition falls short. A production J2EE application build system will typically need to do much more than that. Some sample tasks that can be performed by a build include the following:

- **Version control:** Obtaining the latest version of a project's source code from a version control repository

- **Build plan:** Determining what to build

- **Generate:** Generating any source code from several sources such as annotated code, database tables, UML diagrams

- **Formatting:** Correcting syntax and style

- **Checking:** Validating syntax and style

- **Compiling:** Generating .class files from .java files

- **Testing:** Running automated tests

- **Validating:** Verifying components' validity

- **JavaDoc:** Generating API documentation

- **Metrics:** Generating code metrics reports

- **Packaging:** Generating JAR, WAR, and EAR files

- **Deploying:** Deploying applications to servers

- **Distributing:** Distributing packaged applications

- **Notifying:** Notifying developers and managers of important build-related events

This relatively short list of activities should give you an idea of how involved the build process can become. How many times have you heard the dreaded "But it was working just fine on my machine!" A reproducible build is of paramount importance for keeping your code base healthy and your project in a known state at all times. Having a reproducible and stable build process takes more than just having a dedicated team of developers. Without automation even a small project with few developers can rapidly get out of hand.

By using an automated build tool, developers can define the steps in the process of building their software and execute those steps reliably under different environments and circumstances. Typically such tools will account for individual configuration differences between developers' environments and production systems. Most build tools have some sort of configuration or script that describes the build process in discrete, atomic steps.

A typical build process also covers aspects of both the production and the development stages of an application. For example, in a database-driven application, individual developers might need to initialize a database with sample data needed for testing, while in a production environment such a step would not be required.

Although integrated development environments (IDEs) have always provided a level of support for the building process, this support usually falls short of developers' needs and expectations. Most of these build solutions aren't portable across environments; it's hard enough to get one developer's IDE project file to work on any environment except for its creator's. Not only are these facilities IDE-dependent, but they're also very different from the work that an application assembler or deployer has to do for a production application. Common sense should tell you that the closest your development environment is to the production environment the least amount of problems you'll have going into production. By having a build process that is consistent across development and production environments (and any other environments in between), you can eradicate many of the development difficulties of using multiple IDEs, operating systems, and Java versions.

As the build process is automated and becomes transparent to programmers, other issues such as testing and documentation generation find their way into the build process. Most developers find that they begin with a simple build system that evolves to accomplish more than simply "building." From testing to document generation, a finely crafted build process eventually becomes a reflection of a team's development process.

In J2EE a consistent build system brings together the roles of the application developer, assembler, and deployer. As part of the J2EE specification, Sun defined several roles in its definition of the J2EE platform. Newcomers to J2EE might quickly put themselves in one these categories and disregard the details of the other roles. But the reality is that unless you have an understanding of every role's responsibility, your understanding of the J2EE platform will not be complete. In particular, the roles of the "application assembler" and the "application deployer" are reflected in the build process, and unless your developers can duplicate what happens in production you're likely to experience a painful transition from development into production.

Continuous Integration

One modern software development practice that's embraced by many methodologies and promoted, particularly by the Extreme Programming (XP) movement, is the practice of continuous integration. This practice might be one of the most important lessons you'll ever learn from the XP and agile movement. The main idea is that developers working on a project should integrate changes to their code at least on a daily basis. In Chapter 4, the topic of testing is covered in the context of continuous integration. The basic steps to accomplish continuous integration are simple:

- **Integrate:** Changes are checked into a central repository (code that adds new features requires new test cases that must also be checked in).

- **Test:** All tests are performed. A successful integration is bound by a 100-percent success of the testing stage. If any tests fail, the offending code is rolled back and code is refactored until it passes the respective test(s).

- **Repeat:** With the help of automation, you can run this process at well-defined intervals (ideally a minimum of once a day). This ensures that the system's codebase remains fully tested at all times and that bugs and missing features are addressed as soon as possible.

Continuous Integration, as championed by XP and agile-methodology proponents, is one of those concepts that most developers agree with, but few teams ever implement. You should only build what's necessary and it should be tested for compliance with the requirements as often as possible. You also should understand that making lots of changes at once leads to hours of "big-bang" integration testing later on.

By never holding on to changes in the code for more than a day, a team can minimize the chances that the code will become fragmented. These "unofficial forks" to a code base (they occur when a developer never integrates changes to the code base and is effectively working on an older version) lead to hard-to-find bugs and countless hours of integration effort.

By adopting a test-driven approach to development (see Chapter 4) in combination with build-process automation, a team can achieve Continuous Integration and build only what's needed when it's needed, and build it right. Continuous Integration increases the team's knowledge about the system being built, thereby boosting its reaction time to feedback from the system and the system's stakeholders.

Automating the Build Process with Apache's Ant

A project with a few files and very little dependencies makes the process of building almost not a process at all. By simply using the Java compiler and maybe the JAR command-line utility, you can build simple Java applications.

Before Ant, developers typically started with a set of simple batch files or shell scripts as an initial step towards automation. But as the number of files, components, target platforms, and View Mail (VM) versions increases so does the build time, the complexity of the build, and the likelihood that human errors will contribute to irreproducible and inconsistent builds. After a while you end up realizing that maintaining a nonportable, platform-dependent homemade solution is cumbersome and error prone.

For the few teams in which developers actually agree on a choice of an IDE, the first choice is usually to use the build facilities provided. Most IDEs provide wizards that build simple applications. These wizards cover only part of the equation and they tie your team to the particular IDE.

Besides the aforementioned problems, both approaches treat development and production environments as being conceptually separate. What's needed is a low-level tool that can unify the build process across multiple IDEs, stages of development, platforms, and so on.

For many years UNIX programmers have had a way to build their applications via the make utility and all of its variants (GNU Make, nmake, and so on). Like make, Ant (Another Neat Tool) is at its core a build tool, but as the Ant website states that Ant "is kind of like Make, but without Make's wrinkles."[2]

Ant's simplicity has contributed to its rapid adoption and made it the de facto standard for building applications in the Java world. Ant, together with the Concurrent Versions System (CVS), has played an important role in fostering Open Source by providing a universal way for individuals to obtain, build, and contribute to the Open Source community. Ant has also become an indispensable tool for most Java developers, especially those developing J2EE applications.

---

2. See http://ant.apache.org/.

History

Ant is a pure Java application that was originally developed by James Duncan Davidson during a transatlantic flight back to the United States in 1999. Duncan, also the original author of the Apache Tomcat Servlet reference implementation (and one of the J2EE architects), wrote Ant as a tool to ease Tomcat's building process. As a Sun engineer, he lobbied for Sun to make both projects Open Source by donating the code to the Apache Software Foundation's Jakarta project. As a reflection of its rising popularity, Ant became an Apache Software Foundation top-level project late in 2002.

Ant has made life easier for Java developers worldwide. Although far from perfect, it has demonstrated that it can cover what Java developers need, from gaining control over the build process to cutting the umbilical cord from proprietary build systems.

The Make Utility and Ant

The make utility is a command-line utility that uses a descriptor or script file (referred to as a "makefile") that contains dependency rules, macros, and suffix rules that build and test a program. Makefiles contain inference "rules" that describe how to create a "target." A target is either a file to be created or an action to be taken. Targets can have dependencies, which might also be targets. Rules in a makefile can form a chain of dependencies that are traversed to accomplish the build. In the C/C++ world, makefiles build object files from source files and then link the object files to create an executable.

A great utility, make does have some "wrinkles," such as its dependency on UNIX shell scripting and the correlation of targets with files. The make utility's flexibility and power comes from the fact that it can become a full-blown scripting language that at the same time makes it easier for a makefile to grow rapidly out of control. The same can be said of an Ant build description file, but it seems more likely that problems could occur with the make utility. The make utility's extensibility comes from the capabilities of the UNIX shell. Ant on the other hand is extended with simple Java classes.

Comparing Ant with the make utility is similar to comparing Java and C or C++. Java was born from some of the lessons learned with C++: Too much flexibility can lead to trouble. Most Ant build scripts are somewhat easier to understand than a corresponding makefile. You've probably seen makefiles ranging from difficult to plain cryptic. Makefiles have many features of a bygone developer era such as the need to use control characters like Tab as part of the syntactic rules of the file.

Ant provides a simpler and cleaner way to handle the process of building a Java application. It's important to acknowledge that the make utility has been around for many years and has benefited from the lessons developers have learned from building a countless number of applications. Some of these lessons are reflected in Ant's design.

Another marked difference between Ant and the make utility is the fact that Ant is 100-percent Java and thus inherits all of the pros and cons of platform independence. The make utility on the one hand depends on the operating system shell, which gives you all of the power of the UNIX shell but at the same time makes the shell platform dependent. If an application isn't a Java application there is very little reason to switch from the make utility to Ant. Ant is certainly a Java-centric tool and benefits of its use are seen on Java applications. Although you can make it work with any language due to its extensibility, it isn't clear that doing so will contribute greatly to the build process of a non-Java application.

Why Choose Ant?

Many people, especially those coming from the UNIX world, ask this question, but the answers seem rather extreme, ranging from the evangelization of Ant to total avoidance. The main point is that Ant does simple things very well. It isn't perfect and it doesn't cover every conceivable scenario that can occur in a build, but for the majority of cases it does the job well. The most relevant reasons to choose Ant are as follows:

- **Platform independence:** A typical corporate Java environment includes development teams that work on Wintel machines and deploy to UNIX machines for production. Ant, being a pure Java tool, makes it possible to have a consistent build process regardless of the platform, thereby making the development, staging, integration, and production environments closer to each other. Ant also has built-in capabilities that handle platform differences. Your Java code is portable, therefore your build should be, too!

- **Adoption:** Ant is everywhere! Yes, by itself this is a poor reason to favor a technology but the strengths that ubiquity brings to the table are many including hiring, training, and skills marketability. Ant also has been easily incorporated into many of the leading IDEs, thereby making it the one consistent factor between developers. This is partly due to the choice, for good and bad reasons, of XML as its language.

- **Functionality and flexibility:** For the majority of Java projects, Ant is extensible and highly configurable; it provides the required functionality right out of the box. For Java developers any class can easily become an Ant task, although in our experience we seldom have to write our own tasks (because someone in the Open Source community always seems to beat you to the punch). If desired, you can plug scripting engines (see the Bean Scripting Framework) and run platform-specific commands.

- **Syntax:** Like it or not, XML has become a globally recognized data format. Most Java developers have worked with XML, and J2EE developers deal with XML on a daily basis. XML makes Ant buzzword-compliant. But XML also has some positive advantages. XML is ideal for representing structured data because of its hierarchical nature. The abundance of commercial and Open Source parsers, and the ability to easily check an XML file for well-formness and validation has made the use of XML pervasive in the industry.

Introduction to Ant

Ant's architecture is similar to the make utility in that it's based on the concept of a target. In Ant a target is a modular unit of execution that uses tasks to accomplish its work. An Ant target has dependencies and can be conditionally executed. A build is usually composed of some main targets that will typically accomplish some coarse-grain process related to an application's build, such as compiling the code or packaging a component. These main targets might make use of other subtargets (usually via dependencies) to accomplish their job.

Underneath the covers, tasks are plain Java classes that extend the org.apache.tools.ant.Task class although any class that exposes a method with the signature void execute() can become an Ant Task. One of Ant's great advantages is its extensibility. Ant tasks are pluggable plain Java classes. To write a task all you need to do is extend the Task class and add some code to the execute method. Ant comes loaded with myriad tasks to accomplish many of the things needed during a typical build. These tasks are referred to as the "core tasks" and the "optional tasks." There are also a countless number of third-party tasks, whether they're commercial, freeware, or open-sourced.

The scope of Ant's contribution to Java development isn't obvious at first, especially on small projects. But once complexity begins to creep in and you have multiple developers, you'll find that Ant becomes the glue that can help your team work in synchronization. It can basically remove the need for a full-time build "engineer." This is largely the case with most Open Source Java projects and their success should be a testament to the effectiveness of continuous integration using Ant.

Ant isn't without its critics, however. Many have failed to understand that Ant was never meant to be a full-fledged scripting language but a Java-friendly way to automate the build process in a simple declarative, goal-oriented fashion. Since its inception, many scripting-like features have been added to Ant in the form of custom tasks, and the arguments between camps that want a full-scripting language and ones that want a simple, dependency-driven build system continue to this day. In our opinion there is no right answer; scripting is programming and you know the issues that arise with that. On the other hand, Ant's simple declarative ways make it hard to do write-once and reuse builds across different projects. Ant's reusability is at the task level. In his essay, "Ant in Anger," Steve Loughran recommends that to achieve the level of complexity that most developers turn to scripting to achieve, Ant builds can be dynamically generated on a per-project basis using something like eXtensible Stylesheet Language Transformations (XSLT).[3] For those looking for a full-fledged scripting engine based on XML, the Apache Jakarta Commons project provides Jelly.

Obtaining and Installing Ant

Ant can be obtained from `http://www.ant.apache.org` in binary and source distributions, or you can obtain the source code through CVS. Ant is a pure Java application, therefore the only requirement to run it is that you have a compliant JDK installed and a Java API for XML Processing (JAXP)–compliant parser (Ant ships with the latest Apache Xerces2 parser). Ant is distributed as a compressed archive (.zip, tar.gz, and tar.bz2). Once the archive has been uncompressed to a directory (this directory is referred to as ANT_HOME), it's recommended that you add the environment variable ANT_HOME to your system and the bin directory under the ANT_HOME directory to your system's executable path. The bin directory contains scripts in many different formats for the most popular platforms. These scripts facilitate the execution of Ant and include DOS batch, UNIX shell, and Perl, and Python scripts. Ant also relies on the JAVA_HOME environment variable to determine the JDK to be used.

 CAUTION   If you only have the JRE installed (a rare case for most Java developers) many of Ant's tasks will not work properly.

---

3.   See `http://ant.apache.org/ant_in_anger.html`.

To verify that Ant is installed correctly, at the command prompt type:

```
ant -version
```

If the installation was successful you should see a message showing the version of Ant and the compilation date:

```
Apache Ant version 1.6.0 compiled on December 18 2003
```

Ant's Command-Line Options

Ant is typically used from the command line by running one of the scripts in the bin directory. Ant's command line can take a set of options (prefixed with a dash) and any number of targets to be executed, as follows:

```
ant [options] [target target2 ... targetN]
```

Table 3-1 shows the options available from the command line. You can access them by typing **ant -help.** By default Ant will search for a file named build.xml unless a different file is specified via the Buildfile option.

Table 3-1. Ant Command-Line Options

Option	Purpose
help	Prints the help message showing all available options.
projecthelp	Displays all targets for which the description attribute has been set.
version	Prints the version of Ant.
diagnostics	Prints a diagnostics report that shows information like file sizes and compilation dates; useful for reporting bugs.
quiet	Minimizes the amount of console output produced by Ant.
verbose	Maximizes the amount of console output produced by Ant.

Table 3-1. Ant Command-Line Options (Continued)

Option	Purpose
debug	Prints debugging information to the console.
emacs	Removes all indentation and decorations from the console output.
lib	A path to search for libraries including Jars and Java classes.
logfile <file>, l <file>	Redirects all console output to the specified log file.
logger <classname>	Uses the specified class for logging (it must implement org.apache.tools.ant.BuildLogger).
listener <classname>	Adds an instance of a class that can receive logging events from the build (it must implement org.apache.tools.ant. BuildListener).
noinput	Does not allow the user to interact with the build.
buildfile <file>, file <file>, f <file>	Specifies the build file to be processed.
D <property>=<value>	Passes a property to the build.
propertyfile <filename>	Loads all properties in a properties file. Properties passed with the D option take precedence.
inputhandler <class>	Ant will use this class to handle input request. By default input requests are handled via the standard in (stdin).
find <file>	Ant will search for the given filename by traversing upwards from the current directory until it finds the file.
s	The file system to use.

A Simple Ant Example

Figure 3-1 shows a simplified view of what a simple Ant build entails. The root of an Ant build is the project element, which contains one or more targets and at least one default target. In this case the simple build contains three targets named Target A, Target B, and Target C, with Target C being the default target. As shown in the zoomed view of Target B, a target can contain zero or more tasks.

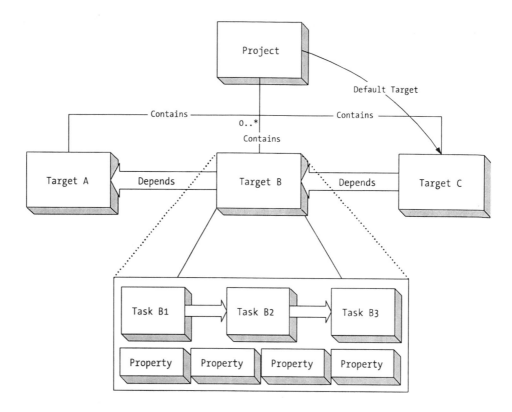

Figure 3-1. A simplified view of an Ant build

Ant controls the build process with a description file. In Ant the description file is typically referred to as a "buildfile" or "build script." The Ant buildfile is an XML file whose root is the project element that contains child nodes that represent the targets. An Ant buildfile representing a build similar to the one depicted in Figure 3-1 would look like this:

```
<?xml version="1.0" encoding="UTF-8"?>
<project basedir="." default="Target C" name="MyProject">

    <target name="Target A" description="Performs Step A">
        <echo>Performing Step A</echo>
    </target>

    <target name="Target B" depends="Target A" description="Performs Step B">
        <echo>Performing Step B</echo>
        <echo>Echo is one of many Core Tasks</echo>
    </target>
```

```
<target name="Target C" depends="Target B" description="Performs Step C">
    <echo>Performing Step C</echo>
</target>

</project>
```

As you can see, for a simple buildfile the XML format makes it easier to discern targets from one another.

Project

The project element can have three attributes: name, default, and basedir. Only the default attribute is required, but we recommend that you use the name attribute especially because many IDE Ant editors use this attribute for display purposes. The name attribute comes in handy when dealing with more than one buildfile.

 BEST PRACTICE   For a project with a single buildfile (build.xml) we recommend that you use the name of the project for the name attribute of the project element. For projects with multiple buildfiles we recommend that you name each one according to its intended functionality and that the name attribute should be the same as the filename without the .xml extension.

The default attribute determines the default target to be executed for the buildfile. Finally the basedir attribute determines the base directory for all file-related operations during the course of a build. In the previous example it's simply the current directory where the buildfile resides, and because this is the default value the attribute could have been omitted. This setting is important especially if you're using multiple buildfiles in different subdirectories of an application directory structure and you want a uniform way to refer to paths across all buildfiles.

The Build Stages

An Ant build has two stages: the parsing stage and the running stage. During the parsing stage the XML buildfile is parsed and an object model is constructed. This object model reflects the structure of the XML file in that it contains one project object at the root with several target objects, which themselves contain other objects representing the contents of a target such as tasks, datatypes, and properties.

NOTE Ant scripts can contain top-level items other than targets. These can include certain tasks and datatypes. These elements are grouped in order of appearance into an implicit target that gets executed right after the parsing process ends and before any other targets are executed.

During the runtime phase Ant determines the build sequence of targets to be executed. This sequence is determined by resolving the target's dependencies. By default, unless a different target is specified, Ant will use the default target attribute as the entry point so it can determine the build sequence.

Let's execute the sample buildfile for the sample build shown in Figure 3-1 in order to get acquainted with Ant and some of the command-line options shown in Table 3-1. First type the contents shown in the listing to a text file and save it as build.xml. To run it, simply change to the directory where the buildfile is located and type the following:

```
ant
```

The output should look like this:

```
Buildfile: build.xml

Target A:
     [echo] Performing Step A

Target B:
     [echo] Performing Step B
     [echo] Echo is one of many Core Tasks

Target C:
     [echo] Performing Step C

BUILD SUCCESSFUL
Total time: 1 second
```

The output shows that Ant executed the build file successfully and that it took 1 sec to execute (execution times will vary from system to system.) From the output, you can see that the targets were executed in the following sequence: Target A, Target B, and Target C. To see a bit more detail you can run Ant again using the -v command-line option, which will show you some extra information as shown:

```
Apache Ant version 1.5.3 compiled on April 16 2003
Buildfile: build.xml
...
Build sequence for target 'Target C' is [Target A, Target B, Target C]
Complete build sequence is [Target A, Target B, Target C]
...
BUILD SUCCESSFUL
Total time: 1 second
```

First, notice that the output shows that the intended target is Target C, which was defined as the build's default target. Ant resolved the default target dependencies to arrive at the build sequence [Target A, Target B, Target C] as shown at the top of the console output.

The text enclosed in the <echo> elements in each of the targets is shown on the console as each target is executed. The <echo> task is one of many built-in tasks provided by Ant. For example, a quick browse of the online documentation shows that the Echo task sends the text enclosed to an Ant logger. By default Ant uses the DefaultLogger, which is a class that "listens" to the build and outputs to the standard out. Specific loggers can be selected on the command line by using the –logger option. Further examination shows that the Echo task is well integrated with the logging system and that it can be provided with a level attribute to control the level at which the message is reported.

 NOTE We decided against regurgitating the contents of the online documentation, therefore we'll explain some of Ant's tasks in context as you set out to build the tiers of the TCMS system. The best place to learn about all the available Ant tasks is from the online manual located at http://ant.apache.org/manual/index.html.

The previous run of the sample script assumed that you wanted to run the default target. To run a specific target you can indicate the target in the command line as follows:

```
ant "Target A"
```

Notice that target names are case sensitive and that double quotes are required for any target names that contain spaces. The resulting output should look like this:

```
Buildfile: build.xml

Target A:
    [echo] Performing Step A

BUILD SUCCESSFUL
Total time: 1 second
```

More on Targets

Targets are meant to represent a discrete step in the build process. Targets use tasks, datatypes, and property declarations to accomplish their work. Targets are required to have a name attribute and an optional comma-separated list of dependent targets.

 BEST PRACTICE   Use action verbs to name your targets, such as "build," "test," or "deploy."

A typical buildfile is composed of several main targets: those that are meant to be called directly by the user and subtargets, which are targets that provide functionality to a main target.

 BEST PRACTICE   Add a description attribute to a build's main targets. Targets containing a description are shown in the automatic project help, which is displayed when Ant is invoked with the -projecthelp command-line option. For subtargets, prefix the name with a hyphen to make it easy to differentiate them from main targets.

Targets can be conditionally executed, for this purpose Ant supports the if and unless attributes. Targets using either or both of these are said to be conditional targets. Both if and unless take the name of a property as value, which is tested for existence. You can see an example of this if you modify Target A from the sample buildfile and add an if attribute with a value of do_a as shown here:

```
<target name="Target A" description="Performs Step A" if="do_a">
    <echo>Performing Step A</echo>
</target>
```

The target should only be executed if the Ant property by the name do_a exists in the context of the build. Executing the buildfile produces the following result:

```
Buildfile: build.xml

Target A:

Target B:
    [echo] Performing Step B
    [echo] Echo is one of many Core Tasks

Target C:
    [echo] Performing Step C

BUILD SUCCESSFUL
Total time: 1 second
```

Notice that the output shows the banner for Target A but the echo tasks contained within were never executed. You can run the buildfile again using the -D option to pass the property do_a to the build as shown:

```
ant -D"do_a="
```

The output now shows that Target A is being executed. You add the double quotes around the name-value pairs for the command-line argument parser so you can recognize the end of the argument. Any value could have been passed and the results would have been the same. Remember with if and unless, the value of the property is irrelevant; what matters is whether the property has been defined or not.

Target Dependencies

From the simple buildfile shown previously you can see that targets can depend on other targets. This example shows a very simple and linear dependency chain in which Target C depends on Target B, which in turn depends on Target A.

Ant will resolve any circular dependencies and will consequently fail the build. For example, you can modify the sample script to add Target C as a dependency of Target A as shown in the following buildfile target:

```
<target name="Target A" depends="Target C" description="Performs Step A">
    <echo>Performing Step A</echo>
</target>
```

The resulting execution of the script will produce output similar to the following:

```
Buildfile: build.xml

BUILD FAILED
Circular dependency: Target C <- Target A <- Target B <- Target C

Total time: 1 second
```

Dependencies are resolved recursively using a topological sorting algorithm. The resulting build sequence ensures that a target in the dependency chain will only get executed once. You can see a great example of this in the Ant online manual, which shows a build with dependencies as shown in Figure 3-2.

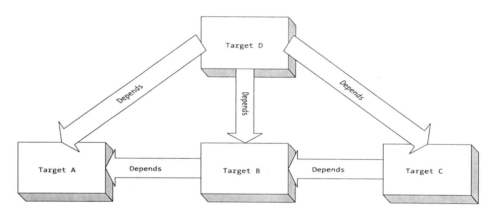

Figure 3-2. Script dependencies

A buildfile for the build in Figure 3-2 would look like the following:

```xml
<?xml version="1.0" encoding="UTF-8"?>
<project basedir="." default="D" name="dependencies">
    <target name="A"/>
    <target name="B" depends="A"/>
    <target name="C" depends="B,A"/>
    <target name="D" depends="C,B,A"/>
</project>
```

Understanding how dependencies work is very important as your build process grows in complexity. Figure 3-3 shows a depiction of the dependency resolution process.

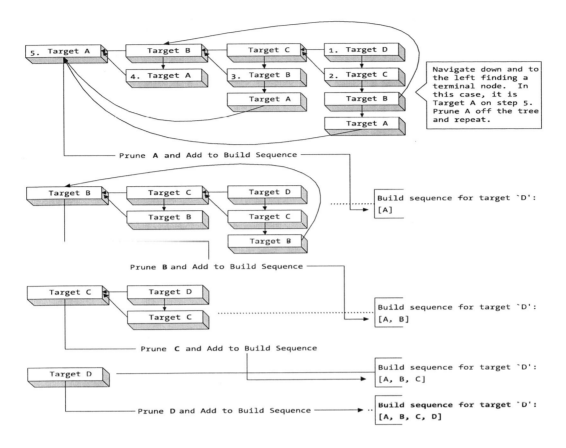

Figure 3-3. Dependency resolution in Ant

To test the dependencies example, save the buildfile as dependencies.xml and
run it using Ant's -f parameter in order to indicate the buildfile as follows:

```
ant -f dependencies.xml -v
```

The output should look like this:

```
...
Buildfile: dependencies.xml
...
Build sequence for target `D' is [A, B, C, D]
Complete build sequence is [A, B, C, D]

A:

B:
```

```
C:

D:

BUILD SUCCESSFUL
Total time: 1 second
```

 BEST PRACTICE   Whenever possible keep a build's dependencies as simple and linear as possible.

Tasks

Tasks are used within a target to achieve certain functionality. Think of a task element as a way to invoke a Java class's functionality. Ant provides a plethora of tasks that are divided in the following two categories:

- **Core:** Core tasks include basic foundational facilities needed in the build process like file manipulation, file dependencies, directory operations, source-code compilation, API document generation, archiving and packaging, XML file manipulation, SQL execution, and others.

- **Optional:** This includes tasks for some commercial products (like EJB/J2EE servers and third-party Version Control Systems) as well as nonbuild-specific tasks like unit testing, XML validation, and others.

Properties

Ant provides the ability for a project to have a set of properties. Properties are simple strings that you can access using the ${propertyName} notation. Whether you need to specify the location of a needed library many times or the name of a CVS repository, properties give you the flexibility to defer until runtime a set of values to be used in the build.

There are several ways to set a property. You can set it individually to the Ant buildfile via the D command-line option (see Table 3-1), or in bulk, from standard Java properties files by using the propertyfile option.

There are also several tasks that deal with properties. The property task enables the setting of a property by name. All property tasks are idempotent, which means that once a property's value has been set it will remain unchanged for the remainder of the build. The immutability of properties in Ant is often a source of confusion, because as developers you often tend to think of them as variables.

NOTE The <ant> and <antcall> tasks both span a new build by starting another instance of an Ant project. The <ant> task calls an external buildfile, and the <antcall> task calls a target on the current buildfile. For both tasks, all of the properties of the calling project become available on the spawned projects, unless you set the inheritAll attribute to false, in which case only those properties passed on the command line become available to the spawned projects.

The simplest way to set a property's value is to use the property task. For example. To set a property named src, which could be later accessed using ${src}, you would use the property task as follows:

```
<property name="src" location="src" />
```

The src property would be an absolute path that refers to the location of the src directory relative to the basedir directory.

BEST PRACTICE Properties should be used with care. The two main uses of properties are, for items whose value might change from build to build or for items whose value is calculated and used more than once during the build.

Many Ant properties are also available implicitly and are composed from the system properties such as ${java.version}.

For any but the simplest project you can load a property file using the file attribute of the property task, thereby taking into account differences in user configurations, as follows:

```
<property file="build.properties"/>
```

Other tasks that deal directly with properties include the following:

- **LoadProperties:** Loads the contents of a file as properties (equivalent to using the file attribute for the property task.

- **LoadFile:** Loads a text file into a single property.

- **XMLProperty:** Loads properties from an XML file. See the Ant documentation for the specific format of the XML file.

- **EchoProperties:** Displays all available properties in the project.

Many other tasks use properties as a way to take parameters in or out. For example, a common practice is for a task to have an attribute that takes the name of an nonexistent property to be set in case of a specific event, such as the possibility of the task failing.

 BEST PRACTICE   We recommend using a properties file named build.properties to store any overridden default values. This property file shouldn't be kept in the source-code repository, but instead you should add a sample properties file named build.properties.sample along with instructions on how to configure the build.properties file.

Datatypes

Ant's datatypes are primitive constructs that provide frequently required information in the processing of a buildfile. Their purpose is to simplify a task by encapsulating some information required and providing a simple way to manipulate it.

Several of Ant's built-in datatypes provide a structure that encapsulates information about a set of related resources such as files, environment variables, or even complex mappings between input and output files. Knowing how to properly use the Ant's datatypes will help you kept your buildfiles simple and efficient.

Datatypes and Properties in Action: A Simple Example

Many of Ant's tasks need to manipulate a file or groups of files. A typical need in a build is to specify a set of JAR files to be included in the classpath for certain tasks. Imagine that you're building a simple application with a directory structure, as shown in Figure 3-4.

Figure 3-4. Sample directory structure for datatypes and properties

The following sample buildfile snippet shows a build for which two path structures (datatypes) are defined, one with an id of class.path and the other with an id of all.source.path. These two datatypes are then used in the target named compile, which uses the javac task to compile the classes referenced by the path reference by the id all.source.path.

```xml
<?xml version="1.0"?>
<project name="My Build" default="all" basedir=".">
...
    <property name="lib" location="lib"/>
    <property name="src" location="src"/>
    <property name="classes" location="classes"/>
    <property name="build" location="build"/>

    <property name="src-java" location="${src}/java"/>
    <property name="src-generated" location="${build}/generated-code/java"/>
    <property name="struts-lib" location="${lib}/struts"/>
...
    <path id="class.path">
        <fileset dir="${lib}">
            <include name="*.jar"/>
        </fileset>
        <fileset dir="${struts-lib}">
            <include name="*.jar"/>
        </fileset>
    </path>

    <path id="all.source.path">
        <pathelement path="${src-java}"/>
        <pathelement path="${src-generated}"/>
    </path>
...
    <target name="compile" description="Compiles all sources.">
...
        <javac
            destdir="${classes}"
            classpathref="class.path"
            debug="on"
            deprecation-"on"
            optimize="off">
            <src>
                <path refid="all.source.path"/>
            </src>
        </javac>
    </target>
```

The class.path path structure uses two instances of the fileset datatype to group under a common classpath all the JAR files included in the directories referenced by the lib and struts-lib properties. The path element is an example of an indispensable datatype that enables you to reuse path information in your builds. The fileset datatype is a typical example of Ant's pathlike structures. It encapsulates a group of files defined via nested patternset structures. For example, to create a fileset that includes all JAR files under the ${lib} directory, you can use the following fileset definition:

```
<fileset dir="${lib}">
    <patternset>
        <include name="*.jar"/>
    </patternset>
</fileset>
```

The fileset datatype contains an implicit patternset structure, which means that you can use shorthand to rewrite the fileset definition as follows:

```
<fileset dir="${lib}">
    <include name="*.jar"/>
</fileset>
```

You can further compact the fileset definition by using the include in the property form, rather than as a nested element:

```
<fileset dir="${lib} include="*.jar" />
```

The path datatype can also make use of nested pathelements, as shown in the definition of the all.source.path path structure. It uses the pathelement datatype to reference the locations defined by src-java and src-generated properties.

Path is a typical Ant pathlike structure. When dealing with paths or classpaths, Ant provides pathlike structures that can be used as nested elements on most tasks. In the previous example, you can see that the two pathelements defined at the top of the buildfile are then used by reference in the context of the javac task. The class.path path is passed to the classpathref attribute of javac to determine the classpath for compilation and the all.source.path is used by creating a new pathelement, which is nested inside the src nested element of the javac task.

As a build's complexity increases so do the patterns for selecting files. Pathlike structures enable the reuse of path information and help keep the growth of buildfiles under control.

NOTE One of the criteria used in choosing many of the tools in this chapter was whether the tool provided an Ant task.

Case Study: Building the Technology Conference Management System with Ant

To set the stage for the development throughout the rest of the book, you need to first create a suitable directory structure (see Figure 3-5) as well as an initial Ant buildfile for the TCMS system.

Figure 3-5. Sample directory structure for the TCMS project

The project's root directory is tcms. Under this directory you'll place the project's main buildfile named build.xml. The subdirectories under tcms are organized as follows:

- **lib:** Contains any libraries required at runtime by the application(s).

- **lib/development:** Contains any libraries required at development time.

- **src:** The root directory for all nongenerated sources.

- **src/java:** The root directory for all Java sources.

From the previous directory structure, it should be clear that you must take measures to differentiate the needs of the application at development or build time vs. the needs of the runtime environment.

Now that you have a suitable directory structure, your next step should be to start putting together the tcms buildfile. The project element contains the name of your project and a nested description element.

BEST PRACTICE Use the project element nested description. This
description is shown on the console when invoking Ant with the
-projecthelp command-line option.

The default target will be the all target, which you'll develop later in the chapter.
The basedir is set to be the directory where the buildfile resides, which in this case
is the tcms directory.

```xml
<?xml version="1.0"?>
<project
    name="Enterprise Java Development on a Budget"
    default="all"
    basedir="."
    >

    <description>
    This build script was developed to be a generic enterprise development
    build script using ANT 1.5.3 (ant.apache.org). To customize it or use it for
    other projects modify the build.properties file.
    </description>
...
```

Next, properties are defined for the created directories. Notice that you can
define properties using other properties as with the lib-dev property. Properties
that represent a directory are defined using the location attribute instead of the
value attribute. The location attribute gets resolved to the full path relative to the
basedir specified in the project element.

 BEST PRACTICE Making all paths relative to the project's basedir
directory and avoiding the use of absolute paths guarantees that your
buildfile will work anywhere. If your build depends on a resource whose
location might change from environment to environment, you should
place the location of said resource in a properties file or use environment
variables such as ${os.name}.

The build directory is the root directory for all products of the build process,
such as the classes directory, where the results of compiling the classes under
src/java will be placed.

```
<!-- ==================================================================== -->
<!-- Initialization                                                       -->
<!-- ==================================================================== -->

<property name="build" location="build"/>
<property name="lib" location="lib"/>
<property name="lib-dev" location="${lib}/development"/>

<!-- Directories -->
<property name="src" location="src"/>
<property name="src-java" location="${src}/java"/>
<property name="classes" location="${build}/classes"/>
<property name="docs" location="docs"/>
<property name="api" location="${docs}/api"/>
```

Paths representing all the JAR files under the lib directory (class.path) and all class files under the classes directory are created.

 BEST PRACTICE   A common practice in Ant buildfiles is to have an init task that all other tasks depend on. We advocate not using the init task for setting up properties, loading properties files, paths, patternsets, or taskdefs. Instead just place them before the first target and they will be added to the implicit target. As mentioned earlier, the contents of the implicit target always get called and you don't have to remember making all other targets dependent on an init target.

A patternset is also used to filter a directory for nonsource files. In the case where resources are part of the source directory, such as property files or images, you can use a patternset to copy them to the location of the compiled classes, which will require said resources.

```
<!-- Paths -->
<path id="class.path">
    <fileset dir="${lib}">
        <include name="*.jar"/>
    </fileset>
</path>

<path id="app.class.path">
    <pathelement location="${classes}"/>
    <path refid="class.path"/>
</path>
```

```
<!-- Patternsets -->
<patternset id="non.source.set">
    <exclude name="**/*.java"/>

    ...

    <exclude name="**/read-me.txt"/>
    <exclude name="**/package.html"/>
</patternset>
```

Compiling

Now it's time to add the first target to the buildfile, the compile target. This target will make use of the javac task, which is a wrapper to the javac command. Notice that before the javac task is invoked, all files under the ${src-java} directory that match the patternset non.source.set are copied to the ${classes} directory. This is done so that any resources such as Java properties files, images, and others are available to the compiled code under the classes directory. This is a common practice for many IDEs.

```
<!-- ===================================================================== -->
<!-- Compiles all the classes                                            -->
<!-- ===================================================================== -->

<target
    name="compile"
    depends="compile-init"
    description="Compiles all classes.">
    <javac
        destdir="${classes}"
        classpathref="class.path"
        debug="on"
        deprecation="on"
        optimize="off"
        >
        <src>
            <path refid="ejb.source.path"/>
        </src>
    </javac>
```

```
<!-- copy non-source resources only if the compilation is successful -->
<copy todir="${classes}">
    <fileset dir="${src-java}">
        <patternset refid="non.source.set"/>
    </fileset>
</copy>
</target>

<target name="compile-init">
    <mkdir dir="${classes}"/>
</target>

<target name="compile-clean">
    <delete dir="${classes}"/>
</target>
```

Notice that you added two more targets other than compile. These are compile-init and compile-clean. The compile-init target simply creates the classes directory by making use of the mkdir task. The compile-clean uses the delete task to remove the directory and all of its contents.

BEST PRACTICE   For each main target in the buildfile, add a target-init and a target-clean, where target is the name of the main target. This makes it fairly straightforward to determine the resources needed and created by a target and also makes it easier to maintain large buildfiles. For simple buildfiles a single clean target will usually suffice.

JavaDoc Generation

For proper team communication and for enabling code reuse you must have a consistent up-to-date set of API documentation. The Javadoc tool has existed for as long as Java has been around and all developers are well acquainted with it. The problem has been that developers feel that they can run Javadoc only after they're finished with the code (which might be never). Running Javadoc at the end of a project provides very little help to others in the team and moves documentation to the end of process, when it isn't as helpful (waterfall).

With Ant you can ensure that Javadoc is generated as part of the daily build and that you don't hide the documentation process until the "end" of the development phase. The Ant Javadoc task provides a convenient way to generate Javadoc from within Ant, as shown here:

```
<!-- ===================================================================== -->
<!-- JavaDocs                                                              -->
<!-- ===================================================================== -->

<target
    name="docs"
    depends="compile,docs-init"
    description="Generate JavaDocs."
    >
    <javadoc
        destdir="${api}"
        author="true"
        version="true"
        use="true"
        windowtitle="${ant.project.name}"
        sourcepathref="all.source.path"
        classpathref="doc.class.path"
        packagenames="com.*"
        verbose="false">
        <doctitle><![CDATA[<h1>${ant.project.name}</h1>]]></doctitle>
        <bottom>
            <![CDATA[<i>Copyright &#169; 2003 All Rights Reserved.</i>]]>
        </bottom>
        <tag name="todo" scope="all" description="To do:"/>
    </javadoc>
</target>

<target name="docs-init">
    <mkdir dir="${api}"/>
</target>

<target name="docs-clean">
    <delete dir="${api}"/>
</target>
```

Notice that the doctitle and the bottom nested elements make use of the XML character data (CDATA) section in order to be able to use HTML markup and not have it interfere with the markup of the buildfile.

Formatting Source Code with Jalopy

Code format and style is a subject that is sometimes discussed with religious fervor and it's one of places where developers feel they shouldn't be forced to follow a standard. Yet determining how clean a piece of code is seems to be a subjective task, and a code base that is in disarray will prevent teamwork and the XP ideal of collective code ownership. We suggest that instead of forcing programmers to code a certain way, you should simply automate the process of formatting the code to a known standard that has been agreed on. For the TCMS system you format all source code as part of the build process. To do so you rely on a handy utility called Jalopy. Jalopy is a Java source-code formatter that reads an XML configuration file that determines the style to apply to the code. By default it's configured to follow the Sun code conventions for the Java programming language (see http://java.sun.com/docs/codeconv/). Jalopy can format brace style, spacing, indentation, code separation (blank lines), as well as control the generation of missing Javadoc comments, and Java file headers and footers.

Jalopy provides an Ant plug-in that is distributed as a single ZIP file (for Ant 1.4 or higher) that can be downloaded from http://jalopy.sourceforge.net/. Unzip the file to a suitable directory. You should have a bin, docs, and a lib directory. The first step is to run the Jalopy GUI configuration utility to fine-tune the settings for the purposes of the application. To do so, change directories to the Jalopy distribution bin directory and execute the preferences script (in this case preferences.bat) as follows:

```
preferences.bat
```

The Jalopy GUI configuration utility should now be up and running as shown in Figure 3-6.

The GUI utility allows you to modify the settings for a given code convention. The application is a simple tree-driven GUI. As you can see from the General node, the default loaded is the Sun Java Coding Convention (simply named "Sun"). Jalopy allows you to save your settings on a "per-project" basis or by modifying the configuration via the GUI and exporting the configuration to an XML file using the export utility in the General node. You can then use the resulting XML file from within Ant with the Jalopy task.

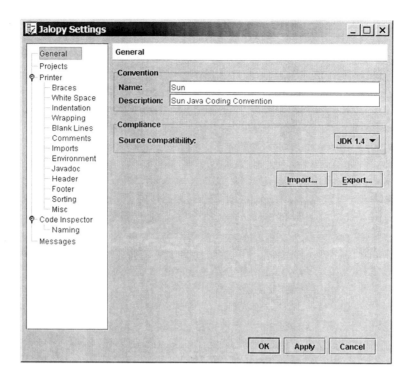

Figure 3-6. The Jalopy GUI configuration utility

The only customization needed for the TCMS system is to add an appropriate header that will be placed on all source files in the application. To accomplish this, switch to Printer ➤ Header (all formatting options are under the Printer node). The Header pane has two tabs, Options and Text. Select the Text tab and enter the header text as shown in Figure 3-7.

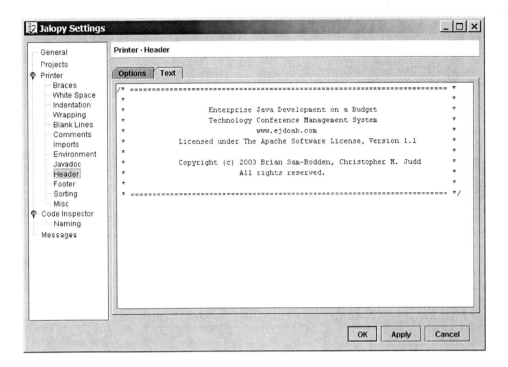

Figure 3-7. Configuring Java Headers in Jalopy.

The Jalopy preview window should display a sample of what the header will look like after it has been applied to a Java file, as shown in Figure 3-8.

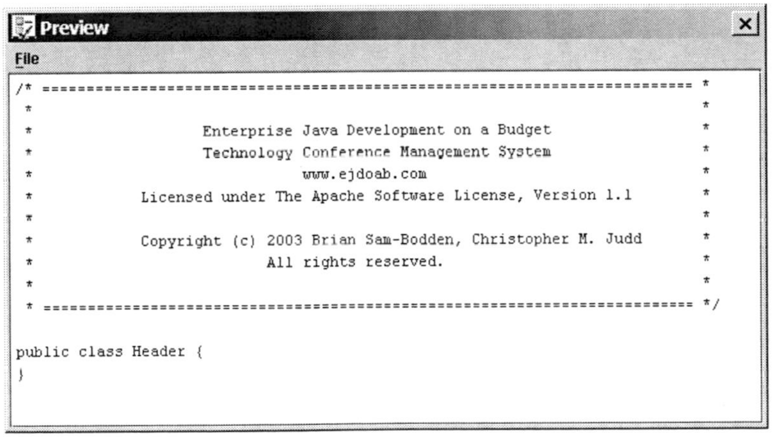

Figure 3-8. Jalopy Header preview

Next, you need to make sure that Jalopy doesn't add the header to a file that already contains it. To accomplish this you need to give Jalopy a sequence of characters that it can use to determine whether the file has a header or not. In this case, the string selected is "Copyright (c) 2003 Brian Sam-Bodden, Christopher M. Judd," as shown in Figure 3-9.

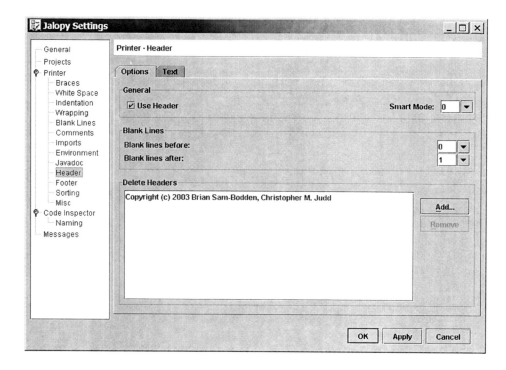

Figure 3-9. Jalopy Header identifying key configuration

You're now ready to export the configuration to an XML file that you can use from within Ant. Switch to the General pane and click the Export button. Save the file as jalopy-sun-convention.xml under the lib/development/jalopy directory under the TCMS project root.

For the purposes of the TCMS application you'll place the files under the Jalopy distribution's lib directory in a directory under the TCMS project root directory named lib/development/jalopy.

Now it's time to modify the Ant buildfile to format the source code as part of the build. The first step is to load the Jalopy task so that it can be used in the context of the build. To load an external task you use one of Ant's built-in tasks, the taskdef task, which is specially designed to load other tasks. Notice that you've set two properties and a pathelement to simplify the format target. The jalopy-lib property points to the location of the Jalopy JAR files. The jalopy-convention-file property points to the XML file that you previously saved with your modified source-code conventions. Finally, the jalopy taskdef loads the Task class by specifying the classname and the classpath to search for the specified class, as shown here:

```
<property name="jalopy-lib" location="${lib-dev}/jalopy" />
<property
    name="jalopy-convention-file"
    location="${jalopy-lib}/jalopy-sun-convention.xml"
    />

<path id="jalopy.class.path">
    <path refid="class.path"/>
    <fileset dir="${lib-dev}/jalopy">
        <include name="*.jar"/>
    </fileset>
</path>

<!-- Jalopy - jalopy.sourceforge.net -->
<taskdef
    name="jalopy"
    classname="de.hunsicker.jalopy.plugin.ant.AntPlugin"
    classpathref="jalopy.class.path"
    />
```

You can now define the format target. The format target is dependent on the compile target. You don't want to try to format code that doesn't compile. The jalopy task takes the name of the convention file to use and a fileset that contains all the Java source files that will be formatted. Notice the use of a nested patternset to filter out unwanted files. The target definition looks like this:

```
<!-- ========================================================================= -->
<!-- Formats all non-generated source code                                     -->
<!-- ========================================================================= -->

<target
    name="format"
    depends="compile"
    description="Formats all source code."
    >
    <jalopy
        convention="${jalopy-convention-file}"
        loglevel="warn"
        classpathref="class.path"
        failonerror="no"
                >
        <fileset dir="${src-java}">
            <patternset refid="non.generated.source.set"/>
        </fileset>
    </jalopy>
</target>
```

Checking Code Conventions with Checkstyle

Even if you're using formatting tools such as Jalopy there are still style checks
beyond the realm of formatting. Checkstyle is a tool that enables code to be checked
against a convention. Like Jalopy it supports the Sun convention by default, although
it can check for more than just simple formatting. For example, it can check for
illegal regular expressions in the code, inline conditionals, double-checked locking,
and other idioms or patterns that might be considered unsafe or problematic.

You can download Checkstyle from http://checkstyle.sourceforge.net. On the
root of the checkstyle distribution you'll find the checkstyle-all-3.1.jar file. Place this
file in a directory named checkstyle under the lib/development/ of the TCMS project
directory. The file containing the XML configuration representing the Sun convention is named sun_checks.xml and it's located under the docs directory of the
distribution directory. Copy this file to the lib/development/checkstyle directory also.

Checkstyle writes its output to the standard out by default or to a file in plain
text or XML format. The checkstyle distribution also provides several XSL stylesheets
that can be used to convert the XML reports to HTML format for easier viewing.
You can find these stylesheets in the checkstyle distribution under the contrib
directory. Copy the checkstyle-noframes-sorted.xsl file to the lib/development/
checkstyle directory.

To use Checkstyle from within Ant you first need to load the Checkstyle task. You also should define some properties and an Ant path to simplify the loading and execution of the task. You define properties for the location of the Checkstyle JARs and the generated reports. You also define the name of the generated XML report and the resulting HTML report.

```
<property name="checkstyle-reports" location="${docs}/checkstyle" />
<property name="checkstyle-lib" location="${lib-dev}/checkstyle" />
<property
    name="checkstyle-xml-report-file"
    location="${checkstyle-reports}/checkstyle-report.xml"
    />
<property
    name="checkstyle-html-report-file"
    location="${checkstyle-reports}/checkstyle-report.html"
    />
<property
    name="checkstyle-checks-file"
    location="${checkstyle-lib}/sun_checks.xml"
    />
<property
    name="checkstyle-stylesheet"
    location="${checkstyle-lib}/checkstyle-noframes-sorted.xsl"
    />

<path id="checkstyle.class.path">
    <path refid="class.path"/>
    <fileset dir="${lib-dev}/checkstyle">
        <include name="*.jar"/>
    </fileset>
</path>

<!-- Checkstyle - checkstyle.sourceforge.net -->
<taskdef
    resource="checkstyletask.properties"
    classpathref="checkstyle.class.path"
    />
```

Notice that the taskdef task for the Checkstyle task uses the resource attribute instead of the name or classname combination used for the Jalopy task. The target named checkstyle uses the checkstyle task to check the code under the ${src-java} directory against the conventions specified by the file ${checkstyle-checks-file} and uses a formatter of type XML to generate the report referred to

${checkstyle-xml-report-file}. The failureProperty attribute is the property that's set if there are any errors encountered during the checking process. You can use this value to determine if any action is to be taken in the case of an error, such as emailing the report.

The second part of the target uses the style task to transform the generated XML into a HTML report. The complete target is shown here:

```
<!-- ====================================================================== -->
<!-- Checks source code for convention violations                          -->
<!-- ====================================================================== -->

<target
    name="checkstyle"
    depends="checkstyle-init"
    description="Generates Code Convention Violations Report."
    >
    <checkstyle
        config="${checkstyle-checks-file}"
        failureProperty="checkstyle.failure"
        failOnViolation="false"
        >
        <formatter type="xml" tofile="${checkstyle-xml-report-file}"/>
        <fileset dir="${src-java}">
            <patternset refid="non.generated.source.set"/>
        </fileset>
    </checkstyle>

    <style
        in="${checkstyle-xml-report-file}"
        out="${checkstyle-html-report-file}"
        style="${checkstyle-stylesheet}"
        />
</target>

<target name="checkstyle-init">
    <mkdir dir="${checkstyle-reports}"/>
</target>

<target name="checkstyle-clean">
    <delete dir="${checkstyle-reports}"/>
</target>
```

A sample checkstyle report is shown in Figure 3-10.

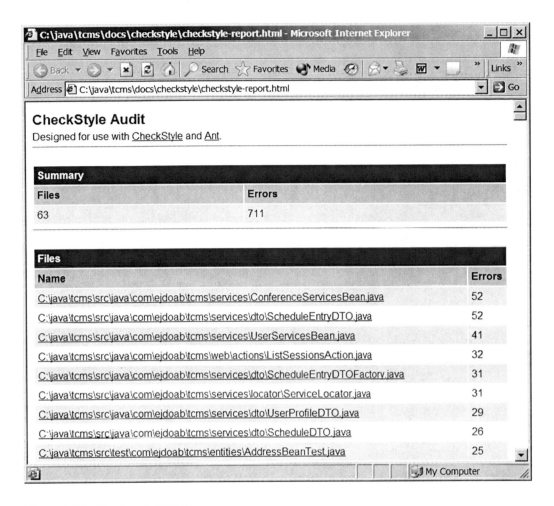

Figure 3-10. Checkstyle HTML report

Generating Source-Code Metrics

Although we don't advocate counting code lines, classes, or methods as a measure of a project's success, static code analysis can help you pinpoint some areas of unnecessary complexity that can lead to the discovery of potential bugs or high-maintenance code.

JavaNCSS is a simple source-measurement tool for Java that provides the following basic types of analysis:

- **NCSS:** Noncommenting source statements provide counts of many features of the code such as lines of code, declarations, methods, statements, constructors, and so on.

- **CCN:** Cyclomatic complexity number (McCabe metric). McCabe's cyclomatic complexity metric looks at a program's control flow graph as a measure of its complexity.

You can download JavaNCSS from http://www.kclee.com/clemens/java/javancss/ as a simple ZIP file that includes an Ant task. Place all JAR files located under the distribution's lib directory in a directory named javancss under the lib/development directory of the TCMS project. Next, create a directory named xslt under the lib/javancss and copy the contents of the xslt directory under the JavaNCSS distribution directory.

The Ant task can generate a report in plain text of the XML format. As with the Checkstyle target, you'll use the style task to transform the reports to HTML, as shown here:

```
<!-- Javancss - kclee.com/clemens/java/javancss -->
<taskdef
    name="javancss"
    classname="javancss.JavancssAntTask"
    classpathref="javancss.class.path"
    />


<!-- ================================================================== -->
<!-- Source Code Metrics                                            -->
<!-- ================================================================== -->

<target
    name="metrics"
    depends="metrics-init"
    description="Generates Code Metrics Reports."
    >
```

```
        <!-- business tier source metrics -->
        <javancss
            srcdir="${src-java}"
            includes="**/*.java"
            excludes="**/entities/*Bean.java"
            generateReport="true"
            outputfile="${javancss-xml-business}"
            format="xml"
            functionMetrics="false"
            />
        <style
            in="${javancss-xml-business}"
            out="${javancss-html-business}"
            style="${javancss-stylesheet}"
            />
/>

<target name="metrics-init">
    <mkdir dir="${metrics-reports}"/>
</target>

<target name="metrics-clean">
    <delete dir="${metrics-reports}"/>
</target>
```

The generated HTML reports look like the one shown in Figure 3-11.

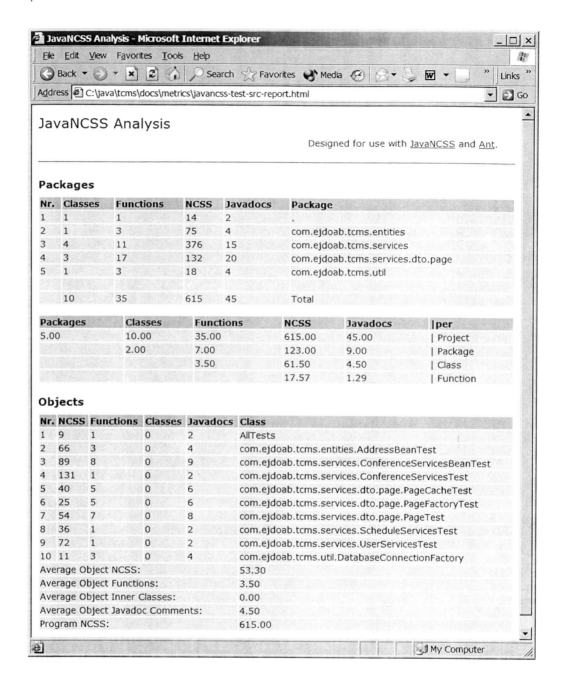

Figure 3-11. A JavaNCSS HTML report

Generating Browseable Source Code

One useful feature for sharing knowledge about a project is the ability to generate a browseable version of the code for viewing online. Many Open Source projects use this as a way to allow others to view the source to a particular class without having to download a source distribution or having to use CVS. Java2Html is a tool that enables you to take a Java class or a snippet of Java code and generate a syntax-highlighted HTML version of the code.

The Java2Html tool can be obtained from http://www.java2html.de as a single ZIP file that contains one JAR file (java2html.jar). As with the other third-party Ant tasks, place the JAR file in a directory named java2html under the TCMS lib directory.

As mentioned previously, you should load the task using the taskdef task. The generated HTML source will be placed under the location pointed to by the property ${browseable-source}, as shown here:

```
<!-- Java2Html - java2html.de -->
<taskdef
    name="java2html"
    classname="de.java2html.anttasks.Java2HtmlTask"
    classpathref="java2html.class.path"
    />


<property name="browseable-source" location="${docs}/browseable-source" />


<!-- ================================================================ -->
<!-- Generates browseable source code in HTML format                  -->
<!-- ================================================================ -->
<target
    name="java2html"
    depends="java2html-init"
    description="Generates browseable HTML version of the source code."
    >
    <java2html
        srcdir="${src}"
        destdir="${browseable-source}"
        includes="**/*.java"
        outputFormat="html"
        tabs="4"
        style="eclipse"
        showLineNumbers="true"
        showFileName="true"
        showTableBorder="true"
        includeDocumentHeader="true"
```

```
            includeDocumentFooter="true"
            addLineAnchors="true"
            lineAnchorPrefix="fff"/>
</target>

<target name="java2html-init">
    <mkdir dir="${browseable-source}"/>
</target>

<target name="java2html-clean">
    <delete dir="${browseable-source}"/>
</target>
```

Figure 3-12 shows an example of an HTML page generated by Java2HTML

Cleaning Up

The build process produces many files and directories. Getting the project directory to the same state as when the source was checked out of a repository is important for determining what has changed. Many Ant users recommend having a "clean" target that can remove all the products of the build process.

The problem with this approach is that for large builds it's easy to accidentally delete files that are needed and it's also easy to miss files or directories that need to be deleted. For this reason you should include a clean subtarget for each main target in the buildfile. By doing this you'll easily be able to determine what needs to be clean at the target level. Then for the global clean target you can simply invoke all individual clean subtargets by adding them to its list of dependencies as shown here:

```
<!-- =================================================================== -->
<!-- Cleans everything                                                   -->
<!-- =================================================================== -->

<target
    name="clean"
    depends="compile-clean,...,target N"
    description="Cleans all build products"
    >
    <delete dir="${build}"/>
</target>
```

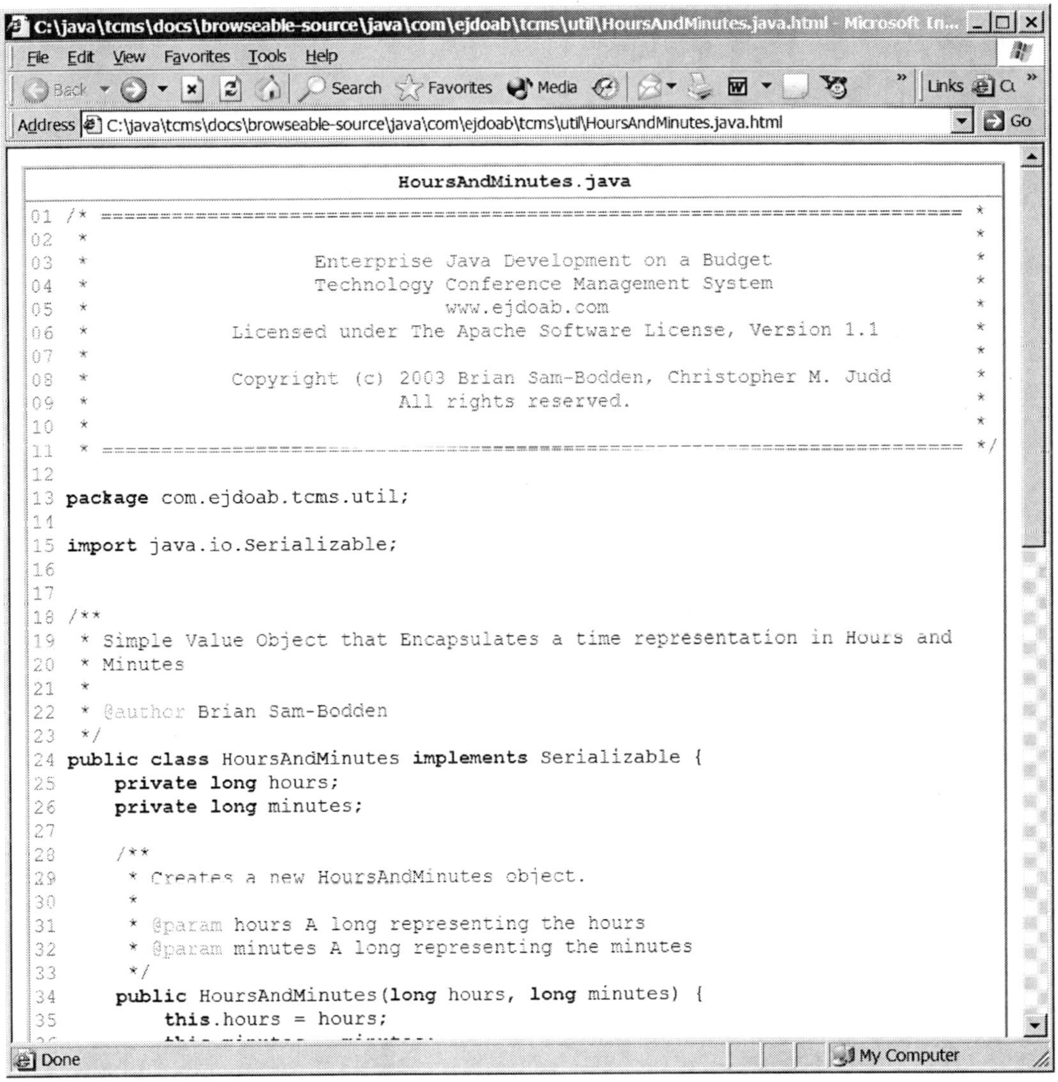

```
C:\java\tcms\docs\browseable-source\java\com\ejdoab\tcms\util\HoursAndMinutes.java.html - Microsoft In...
File   Edit   View   Favorites   Tools   Help
Back              x         Search    Favorites    Media             W              Links
Address    C:\java\tcms\docs\browseable-source\java\com\ejdoab\tcms\util\HoursAndMinutes.java.html           Go
```

```
                            HoursAndMinutes.java
01 /* ================================================================= *
02  *                                                                    *
03  *              Enterprise Java Development on a Budget               *
04  *              Technology Conference Management System              *
05  *                         www.ejdoab.com                            *
06  *         Licensed under The Apache Software License, Version 1.1    *
07  *                                                                    *
08  *         Copyright (c) 2003 Brian Sam-Bodden, Christopher M. Judd   *
09  *                      All rights reserved.                          *
10  *                                                                    *
11  * ================================================================= */
12
13 package com.ejdoab.tcms.util;
14
15 import java.io.Serializable;
16
17
18 /**
19  * Simple Value Object that Encapsulates a time representation in Hours and
20  * Minutes
21  *
22  * @author Brian Sam-Bodden
23  */
24 public class HoursAndMinutes implements Serializable {
25     private long hours;
26     private long minutes;
27
28     /**
29      * Creates a new HoursAndMinutes object.
30      *
31      * @param hours A long representing the hours
32      * @param minutes A long representing the minutes
33      */
34     public HoursAndMinutes(long hours, long minutes) {
35         this.hours = hours;
```

```
Done                                                              My Computer
```

Figure 3-12. An HTML page generated by Java2HTML

The all Target

Finally, it's a common practice to make the buildfile default target a target named "all," which has in its dependencies a list of the targets that represented a full build of the system. If your build process has any noncritical targets that take a fair amount of time to generate, you can create new targets that will do whatever the all target does in addition to any extra work a target such as all-with-docs does. The point is that you want to minimize the amount of time that it takes to build the application so that developers don't have noticeable interruptions in the flow of their work. A typical all target looks like this:

```
<!-- ======================================================================= -->
<!-- Does it all                                                             -->
<!-- ======================================================================= -->

<target
    name="all"
    depends="compile,..."
    description="Generates, compiles, packages and deploys."
/>
```

Conclusions

In this chapter you learned the importance of having a solid build system in place, the basics of the Ant build tool. You tailored an Ant buildfile to automate the build process of the TCMS system. The resulting buildfile reflects our experiences building many Java and J2EE applications. You can apply most of the ideas used in this file to your existing and future projects.

As a programmer, you strive to write reusable software components and it's natural to attempt to do the same with a system's build scripts. It's important to understand that Ant isn't a scripting language and that complex tasks are meant to be encapsulated inside of Ant tasks. Therefore, if your buildfiles become too complex don't feel compelled to stick solely with what's distributed with Ant. Feel free to explore the countless commercial and Open Source Ant tasks available or begin writing your own.

CHAPTER 4
Testing

*"Whenever you are tempted to type something into a print statement
or a debugger expression, write it as a test instead."*

—Martin Fowler[1]

HISTORICALLY, TESTING AND PERFORMANCE are activities saved for the end of a project. For example, testing is the last step of a project in the traditional waterfall approach. But agile methodologies such as Extreme Programming (XP) have proven that testing-and-performance checking early and often leads to better quality software. Testing and performance checking from day one of development can help developers to locate defects and bottlenecks when they're introduced, thereby reducing the time and expense of correcting them. In addition, unit testing improves the refactoring and debugging process. Automated unit testing supports refactoring by quickly determining how small changes affect the entire system. Debugging becomes more challenging as applications grow in size. Debugging failed unit tests rather than debugging entire applications can save valuable time.

Many applications and frameworks have been developed to automate repeatable unit testing and performance checking. The most notable and extended framework is the Open Source JUnit framework. This chapter explains how JUnit and its Cactus and DBUnit extensions can be used to increase software quality.

Testing Best Practices

Even though there are many approaches and philosophies to testing, you can apply the following basic best practices that can immediately improve the software quality and the process of developing it:

- **Establish test harnesses before development begins:** Determine the type of testing needed before the development begins. Download the necessary frameworks and JUnit extensions necessary to support each type of testing.

---

1. *Refactoring: Improving the Design of Existing Code* (Reading, MA: Addison-Wesley, 1999).

- **Task is complete when unit test is complete:** Just like code shouldn't be checked into version control without properly compiling, code shouldn't be checked in unless its unit tests pass.

- **Test first:** Get in the habit of writing the tests before the implementation based on a business interface implemented by a class or against a skeleton class. Then implement enough functionality to pass the tests.

- **Don't over-test:** Write just enough tests to test functionality. Add new tests as defects arise to prevent them from reoccurring.

- **Continuous Integration:** All unit tests should be run by developers before the code is checked into version control. In addition, all unit tests should be executed on version-controlled software at least once a day, but preferably more often than that. If unit tests are run once a day all defects found must have been introduced during the last 24-hour period. This enables you to react more quickly to problems in your codebase.

- **Map test cases to use cases or user stories:** To make sure all use cases are validated at least create a test case for each use case.

 NOTE   Applying these best practices had a major impact on the development of the Technology Conference Management System (TCMS) application. We were able to identify and communicate defects extremely early in the process.

Open Source Project Testing

Many Open Source projects have adopted the practice of unit testing. Many of the Jakarta Commons projects will not release new versions unless each class is accompanied by a unit test. This practice is very advantageous for those using Open Source. When Open Source JARs are upgraded they can be tested against previous-version unit tests to verify consistency and possible problems before the upgrade is even applied. Commercial vendors should consider providing this peace of mind.

JUnit Principles

For many years, unit testing has consisted of System.out.println() functions or testing code in a class's main method. Though this form of testing can be effective, it is a reactive measure that has some drawbacks: it requires human intervention and interpretation, it taints production code and deploys testing code, and the results aren't very repeatable. Today, the de facto standard in unit testing Java is the Open Source framework JUnit, which is hosted at `http://www.junit.org`. The framework includes extendable classes used to create tests and test runners that run the tests and present the results.

The junit.framework package contains the interface and classes used to develop unit tests. The Test interface is a simple interface used to define a test. Rather than implement the Test interface directly, most users extend the abstract base class junit.framework.TestCase or the concrete class junit.framework.TestSuite. A TestCase contains the tests for a single unit while a TestSuite is a collection of Test classes.

In Java, a unit is a class. Therefore, a TestCase typically contains all the tests for a single class. A test tests a single method of a class or a single unit of work. Tests have one of three outcomes: pass, fail, or error. If a test passes, the method or unit of work implements all the functionality as expected. A failure occurs when an expected value doesn't equal an actual value. For example, a test might be written to check that the size is incremented when an object is added to a collection. Assertions are used to compare the actual value to the expected value. Uncaught Exceptions are the cause of errors. A test runner can be used to execute a TestCase and report the results. There are many test runners available; several will be introduced throughout this chapter.

To define a test, extend the junit.framework.TestCase class and add the appropriate test methods similar to those shown in Listing 4-1. A test is a method with no return value, no parameter, and the name testXXXX. In the test method, the Assert class static methods are used to determine if actual result values of a test equal the expected values. The Assert class contains many static assert methods. Aside from the expected and actual parameters, most of the methods have an optional message parameter for describing the failure. An example is the overloaded assertEquals method for comparing just about every defined datatype. In addition to the assertEquals there are assertNotNull, assertFalse, assertNotSame, assertNull, and assertTrue. The Assert class also contains a fail method for explicate failures. The TestCase class extends Assert so it isn't necessary to directly use the Assert class in the TestCase. Adding a throws Exception to a test method makes error and exception handling easy. A Test class can also optionally override the setUp and tearDown methods to prepare and clean up the state of a test. The setUp method is called prior to every execution of a test method and the tearDown is called immediately afterward.

Listing 4-1. PageTest.java test for Page

```java
package com.ejdoab.tcms.services.dto.page;

import com.ejdoab.tcms.services.dto.page.Page;

import junit.framework.TestCase;

import java.util.*;
public class PageTest extends TestCase {

    private Collection list = new ArrayList();
    private static final int SIZE = 10;

    protected void setUp() throws Exception {
        for(int i = 1; i <= SIZE; i++) {
            list.add(new Integer(i));
        }
    }

    protected void tearDown() throws Exception {
        list.clear();
    }

    /**
     * Test getSize, getTotalSize and getIndex
     */
    public void testGetSize() {
        Page page;
        page = new Page(list,0,10);
        assertEquals("Get Size of entire collection.",
            SIZE, page.getSize());
        assertEquals("Get Total Size of entire collection.",
            SIZE, page.getTotalSize());

        page = new Page(list,2,4);
        assertEquals("Get Size of index 2 and size 4.",
            4, page.getSize());
        assertEquals("Get Total Size of index 2 and size 4.",
            SIZE, page.getTotalSize());
    }
```

```
/**
 * Test Page boundaries.
 */
public void testBoundaries() {
    Page page;

    try {
        page = new Page(list, -5, 2);
        fail("Invalid index -5,2");
    } catch (ArrayIndexOutOfBoundsException abex) { /* expected */ }

    try {
        page = new Page(list, -1, 2);
        fail("Invalid index -1,2");
    } catch (ArrayIndexOutOfBoundsException abex) { /* expected */ }

    page = new Page(list, 9, 1);
    assertEquals("Valid range 9,1", 1, page.getSize());
}

}
```

Listing 4-1 shows the TestCase for com.ejdoab.tcms.services.dto.page.Page. The Page class is a subset of a larger collection defined by an initial index and number of elements. This class is useful for listing pages of conference sessions on a website. The PageTest class extends TestCase and contains two tests, testBoundaries and testGetSize. The class also overrides the setUp and tearDown methods to ensure consistent test data in the list Collection, because tests aren't guaranteed to run in any order. Notice that in testGetSize pages of elements from the list Collection are created. Immediately following this, assertEquals is used to test the actual size of the Page and total size of the collection to the expected values. If the numbers aren't equal, a failure occurs.

Even though a TestCase may be run individually, it's often advantageous to run a complete set of tests at one time. JUnit supports a collection of TestCases with the TestSuite class. Listing 4-2 shows the TCMS AllTests class, which creates a TestSuite in the static suite method and adds the TestCases to it using the addTestSuite() method.

Listing 4-2. TCMS's TestSuite

```
/**
 * Executes all tests in the System.<p>
 * Useful for creating a single JUnit test report to review.
 */
public class AllTests {

    public static Test suite() {
        TestSuite suite = new TestSuite("Test for default package");

        // Plain old Java Object Tests
        suite.addTestSuite(PageTest.class);
        suite.addTestSuite(PageCacheTest.class);

        // Session Bean Tests
        suite.addTestSuite(ConferenceServicesBeanTest.class);

        // In-container Tests
        suite.addTestSuite(PageFactoryTest.class);
        suite.addTestSuite(AddressBeanTest.class);

        return suite;
    }
}
```

Tests must be run and the results must be evaluated. This is the responsibility of the test runners. JUnit contains three test runners. It contains an Abstract Window Toolkit (AWT) implementation in junit.awtui.TestRunner, a Swing implementation in junit.swingui.TestRunner, and a plain text implementation in junit.textui.TestRunner. The text TestRunner displays the text summary of the results unless an error or exception occurs. Listing 4-3 shows an example of a text summary containing a failure. Notice the failure prints out the reason for the failure and the call stack. Likewise, an error would also print out a reason and call stack.

Listing 4-3. Example of a Failure Using the Text TestRunner

```
..F............
Time: 4.826
There was 1 failure:
```

```
1) testBoundaries(com.ejdoab.tcms.services.dto.page.PageTest)junit.framework.
AssertionFailedError:
Valid range 9,1 expected:<6> but was:<1>
    at com.ejdoab.tcms.services.dto.page.PageTest.testBoundaries(PageTest.java:90)
    at sun.reflect.NativeMethodAccessorImpl.invoke0(Native Method)
    at sun.reflect.NativeMethodAccessorImpl.invoke(NativeMethodAccessorImpl.java:39)
    at sun.reflect.DelegatingMethodAccessorImpl.invoke(DelegatingMethodAccessorImpl.
java:25)
    at AllTests.main(AllTests.java:46)


FAILURES!!!
Tests run: 14,   Failures: 1,   Errors: 0
```

The Swing TestRunner shown in Figure 4-1 is a more user-friendly TestRunner. In this example, the TestSuite AllTests is run by executing 14 tests. The results were 6 errors and 5 failures. Besides the results, this TestRunner provides a status bar that grows as the tests are executed. By selecting the errors or failures in the Results list, the appropriate message and call stack are displayed in the bottom text box.

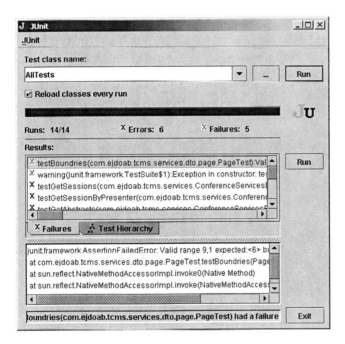

Figure 4-1. Swing TestRunner

IDE Integration

Many IDEs including Eclipse and NetBeans include some kind of JUnit integration. Typically the integration includes wizards to create TestCases and TestSuites and a customized TestRunner.

 NOTE Before you begin creating TestCases or TestSuites in Eclipse, the junit.jar should be in your project build classpath.

Eclipse's TestCase and TestSuite wizards are available by selecting File ➤ New ➤ Other ➤ Java ➤ JUnit. The TestCase wizard is a two-step process. The first step shown in Figure 4-2 involves setting the source folder where the test source file will be placed. It's a good idea to keep testing code and production code in separate directories but corresponding packages. For example, many projects such as the TCMS put the main source in a src/java directory and JUnit tests in a src/test directory. This helps to reduce the size of the deployable application and prevents testing code from accidentally being executed in production. Likewise, the testing source should also be compiled into a separated directory.

The next couple of fields define package and class names. If a class is selected in the Navigator or Package Explorer these values will automatically be filled in. It's customary to make the Test class name the same as the class being tested followed by the word Test. The wizard also makes it easy to generate a main method that runs a selectable TestRunner. Checking the setUp and tearDown boxes generates setUp and tearDown stubs.

The second step shown in Figure 4-3 makes it easy to create the stub test methods by selecting existing methods of the class that's being tested.

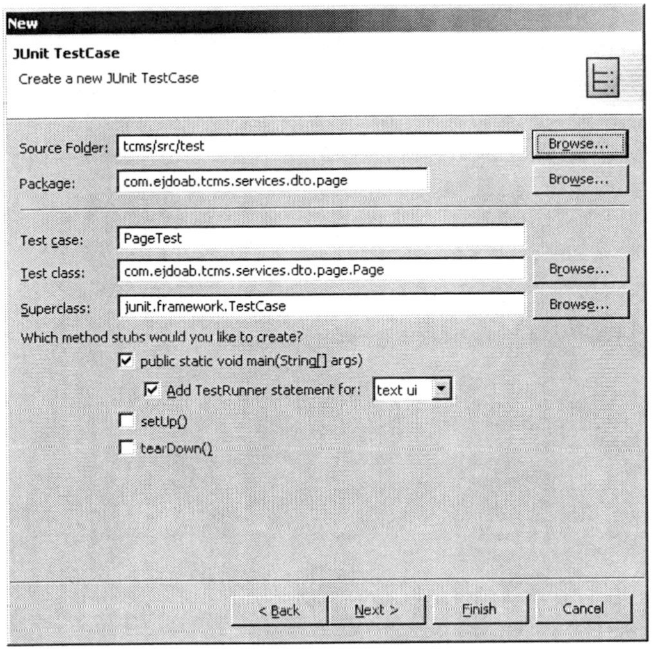

Figure 4-2. First step in Eclipse TestCase wizard

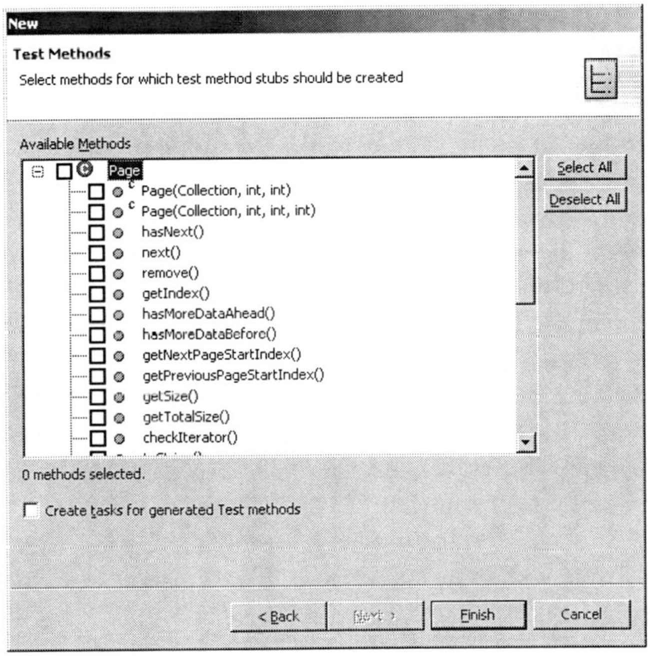

Figure 4-3. Second step in Eclipse TestCase wizard

Integrated development environments (IDEs) typically include a custom TestRunner so developers don't have to leave the environment to execute the tests. Eclipse is no exception. After selecting a TestCase or TestSuite in the Navigator, Java Editor, or Package Explorer, select Run ➤ Run As ➤ JUnit Test. A view like the one in Figure 4-4 is displayed containing the results of the test and a progress bar similar to the Swing TestRunner included with JUnit.

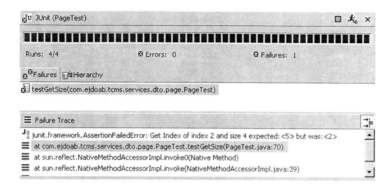

Figure 4-4. Eclipse custom TestRunner

Setting Up a Test Harness

Testing early and often is an important aspect of agile methodologies. A test harness provides necessary automation and repeatability. A test harness usually consists of TestCases, TestSuite(s), and integration with a build tool such as Ant. Depending on the type of code being tested, it may also rely on additional JUnit extensions. Setting the test harness up early before development begins establishes a positive tone for the entire development process. Though it's possible to add automated unit testing in the middle or end of a project, it isn't fun or advisable.

Integration with the build process helps make the test harness automated and repeatable. Ant ships with optional JUnit and JUnitReport tasks to simplify integration. The JUnit task is optional because it requires the junit.jar to be copied to the ANT_HOME/lib directory. The JUnit task can execute a Test class or batch of Test classes. The results of the tests are written to a report file as either plain text or XML. The report file name, unless overwritten, is TEST—followed by the name of the package and Test class with a .txt or .xml extension depending on the formatter type. In the case of batched tests, a separate report file is created for each test, thereby making it difficult to find failures and errors. So, it's a good practice to use the XML formatter and transform the XML results using the JUnitReport into HTML pages. If the harness is run in an automated way, the reports can be uploaded to a web server, or placed in a web archive (WAR) file and deployed to an application server for everybody to see. Figure 4-5 shows an example of the unit test results as a web page.

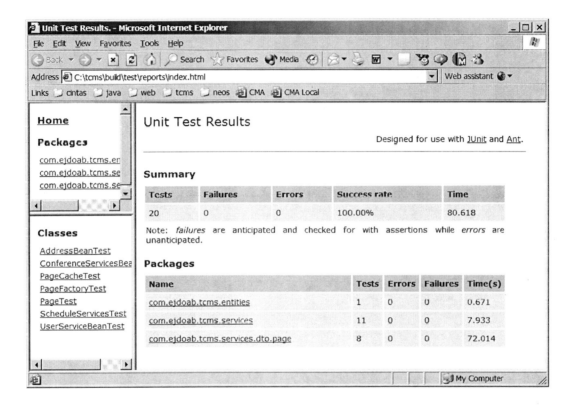

Figure 4-5. Unit test results

The TCMS application relies heavily on the JUnit task to produce results of unit tests throughout the development process. Listing 4-4 shows the testing targets used in the TCMS build.xml file. The details of the test-deploy and test-war targets will be discussed in the "Cactus" section.

Listing 4-4. TCMS Ant Targets from build.xml

```xml
<target name="test"
        depends="deploy,test-properties,test-compile,test-run"
        description="Executes unit tests." />

<target name="test-run" depends="test-deploy">
  <junit printsummary="on">
    <classpath>
      <path refid="test.class.path"/>
    </classpath>
    <formatter type="xml"/>
    <batchtest fork="yes" todir="${test-reports}">
      <fileset dir="${src-test}">
        <include name="**/*Test*.java"/>
      </fileset>
    </batchtest>
  </junit>
  <junitreport todir="${test-reports}">
    <fileset dir="${test-reports}">
      <include name="TEST-*.xml"/>
    </fileset>
    <report format="frames" todir="${test-reports}"/>
  </junitreport>
</target>

<target name="test-deploy" depends="test-war">
  <copy file="${test-war-file}"
        todir="${deploy-dir}"
  />
</target>

<target name="test-war" depends="test-compile">
  <war destfile="${test-war-file}"
      webxml="${test}/WEB-INF/web.xml">
    <lib dir="${lib}">
      <patternset refid="test.lib.set"/>
    </lib>
    <classes dir="${test}"/>
  </war>
</target>
```

```
<target name="test-properties" depends="test-init">
  <concat destfile="${test}/db.properties">
          db.url=${global.db.url}
          db.driver=${global.db.driver}
          db.user=${global.db.userid}
          db.password=${global.db.password}
  </concat>
</target>

<target name="test-compile" depends="test-init">
  <copy todir="${test}">
    <fileset dir="${src-test}">
      <patternset refid="non.source.set" />
    </fileset>
  </copy>
  <javac destdir="${test}"
         classpathref="test.class.path"
         debug="on"
         deprecation="on"
         optimize="off"
   >
      <src>
        <path refid="test.source.path" />
      </src>
  </javac>
</target>

<target name="test-init">
  <mkdir dir="${test}" />
  <mkdir dir="${test-reports}" />
</target>

<target name="test-clean">
  <delete dir="${test}" />
  <delete file="${test-war-file}" />
</target>
```

The TCMS build.xml file contains a collection of testing targets. The test-init target is responsible for creating the output directory used in the test-compilation process. The test-clean target removes all the generated stuff like the class files and directory as well as the report file and testing WAR file used by Cactus. To compile the test code, test-compile first copies all the non-Java files to the test output directory and then uses javac to compile the testing code. The javac process must include the application classes to be tested, as well as the JAR junit.jar and any JUnit extension JARs used. The test-run target executes the JUnit tests. The target forks a new JUnit process. It also enables a summary of the results to be printed to the Ant standard out. The summary contains the TestCase names along with the number of tests run, failures, errors, and the time elapsed. The summary saves time by not requiring the viewing of the report file if all tests complete successfully.

The formatter tag is used to define the format of the report as XML. The XML output is used as the input to a junitreport task to transform the documents into HTML reports. The batchtest is used to instruct JUnit to run all Java files with the Test in the name. The final target is the compressive test target. The test target will even ensure that the application is up to date and if it isn't, the test target will rebuild and redeploy it before it executes.

All the JUnit resources, including the TestCase and TestSuite classes, are contained in the junit.jar file. This JAR file must be included in the classpath when testing. In the case of tests needing to be tested in the context of a application server, the junit.jar must be deployed with the tests or in the classpath of the application server. JUnit extensions will also require the inclusion of JARs in the classpath. Later, the Cactus and DBUnit extension JARs will be discussed. We recommend you review other JUnit extensions to determine if they cover any of your testing needs.

Continuous Integration

Some organizations have integrated unit testing with version-control software so that they can provide a Continuous Integration test harness. Some version-control software like Concurrent Versions System (CVS, see Appendix B) can support custom listeners. Organizations have developed custom listeners that wait for a duration of time (15 minutes for example) after the last file has been checked in. The custom listener then executes an Ant script, which builds, deploys, and executes unit tests. Systems like AntHill, Centipede, and CruiseControl can be used in conjuction with Ant and JUnit to achieve continuous integration.

JUnit Extensions

JUnit is primarily capable of unit testing plain old Java objects. Because JUnit is a framework and not a product many groups have extended JUnit to test other units such as J2EE components, web components, and SQL scripts. You can find JUnit extensions at http://www.junit.org/news/extension/index.htm. The next two sections cover the Cactus and DBUnit extensions.

Jakarta Cactus

Many enterprise applications contain components such as Enterprise JavaBeans (EJB), servlets, tag libraries, and filters that must execute in the context of an application server, thereby making unit testing a challenge. One solution is to create mock or simulated objects to act like those found in an application server. This is a long and difficult process, plus it doesn't test the components in a real application server environment. A better option is to run the tests within the application server itself (referred to as in-container unit testing). The Jakarta Cactus project, found at http://jakarta.apache.org/cactus/index.html, is a JUnit extension for server-side testing.

Cactus's support for in-container testing is almost transparent. The difference is the tests must extend ServletTestCase instead of TestCase (see Listing 4-5). Tests must be deployed to the application server and some additional configuration files are needed.

Listing 4-5. Example of a Cactus Unit Test

```
package com.ejdoab.tcms.services.dto.page;

import com.ejdoab.tcms.entities.*;
import com.ejdoab.tcms.services.dto.*;
import junit.framework.*;
import org.apache.cactus.*;
import java.util.*;
public class PageFactoryTest extends ServletTestCase {

    private SessionDTOFactory dtoFactory = null;


    public void setUp() {
        dtoFactory = (SessionDTOFactory) DTOAbstractFactory
            .getInstance()
            .getDTOBuilder(
                    SessionDTO.class);
    }

    public void testBuildPage() throws Exception {
        SessionLocalHome slh;

        slh = SessionUtil.getLocalHome();
        Collection c = slh.findAll();
```

```
        Page page = PageFactory.buildPage(c, 0, 5, dtoFactory);
        assertNotNull("Page object", page);
        assertEquals("Page size", 5, page.getSize());
        assertEquals("Page total size", 16, page.getTotalSize());
        while(page.hasNext()) {
            Object obj = page.next();
            assertTrue("Instance of Session",
                obj instanceof SessionDTO);
        }
    }

    public void testEmptyCollection() throws Exception {
        Page page;
        page = PageFactory.buildPage(new ArrayList(), 0, 5, dtoFactory);
        assertEquals("Page size", 0, page.getSize());
        assertEquals("Page total size", 0, page.getTotalSize());
        assertEquals("Page.EMPTY_PAGE", Page.EMPTY_PAGE, page);
    }

}
```

The only required code change to implement in-container testing, rather than testing in the TestRunner JVM, is extending test classes from ServletTestCase. By extending ServletTestCase, the life cycle of the testing changes slightly. Figure 4-6 shows a UML sequence diagram of a Cactus test life cycle.

For JUnit, the life cycle involves a TestRunner that executes the run method, which calls the setUp, test, and tearDown methods before returning the results. This all takes place in the Java Virtual Machine (JVM) of the TestRunner. In the case of a Cactus test life cycle though, the run method is invoked on the ServletTestCase which causes an HTTP request to be sent to the ServletTestRedirector that's running in the application server. To see an example of a Cactus request, after deploying the test WAR you can use the an HTTP request like `http://localhost:8080/tcms_test/ServletRedirector?Cactus_TestMethod=testBuildPage&Cactus_TestClass=com.ejdoab.tcms.services.dto.page.PageFactoryTest&Cactus_AutomaticSession=true&Cactus_Service=CALL_TEST` to manually execute a server side unit test. Notice that the URL contains the class and method to test which will be executed by the CALL_TEST service. The ServletTestRedirector acts as a proxy and invokes the tests on the same ServletTestCase class but in the context of the application server. The tests run as any other JUnit test would, but in the container. When the test is complete, the ServletTestCase makes a second request to get the results of the test using the following URL: `http://localhost:8080/tcms_test/ServletRedirector?Cactus_Service=GET_RESULTS`. This URL just requests the GET_RESULTS service.

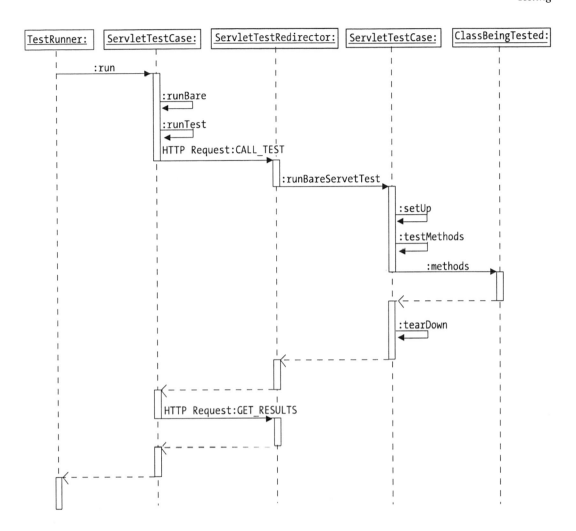

Figure 4-6. Cactus sequence diagram

For the tests to run in the context of an application server, they must be packaged and deployed to the application server just like the application. As mentioned earlier, keeping the tests separate from the production application is a good idea. This is accomplished by creating and deploying a separate WAR file that contains only the testing code. In the TCMS project, the build.xml file contains test-war and test-deploy targets used for packaging and deploying a tcms_test.war file (see Listing 4-6).

Listing 4-6. TCMS test-deploy and test-war Targets

```
<target name="test-deploy" depends="test-war">
    <copy
        file="${test-war-file}"
        todir="${deploy-dir}"
    />
</target>

<target name="test-war" depends="test-compile">
    <war destfile="${test-war-file}" webxml="${test}/WEB-INF/web.xml">
        <lib dir="${lib}">
            <patternset refid="test.lib.set"/>
        </lib>
        <classes dir="${test}"/>
    </war>
</target>
```

Cactus does require a certain amount of configuration, which includes JAR files, properties files, and a web.xml file used in the WAR file.. Both the client and server will need to have cactus-VERSION.jar, commons-logging.jar, httpunit-VERSION.jar, aspectjrt-VERSION.jar, log4j-VERSION.jar, and junit-VERSION.jar files in the classpath. In addition, the client-side classpath needs to include commons-http-client-VERSION.jar. The test-war target in Listing 4-7 shows how using the lib tag can automatically include the JARs in the server-side classpath. Cactus includes three properties files. You can place all three files in the root of the testing source directory. Two of the files configure logging. The log_client.properties shown in Listing 4-7 configures Log4j in the TestRunner JVM.

Listing 4-7. Cactus Client-Side Log4j Configuration File log_client.properties

```
# Properties for configuring Log4j
# This is the configuration for logging on the JUnit side (i.e. the client side)

log4j.appender.cactus = org.apache.log4j.FileAppender
log4j.appender.cactus.File = cactus_client.log
log4j.appender.cactus.Append = false
log4j.appender.cactus.layout = org.apache.log4j.PatternLayout
log4j.appender.cactus.layout.ConversionPattern = %d{ABSOLUTE} [%t] %-5p %-
30.30c{2} %x - %m %n

# Any application log which uses Log4J will be logged to the Cactus log file
log4j.rootCategory=DEBUG, cactus
```

```
# By default we don't log at the DEBUG level for Cactus log, in order not to
# generate too many logs. However, should a problem arise and logs need to be
# sent to the Cactus dev team, then we will ask you to change this to DEBUG.
log4j.category.org.apache.cactus = WARN, cactus
log4j.additivity.org.apache.cactus=false
```

The log_server.properties shown in Listing 4-8 configures Log4j in the application server JVM.

Listing 4-8. Cactus Server-Side Log4j Configuration File log_server.properties

```
# Properties for configuring Log4j
# This is the configuring for logging on the JUnit side (i.e. the client side)

log4j.appender.cactus = org.apache.log4j.FileAppender
log4j.appender.cactus.File = cactus_client.log
log4j.appender.cactus.Append = false
log4j.appender.cactus.layout = org.apache.log4j.PatternLayout
log4j.appender.cactus.layout.ConversionPattern =
%d{ABSOLUTE} [%t] %-5p %-30.30c{2} %x - %m %n

# By default we don't log at the DEBUG level for Cactus log, in order not to
# generate too many logs. However, should a problem arise and logs need to be
# sent to the Cactus dev team, then we will ask you to change this to DEBUG
# then we will ask you to change this to DEBUG.
log4j.category.org.apache.cactus = WARN, cactus
log4j.additivity.org.apache.cactus=false
```

In addition to the logging configuration, the client needs a cactus.properties file that contains the information necessary to create the URL that's used to request the ServletTestRedirector. Listing 4-9 is an example of the cactus.properties file, which requests the servlet from the local machine, using the ServletRedirectorName specified in the web.xml file that's discussed in the next paragraph, and the name of the test WAR file. Logging may also be enabled here.

Listing 4-9. Example of the cactus.properties File

```
cactus.contextURL=http://localhost:8080/tcms_test
cactus.servletRedirectorName=ServletRedirector
cactus.enableLogging=true
```

The cactus-X.jar contains the ServletTestRedirector Servlet. A web.xml file is used to map org.apache.cactus.server.ServletTestRedirector to the /ServletRedirector URL. An example of the web.xml file is shown in Listing 4-10.

Listing 4-10. Cactus web.xml File

```
<?xml version="1.0" encoding="UTF-8"?>
<!DOCTYPE web-app PUBLIC "-//Sun Microsystems, Inc.//DTD Web Application 2.2//EN"
    "http://java.sun.com/j2ee/dtds/web-app_2_2.dtd">

<web-app id="WebApp">
    <display-name>TCMS Unit Testing</display-name>

    <servlet>
        <servlet-name>ServletRedirector</servlet-name>
    <servlet-class>
                org.apache.cactus.server.ServletTestRedirector
          </servlet-class>
        </servlet>

    <servlet-mapping>
        <servlet-name>ServletRedirector</servlet-name>
        <url-pattern>/ServletRedirector</url-pattern>
    </servlet-mapping>
</web-app>
```

 NOTE   Cactus 1.5 contains a cactifywar Ant task that can create the web.xml in Listing 4-10.

DBUnit

Most enterprise applications store data in a relational database. Conducting valid unit tests of classes that depend on database interaction requires you to have a way to know the database state before the tests are performed. In addition, changes to the state of the database must be verified. You can set the initial database state by loading SQL scripts. Unfortunately, JUnit doesn't guarantee the order in which tests are run so tests may adversely affect the state of the database. DBUnit, found at http://www.dbunit.org/, extends JUnit functionality to provide data loading and change verification using XML files.

You can use DBUnit in one of two ways to configure the state of the database. The first method allows the JUnit framework to implicitly do the loading by extending DatabaseTestCase rather then TestCase and overriding the getConnection() and getDataSet() methods. The alternative is to call the DBUnit methods explicitly from the setUp method. Listing 4-11 shows how the TCMS project explicitly calls the DBUnit code in order to load the database from ConferenceServicesBeanTest.java. The TCMS project uses the explicit method so that tests can easily be modified to not use Cactus if necessary.

Listing 4-11. The ConferenceServicesBean Explicit Calls to DBUnit Classes

```
public class ConferenceServicesBeanTest extends TestCase {

    private Context ctx = null;
    private ConferenceServices cs = null;


    public void setUp() throws Exception {
        if(ctx == null) {
            ctx = new InitialContext();
        }

        if(cs == null) {
            // look up the home interface
            Object obj = ctx.lookup("ejb.ConferenceServicesHome");
            assertNotNull("ejb.ConferenceServiceHome lookup", obj);

            // cast and narrow
            ConferenceServicesHome csHome =
                (ConferenceServicesHome) PortableRemoteObject.narrow(
                    obj,
                    ConferenceServicesHome.class);
            assertNotNull(
                "ejb.ConferenceServiceHome interface",
                csHome);

            cs = csHome.create();
            assertNotNull("ConferenceServices remote interface", cs);
        }
```

```
IDatabaseConnection conn =
    DatabaseConnectionFactory.createConnection();
try
{
    DatabaseOperation.CLEAN_INSERT.execute(
        conn,
        DatabaseConnectionFactory.createBaseDataSet());
}
finally
{
    conn.close();
}
}
...
}
```

In Listing 4-11, explicit calls are made to DBUnit to set the database in a known state before each test run. This is done by getting a DBUnit specific IDatabaseConnection. To reduce redundant code, TCMS uses an internal DatabaseConnectionFactory class to get DBUnit IDatabaseConnections and IDataSets. After the connection is established, different DBUnit DatabaseOperations can be performed. The CLEAN_INSERT operation causes all the database rows to be deleted and inserts records from the XML document.

To load the data, you must initially put it into a specific XML format. The easiest way is to export the data from an existing database in the desired state. DBUnit includes an export utility and Ant task for performing this activity. The build.xml file contains an export task that exports the data to a file named exportFile.xml in the src/test/data directory. This task provides a good starting point. The XML file can be renamed and edited for a specific state.

 NOTE The TCMS initial XML dataset had to be organized so tables were inserted in the proper order because of referential integrity constraints.

DBUnit can also be used to compare changes to the database. Listing 4-12 is a test that submits an abstract to a Session Bean, thereby ultimately causing a SQL insert. DBUnit is used to verify that the insert is made by comparing the contents of the database with an exported and edited XML file named AfterAbstractSubmitted.xml, using an Assertion class from DBUnit.

Listing 4-12. Submit Abstract Test Using DBUnit to Verify the Insert

```java
public void testSubmitAbstract() throws Exception {
    Page page;
    ConferenceAbstractDTO ca;

    page = cs.getAbstracts(0, 5);
    int totalAbstracts = page.getTotalSize();

    String aBody =
        "A panel of experts discuss the future of the Java platform";

    ConferenceAbstractDTO dto =
        new ConferenceAbstractDTO(
            "The future of Java",
            "Panel",
            "Management",
            "Intermediate",
            aBody,
            "bsb@isllc.com");

        boolean submitted = cs.submitAbstract(dto);
        assertTrue("Submitted abstract", submitted);


        // An uncached result
        page = cs.getAbstracts(0, 6);
        assertEquals(
            "Uncached total size",
            totalAbstracts + 1,
        page.getTotalSize());

        // compare contents ignoring PK_ID because it's generated
        IDatabaseConnection conn =
            DatabaseConnectionFactory.createConnection();
        ITable actualTable = conn.createQueryTable(
            "ABSTRACTS",
          "select TITLE,TYPE,TOPIC,LEVEL,BODY,STATUS,FK_PRESENTERID from ABSTRACTS");
```

```
        IDataSet expectedDataSet =
            DatabaseConnectionFactory.createDataSet(
                "AfterAbstractSubmit.xml");
            ITable expectedTable = expectedDataSet.getTable("ABSTRACTS");

        Assertion.assertEquals(expectedTable, actualTable);
    }
```

Conclusion

This chapter explained the importance of unit testing and identified some of the best practices to consider while unit testing. The chapter also demonstrated how JUnit can be used in combination with Ant to create an automated test harness that can produce repeatable results. You learned how to use JUnit to create unit tests for plain old Java objects, and the Cactus JUnit extension was used to test components within a J2EE application server. You also learned how to perform a database-dependent test using DBUnit to set the database to a known state before a test and checking the state after the test. To learn more about unit testing and the many JUnit extensions available, we recommend that you visit `http://www.junit.org`.

CHAPTER 5

Business Tier
with JBoss

"I choose a block of marble and chop off whatever I don't need."

—Francois-Auguste Rodin

THE BUSINESS TIER is where the application logic or business rules reside. It's a slice of functionality that represents a solution to a set of problems in a particular business domain. There are many names being used today for the business tier, such as the middle tier, the application tier and the server tier. But they all imply the same thing: the brains of your application where the computation of business rules occurs. The business tier performs business processing on behalf of the presentation tier (either a web tier or a client tier). To fulfill those processes it communicates with back end data stores and the Enteprise Information Systems tier (EIS) to retrieve any persistent business data that needs to be manipulated or transformed during the course of a business transaction.

In contemporary enterprise development the J2EE application server is positioned at the heart of it all and has come to replace the operating system as the new layer of abstraction upon which enterprise applications and services are created. The J2EE architecture represents the state of the art in middleware technology, drawing on the lessons learned from the fields of transaction processing (TP) monitors, object request brokers (ORBs), component technologies, distributed computing and relational and object databases.

There are many considerations and choices faced by Java developers when designing and implementing an enterprise application business tier. The J2EE platform is a highly modular, well-integrated yet loosely coupled set of APIs that gives developers the ability to "chop off" whatever they don't need.

This chapter focuses on extracting the essential services and processes from the design of the Technology Conference Management System (TCMS) and translating them into a system of components that provide business services to the user-facing areas of the system. The complicated nature of enterprise development and the high entry cost typically associated with J2EE applications has made it an ideal area for the Open Source movement to tackle. This chapter will show you how to develop your application's business tier using the JBoss application server in conjunction with Open Source tools. You'll combine them in synergistic ways to streamline, simplify, and reduce the overall cost of developing enterprise Java applications.

J2EE: A Different Development Paradigm

There are many new aspects that make J2EE development different from traditional application development, especially when it comes to developing Enterprise JavaBeans (EJB). The J2EE platform does, in general, make programmers' lives easier by removing a great deal of the complexity previously required to handle the needs of an enterprise application.

A consequence of the effort to simplify enterprise computing is that it forces certain restrictions and radical changes to the way programmers do their jobs. There are three prominent factors that J2EE development introduces that represent a radical departure from the traditional ways of developing applications. These are as follows:

- **Declarative control:** J2EE introduces the notion of declarative control of the runtime environment. This is by far the most radical of departures for newcomers to the J2EE world. J2EE uses XML deployment descriptors that declare the way applications and components interact with the application server and clients. Declarative control is used in many areas including security, naming, transactions, and intracomponent relationships. In J2EE a great deal of the runtime behavior of an application is decided at deployment time. This flexibility leads to a more complex code-compile-debug cycle than most programmers are used to.

- **Programmatic restrictions:** EJBs are restricted in several ways to ensure that they don't interfere with the responsibilities of the container they live in. These restrictions, in combination with the fact that EJBs only work in the context of an EJB container, prevent programmers from using typical development techniques (like unit testing a class) by adding a simple main() method (console-driven testing). These restrictions aren't handled at compilation time, therefore developers who are unaware of them have no way of knowing they're violating the specification.

- **Indirection levels:** J2EE introduces a level of abstraction and indirection that most developers aren't accustomed to. A single EJB includes several Java files and deployment descriptors that can distract the developer from its "development"-time responsibilities, which should be the creation of business logic of value to the enterprise. It's important to understand that these extra layers of abstraction are usually the result of the flexibility and vendor independence designed from the ground up into the J2EE platform.

J2EE effectively changes the way programmers work, but without the right combination of tools it can be an overwhelming experience. The most common complaints from beginners about J2EE, and EJB development in particular, involve the differences in the day-to-day development processes that most programmers have grown accustomed to. At first it might seem that most of the old techniques for rapid prototyping learned in the J2SE world no longer apply, but as you continue exploring enterprise Java you'll learn that most of these techniques are adapted to work in this new environment.

NOTE   The EJB specification lays the groundwork for tool developers to automate and streamline EJB development. Unfortunately, the state of the existing tools isn't at the point where all of the benefits promised by the many vendors are a reality. The J2EE tools market is evolving rapidly and vendors are learning to read between the lines of the specifications and have begun to implement time-saving techniques for the development of J2EE-based applications. The Open Source movement has been one of the primary forces in the evolution of the J2EE tool landscape. It's now common to see an API reference implementation emerge as an Open Source project and vice versa (Open Source projects driving new JSRs).

The development of a J2EE application requires a certain amount of planning and preparation. J2EE development centers on the construction of J2EE components such as Java Server Pages (JSP), servlets, and EJBs. These components are then packaged with a module-level deployment descriptor to create what is referred to as a J2EE module. J2EE modules, in the form of Java JAR files (for EJBs) and WAR files (for servlets and JSPs), are autonomous deployable units that can also be assembled with other modules to form J2EE applications (EAR files). Unfortunately, the J2EE assembly and packaging processes have been, until recently, a very manual process, which by its very nature hinders some of today's accepted best practices for development such as Continuous Integration. Ant, the now de facto, independent development environment (IDE)-independent way to build a Java application, has streamlined many of these manual processes. Later in this chapter you'll expand on your use of Ant to deal with the particulars of a J2EE application.

EJB—to some the cornerstone of enterprise Java development—can be difficult and cumbersome to develop. Besides the creation of the numerous deployment descriptors required, EJBs require the creation of many other "glue" files. The creation, maintenance, and synchronization of these files present a significant amount of overhead. Figure 5-1 shows a breakdown of the activities involved in J2EE-component development. As a developer you should know which of these activities you can automate and which ones you can streamline by using the right tools such as XDoclet for the generation of many of the supporting glue files and descriptors. You'll explore XDoclet in greater detail later in this chapter.

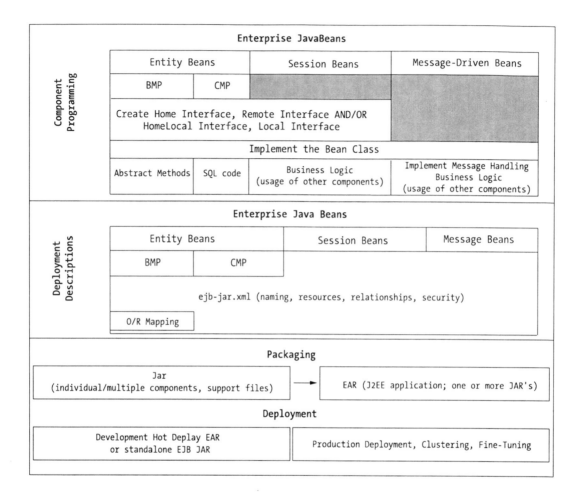

Figure 5-1. Business tier J2EE development

Open Source tools like Ant, XDoclet, and Middlegen can help streamline and reduce the overhead of J2EE development. In combination with freely available J2EE servers and EJB containers from projects like JBoss, OpenEJB, and JOnAS, these tools lessen the complexity of entering into J2EE. Open Source provides zero cost for infrastructure and a large pool of worldwide developer resources behind the refinement and troubleshooting of the tools and frameworks. Open Source makes the rapid development of enterprise Java applications on a budget a reality. After all, development time—not application server cost—usually has the highest impact on a new J2EE project.

Considerations for the Business Tier

The J2EE platform was born out of the lessons learned through the years in component-oriented technologies. Originally, Sun envisioned a thriving reusable component market that would rapidly evolve. This dream hasn't come to fruition like it happened with the visual-component market created by products like Visual Basic and Delphi Rapid Application Development (RAD) tools. Although Sun strongly directed the early push toward building reusable components, the emphasis has shifted toward ease of development and performance as the J2EE technology has been battle tested. The early analogies with the visual RAD world have proved a little misguided. Visual components are radically different than middleware components and visual-application developers work in very different ways than middle-tier developers. Visual component developers usually have a much better defined environment, well-established contracts for containment, and a much simpler set of resources to manage for their components. When one adds distribution, fault tolerance, data awareness, and many more degrees of freedom in terms of component usage, it's easy to see the differences. We predict that the market for reusable components will flourish after the tools market matures and we, as an industry, find the right paradigm for the component-based rapid construction of enterprise applications.

Before you get started building the business tier for the TCMS system it's important to get a basic understanding of the issues and choices that you'll be faced with in a typical J2EE project. The considerations are many, from the actual processes involved in the day-to-day development, to the choices between the different API and technologies offered by the J2EE platform. Issues such as which design patterns and which best practices to apply to a project are key ingredients in building a successful J2EE application. This section provides some insight into some of these issues and offers some general guidance for those who are relatively new to the J2EE platform.

Write Once Run Anywhere

The concept of Write Once Run Anywhere (WORA) is one of the stated goals of J2EE and Java in general. WORA still isn't something that you automatically get simply because you're using J2EE technologies, and how much importance you place into attaining it can be crucial to the success of a J2EE project. You must work to achieve WORA and in the current state of affairs being able to just switch application servers or databases isn't a matter of hours or days but rather a task that can take weeks . Portability most of the time is an afterthought to the driving forces of corporate America and it's rarely a business requirement for most projects. If your application isn't solving a particular business problem well, odds are that it won't survive long enough to be ported anyways. WORA is a more important consideration if you're planning to sell off-the-shelf packaged third-party components.

In general you should strive to make your applications as portable as possible without hampering their capability to deliver business value. The next two sections discuss the two most likely places where you might be faced with a decision between maximizing functionality and marginalizing portability.

Proprietary J2EE Container Features

The J2EE specification aims at creating competition amongst vendors' implementations while adhering to a standard set of APIs. Unfortunately, there are plenty of gaps in the J2EE specifications that vendors must fill without the guidance of a well-defined set of APIs. Poor planning in the usage of these value-added features can become a major roadblock if you decide to port your J2EE application to a different vendor's server. Yet, for most companies switching, an application server is a rarely seen concern ranking very low in comparison with having an application that truly fulfills a business need.

Many times you'll find that a particular vendor implements a specific non-J2EE value-added feature based on a submitted JSR. In the case of a company that is leading the pack, it might submit a JSR for a particular feature. The point here is that choosing an implementation that is aligned closely with a JSR makes the portability issues less marked. Also, good object orientation should tell you that when plugging a proprietary feature into an application, the standard approach is to "adapt" it using an existing API or JSR as a guideline.

Proprietary Database Features

Although EJBs make a natural choice for caching data, for certain types of operations on data it's just much more efficient to let the database handle them. Store procedures and custom-database functions might be the best choice when dealing with bulk management of data. For example, for data that's read repeatedly from the database, store procedures provide a tremendous performance boost by taking advantage of precompilation, in which each store procedure is compiled once and the execution plan is reused many times. Store procedures have access to query optimizers and other performance-boosting facilities that application programmers cannot access from the confines of the application server.

It's important to understand the difference between business logic and persistence logic (with data-integrity logic spread between the two). Persistence logic deals with how to reflect the effect of a business process on the persistent data. If your application deals primarily with persistence logic and if your database structure is likely to change often, then store procedures provide a convenient extra layer of abstraction between your application and the data. EJB-based applications (CMP 2.0) are strongly coupled to the database structure (one-to-one, table-to-Bean relationships).

CMP 2.0 Entity Beans provide a place at the application level to handle persistence logic and handle complex data model relationships better than the previous versions of the specification. But you have to remember that the strength of the J2EE platform is in providing an enterprise-level execution environment for business logic—persistence logic is just a necessary evil. One of the greatest problems in enterprise development is the object-relational impedance mismatch; CMP 2.0 is J2EE's answer to that problem. But it should be carefully evaluated as a solution. Java code cannot provide the level of optimization that you can achieve at the database level.

 NOTE   It's relevant to mention that the CMP specification provides several commit options that provide the flexibility to optimize the interaction with the database. For example when there is prior knowledge that the database will only be accessed by the EJB container, the container can cache a Bean's state between transactions using commit Option A. The CMP commit options are transparent to the Entity Bean developer and are specified by the J2EE server administrator. To learn more about CMP commit options see EJB 2.1 Specification section 10-5-10.

That said, it's important to plan in the event that the underlying database needs to be replaced. One key example of the differences between database vendor implementation is unique key generation, which you'll explore later in this chapter.

Enterprise JavaBeans

Typically the first question that many developers ask when making the transition into the J2EE platform is whether to use EJB or not. EJBs are distributed, network-aware components for developing secure, scalable, transactional, and multiuser applications in a J2EE environment. EJBs, as part of the J2EE architecture, advocate a 3+ tier architecture, which, according to a Software Engineering Institute (SEI) article, "has been shown to improve performance for groups with a large number of users (in the thousands) and improves flexibility when compared to the two tier approach."[1]

But, what does that mean to you? And how do you determine whether you need EJBs in your current application? To start with, it's important to understand that EJBs aren't the core or foundation of the J2EE platform; they're just one of the APIs available, though one that can cover a wide range of enterprise-application needs. Also it's important to understand that there are several different types of EJBs and though some might be applicable to certain problems others might not be. There is still a lot of fear, uncertainty, and doubt being spread in the industry about EJBs. The opinions in the industry can be classified on three different levels:

- **The Good:** Based on real limitations or questionable designs in the EJB specification. Like any approach to distributed computing, EJBs are far from perfect and are under greater scrutiny than most technologies given the extent of their usage. The EJB specification is evolving to cover web services integration (JavaBeans as SOAP-based services) and better integration with legacy and third-party messaging systems.

- **The Bad:** Those based on problems found in earlier EJB specifications, but which are still driving newcomers away from the technology. Problems like the dreaded n+1 database call problem present in early Entity Bean specifications (caused by containers requiring n+1 database calls and network trips to load an Entity Bean and its dependent child objects in a parent-child relationship).

- **The Ugly:** As with any far-reaching technology, there are opinions that are market driven or based on a lack of understanding of the needs of enterprise applications in general. EJBs are by far the most controversial technology in Sun's repertoire and we've seen both sides of the spectrum, from high praise to no-holds-barred bashing.

One of the key considerations when deciding whether to use EJBs is distribution. How will your application be architected? How would the tiers be partitioned physically? Are the web container and the EJB container running on the same machine? How would you handle concurrency and load issues? How would your transactions be distributed? What level of security will your business services need? What about quality-of-service requirements? The J2EE EJB container is a marvelous piece of middleware that does a lot of the things that as programmers you previously had to deal with on every application that was built. Before the rise of the J2EE application server most companies slowly and painfully built the

---

1. Carnegie Mellon University, Software Engineering Institute (SEI), Jan 1997. See http://www.sei.cmu.edu/str/descriptions/clientserver_body.html.

equivalent infrastructure on an as-needed basis. These efforts usually distracted application developers from their goal: the development of applications that improve the bottom line of their employers. Also, the consistency in the quality of the plumbing code produced is always questionable. The resulting products were usually a clear case of jack-of-all-trades and master-of-none syndrome.

The main goal of EJBs is to simplify enterprise-server computing. But it's important to understand where this "simplification" takes place. Entity Beans hide the complexities of multithreading, transactions, connection pooling, scalability, object-relational mapping, and security. Hiding these complexities comes with a price. The price is in the form of overhead and complexity in other areas such as development, testing, and deployment. Achieving the enterprise capabilities on your own, without an EJB container, is extremely difficult, yet at the same time EJBs are still more complex to develop and use than plain JavaBeans or simple Java Objects. The common rule that the more generic a solution the slower it will perform holds particularly well for EJBs if used in the wrong scenario.

The earlier EJB specification went through a lot of criticism for issues such as forcing every interBean interaction to be a remote call at the specification level. This has now changed with the introduction of local interfaces. EJB 1.1 generalized the remoteness and distribution aspects, making all JavaBeans locations independent (also know as location transparency). Local interfaces allow co-located clients and EJBs to be accessed using pass-by-reference semantics instead of pass-by-value semantics.

NOTE   Contemporary programming languages implement two common parameter passing models: pass by value and pass by reference. Pass by value entails that the parameters and return values are copied for each method call, and pass by reference passes a reference to the actual object to the method. Pass by reference improves performance by not having to clone objects. Pass by reference also allows the caller to modify the state of the passed object.

EJB, as with any other standard, makes you fit your problem into a specific solution space. Even if you use EJBs, you don't have to make everything an EJB. It's obvious that if your application needs a large percentage of the capabilities that are provided by EJBs then you should consider EJBs as a viable solution. It's important to understand the point of diminishing returns with EJBs and where on that line your application lies. It's typical to hear claims of projects that have seen performance gains in order of ten or more by not using EJBs, yet once you examine their architectures it's hard to see why they used them in the first place.

Later on, in Chapter 7, you'll see what technologies you can use in conjunction or as alternatives to EJBs. Compelling reasons to go the EJB route are as follows:

- **Transactions:** If your application deals with well-defined transactions against a data store. Container-managed transactions are one of the most powerful features of EJB technology. Declarative-transaction management, the ability to change transactional characteristics without changing code, is one of the jobs that Enterprise JavaBeans does well.

- **Concurrency:** Concurrency control for operation on shared data.

- **Expected load:** If you expect more than a thousand users, EJBs offer advanced, tunable instance pooling to effectively manage resources in such conditions.

- **Components:** If you're looking for a platform that encourages the use of third-party components.

- **Data integrity:** If data integrity is a must, container-managed persistence provides a reliable, proven solution.

- **Session management:** If you need reliable session management.

- **Layering:** If you need strong separation of presentation and business tiers.

- **Support:** Easier to find qualified people. As with any standard, it's easier to discern a person's level of understanding of a particular technology. Most proprietary in-house approaches are rarely documented well enough to be learned in a reasonable amount of time. Prospective candidates might shy away from working with a proprietary framework (job portability).

- **Channels:** If you're expecting to handle many different types of client applications.

On the other hand reasons to avoid EJBs are as follows:

- **Testing:** More complex testing.

- **Development time:** More complex development and longer deployment cycles.

- **Cost:** EJB container cost (see the discussion of JBoss later in this chapter).

- **Training:** Steeper learning curve.

- **Expected load:** If you have a fairly small user load, and performance is your primary goal, the overhead of the container services might not be worth the performance penalties incurred.

- **Tabular data:** If you're only providing a nonobject-oriented view of a set of database tables, your application can tolerate stale data and the data is mostly read-only, nontransactional.

- **Data warehousing:** Massive data-manipulation operations such as a data-warehousing aren't well suited for EJBs. This is an area where programming to the database excels.

- **Prototypes:** If you're prototyping a simple application or a proof of concept, use a lighter, nonenterprise solution.

- **Complex object models:** EJBs don't support complex object models well. They don't support domain inheritance and aren't truly polymorphic. A complaint from purists is that the resulting object models are overly data-driven, which makes it difficult to implement nontrivial best practices when it comes to modeling your application.

EJBs, like any other technology, aren't perfect and aren't a perfect fit for every problem. They're by far the most complex technology in the J2EE stack and might not be the best entry point into the J2EE arena. If you're prototyping an application, EJBs might not be the best choice. You can build a simple prototype using Struts or JSPs, servlets, JavaBeans, and JDBC in a fraction of the time that it takes you to get a simple EJB-based application up and running.

Entity Beans

Of all the EJB types, Entity Beans are the ones that have been criticized the most. Given that a large percentage of applications will be database-driven applications, it's no surprise that this API has fallen under such scrutiny. One of the arguments against Entity Beans that you can find in discussion groups is that everything that you can do with EJBs can also be accomplished with JSP, servlets, JavaBeans, TagLibs, and plain JDBC. Though this is certainly true in a lot of cases, the problem with this type of overgeneralization is that the gains of Entity Beans aren't easily perceived in systems with a small number of users (< 1000). To reap the benefits you have to be past the point where a typical JSP/servlet/JavaBeans application that does straight JDBC begins to have problems. These problems are typically related to the ability for the application to cache data. The main culprit when it comes to the performance problems of a multitier application is serialization.

Entity Beans, for example, minimize the amount of serialization by providing a cache for database data. With smart container optimizations, Remote Procedural Call (RPC) optimizations, and a well-architected CMP engine, EJBs provide a viable choice for caching data.

The introduction of container-managed relationships has alleviated some of the complaints about EJBs being poor object-oriented artifacts by allowing complex relationships in the data model to be mirrored at the EJB level. As you learned in the "design" chapter, a sound object-oriented design should always prevail over any technology-specific workaround. We see the difficulty of implementing a complex object model in EJBs as one of the main detracting points for using the technology. On the other hand, the enterprise Java community is very skilled and very proactive at taking what it has been given by the specifications and making it work in the real world. As a result a lot of "design patterns" have emerged to deal with the shortcomings of the J2EE platform, mainly in the area of EJB development. Some of these so-called "design patterns" could be better labeled as "implementation patterns" or "strategies" to deal with the shortcomings of the technology, while they attempt to support a sound object-oriented design. With the now available EJB 2.1 specification and the introduction of container-managed relationships, you can now use Entity Beans to model finer-grained domain entities. The object-relational impedance mismatch existed long before the introduction of EJBs, and as long as your data continues to live in the relational world the problem will exist.

Asynchronous Processing

Synchronous processing is the primary modus operandi of contemporary computing. The traditional client-server paradigm of the Web is a perfect example of the request-response synchronous system in which a caller blocks until receiving a response from the server. As you know, the Web is a stateless environment and a synchronous one. This means that long-running processes aren't well suited for this environment. In stand-alone applications you can use background threads and callbacks for long-running processes. In a synchronous invocation environment such as the Web, the server side of the equation must process and return a response before the client on the other end of the line times out.

At the application level, a synchronous call between processes is handled with RPC-like mechanisms. In Java and J2EE this is accomplished via the Remote Method Invocation (RMI) subsystem, which provides synchronous RPC services.

Another way for processes to communicate with one another is asynchronously, in which one process sends a message and doesn't block for an answer. For a long-running process such as calculating a credit score for a home loan, a client could send the request and later (without blocking) receive a message containing the result of the requested operation.

You can extend this paradigm further by decoupling the senders from the receivers by placing an entity in the middle that enables both parties to be unaware of each other. In enterprise messaging this entity is referred to as the message broker. A message broker offers a very flexible type of interapplication communication by simplifying the logical connections among multiple application systems. Message brokers are logical entities, distinct from senders and receivers, which coordinate message distribution.

Going back to the credit score example, imagine that the entity that processes the credit applications is the credit processor. In an enterprise-messaging scenario the credit processor will be able to process "credit application" messages. Now you can see that by decoupling the credit processors from the client applications, you now have the ability to scale the system by simply adding more credit processors.

TIP A system's scalability will typically increase as you decouple its components and remove any unnecessary "state" that's being kept.

Enterprise messaging provides a reliable, flexible service for the asynchronous exchange of critical business data and events throughout an enterprise. Java Message Service (JMS) provides a common API and a provider framework that enables the development of portable, message-based applications.

One of the missing ingredients in the EJB mix was a better integration with message-oriented middleware (MOM). With the introduction of JMS and message-driven Beans (MDBs) to the J2EE and EJB specifications respectively, Enterprise Java developers now have at their disposal the tools of enterprise messaging. MDBs made their debut in version 2.0 of the EJB specification. As you learned in the J2EE primer, unlike Session and Entity Beans, MDBs aren't directly accessible by a client. Instead they operate on messages received either from a JMS queue (point-to-point) or a JMS topic (publish-subscribe).

The use of messaging can change the perceived performance of an EJB-based application by providing a way to accomplish parallelism in an otherwise (from the point of view of the developer) single-threaded environment. JMS can enable coordination of long-running tasks by allowing developers to handle specific workflow items in "set-it-and-forget-it" fashion.

Integration with external non-J2EE sources is also facilitated with MDBs. For example, imagine a J2EE system that needs to interact with a non-J2EE order-fulfillment subsystem. In such a case you could expose an HTTP interface or a web service that in turn uses messaging in the form of an MDB to alert a J2EE application of a relevant event in the processing flow of an order.

Another advantage of messaging systems is that messaging technologies have been around for quite a while now. And with the reliability of the mature MOM systems, along with features like "guaranteed delivery" and "durable subscribers," recovery from failure is easier to accomplish than with traditional RPC-based architectures.

JBoss: The Open Source Choice for the Business Tier

The JBoss application server started life as the EJBoss project back in March 1999. Spearheaded by Marc Fleury, a former Sun Microsystems engineer, along with an enthusiastic group of programmers ready to embrace the then-new EJB specification, it has grown to be the most popular Open Source application server in the market and a worthy contender to the likes of BEA WebLogic, IBM Websphere, and the Borland application server.

Distributed under the GNU Lesser General Public License (LGPL) Open Source license, JBoss is a 100-percent compliant clean-room implementation that provides the full gamut of J2EE services, and it's built on a pluggable architecture that leverages the Java Management Extensions (JMX) specification and recent academia-driven advances in software engineering such as aspect-oriented programming (AOP). JBoss was also one of the first application servers tailored to developers, with dynamic features like hot deployment. It featured the ability to load and unload libraries at runtime as well as dynamic generation of container stubs and skeletons. Many of these features aren't found in commercial offerings.

JBoss is more than an application server. It's a full-featured platform for enterprise development that provides the full J2EE stack of services. Under the umbrella of the JBoss project you'll find the following:

- **JBossServer:** An advanced EJB container and JMX "bus"

- **JBossMQ:** A JMS provider

- **JBossTX:** For Java Transaction API (JTA) and Java Transaction Service (JTS) transactions

- **JBossCMP:** Container-managed persistence engine

- **JBossSX:** For JAAS-based security

- **JBossCX:** For Java Connector Architecture (JCA) connectivity

- **JBossMail:** Java mail provider

- **JBossWeb:** A slightly customized version of the popular Jetty web container for servlets/JSPs (or alternatively Tomcat or another container for which a JBoss service exists)

The JMX specification allows for the control and configuration of managed Beans (MBeans). MBeans are components that wrap the network entities, which include other components, applications, and hardware devices. MBeans, just like EJBs, live in a container that abides by the JMX server standard: the MBean server. The MBean server is a lightweight process, similar to a Common Object Request Broker Architecture (CORBA) ORB, which serves as a repository or registry for MBeans. The JMX server in JBoss is the spinal cord of the system where MBeans plug in and interact with other MBeans. JMX was designed as a bridge and a consolidation point for other network management systems, just like JMS and JDBC are for the areas of enterprise Messaging and database connectivity.

MBeans are designed for management and they provide clients with the ability to receive notifications of relevant management events by registering with the MBean. JBoss's JMX-based flexible architecture allows you to select which components (or services) you want in a running server. JBoss enables developers to mix and match different implementations of specific J2EE services as long as there is a compliant JMX MBean. MBeans are registered and instantiated using MLets. MLets are management applets; the MBeans server provides an MLet service that loads a text file that specifies the information on the MBean(s) that will be loaded. JBoss can be extended and customized by creating MBean services.

Since its inception JBoss's extreme flexibility has greatly contributed to its meteoric rise to stardom. It's consider by many in the industry as a prime example of the viability of the Open Source model in the area of enterprise infrastructure. The JBossGroup, headed by Fleury, is also one of the first in a breed of companies embracing the Open Source service-oriented revenue model. Many commercial vendors of J2EE value-added software and development tools are partnering with JBoss—a testament to its success. You could argue that the JBoss application server's success has been one of the main driving forces in the recent drop in application server prices and licensing flexibility. Today major vendors are offering "community" editions or giving the application servers away as part of a bundle that might include an operating system or hardware.

JBoss is an application-server build for developers by developers. JBoss uses dynamic proxies during deployment to generate the server-side "glue" code dynamically. No longer do you have to run a proprietary server-side code generator as you would with many commercial application servers. Static glue approaches tend to muddy the business objects in a swamp of proprietary files. Dynamic glue generation facilitates fast prototyping and supports the evolution of the codebase in short phases (Continuous Integration).

JBoss is leading the pack as an enterprise platform that's moving towards embracing aspect-oriented concepts such as enabling developers to work with plain old Java objects (POJOs) In the context of an enterprise application that's still gaining all the advantages of distributed-component architectures.[2] Expect to see many new advanced features in the upcoming 4.0 versions of the platform.

---

2.   Fowler. *Patterns of Enterprise Application Architecture* (Boston, MA: Addison-Wesley, 2003).

Readers interested in finding out more on the inner working of the JBoss application server should start by getting an overview of the JMX API, the Dynamic Proxy API and Rickard Oeberg's "Interceptor Stack," which is the pattern at the heart of the JBoss containers. To learn more about the JBoss server architecture see Stark et al. *JBoss Administration and Development.*[3] Figure 5-2 shows an overview of the JBoss server architecture.

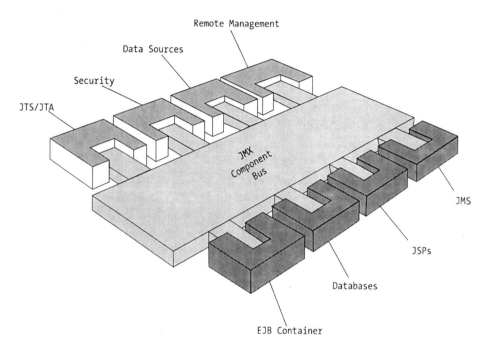

Figure 5-2. JBoss architecture

Setup and Configuration

As with most other Open Source projects, you can obtain JBoss in source form or in binary form. In this chapter you'll use the binary ready-to-run distribution. To obtain the latest development release you can use the Concurrent Versions System (CVS).

In this book we're promoting the collocation of the EJB container and the web container; therefore you'll be using JBoss and the embedded JBossWeb web container.

3. Stark, Fleury, et al. *JBoss Administration and Development* (SAMS, March 2002).

NOTE Collocating the web tier and the EJB container was sometimes frowned upon as a technically incorrect layering of the architecture. An underlying reason not to collocate was the fact that licensing costs normally made such an arrangement cost-prohibitive. Remember, with JBoss the cost per CPU is always constant: zero dollars and the performance gains due to container-to-container optimizations (reduction in serialization) are remarkable. If your network topology and security constrains enable you to collocate the two tiers we highly recommend that you do so.

Properly configuring and fine-tuning your application is one the most important aspects of a J2EE deployment. In this chapter though you'll concentrate only on the definitions and development of the components.

Download and Install JBoss

The JBoss distribution consists of one single compressed archive following the naming convention jboss-[JBoss-Version].zip. In this case the archive file is jboss-3.2.1.zip and you can obtain it from http://www.jboss.org/downloads.jsp. The following instructions should work on any JBoss 3.2.x distribution.

NOTE In this book we've decided to use the JBoss version that uses the JBossWeb web container. The JBossWeb container, a customized version of the Open Source Jetty web container, is reported to provide better performance that the Tomcat reference implementation.

Next, proceed to extract or unzip the downloaded file to a suitable directory using the Java JAR tool (on any platform), Winzip, the Windows XP built-in extract utility, or unzip in Linux. In this case we're using c:\java\ so the JBoss distribution directory (JBOSS_DIST) is C:\java\jboss-3.2.1.

CAUTION The JBoss group recommends that you select a directory structure that contains names without spaces, which seem to cause problems with certain Sun Java Virtual Machines (JVMs).

The resulting directory structure should resemble the one shown in Figure 5-3.

```
□ 🗀 jboss-3.0.6
    🗀 bin
    🗀 client
  ⊞ 🗀 docs
    🗀 lib
  □ 🗀 server
    ⊞ 🗀 all
    ⊞ 🗀 default
    ⊞ 🗀 minimal
```

Figure 5-3. JBoss directory structure

Next, proceed to start the JBoss server by opening a command prompt under Windows, or the shell terminal under Linux, or the console under UNIX. Change the active directory to the bin directory under the JBoss installation and enter the following:

```
C:\java\jboss-3.2.1\bin>run
```

If the server starts correctly you should see a great deal of logging information scroll by without any Java exceptions. If you're a longtime Java developer you're probably going to be able to catch a glimpse of a Java exception scrolling regardless of how fast is goes by.

The batch file run.bat (or run.sh if running under Linux or Unix) uses the default configuration, which is located in the JBOSS_DIST/server/default. JBoss also ships with "minimal" and "all" services–enabled configurations under the JBOSS_DIST/server/ directory.

NOTE   For those familiar with the WebLogic application server, the directories under the JBoss distribution "server" directory serve a similar function to the concept of a domain in WebLogic. The domain can host a collection of applications under a common set of resources and configuration options.

Let's examine some of the console output to get an understanding of the JBoss runtime environment. At the very top you should see the definition of the environment variable JBOSS_HOME, your current JAVA_HOME—the classpath available to JBoss at startup—as well as some other environment variables. You would see several MBean services go through a progression of states, typically the following: creating, created, starting, and started.

The output results for a successful server startup should resemble the following:

```
...
21:28:11,495 INFO  [Server] Starting JBoss (MX MicroKernel)...
21:28:11,515 INFO  [Server] Release ID: JBoss [WonderLand] 3.2.1 (build:
CVSTag=JBoss_3_2_1 date=200305041533)
...
21:28:11,525 INFO  [Server] Root Deployemnt Filename: jboss-service.xml
21:28:11,535 INFO  [Server] Starting General Purpose Architecture (GPA)...
21:28:12,006 INFO  [ServerInfo] Java version: 1.4.2_03,Sun Microsystems Inc....
...
21:28:42,099 INFO  [Server] JBoss (MX MicroKernel) [3.2.1 (build:
        CVSTag=JBoss_3_2_1

date=200305041533)] Started in 30s:564ms
```

To test the installation and inspect the runtime environment go to
http://localhost:8080/jmx-console/, which should display the JBoss JMX
console as shown in Figure 5-4.

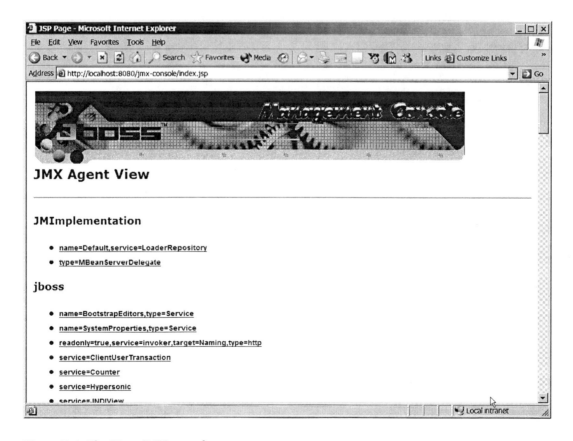

Figure 5-4. The JBoss JMX console

A more comprehensive set of tests is available in the JBoss TestSuite, which is a collection of unit tests used by the JBoss team to provide Continuous Integration to their development process. Running the TestSuite is outside of the scope of this book but we recommend doing so, especially when building JBoss from CVS or a source-code distribution.

JBoss Management with Java Management Extensions

The runtime management of the JBoss server is currently performed via the JBoss JMX console web application shown in Figure 5.4. The JBoss services are exposed as MBeans, which you can inspect with the console. The console provides a listing of all JBoss services (JMX agent view). From this list of services you can drill down to an individual view of the service to the MBean view in order to perform an operation on a particular MBean.

For example, to view the contents of the Java Naming and Directory Interface (JNDI) tree select the service=JNDIView hyperlink under the JBoss heading, which will take you to the MBean view for the JNDIView service. MBean operations are exposed in the raw in the JBoss console as method signatures that you can click to execute. On this page you'll see a list of MBean operations; select the list() operation. The list() operation will give you a listing of the items in the JNDI tree. Notice that you're able to select the value of the Boolean parameter. If you wonder about the meaning of the parameter, check the JavaDoc documentation for the org.jboss.naming.JNDIView class and you'll find that the parameter is a verbose flag.

```
public java.lang.String list(boolean verbose)
```

The JavaDoc also reveals the purpose of the method: "List deployed application java:comp namespaces, the java: namespace as well as the global InitialContext JNDI namespace."

 TIP   It comes in handy to bookmark the JBoss JavaDoc API because the JMX console doesn't provide MBeans method details.

The java:comp/env namespace, also referred to as the environment naming context (ENC), provides a namespace that links logical resource names to their physical counterparts, thereby avoiding the hard coding of values in EJB lookups. The logical-physical mapping is configured via the ejb-ref, ejb-local-ref, resource-ref, and resource-env-ref elements of the ejb-jar deployment descriptor.

 TIP Always use the java:comp/env namespace for looking up other components and resources from within a Bean. This technique allows applications to be deployed without the components having any knowledge of the actual JNDI names of the components they reference.

The JMX standard makes it relatively simple for any JMX-compliant management application to be used with JBoss. The JBoss Group is working on JBossMGT, an advanced management console project based on the JSR-77, which specifies a management specification for the J2EE platform.

As mentioned before, MBeans live in the JMX container. In JBoss they provide a way for JMX-compliant tools to manage services through management interfaces exposed through an MBean. MBeans can notify registered listeners of changes to a managed service. By writing custom MBeans you can access and control certain advanced features of the application server such as cache-invalidation schemes and advanced clustering techniques.

JMX management tools are slowly appearing in the market both from commercial vendors and from the Open Source community. One such JMX Open Source management console is provided by the EJTools project, hosted on SourceForge. It provides both web-based and Java swing client-management tools that work with the JBoss server. The EJTools utilities will give you better control over the deployment of the TCMS application.

Go to http://www.ejtools.org/ and download the current distributions of jmx.browser and the jndi.browser WAR archives: At the time of this writing these were jmx.browser-1.1.1.sar and jndi.browser-1.0.1.war. To deploy them simply copy both archives to the JBOSS_DIST/server/default/deploy directory. JBoss monitors this directory for changes; when it detects a deployable file it attempts to locate a suitable deployer for it.

To view the EJTools JMX browser, point your web browser to `http://localhost:8080/jmx.browser/` as shown in Figure 5-5. As you can see, the functionality is very similar to that which is provided by the JBoss JMX console.

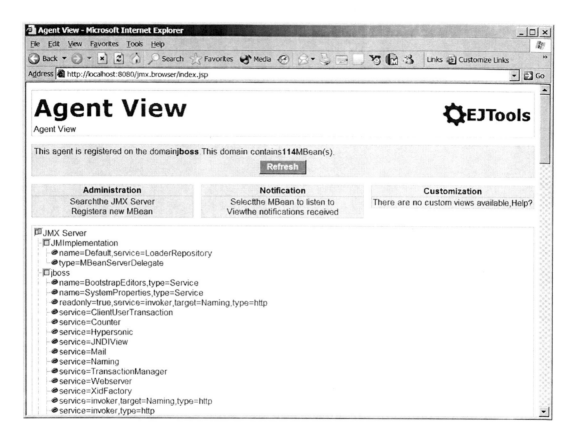

Figure 5-5. The EJTools JMX browser

More useful than the EJTools JMX browser is the JNDI browser, which you can see at `http://localhost:8080/jndi.browser-1.0.1/`. The view it provides of the JBoss JNDI tree is a little cleaner than the one provided by the JBoss JMX console as it's shown in Figure 5-5.

As you can see the JMX API creates the same type of open standards–based competition that you see in other areas of J2EE development.

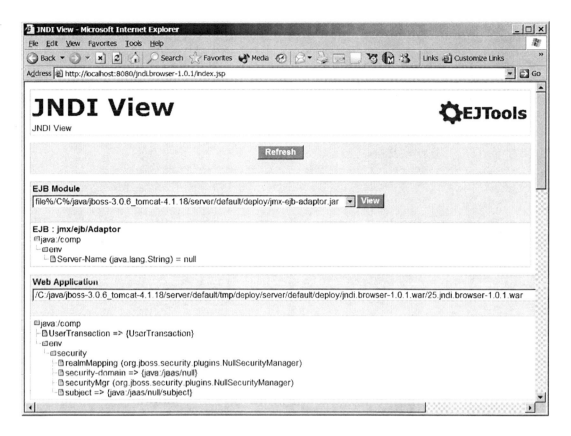

Figure 5-6. The EJTools JNDI browser

Case Study: Technology Conference Management System Business Tier on JBoss

The architectural guidelines and initial design produced in Chapters 1 and 2 will guide the decisions made in the implementation of the business tier. The business tier encapsulates the system's business rules and logic. The business tier provides services needed for the realization of the use cases or user stories. In developing the business components necessary to fulfill the use cases, you typically move back and forth between different levels of abstraction, namely, the abstract object model, the concrete Java classes representing that model, the J2EE components built from the concrete classes, and the higher level of services provided by collaborating sets of components. Figure 5-7 shows the different levels of abstraction J2EE developers find themselves dealing with.

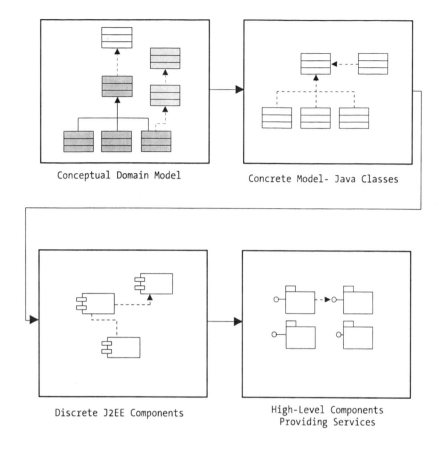

Figure 5-7. Levels of abstraction in J2EE development

Mapping the UML Object Model to J2EE Components

The following set of simple guidelines can help you arrive at the initial J2EE component diagram. These rules for turning your domain model into a set of J2EE components are as follows:

- **Coarse components:** Group fine-grained objects into coarse components. Objects that exhibit high cohesion are good candidates to be part of the same component.

- **Uses cases to facades:** Group related use cases (look at the Moment-Interval classes in your domain model) under the control of a Session or Message Facade.

- **Entities with Entity Beans:** Party, Place, or Things classes are usually good candidates to become Entity Beans.

Mapping a UML model to the J2EE framework is a very subjective task. Take three different architects and you're likely to end up with three completely different systems. By following the guidelines in this section we hope that you can repeatedly and consistently produce sound J2EE systems. The approach is simple; after obtaining a suitable representation of your problem space in the form of a domain class diagram (structure plus implicit dynamism), uses cases, and interaction diagrams (explicit dynamism), you should use the previous three rules to arrive at a first draft of an object-oriented component-based solution. From there you apply design and implementation patterns or strategies to refine the application.

Plain Old Java Objects and the Business Tier

Just because we've chosen to use Enterprise JavaBeans in the TCMS system doesn't mean that everything will be an EJB. Actually, most EJBs of medium to high complexity are actually patterns of Plain Old Java Objects (POJOs) that interact with each other and use the services provided by the EJB container to expose a cohesive set of functions to a client.

What does that mean to you? First, it means that some of the complex business logic interactions of a J2EE system can be coded and tested outside of the realm of the J2EE application server. Many introductory books, for the sake of brevity, choose to show all the relevant operations of an EJB in the code of the EJB itself. Again, good object-oriented practices tell you that this will lead to business code that's tightly coupled with your choice of technologies. What if that functionality needs to be reused in a personal, nonnetworked version of the system such as a commercial swing application?

Using well-designed POJOs in your J2EE application will lead to easier testing (see "JUnit" in the "Testing" chapter), and they will let you easily discern if adding distribution into the equation is what might be causing problems in your application. Remember the harder something is to test the less likely it will be thoroughly tested.

Many projects using aspect-oriented techniques are hinting toward using J2EE technologies as aspects that apply to POJOs. If this prediction becomes a reality, expect to see enterprise-level J2EE applications being produced without developers having to write a single EJB.

Configuring the TCMS JBoss Server

Before you get started with the development you need to configure JBoss for the TCMS system. To configure an application domain or server for the TCMS system under JBoss you'll use the "default" configuration as a base. To get started, copy the JBOSS_DIST/server/default directory recursively into a JBOSS_DIST/server/tcms directory. This directory will be the tcms server directory for the remainder of the chapter.

Earlier in the chapter the JBoss installation section described how to start the "default" server by using the run.bat or run.sh scripts under the bin directory. To start the tcms server type the following:

```
run —c tcms
```

The output should resemble the output previously seen when starting the default server.

Data Model and Database Setup

The database for the TCMS system is composed of the following tables, as shown in Table 5-1:

Table 5-1. TCMS System Database Tables

Table Name	Description
Abstracts	Holds a list of all submitted presentation abstracts and their status.
AbstractStatus	Holds a list of the possible status for a submitted abstract.
Addresses	Holds addresses for any entity in the system that can have an address.
Answers	Holds answers to evaluations submitted by attendees of a conference session.
Attendees	Holds a list of all conference attendees (role).
Booths	Holds a list of conference booths associated with a venue.
Conferences	Holds a list of the conferences being managed by the system.
GroupPricingRules	Holds the pricing structure for groups of attendees.
PresentationLevels	Holds a list of the levels that can be associated with a presentation.
Presentations	Holds information related to a presentation.
PresentationTopics	Holds a list of the topics that can be associated with a presentation.
PresentationTypes	Holds a list of the types of presentations available.

Table 5-1. TCMS System Database Tables (Continued)

Table Name	Description
Presenters	Holds a list of all conference presenters (role).
Questionnaires	Maps a group of questions to a particular presentation.
Questions	Holds a collection of reusable questions.
RegistrationDatePricingRules	Holds the pricing structure for registration based on registration date.
Reminders	Holds reminders to be sent for a given scheduled item.
Roles	Holds a description of the available roles.
Rooms	Holds a list of conference rooms associated with a venue.
ScheduleEntries	Holds a list of the sessions to be attended for an attendee or presenter.
Sessions	Holds a list of all available sessions (an instance in time of a presentation).
Tracks	Holds a list of the available tracks for a given conference.
UserRoles	Holds a map of users to roles (one role per user in our current implementation).
Users	Holds a list of all users in the system and their identity and authentication information.
Venues	Holds a list of venues where conferences are held.

In this chapter you'll create the tables needed for the examples. As part of the source-code distribution you'll find the SQL scripts needed to configure the entire database under several different relational database management system (RDBMS) vendors.

In the case of the TCMS systems we had the luxury of creating a database schema from scratch suitable to our application's business-data needs. This is rarely the case; typically most people end up working with an existing schema that might not map quite directly to an object model. As mentioned previously in this chapter, the object-relational impedance mismatch is a problem that you as an architect or developer will encounter over and over. The TCMS database is shown in Figure 5-8.

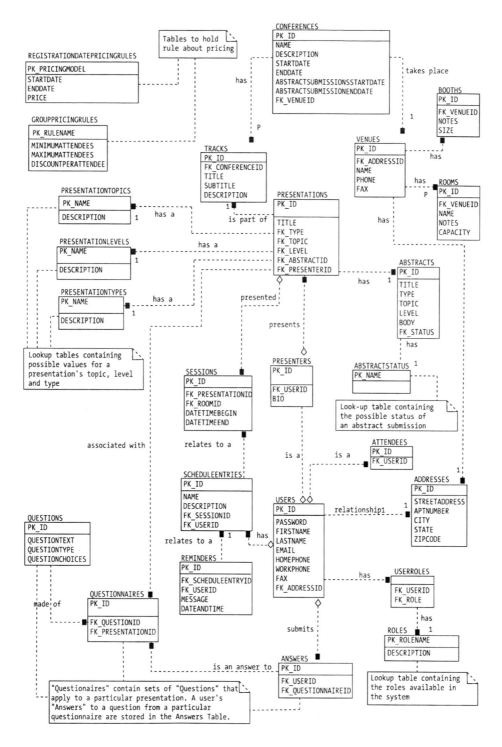

Figure 5-8. TCMS database Entity Relationship Diagram (ERD)

As guidelines for the creation of the TCMS schema, you should follow these simple rules:

- **Use numeric primary keys:** It will speed up access and indexing times.

- **Do not over-constrain tables:** Over-constraining a set of tables might lead to applications that are difficult to test. Focus on the functionality of the application first and then move on to database-integrity issues. It will make for an easier time during the initial iterations or prototyping stages of development.

- **Denormalize for performance:** If query performance is a high priority, then it's sometimes useful to denormalize a table. Several vendors offer the option of mapping an Entity Bean to database objects other than a table such as a View.

Creating the Database Tables

The JBoss server distribution comes with the hsqldb (formerly HypersonicDB). The hsqldb is a 100-percent Java relational database that supports both in-memory and file-based database tables and it can be run in embedded and server modes. It implements a large subset of the ANSI-SQL 92 standard. Hsqld is a very popular database platform that's being used in a large variety of commercial as well as Open Source offerings, including both JBoss and Middlegen. You can find more information on the Open Source catalog or at http://hsqldb.sourceforge.net.

The next step is to create the tables. To do this you need a SQL client and the right JDBC driver. Using iSQL or your favorite SQL client along with the following parameters in Table 5-2 to get a connection to the embedded hsqldb database:

Table 5-2. TCMS System JDBC Connection Properties

Property	Value
JDBC driver	org.hsqldb.jdbcDriver
JDBC URL	jdbc:hsqldb:hsql://localhost:1701
Username	sa
Password	-- blank --
Driver JAR	JBOSS_DIST\server\tcms\lib\hsqldb.jar

NOTE   For JBoss version 3.0.X the port for the embedded HSQLDB is 1476.

Once you've established a connection, execute the SQL statements to create the tables Conference and Tracks. Note that the foreign key and constraint to the Venues table is commented out for purpose of this example. The create statements for the Conferences and Tracks tables are as follows:

```
CREATE TABLE Conferences (
  pk_Id INTEGER NOT NULL PRIMARY KEY,
  Name varchar(64),
  Description LONGVARCHAR,
  StartDate DATETIME,
  EndDate DATETIME,
  AbstractSubmissionStartDate DATETIME,
  AbstractSubmissionEndDate DATETIME
  -- fk_VenueId int NULL,
  -- CONSTRAINT ConferencesVenuesFK FOREIGN KEY(fk_VenueId) REFERENCES Venues(pk_Id)
);

CREATE TABLE Tracks (
  pk_Id INTEGER NOT NULL PRIMARY KEY,
  fk_ConferenceId INTEGER,
  Title VARCHAR(32),
  Subtitle VARCHAR(32),
  Description LONGVARCHAR,
  CONSTRAINT TracksConferencesFK FOREIGN KEY(fk_ConferenceId) REFERENCES
    Conferences(pk_Id)
);
```

Creating a JBoss Datasource

Now that you've created the tables, you need to provide a way for your components to access them. For this you need to define a JBoss service, in particular a JBoss datasource. JBoss services are defined as XML files located in the deploy directory under the server directory. For the tcms example look at the file hsqldb-ds.xml, which is located in the deploy directory of the tcms JBoss server (JBOSS_DIST/server/tcms/deploy/hsqldb-service.xml).

Make a copy of this file and rename it tcms-ds.xml. Using a text editor, edit the file and find the element <jndi-name> under the <local-tx-datasource> tag. Change the value to tcmsDS. Also, near the end of the file you'll find an element of type mbean. Comment-out this element because the MBean is already registered in the file hsqldb-ds.xml.

NOTE   For JBoss version 3.0.X edit the file hsqldb-service.xml. Find the element <depends optional-attribute-name="ManagedConnectionFactoryName"> under the <server> tag. Change the value of the JndiName attribute to tcmsDS and save the file.

There's no need to stop the server for the tcmsDS Data Source to be available. Simply make the changes, save the file, and you should see the changes take place on the console.

The Project Directory Structure

To facilitate the development of the tcms system, you need a suitable directory structure. By following the guidelines set in Chapter 3 you should have the directory structure shown in Figure 5-9. As the chapter progresses you'll learn the role played by each of the directories shown.

Figure 5-9. TCMS project directory structure

Entities with Entity Beans

Entity Beans are components that model business concepts from the domain whose lifespan extends beyond the scope of the running application. They play a dual role as an object-oriented window into the data stored in a database and serve as general-purpose business objects in a system. This dual role brings a lot of confusion to new Bean developers, especially when they take the definition of a pattern like the Session Facade (see the "TCMS Services" section) and blindly apply it without understanding it. The fact is that Entity Beans should follow common rules of good object-oriented design, which tells you that an object is composed of data and behavior that applies to the data.

With that in mind you'll notice that the Entity Beans provide a window into one or more database tables, and they also provide methods that act upon that data. Selecting which methods belong in the Entity Bean and which methods belong in a Session Facade can be a little confusing. A good design mnemonic is to question whether an action that is represented by a method is a defining characteristic of what it means to be a particular entity. If the method represents an action performed as a collaborative activity with other entities or processes then it's probably wiser to place it in a Session Facade. Also, from the Session Facade point of view, choosing an appropriate name for your facade will help you determine whether a method belongs in there.

For the Entity Beans in this example, we've chosen to use container-managed persistence (CMP 2.0). CMP 2.0 supports new features that provide powerful data management and persistence functionality while allowing the EJB developer to focus on business logic.

BEST PRACTICE   When possible, you should use CMP Entity Beans instead of Bean-managed persistence (BMP) to take advantage of the container optimizations and the deployment time flexibility they provide.

For those familiar with previous versions of CMP, it's important to note that in the 2.x specification CMP fields aren't declared using class fields in the Bean implementation, but instead are declared with a set of abstract assessor methods. This is a good addition to the specifications in that it forces strict encapsulation, thereby making a clearer separation between the persistence part of an Entity Bean and the business- or application-logic parts of it.

Using the domain class diagram in conjunction with the use cases created during the analysis and design, two design diagrams are created that describe the structure and behavior of the system in terms of components. The first diagram contains the domain-entity components, as shown in Figure 5-10. You might be wondering about the similarities with the database schema diagram shown in Figure 5-8. If you worked with CMP EJBs prior to version 2.0, you know that a well-known best practice was to only model coarse-grained components using EJBs, and you also know that Sun didn't recommend direct one-to-one mappings to a database schema. CMP 2.0 changes all of that in that Entity Beans are now well suited to represent fine-grained persistent objects thanks to the addition of local interfaces and EJB relationships.

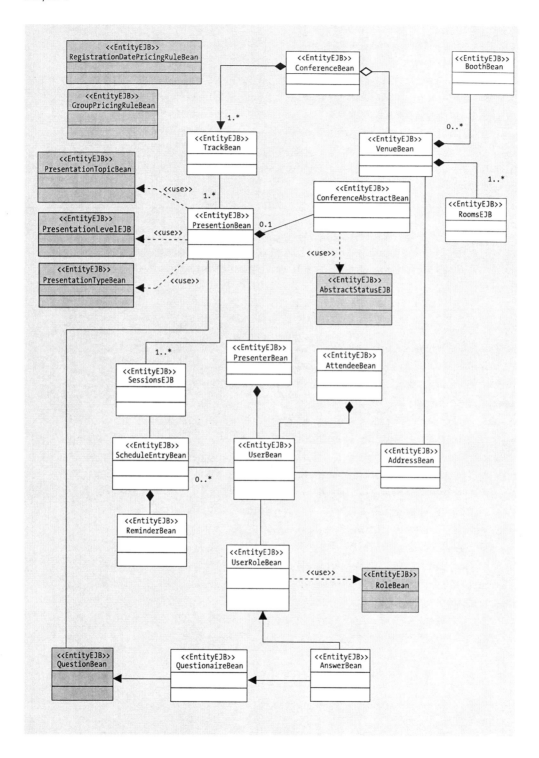

Figure 5-10. TCMS domain entity components

Writing the Beans

For a practical example of building a J2EE component-based business tier, you'll now implement a nontrivial set of Entity Beans and the corresponding Session Facade Bean. We've chosen to use the ConferenceEJB and TrackEJB Entity Beans as part of the ongoing development of the TCMS system. The ConferenceEJB and the TrackEJB Beans map to the "Conferences" and "Tracks" tables, respectively.

This simple example shows a very typical situation in EJB Entity Bean development—that of having a one-to-many relationship among Beans that highlights many of the new facilities found in the new EJB specifications, in particular the CMP 2.0 specification for container-managed relationships.

The next sections will walk you through the manual process of creating the Conference CMP 2.0 Entity Bean and its deployment under the JBoss application server. In order to make the example easier to understand the Bean has been greatly simplified and the amount of code has been reduced for the purposes of the example.

Remote and Local Interfaces

Both the remote and local interfaces serve to expose methods that a Bean's client can call to perform work. These two classes expose the methods of a Bean to the outside world (remote) or to its immediate neighborhood (local).

 NOTE The remote interface must abide by the limitations imposed by the Java to IDL Mapping Specification, which dictates what types of return values, parameters, and exceptions are valid. For more information see http://java.sun.com/j2se/1.4.2/docs/guide/idl/mapping/jidlMapping.html.

The remote interface declares methods available remotely using Remote Method Invocation (RMI) syntax. It plays the role of a proxy and provides the Bean with location transparency. Remote interfaces embody the notion of a distributed component and all of the implications of distribution such as the following:

- Pass-by-value semantics.

- Strong isolation between caller and callee.

- Acknowledgment of remote communication errors.

- Overhead of network latency, client-and-server marshaling and demarshaling code, argument handling, and so on.

You must take these implications into account when designing a component's remote interface. The main factor in whether to provide remote access to a component must be the distribution requirement. In stateless environments there's little to no reason to distribute an object that has no identity.

The EJB container is responsible for providing an implementation to this interface, which is either generated statically or dynamically (JBoss does this dynamically at deployment time).

Notice the package definition for the remote interface (com.ejdoab.tcms.entities). For the rest of this example this package will contain all domain-entity components, therefore under tcms\src\java you'll now need to create a com\ejdoab\tcms\entities set of directories in which you'll place the files you're about to create.

The code for the remote interface is as follows:

```
package com.ejdoab.tcms.entities;

import javax.ejb.EJBObject;
import java.rmi.RemoteException;
import java.util.Date;

/**
 * Conference Bean - Remote Interface
 */
public interface Conference extends EJBObject {
    public Integer getId() throws RemoteException;
    public String getName() throws RemoteException;
    public String getDescription() throws RemoteException;
    public Date getStartDate() throws RemoteException;
    public Date getEndDate() throws RemoteException;
    public Date getAbstractSubmissionStartDate() throws RemoteException;
    public Date getAbstractSubmissionEndDate() throws RemoteException;

    public void setId(Integer id) throws RemoteException;
    public void setName(String name) throws RemoteException;
    public void setDescription(String description) throws RemoteException;
    public void setStartDate(Date startDate) throws RemoteException;
    public void setEndDate(Date startDate) throws RemoteException;
    public void setAbstractSubmissionStartDate(Date abstractSubmissionStartDate)
        throws RemoteException;
    public void setAbstractSubmissionEndDate(Date abstractSubmissionEndDate)
        throws RemoteException;
}
```

The local interface provides in-JVM access to a component. As opposed to the remote interface in all methods of the local interface (and the local home interface), return values and parameters are passed by reference. This brings up an interesting difference between the use of local interfaces and the use of remote interfaces. With local interfaces there's a strong coupling between the caller and the callee. This requires extra care from the programmer for there exists the potential to unknowingly have the same instance of a component referenced in another context. For this reason it's recommended that you avoid storing references to a Bean obtained locally as part of the state of another component. Whenever possible the specification recommends using the local reference only in the scope of the method that obtained it.

For the Conference Bean the local interface is identical to the remote interface with the exception being that it doesn't have to declare its methods as throwing a RemoteException, as shown in the following code:

```
package com.ejdoab.tcms.entities;

import javax.ejb.EJBLocalObject;
import java.util.Date;

/**
 * Conference Bean - Local Interface
 */
public interface ConferenceLocal extends EJBLocalObject {
    public Integer getId();
    public String getName();
    public String getDescription();
    public Date getStartDate();
    public Date getEndDate();
    public Date getAbstractSubmissionStartDate();
    public Date getAbstractSubmissionEndDate();

    public void setId(Integer id);
    public void setName(String name);
    public void setDescription(String description);
    public void setStartDate(Date startDate);
    public void setEndDate(Date startDate);
    public void setAbstractSubmissionStartDate(Date abstractSubmissionStartDate);
    public void setAbstractSubmissionEndDate(Date abstractSubmissionEndDate);
}
```

Home Interfaces

The home interface specifies how a new Bean is created and how existing Beans are found and deleted. It's a factory for Beans of a given type. In the home interface you define creation and finder methods. In the case of the conference Bean you've defined a create method, which takes the ID and name of the conference, and a finder, which locates a conference Bean given its primary key. The code for ConferenceBean Remote Home Interface is shown here:

```
package com.ejdoab.tcms.entities;

import javax.ejb.EJBHome;
import javax.ejb.CreateException;
import javax.ejb.FinderException;
import java.rmi.RemoteException;

/**
 * Conference Bean - Remote Home Interface
 */
public interface ConferenceHome extends EJBHome {
    public Conference create(int id, String name)
        throws CreateException, RemoteException;
    public Conference findByPrimaryKey(Integer pk)
        throws FinderException, RemoteException;
}
```

The local Home Interface is again very similar to its remote counterpart, as shown here:

```
package com.ejdoab.tcms.entities;

import javax.ejb.EJBLocalHome;
import javax.ejb.CreateException;
import javax.ejb.FinderException;

/**
 * Conference Bean - Local Home Interface
 */
public interface ConferenceLocalHome extends EJBLocalHome {
    public ConferenceLocal create(int id, String name) throws CreateException;
    public ConferenceLocal findByPrimaryKey(Integer pk) throws FinderException;
}
```

Notice that the main difference between the home and remote interface is that the possible consequence of remote communication is removed from the interface definition. Mainly there's no need to worry about RemoteExceptions.

Bean Implementation

The Bean implementation defines the methods specified by the exposed interfaces. The code for your CMP 2.0 Bean provides pairs of abstract setters and getters that the container will use (most likely by extending the Bean class) in order to save and populate the Bean's data to and from the database. Notice that it isn't necessary to provide any class members to store the data; this is handled by the EJB container's internal representation of the Bean. The Entity Bean implementation class is also marked abstract (a consequence of the CMP field getters and setters being abstract).

```
package com.ejdoab.tcms.entities;

import javax.ejb.EntityBean;
import javax.ejb.CreateException;
import javax.ejb.EntityContext;
import java.util.Date;

/**
 * The conference EJB maintains information related to the conference
 */
public abstract class ConferenceEJB implements EntityBean {
    // ----------
    // CMP Fields
    // ----------

    public abstract Integer getId();
    public abstract String getName();
    public abstract String getDescription();
    public abstract Date getStartDate();
    public abstract Date getEndDate();
    public abstract Date getAbstractSubmissionStartDate();
    public abstract Date getAbstractSubmissionEndDate();
```

```
public abstract void setId(Integer id);
public abstract void setName(String name);
public abstract void setDescription(String description);
public abstract void setStartDate(Date startDate);
public abstract void setEndDate(Date startDate);
public abstract void setAbstractSubmissionStartDate(
    Date abstractSubmissionStartDate);
public abstract void setAbstractSubmissionEndDate(
    Date abstractSubmissionEndDate);


// -----------------------
// EJB Methods - Callbacks
// -----------------------

public Integer ejbCreate(int id, String name) throws CreateException {
    this.setId(new Integer(id));
    this.setName(name);
    return null; // See 14.1.2 of the EJB 2.1 specification
}

public void ejbPostCreate(int id, String name) throws CreateException {}
public void setEntityContext(EntityContext ctx) {}
public void unsetEntityContext(EntityContext ctx) {}
public void ejbActivate() {}
public void ejbPassivate() {}
public void ejbLoad() {}
public void ejbStore() {}
}
```

An ejbCreate (and a corresponding ejbPostCreate) method must be defined and implemented for each way that you want a new instance of an enterprise Bean to be created. Each ejbCreate method corresponds to a create method in the home interface. The client actually uses the home-interface counterparts to the ejbCreate method; the container then invokes the ejbCreate method followed by the ejbPostCreate method. If both methods execute successfully an EJB object is instantiated and the persistent data associated with that object is inserted into the database.

For CMP Entity Beans the container handles the required interaction between the Entity Bean instance and the datasource. For BMP Beans, the ejbCreate method must contain the code to directly handle the interaction with the database. For more information on writing BMP Entity Beans, see *Enterprise Java Beans 2.1.*[4]

---

4. Denninger, Peters, and Castaneda. *Enterprise Java Beans 2.1* (Berkeley, CA: Apress, 2003).

The EJB specification lays out the following rules for the ejbCreate and ejbPostCreate methods:

- Both methods must be public and must return the same type as the primary key. Yet the actual value returned must be null. This is required for backward compatibility in order to enable a BMP Entity Bean to inherit from a CMP Bean.

- The arguments must be valid RMI-IIOP types. These include Java primitives, strings, java.rmi.Remote types, and any class that implements the serializable interface.

- Both methods must be prefixed with ejbCreate and ejbPostCreate, respectively.

- Both methods must be nonfinal and nonstatic.

The ejbPostCreate method must have the same arguments as the matching ejbCreate method. Both methods can throw the javax.ejb.EJBException exception or one of its subclasses, typically a CreateException. It was customary in EJB 1.0 specification to throw a java.rmi.RemoteException exception to indicate nonapplication exceptions; this practice is deprecated in EJB 1.1 or higher specifications.

Deployment Descriptors

The J2EE platform takes a declarative programming approach that isolates the developer from runtime details or the specific use of a component and frees the developer to concentrate on the actual functionality of the component.

Container-managed persistence is an example of the declarative programming paradigm at work. EJB CMP enables the developer to access persistent datasources for Entity Beans by declaring the mappings and relationships in XML deployment descriptors rather than by hand-coding complex data-access logic in the actual components. The components are then deployed as a unit that includes the deployment descriptors, which are then used by the EJB container to handle the complex logic of synchronizing the Entity Bean's state with that of its source of data.

The deployment descriptors contain structural and application assembly information for an enterprise Bean. You specify this information by specifying values for the deployment descriptors in three XML files. These files are as follows:

ejb-jar.xml

This file is a vendor-independent J2EE deployment descriptor as defined in the EJB 2.1 specification. It can hold the definitions of one or more enterprise Beans that will be packaged together in the same JAR file.

Each Bean declaration is contained under the <enterprise-beans> element and falls under one of the three categories: entity, session, or message (you'll learn about session Beans later in this chapter as you implement the Session Facade pattern). A Bean declaration consists of a description of the Bean, the full class name for Home, Remote, HomeLocal, and Local interfaces.

For CMP Entity Beans the CMP version, schema name, primary key field, primary key Java type as well as a complete list of all CMP fields must be present as you can see in the following ejb-jar.xml for the Conference Bean:

```xml
<?xml version="1.0" encoding="UTF-8"?>
<!DOCTYPE ejb-jar PUBLIC
    "-//Sun Microsystems, Inc.//DTD Enterprise JavaBeans 2.0//EN"
    "http://java.sun.com/dtd/ejb-jar_2_0.dtd">
<ejb-jar >
   <description><![CDATA[Conference Entity Bean]]></description>
   <display-name>Conference Entity Bean</display-name>
   <enterprise-beans>
     <entity>
        <description><![CDATA[Conference]]></description>
        <ejb-name>Conference</ejb-name>
        <home>com.ejdoab.tcms.entities.ConferenceHome</home>
        <remote>com.ejdoab.tcms.entities.Conference</remote>
        <local-home>com.ejdoab.tcms.entities.ConferenceLocalHome</local-home>
        <local>com.ejdoab.tcms.entities.ConferenceLocal</local>
        <ejb-class>com.ejdoab.tcms.entities.ConferenceEJB</ejb-class>
        <persistence-type>Container</persistence-type>
        <prim-key-class>java.lang.Integer</prim-key-class>
        <reentrant>False</reentrant>
        <cmp-version>2.x</cmp-version>
        <abstract-schema-name>Conference</abstract-schema-name>
        <cmp-field>
            <field-name>id</field-name>
        </cmp-field>
        <cmp-field>
            <field-name>name</field-name>
        </cmp-field>
```

```
        <cmp-field>
            <field-name>description</field-name>
        </cmp-field>
        <cmp-field>
            <field-name>startDate</field-name>
        </cmp-field>
        <cmp-field>
            <field-name>endDate</field-name>
        </cmp-field>
        <cmp-field>
            <field-name>abstractSubmissionStartDate</field-name>
        </cmp-field>
        <cmp-field>
            <field-name>abstractSubmissionEndDate</field-name>
        </cmp-field>
        <primkey-field>id</primkey-field>
    </entity>
  </enterprise-beans>
</ejb-jar>
```

jboss.xml

The jboss.xml file provides a mapping between the Beans declared in the ejb-jar.xml and the JNDI names used in the application. In the following code sample both the remote and local interface JNDI names are defined as ejb/Conference and ejb/ConferenceLocal, respectively.

```
<?xml version="1.0" encoding="UTF-8"?>
<!DOCTYPE jboss PUBLIC
    "-//JBoss//DTD JBOSS 3.0//EN"
    "http://www.jboss.org/j2ee/dtd/jboss_3_0.dtd">
<jboss>
    <enterprise-beans>
      <entity>
        <ejb-name>Conference</ejb-name>
        <jndi-name>ejb/Conference</jndi-name>
        <local-jndi-name>ejb/ConferenceLocal</local-jndi-name>
      </entity>
    </enterprise-beans>
    <resource-managers>
    </resource-managers>
</jboss>
```

jbosscmp-jdbc.xml

The jbosscmp-jdbc.xml provides the actual mapping between the Entity Bean
and a table and between the CMP fields and the table columns. It also specifies
the datasource that you should use to connect as well as an optional database-
type to Java-type mapping.

In the following sample, you can see that you're using the java:/tcmsDS datasource to connect to the database and that you're also using the Hypersonic SQL
mapping. In the <enterprise-beans> section you have the mapping of the Bean to
the table in the <ejb-name> and <table-name> elements as well as the list of the
CMP fields in one or more <cmp-field> elements.

```xml
<?xml version="1.0" encoding="UTF-8"?>
<!DOCTYPE jbosscmp-jdbc PUBLIC "-//JBoss//DTD JBOSSCMP-JDBC 3.0//EN"
    "http://www.jboss.org/j2ee/dtd/jbosscmp-jdbc_3_0.dtd">
<jbosscmp-jdbc>
   <defaults>
      <datasource>java:/tcmsDS</datasource>
      <datasource-mapping>Hypersonic SQL</datasource-mapping>
   </defaults>

   <enterprise-beans>
     <entity>
        <ejb-name>Conference</ejb-name>
        <table-name>CONFERENCES</table-name>
        <cmp-field>
           <field-name>id</field-name>
           <column-name>pk_Id</column-name>
        </cmp-field>
        <cmp-field>
           <field-name>name</field-name>
           <column-name>Name</column-name>
        </cmp-field>
        <cmp-field>
           <field-name>description</field-name>
           <column-name>Description</column-name>
        </cmp-field>
        <cmp-field>
           <field-name>startDate</field-name>
           <column-name>StartDate</column-name>
        </cmp-field>
```

```
        <cmp-field>
            <field-name>endDate</field-name>
            <column-name>EndDate</column-name>
        </cmp-field>
        <cmp-field>
            <field-name>abstractSubmissionStartDate</field-name>
            <column-name>AbstractSubmissionStartDate</column-name>
        </cmp-field>
        <cmp-field>
            <field-name>abstractSubmissionEndDate</field-name>
            <column-name>AbstractSubmissionEndDate</column-name>
        </cmp-field>
    </entity>
  </enterprise-beans>
</jbosscmp-jdbc>
```

Packaging and Deployment

The next step is to compile, package, and deploy the ConferenceEJB. EJBs are packaged in the JAR format, which is a subset of the widely known ZIP compression format. This can be accomplished by using the JAR tool that ships with the JVM.

The first step is to compile the source code. Make sure that the jbossall-client.jar file (located under the JBOSS_DIST/client directory) is in your classpath by either modifying your classpath globally or by using the -classpath option with javac. Once your classpath is properly set, switch directories to tcms\src\java and use the following command to compile the sources:

```
javac -d ..\..\classes com\ejdoab\tcms\entities\Conference*.java
```

Notice that you're using the -d switch with javac to specify the destination for your compiled classes. Place the three xml deployment descriptors in a directory named META-INF, which should be at the same level as the com directory where your compiled code resides (in this case the classes directory). After successful compilation, you should package the compiled classes and the deployment descriptor in a JAR file named conference-ejb.jar by using the following command:

```
jar cf conference-ejb.jar com\ejdoab\tcms\entities\*.class META-INF\*.xml
```

The JAR file should now be in classes directory. Next, deploy the JAR by copying the file to the deploy directory under tcms/deploy directory. If everything goes as planned you should see output on the console similar to the following:

```
18:32:07,615 INFO  [MainDeployer] Starting deployment of package:
    file:/C:/java/jboss-3.2.1/server/tcms/deploy/conference-ejb.jar
18:32:07,665 INFO  [EjbModule] Creating
18:32:07,675 INFO  [EjbModule] Deploying Conference
18:32:07,695 INFO  [EjbModule] Created
18:32:07,695 INFO  [EjbModule] Starting
18:32:07,805 INFO  [Conference] Table 'CONFERENCES' already exists
18:32:07,805 INFO  [EjbModule] Started
18:32:07,805 INFO  [MainDeployer] Deployed
```

package: file:/C:/java/jboss-3.2.1/server/tcms/deploy/conference-ejb.jar

JBoss by default verifies all EJB deployments against the specifications for compliance. This is a needed feature that reflects the error-prone nature of the EJB manual code–compile-declare-package-deploy cycle. Also notice the message [Conference] Table 'CONFERENCES' already exists. If desired, you can configure a JBoss deployment to automatically create the tables.

Testing the Conference Bean

Now you're ready to test the conference Bean. There are two ways to access the Bean:

- **Locally:** From within the container of another J2EE component by using the local home and local interfaces.

- **Remotely:** From outside of the container over a network by using the remote home and remote interfaces.

For this first example you'll access the Entity Bean remotely. There is rarely a need to access an Entity Bean remotely from a client. As previously mentioned we're promoting a service-based architecture where the details of the domain entities and the underlying data store are hidden from the outside world. A service-based architecture exposes services to its clients.

Our simple test class ConferenceEJBTest.java performs the following steps:

- Obtains a JNDI initial context.

- Looks up the conference remote home interface using its JNDI name.

- Obtains a remote reference to the conference it creates via the home interface create method.

- Manipulates the Bean by setting some of its fields.

- Looks up the previously created instance using the findByPrimaryKey method.

The simple client is shown here:

```
package com.ejdoab.tcms.entities;

...

/**
 * Simple EJB Test - ConferenceEJBTest.java
 */
public class ConferenceEJBTest {
    private static final String ICF = "org.jnp.interfaces.NamingContextFactory";
    private static final String SERVER_URI = "localhost:1099";
    private static final String PKG_PREFIXES =
        "org.jboss.naming:org.jnp.interfaces";

    public static void main(String args[]) {
        Context ctx;
        ConferenceHome confHome;
        Conference conf;

        // initial context JBossNS configuration
        Hashtable env = new Hashtable();
        env.put(Context.INITIAL_CONTEXT_FACTORY, ICF);
        env.put(Context.PROVIDER_URL, SERVER_URI);
        env.put(Context.URL_PKG_PREFIXES, PKG_PREFIXES);

        try {

            // ----------
            // JNDI Stuff
            // ----------

            ctx = new InitialContext(env);
            // look up the home interface
            System.out.println(
                "[jndi lookup] Looking Up Conference Remote Home Interface" );
            Object obj = ctx.lookup("ejb/Conference");
```

```
            // cast and narrow
            confHome = (ConferenceHome) PortableRemoteObject
                .narrow( obj, ConferenceHome.class);

            // ----------
            // Write Test
            // ----------

            System.out.println("[write test] begin...");
            System.out.println(
                "[ejb create] Create an Instance of Conference Bean");
            // create
            conf = confHome.create(0, "EJDOAB");
            // add some data
            conf.setDescription("Enterprise Java Development on a Budget");
            // null to reuse
            conf = null;

            // ---------
            // Read Test
            // ---------
            System.out.println("[read test] begin...");
            // find the bean - pk has to be an object
            conf = confHome.findByPrimaryKey(new Integer(0));
            System.out.println("[ejb find] Retrieved conference with id (pk) = "
                + conf.getId());
            System.out.println("    [name] " + conf.getName());
            System.out.println("    [description] " + conf.getDescription());
        }
        catch (RemoteException re) {
            System.out.println("[rmi] remote exception: " + re.getMessage());
        }
        catch (NamingException ne) {
            System.out.println("[naming] naming exception: " + ne.getMessage());
        }
        catch (FinderException fe) {
            System.out.println("[ejb] finder exception: " + fe.getMessage());
        }
        catch (CreateException ce) {
            System.out.println("[ejb] create exception: " + ce.getMessage());
        }
    }
}
```

Now it's time to run the test. Your test class needs to find the jbossall-client.jar and the log4j.jar in its classpath to be able to run. Both of these are located in the JBOSS_DIST\client directory. The client also needs some of the compiled classes under the tcms\classes directory.

TIP   If you're using a J2SE version prior to 1.4.x you'll also need the jnet.jar file. This is a utility that provides implementation for the Java Secure Socket Extension (javax.net.ssl).

Compile the test client class using the following command from the tcms\src\java directory (the -d parameter places the compiled class under the classes directory):

```
javac d ..\..\classes com\ejdoab\tcms\entities\ConferenceEJBTest.java
```

Execute it by issuing the following command:

```
java com.ejdoab.tcms.entities.ConferenceEJBTest
```

During the first run you should see the following output:

```
[jndi lookup] Looking Up Conference Remote Home Interface
[write test] begin...
[ejb create] Create an Instance of Conference Bean
[read test] begin...
[ejb find] Retrieved conference with id (pk) = 0
    [name] EJDOAB
    [description] Enterprise Java Development on a Budget
```

Running it a second time should throw an EJBCreate exception and tells you that a Bean with the primary key 0 is already in the database as shown in the following output:

```
[jndi lookup] Looking Up Conference Remote Home Interface
[write test] begin...
[ejb create] Create an Instance of Conference Bean
[ejb] create exception: Entity with primary key 0 already exists
```

Attribute-Oriented Programming with XDoclet

By this time you should realize that there must be a faster way to develop an enterprise Java component. Although there are many IDEs in the market with EJB Creation wizards, their solutions are proprietary and mostly confined to the "preferred" application server of the IDE vendor (normally the one that they make!). IDEs are wonderful tools that can increase an individual's productivity. But enterprise development is about more than just the productivity of a single programmer but rather the productivity of the team as a whole. In the "Development and Build System with Ant" chapter you learned that Ant is a powerful ally when it comes to fulfilling the task of Continuous Integration because you can help a team to have a project-level build that you can run on a daily basis (or as often as possible), and it's independent of any particular IDE.

In the previous example you had to create three separate Java files with syntactic interdependencies that are hard to keep in synchronization, even for the simplest of Beans. Even for the simple ConferenceEJB.java we made more than three passes until we had all of the errors corrected. The most common mistake we've seen is mismatched method signatures. This simple problem has plagued EJB development and it certainly has had an effect in terms of lost productivity.

Aside from the interfaces you also had to create three XML deployment descriptors. Although most developers never write an XML descriptor from scratch, most use an existing one as a template for their work. This practice can lead to potential oversights in the configuration parameters, which might have been well suited for the original Bean but not for the work at hand (the same reuse by copy-and-paste antipattern that gets programmers in trouble very often). If it wasn't bad enough already, vendors add their own, fairly dissimilar XML deployment descriptors to the mix, thereby increasing the likelihood of mistakes.

To cope with the deficiencies (in terms of the development process) in the EJB specification, several code generators have appeared in the market, the most popular being XDoclet. XDoclet reduces the workload to the writing of just the Bean implementation code and the annotating of the source by adding JavaDoc style comments that determine the generation of all the other plumbing files. This is referred to as attribute-oriented programming (AOP) (not to be confused with the other AOP, aspect-oriented programming). Attribute-oriented programming is a method by which metadata attributes are used to guide a code-generation engine to produce otherwise redundant plumbing code. It works under the Don't Repeat Yourself (DRY) principle, given the dynamically enforced redundancy between all the EJB glue files and deployment descriptors. The DRY principle tells you that there should exist a single representation of a specific piece of knowledge (for more on the DRY principle see *The Pragmatic Programmer: From Journeyman to Master.*)[5]

XDoclet is a Java doclet. A doclet is a pluggable component written to the doclet API specification that determines the content and format of the output resulting from running the Javadoc tool on a Java source file. By default the Javadoc tool is configured to use the "standard" doclet, which generates the familiar HTML API documentation you're all accustomed to.

XDoclet instead is configured to read XDoclet specific javadoc tags (also know as @ tags), which control the creation of other Java files, XML deployment descriptors, primary key classes, data-access objects, web-services code, web-application descriptors, and many more. XDoclet started as a project by Rickard Oeberg's (same person who brought you the interceptor stack in JBoss along with most of JBoss's new architecture) named EJBDoclet. XDoclet, like many of the projects used in this book, is hosted at sourceforge. Like other Open Source projects, XDoclet is built on a customizable, modular design that enables developers to create and plug their own modules if the need arises. XDoclet has a wide array of plug-ins for generating many application server–specific files as well as files for presentation engines and persistence frameworks.

XDoclet runs within the context of an Ant build only. This is by no means a limitation; on the contrary Ant is probably the best delivery vehicle for any utility that touches any part of the build process because Ant is the de facto standard for performing Java builds. XDoclet requires an Ant version greater or equal to 1.5 and a J2SE version 1.2 or higher (for a comprehensive coverage of Ant see Chapter 3).

Download and Installation

In this book you'll be using version 1.2 of XDoclet. The XDoclet distribution consists of a single ZIP file that you can obtain from `http://xdoclet.sourceforge.net`. Download and unzip the file. The file contains all the necessary JAR files in the lib directory as well as samples that show you how to use XDoclet.

For the purpose of your application you'll copy the JAR files contained in the XDoclet distribution lib directory under the /lib/development/xdoclet directory of the TCMS project. As you learned in the "Development and Build System" chapter, this is the directory where all of your third-party development time libraries reside.

---

5. Hunt, Thomas, and Cunningham. *The Pragmatic Programmer: From Journeyman to Master* (Addison-Wesley, 1999).

XDoclet Ant Tasks

XDoclet is organized as a set of Ant tasks that include the following:

- **ejbdoclet:** Executes various specific subtasks for the business and integration tiers. Includes subtasks that handle several application servers such as JBoss, JOnAS, JRun, Resin, Orion, Pramati, Borland EAS, Sybase EAServer, and WebLogic. It enables the creation of all EJB "glue" files, deployment descriptors, data objects for Entity Beans, and some application server-specific descriptors.

- **webdoclet:** Executes various specific subtasks for the presentation tier such as the creation of XML web-deployment descriptors for generic WAR files as well as descriptors for presentation frameworks like Struts and WebWork and web-container descriptors for JBossWeb, JOnAS, Resin, WebLogic, and Websphere.

- **hibernatedoclet:** Executes various subtasks to integrate the hibernate object-relational persistence and query service, including automatic integration with JBoss by creating a JBoss-specific service.

- **jdodoclet:** Executes various specific subtasks for the integration tier related to the generation and integration of JDO-compliant persistence frameworks such as Lido, Kodo, and Triactive.

- **jmxdoclet:** Executes various specific subtasks for the management tier related to the JMX standard such as MBean interface and MLet descriptor generation as well as JBoss-specific JMX files.

- **doclet:** The base class for all other tasks. It can be used standalone to execute a template file without having to write a new task.

- **documentdoclet:** Executes subtasks related to the profiling of XDoclet use in an application.

In this chapter you'll concentrate on the <ejbdoclet> task.

XDoclet Tags

XDoclet tags are JavaDoc block style tags and as such are contained inside a doc comment. XDoclet tags start with the @ symbol, followed by a combination of namespace and name. Specific namespaces map to specific XDoclet doclets. For example, the namespace ejb map to the doclet EJBDoclet. The name of the tag is unique within a given namespace. The name and the namespace are separated by a colon or a period and followed by one or more attributes. Attributes are simple name-value pairs that further define the purpose of the tag. For example an XDoclet tag to define a CMP Entity Bean with a logical name "Conference" would look like this:

```
/**
 * @ejb.bean type="CMP" name="Conference"
 */
```

Tags are also differentiated based on their positioning within the file. Just like with JavaDoc tags there are class-level tags and method-level tags. XDoclet provides tags under many namespaces. The XDoclet project is a thriving Open Source project and it's easy to get lost in the sea of new tag namespaces. Figure 5-11 provides a map of sorts that should give readers a bird's-eye view of the most relevant XDoclet tag namespaces.

	EJB	WEB	PERSISTENCE
GENERIC	@ejb @dao	@jsp @web @javabean @msg	@jdo
APP SERVER SPECIFIC	@jboss @jonas @resin @weblogic @websphere @orion @easerver @hpass @pramati @jrun	@strusts @webwork	@castor @hibernate @mvcsoft

Figure 5-11. XDoclet namespace map

ConferenceEJB with XDoclet

As an example of XDoclet usage the previously hand-coded glue files and deployment descriptors for the ConferenceEJB Bean will be generated automatically by coding only the Bean implementation and annotating it with XDoclet tags. As mentioned before XDoclet only works from within a Ant script.

Before you get on with creating a suitable Ant script for your XDoclet example you need to place the needed JARs in the classpath.

Configuring the ClassPath

The <ejbdoclet> needs several classes to be available in the classpath in order to function correctly. To execute the <ejbdoclet> target XDoclet is dependent on the following:

- **Jakarta Commons:** Collections (commons-collections-2.0.jar) and logging (commons-logging.jar).

- **XDoclet:** xdoclet-1.2.jar, xdoclet-jboss-module-1.2.jar, xdoclet-xjavadoc-1.2.jar, xdoclet-ejb-module-1.2.jar, xdoclet-jmx-module-1.2.jar, xdoclet-web-module-1.2.jar.

- **J2EE implementation:** As with the previous example you need to add the JBoss implementation of the javax.* classes required for EJBs contained in jbossall-client.jar.

You can find both the Jakarta Commons and XDoclet-specific JAR in the lib directory of the xdoclet distribution. The JBoss JAR is located in the client directory of the JBoss distribution. For this example copies of those JARs are placed in the tcms lib (jbossall-client.jar) and lib/development (all Xdoclet jars) directories.

Simple Ant Script

To use XDoclet you need a simple Ant script, which needs to accomplish the following tasks:

1. Load the needed JARs needed for the <ejbdoclet> task.

2. Add the <ejbdoclet> task to the context of the Ant script.

3. Execute the <ejbdoclet> task on the annotated ConferenceEJB.java.

4. Compile the sources (both the annotated class and the generated ones).

5. Package the Bean in the JAR file conference-ejb.jar.

The Ant script is shown here:

```xml
<?xml version="1.0"?>
<project name="xdoclet test" default="package" basedir=".">
    <!-- ================================================================= -->
    <!-- Configures the ClassPath                                          -->
    <!-- ================================================================= -->
    <path id="class.path">
        <fileset dir="lib">
            <include name="*.jar"/>
        </fileset>
        <!-- Step 1 -->
        <fileset dir="lib/development/xdoclet">
            <include name="*.jar"/>
        </fileset>
    </path>


    <!-- ================================================================= -->
    <!-- Initializes the Project Paths                                     -->
    <!-- ================================================================= -->
    <target name="init">
        <echo>initializing...</echo>
        <property name="root" location="${basedir}" />
        <property name="src" location="${root}/src/java" />
        <property name="lib" location="${root}/lib" />
        <property name="classes" location="${root}/classes" />
        <property name="generated-ejb" location="${root}/generated/ejb-src" />
        <property name="descriptors-ejb"
            location="${root}/generated/descriptors/ejb"
        />
        <property name="dist-jar" location="${root}/dist/jar" />
        <property name="build" location="${root}/build" />

        <!-- Step 2 -->
        <taskdef
            name="ejbdoclet"
            classname="xdoclet.modules.ejb.EjbDocletTask"
            classpathref="class.path"
            />
    </target>
```

```xml
<!-- ===================================================================== -->
<!-- Prepares the directory structure                                      -->
<!-- ===================================================================== -->
<target name="prepare" depends="init">
    <echo>preparing...</echo>
    <mkdir dir="${classes}"/>
    <mkdir dir="${generated-ejb}"/>
    <mkdir dir="${descriptors-ejb}"/>
    <mkdir dir="${build}"/>
    <mkdir dir="${dist-jar}"/>
</target>


<!-- ===================================================================== -->
<!-- Generate EJB glue files using XDoclet's ejbdoclet - Step 3            -->
<!-- ===================================================================== -->
<target name="generate" depends="prepare">
    <echo>generating...</echo>
    <ejbdoclet
        destdir="${generated-ejb}"
        excludedtags="@version,@author,@todo"
        ejbspec="2.0"
        force="true"
        >
        <fileset dir="${src}">
            <include name="com/ejdoab/tcms/entities/*EJB.java"/>
        </fileset>
        <remoteinterface/>
        <localinterface/>
        <homeinterface/>
        <localhomeinterface/>
        <valueobject/>
        <entitycmp/>
        <utilobject cacheHomes="true" includeGUID="true"/>
        <deploymentdescriptor
            destdir="${descriptors-ejb}"
            validatexml="true"
        />
```

```
        <jboss
            version="3.0"
            unauthenticatedPrincipal="nobody"
            xmlencoding="UTF-8"
            destdir="${descriptors-ejb}"
            validatexml="true"
            preferredrelationmapping="relation-table"
            typemapping="Hypersonic SQL"
            datasource="java:/tcmsDS"
            />
    </ejbdoclet>
</target>


<!-- =================================================================== -->
<!-- Compiles all the classes - Step 4                                  -->
<!-- =================================================================== -->
<target name="compile" depends="generate">
    <echo>compiling...</echo>
    <javac
        destdir="${classes}"
        classpathref="class.path"
        debug="on"
        deprecation="on"
        optimize="off"
        >
        <src path="${src}"/>
        <src path="${generated-ejb}"/>
    </javac>
</target>


<!-- =================================================================== -->
<!-- Package the EJB JAR - Step 5                                       -->
<!-- =================================================================== -->
<target name="package" depends="compile">
    <echo>packaging...</echo>
    <jar jarfile="${dist-jar}/conference-ejb.jar">
    <metainf dir="${descriptors-ejb}" includes="*.xml"/>
    <fileset dir="${classes}">
        <include name="com/ejdoab/tcms/entities/*.class" />
        <exclude name="com/ejdoab/tcms/entities/*Test.class" />
    </fileset>
    </jar>
</target>
</project>
```

Notice that you purposely placed all generated files in a separate location from the annotated Bean class (tcms/generated/src). This makes for a leaner, easier-to-understand project.

Annotating ConferenceEJB.java with XDoclet Comments

Besides automating the creation of the interfaces for the ConferenceEJB Bean, you'll also do a bit of refactoring about the way the Bean is accessed. In the previous incarnation of the ConferenceEJB Bean all CMP fields were exposed through the interfaces. It's easy to see that with such an approach a remote client would have to make several remote calls to set all the values of the Bean (or you would have to provide a bloated create method that could take all the parameters needed). Instead you'll be using XDoclet to implement a very common inter-tier implementation pattern known as the data transfer object (DTO). For an extensive coverage of this pattern see Floyd Marinescu's *EJB Design Patterns: Advanced Patterns, Processes, and Idioms*. The DTO pattern, as Marinescu points out, is a "deprecated pattern" in a local invocation scenario, but it's a perfectly valid one for intratier communications.[6] It enables the transfer of data in bulk, therefore minimizing the "chattiness" over the wire.

An example of some XDoclet annotated fields in the ConferenceEJB is shown in the following code segment:

```
...
/**
 * // -----------
 * // XDOCLET Tags
 * // -----------
 *
 * @ejb.bean
 *      name="Conference"
 *      type="CMP"
 *      jndi-name="ejb/Conference"
 *      local-jndi-name="ejb/ConferenceLocal"
 *      primkey-field="id"
 *      schema="Conferences"
 *      cmp-version="2.x"
 *      view-type="both"
 * @ejb.value-object
 *      name="Conference"
 *      match="*"
```

---

6. Marinescu, Floyd. *EJB Design Patterns: Advanced Patterns, Processes, and Idioms* (John Wiley & Sons, 2002)

```
 * @ejb.transaction
 *      type="Required"
 * @ejb.util
 *      generate="physical"
 * @ejb.persistence
 *      table-name="Conferences"
 * @ejb.finder
 *      signature="Collection findAll()"
 * @ejb.finder
 *      signature="Conference findByName(java.lang.String name)"
 *      query="SELECT OBJECT(c) FROM Conferences c WHERE c.name = ?1"
 */
public abstract class ConferenceEJB implements EntityBean {
    // ----------------
    // Business methods
    // ----------------

    /**
     * @ejb.interface-method
     */
    public abstract ConferenceValue getConferenceValue();

    /**
     * @ejb.interface-method
     */
    public abstract void setConferenceValue( ConferenceValue data );

    // ----------
    // CMP Fields
    // ----------

    /**
     * @ejb.pk-field
     * @ejb.persistence
     *      column-name="pk_id"
     * @ejb.transaction
     *      type="Supports"
     */
    public abstract Integer getId();
    public abstract void setId(Integer id);
```

```
/**
 * @ejb.persistence
 *         column-name="name"
 */
public abstract String getName();
public abstract void setName(String name);
   ...
}
```

Let's analyze the differences between the annotated XDoclet version and the previous version. Table 5-3 shows the different tags used in the Bean and each tag's purpose.

Table 5-3. XDoclet EJB Tags Used in ConferenceEJB.java

Tag	Level	Purpose
@ejb.bean	class	Required tag that provides general information about the EJB such as name, type, JNDI name(s), primary key field, abstract schema name, and CMP version.
@ejb.value-object	class	Generates a value-object (DTO) and defines its name.
@ejb.transaction	class | method	Provides transaction attributes on a per-class or per-method level. The type attribute corresponds to the <trans-attribute> value in the <container-transaction> section of the assembly descriptor. It's typical to set a default value for all methods at the class level and then apply a per-method value to customize the transaction attributes of a given method.
@ejb.util	class	Generates a utility class. This attribute works in conjunction with the <utilobject/ > task at the Ant buildscript level. The generated utility class serves as a cache for home objects among other miscellaneous uses.
@ejb.persistence	class | method	Information about CMP persistence. When used at the class level it provides bean-to-table mapping and at the method level it provides field-to-column mapping.

Table 5-3. XDoclet EJB Tags Used in ConferenceEJB.java (Continued)

Tag	Level	Purpose
@ejb.finder	class	Defines an EJB-QL query.
@ejb.interface-method	method	Denotes a method to be exposed in the interfaces (local and remote).
@ejb.pk-field	method	Denotes a field as being the primary key for the Bean.
@ejb.create-method	method	Denotes a method as being an ejbCreate method. XDoclet will create methods with matching signatures in the home interfaces and in the Bean implementation.

From the Ant script you control what you want XDoclet to generate, then, using the tags in the Bean implementation, XDoclet determines how to generate the code. Now you can get an understanding of how the ejbdoclet task performs its work in the Ant script. In the Ant script the subtasks <remoteinterface/>, <localinterface/>, <homeinterface/>, <localhomeinterface/>, <valueobject/>, and <entitycmp/> control the generation of the interfaces and other classes.

For example, to stop generating the remote interfaces, you can choose to not include the <remoteinterface/> subtask. Also notice the jboss subtask, which enables you to generate JBoss-specific source and deployment descriptors.

Looking back to the Java code, you'll notice the value of the view-type attribute in the @ejb.bean tag. It's set to the value both, which instructs XDoclet's interface-creation subtasks to generate both remote and local versions of the interfaces.

At the class level you have the declaration of a custom finder method. The @ejb.finder defines a finder named findByName, which takes as parameters a string representing the name of the conference. Notice that to define a finder you must declare its signature and the associated EJB QL query as attributes of the @ejb.finder tag.

EJB QL stands for Enterprise JavaBeans Query Language, which defines the queries for the finder and select methods of an Entity Bean in a container-managed scenario. EJB QL is an objectified subset of SQL92, which allows navigation over the relationships defined in an Entity Bean's abstract schema. You'll learn more about relationships later in the chapter.

TIP   Notice that the EJB QL query for the findAll() method wasn't specified. This is a special case for which XDoclet generates the query for you. You could include something like query="SELECT OBJECT(c) FROM Conferences AS c", but it will be the same as what XDoclet is doing behind the scenes.

XDoclet also supports the inclusion of Ant-style properties (${my-property}) in the context of an XDoclet tag, which further increases the flexibility of the system. The XDoclet design also acknowledges that not all information should exist at the source-code level in XDoclet tags. The design introduces the concept of "merge points" by which you can merge in a template file at a specific point in the source.

Testing the Bean

Before running the Ant script you need to remove the manually generated files that you created for the non-XDoclet example. Delete the files Conference.java, ConferenceHome.java, ConferenceLocal.java, and ConferenceLocalHome.java. Only the Bean implementation and the test client should remain.

To test your new implementation you also need to modify the previously written test client in order to use the DTO pattern to get and set the values of the Bean. As previously mentioned the DTO pattern is a strategy more than a pattern that serves to ease the passing of data from the EJB tier to a remote client. A DTO serves as a carrier of data between tiers in bulk fashion, thereby minimizing the "chattiness" over the wire caused by the invocation of multiple methods that will retrieve an object's state.

In the TCMS system (because you're taking advantage of the collocation of the web and EJB tiers) the main advantage of using the DTO pattern is to provide a lightweight transport for custom presentation objects; this effectively decouples the client from the specifics of how the data is stored in the database. Custom DTOs provide strongly typed objects that the client can access just like any other object. One possible drawback of the custom DTO strategy is that you could potentially end up with a larger number of objects to be maintained. Other strategies for implementing a DTO layer include the use of Java Collections to create weakly typed data containers in which data items are retrieved by name or some sort of index.

In most cases the data for a single DTO comes from a variety of sources, including multiple Entity Beans, Session Beans, or by calculations. DTOs are meant to be lightweight objects and you should refrain from implementing business logic in them. Limit your DTOs' behavior to simple activities like internal consistency checks and basic validation that the client can perform to avoid the perils of multiple trips to the server for validation.

TIP You should base your use of DTOs on an understanding of how the data is being used across tier boundaries, that is, how much data goes back and forth, its size, and the frequency of the communication.

The modifications to the ConferenceEJBTest class are as follows:

```
...
// create
conf = confHome.create(0, "EJDOAB");
// add some data using DTO
ConferenceValue cvalue = conf.getConferenceValue();

cvalue.setDescription("Enterprise Java Development on a Budget");
conf.setConferenceValue(cvalue);

// nulled to reuse
cvalue = null;
conf = null;

// ---------
// Read Test
// ---------
System.out.println("[read test] begin...");

// find the bean
conf = confHome.findByPrimaryKey(new Integer(0));
// retrieve the DTO
cvalue = conf.getConferenceValue();

System.out.println("[ejb find] Retrieved conference with id (pk) = "
                  + cvalue.getId());
System.out.println("    [name] " + cvalue.getName());
System.out.println("    [description] " + cvalue.getDescription());
...
```

To run the Ant script, open a command prompt, change the directory to the root of the TCMS project and type the following:

```
ant
```

The output of the Ant build script is shown here:

```
Buildfile: build.xml

init:
     [echo] initializing...

prepare:
     [echo] preparing...

generate:
     [echo] generating...
[ejbdoclet] Running <remoteinterface/>
[ejbdoclet] Generating Remote interface for
     'com.ejdoab.tcms.entities.conference.ConferenceEJB'.
[ejbdoclet] Running <localinterface/>
[ejbdoclet] Generating Local interface for
     'com.ejdoab.tcms.entities.conference.ConferenceEJB'.
[ejbdoclet] Running <homeinterface/>
[ejbdoclet] Generating Home interface for
     'com.ejdoab.tcms.entities.conference.ConferenceEJB'.
[ejbdoclet] Running <localhomeinterface/>
[ejbdoclet] Generating Local Home interface for
     'com.ejdoab.tcms.entities.conference.ConferenceEJB'.
[ejbdoclet] Running <valueobject/>
[ejbdoclet] Generating Value Object class:
     'com.ejdoab.tcms.entities.conference.ConferenceEJB-->
     com.ejdoab.tcms.entities.conference.ConferenceValue'.
[ejbdoclet] Running <entitycmp/>
[ejbdoclet] Generating CMP class for
     'com.ejdoab.tcms.entities.conference.ConferenceEJB'.
[ejbdoclet] Running <utilobject/>
[ejbdoclet] Generating Util class for
     'com.ejdoab.tcms.entities.conference.ConferenceEJB'.
[ejbdoclet] Running <deploymentdescriptor/>
[ejbdoclet] Generating EJB deployment descriptor (ejb-jar.xml).
[ejbdoclet] Running <jboss/>
[ejbdoclet] Generating jboss.xml.
[ejbdoclet] Generating jbosscmp-jdbc.xml.

compile:
     [echo] compiling...
     [javac] Compiling 7 source files to C:\java\tcms\classes
```

```
package:
    [echo] packaging...
    [jar] Building jar: C:\java\tcms\dist\jar\conference-ejb.jar

BUILD SUCCESSFUL
Total time: 5 seconds
```

To deploy the new conference-ejb.jar simply copy it to the tcms server deploy directory.

Next, compile the modified ConferenceEJBTest.java class using the following:

```
javac -d ..\..\classes com\ejdoab\tcms\entities\ConferenceEJBTest.java
```

Alternatively, if the class is in the same location as the source that will be compiled by the Ant script, you can skip the manual compilation step. To run the same tests as before you need to delete the records previously inserted in the database. Using you favorite SQL client, execute the following statement:

```
delete from conferences;
```

Now you can run the test client again by using the following command:

```
java com.ejdoab.tcms.entities.ConferenceEJBTest
```

Running the class should produce the exactly the same behavior as in the prior run.

Container-Managed Relationships

At the onset of the current example you'll set out to create two Beans, the ConferenceEJB and the TrackEJB, both of which share a one-to-many, bidirectional relationship (or a many-to-one depending on the direction).

Container-managed relationships (CMR) help you model complex database schemas using Entity Beans. As you've seen, the entity components for the TCMS system are interconnected by many relationships.

In the case of the ConferenceEJB and the TrackEJB you need a way for a ConferenceEJB to return all of its associated Tracks and for a Track to return its associated Conference. At the database level you'll see a foreign key on the Tracks table that points to the Conferences table as shown here:

```
CREATE TABLE Tracks (
  ...
  fk_ConferenceId INTEGER,
  ...
  CONSTRAINT TracksConferencesFK FOREIGN KEY(fk_ConferenceId)
  REFERENCES Conferences(pk_Id)
);
```

Both the cardinality and direction of a relationship in EJBs is defined in the deployment descriptors in the form of <cmr-field>. In CMP 2.0 specification there are a few restrictions that you must abide by when defining Bean relationships. Those are as follows:

- Only CMP 2.0 Beans can participate in a relationship.

- Both Beans in a relationship must be declared in the same descriptor. This requirement also implies that Beans in a relationship need to be contained in the same JAR file.

- Relationships are forced to use the local, pass-by-reference interfaces.

- For relationship methods returning more than one reference, you can only use the java.util.Collection and the java.util.Set classes to package collections of references.

The steps required for the creation of the relationship are as follows:

- Define the abstract accessor methods for each relationship field.

- Define the relationship cardinality and direction in the deployment descriptor.

- Select whether to cascade delete for one-to-one, one-to-many, and many-to-many relationships.

The ejb-jar <relationships> section for the ConferenceEJB and TrackEJB relationship is shown here. Notice that there can be many <ejb-relation> descriptors inside the <relationships> descriptors. Each <ejb-relation> descriptor has two participants that play the <ejb-relationship-role>.

```
<relationships>
  <ejb-relation>
    <ejb-relation-name>conference-tracks</ejb-relation-name>
    <ejb-relationship-role>
      <ejb-relationship-role-name>
        track-belongs_to-conference
      </ejb-relationship-role-name>
      <multiplicity>Many</multiplicity>
      <cascade-delete/>
      <relationship-role-source>
        <ejb-name>Track</ejb-name>
      </relationship-role-source>
      <cmr-field>
        <cmr-field-name>conference</cmr-field-name>
      </cmr-field>
    </ejb-relationship-role>

    <ejb-relationship-role >
      <ejb-relationship-role-name>
        conference-has-tracks
      </ejb-relationship-role-name>
      <multiplicity>One</multiplicity>
      <relationship-role-source >
        <ejb-name>Conference</ejb-name>
      </relationship-role-source>
      <cmr-field>
        <cmr-field-name>tracks</cmr-field-name>
        <cmr-field-type>java.util.Collection</cmr-field-type>
      </cmr-field>
    </ejb-relationship-role>
  </ejb-relation>

</relationships>
```

As you can see there are two roles: the track-belongs-to-conference, which has the multiplicity of Many (read it as [multiplicity] + [role-name], that is, "Many Tracks belong to a Conference"). The <cascade-delete> descriptor tells the CMP engine to delete all Tracks when their associated Conference is deleted (ejbRemove). Role player is defined in the <relationship-role-source> and the <cmr-field> descriptors tell you that the conference (getConference method) field provides the linkage from a track back to its parent conference.

The second <relationship-role> conference-has-tracks can be read as "One conference has [many] tracks." You see again that the role player is Conference and its cardinality in the relationship is One. The link from the One Conference to the Many Tracks is provided by the tracks field, which maps to a java.util.Collection type.

Before you can "wire" the Beans together in a relationship you need to create the TrackEJB Bean. The source code for TrackEJB.java is shown here:

```
package com.ejdoab.tcms.entities;
...
/**
 * @ejb.bean
 *      name="Track"
 *      type="CMP"
 *      local-jndi-name="ejb/TrackLocal"
 *      primkey-field="id"
 *      schema="Tracks"
 *      cmp-version="2.x"
 *      view-type="local"
 * @ejb.value-object
 *      name="Track"
 *      match="*"
 * @ejb.transaction
 *      type="Required"
 * @ejb.util
 *      generate="physical"
 * @ejb.persistence
 *      table-name="Tracks"
 * @ejb.finder
 *      signature="Track findByTitle(java.lang.String title)"
 *      query="SELECT OBJECT(t) FROM Tracks AS t WHERE t.title = ?1"
 */
public abstract class TrackEJB implements EntityBean {
    // ----------------
    // Business methods
    // ----------------
...

    // ----------
    // CMP Fields
    // ----------
...
```

```
    // ----------
    // CMR fields
    // ----------

    /**
     * @ejb.interface-method
     * @ejb.relation
     *       name="conference-tracks"
     *       role-name="track-belongs_to-conference"
     *       cascade-delete="yes"
     *
     * @jboss.relation
     *       fk-column="fk_ConferenceId"
     *       related-pk-field="id"
     *       fk-constraint=true
     */
    public abstract ConferenceLocal getConference();
    public abstract void setConference(ConferenceLocal conference);
...
}
```

Notice the section following the method getConference and the JavaDoc comment before it. Compare the values with the expected XML descriptor that was shown previously.

You also need to modify the ConferenceEJB and add the relationship to TrackEJB. The relevant code changes are shown here:

```
package com.ejdoab.tcms.entities;
...


// need implicit imports to avoid warning
import com.ejdoab.tcms.entities.ConferenceValue;
import com.ejdoab.tcms.entities.TrackValue;

/**
...
 */
public abstract class ConferenceEJB implements EntityBean {
```

```
// ----------------
// Business methods
// ----------------

/**
 * @ejb.interface-method
 * @ejb.transaction
 *      type="Supports"
 */
public abstract ConferenceValue getConferenceValue();

/**
 * @ejb.interface-method
 */
public abstract void setConferenceValue( ConferenceValue data );

/**
 * @ejb.interface-method
 */
public void addTrack(int i, String title)
    throws FinderException, CreateException {
    try {
        TrackLocal track = TrackUtil.getLocalHome().create(i, title);
        getTracks().add(track);
    }
    catch ( NamingException ne ) {
        CreateException ce = new CreateException(ne.getMessage());
        // uncomment this line if using JDK 1.4 or greater
        // ce.initCause(ne);
        throw ce;
    }
}

/**
 * @ejb.interface-method
 */
public Collection getAllTrackValues() {
    List trackValues = new ArrayList();
    for (Iterator i = getTracks().iterator(); i.hasNext(); ) {
        TrackLocal track = (TrackLocal)i.next();
        trackValues.add(track.getTrackValue());
    }
    return (Collection)trackValues;
}
```

```
    /**
     * @ejb.interface-method
     */
    public int getHowManyTracks() {
        return getTracks().size();
    }
...
    // ----------
    // CMR fields
    // ----------

    /**
     * @ejb.interface-method
     *      view-type="local"
     * @ejb.relation
     *      name="conference tracks"
     *      role-name="conference-has-tracks"
     */
    public abstract Collection getTracks();
    public abstract void setTracks(Collection tracks);
...
}
```

In order to test the relationship you'll modify the ConferenceEJBTest class one final time. The final version of the test client code is shown here:

```
package com.ejdoab.tcms.entities;
...
public class ConferenceEJBTest {
    ...

    public static void main(String args[]) {
        ...

        try {
            // ----------
            // JNDI Stuff
            // ----------
            ...

            // ----------
            // Write Test
            // ----------
```

```
System.out.println("[write test] begin...");

System.out.println(
    "[ejb create] Create an Instance of Conference Bean");
// create
conf = confHome.create(0, "EJDOAB");
// add some data using DTO
ConferenceValue cvalue = conf.getConferenceValue();

cvalue.setDescription("Enterprise Java Development on a Budget");
conf.setConferenceValue(cvalue);

// get the track count
System.out.println(
    "[ejb cmr access] There are ("+
    conf.getHowManyTracks() +") tracks");

// create 3 new tracks
System.out.println(
    "[ejb create] Creating three Instances of Track Bean");

// add the tracks to the collection of tracks
conf.addTrack(0, "J2SE");
conf.addTrack(1, "J2EE");
conf.addTrack(2, "J2ME");

// nulled to reuse
cvalue = null;
conf = null;

// ---------
// Read Test
// ---------
System.out.println("[read test] begin...");

// find the bean
conf = confHome.findByPrimaryKey(new Integer(0));
// retrieve the DTO
cvalue = conf.getConferenceValue();

System.out.println("[ejb find] Retrieved conference with id (pk) = "
    + cvalue.getId());
System.out.println("    [name] " + cvalue.getName());
System.out.println("    [description] " + cvalue.getDescription());
```

```
        // get the tracks
        System.out.println(
            "[ejb cmr access] Retrieving all tracks for conference");
        Collection tracks = conf.getAllTrackValues();

        for (Iterator i = tracks.iterator(); i.hasNext(); ) {
            TrackValue tv = (TrackValue)i.next();
            System.out.println("[ejb cmr access] track title = "
                + tv.getTitle());
        }
    }
    catch (RemoteException re) {
        System.out.println("[rmi] remote exception: " + re.getMessage());
    }
    catch (NamingException ne) {
        System.out.println("[naming] naming exception: " + ne.getMessage());
    }
    catch (FinderException fe) {
        System.out.println("[ejb] finder exception: " + fe.getMessage());
    }
    catch (CreateException ce) {
        System.out.println("[ejb] create exception: " + ce.getMessage());
    }
    }
}
```

Run the Ant build script and deploy the conference-ejb.jar file. Delete any records from the Conference table as shown previously and run the test class again. The output should resemble the following:

```
[jndi lookup] Looking Up Conference Remote Home Interface
[write test] begin...
[ejb create] Create an Instance of Conference Bean
[ejb cmr access] There are (0) tracks
[ejb create] Creating three Instances of Track Bean
[read test] begin...
[ejb find] Retrieved conference with id (pk) = 0
    [name] EJDOAB
    [description] Enterprise Java Development on a Budget
[ejb cmr access] Retrieving all tracks for conference
[ejb cmr access] track title = J2SE
[ejb cmr access] track title = J2EE
[ejb cmr access] track title = J2ME
```

Automating the Database Setup

As part of the effort to achieve Continuous Integration you need to automate the database table creation and initial configuration. For this we've created three SQL scripts that are executed with Ant (using the script that we'll introduce in the next section). The three SQL scripts are as follows:

- **tcms-create.sql:** This script creates the 25 tables required for the TCMS system. The script is an exact representation of the database-schema diagram seen earlier in the chapter (see Figure 5-8). It correctly defines all relationships among the entities by using foreign key constraints. Notice that you use the prefix "pk_" for primary key fields and "fk_" for foreign keys.

- **tcms-populate.sql:** This script's purpose is to delete the contents of all TCMS tables and insert some sample data.

- **tcms-drop.sql:** This script removes all tables from the TCMS database.

These scripts are available online as part of the book source code. The three SQL scripts must be placed in the setup/db/hsqldb directory under the TCMS project directory. In the next section you'll learn how to have Ant execute the scripts.

Database-Driven Code Generation with Middlegen

Until now, the direction of the development effort has been moving from the domain and the service abstractions to defining the database tables in order to honor the contracts you've established between the entities. Middlegen is a tool that takes the approach of building an application beginning with the data tier and moving outward to the business and presentation tiers.

Middlegen, originally developed by Aslak Hellesøy, is a tool capable of taking several database tables, resolving the relationships between them (using database metadata), creating the corresponding Java code, and marking it up with XDoclet comments. Middlegen is capable of working with many JDBC-compliant databases and can generate EJB, JDO, and Struts modules. Middlegen uses Velocity templates to generate XDoclet-annotated code and it provides an Ant task to invoke the code generation as part of the build process. Middlegen is especially useful in an application where there are multiple relationships between tables, because it can handle the creation of all the necessary @ejb.relation XDoclet tags.

Code generated by Middlegen relies on further processing by XDoclet and takes full advantage of XDoclet's capabilities to generate interfaces, primary key classes, and deployment descriptors. Middlegen works by using several plug-ins that perform different types of code generation. Middlegen ships with the following plug-ins:

- **cmp20:** Generates one or more CMP Entity Beans based on a set of database tables. It can also create code for handling database-independent primary-key generation schemes (GUID-based or table-sequence-block) as well as Oracle-specific sequence. One of its greatest features is that it correctly generates CMR fields representing the relationships among the tables. You'll cover this plug-in extensively in this chapter.

- **sunjdo10:** Generates Sun JDO 1.0–compliant classes and descriptors. It generates one JDO class per table in the database.

- **struts:** Generates Struts actions, forms, and JSP. The generated pages provide basic functionality to create, list, and delete records in each table.

- **servlet:** Generates a simple servlet that provides a simple way to list the contents of the database table with an Entity Bean.

- **html:** Generates a set of HTML pages describing a database; it's provided as an example of how easy it is to extend Middlegen.

- **simple:** The simple plug-in enables the use of custom Velocity templates without having to write a custom plug-in.

- **java:** Base plug-in class from which all plug-ins that generate Java code descend.

Middlegen provides a <fileproducer> nested tag that serves as a way to pipe the input (tables) to a custom Velocity plug-in in order to generate Java code or other file types. Both the simple and java plug-ins make use of <fileproducer>.

Download and Installation

In this book you're using the version 2.0 of Middlegen. The Middlegen distribution consists of a single ZIP file that you can obtain from http://boss.bekk.no/boss/middlegen/. Download and unzip the file. The file contains all the necessary JAR files in the lib directory as well as a sample application (Middlegen Airlines) that shows you how to use Middlegen.

For the purpose of your application you'll copy the JAR files contained in the Middlegen root directory to the lib/development/middlegen and also copy all the JAR files contained under the samples/lib to the lib/development/middlegen/util directory of the TCMS project.

Using Middlegen

Middlegen is currently being used in two very different ways; one way (and by far the easiest) is to let it generate a baseline version of your code, which you can then manipulate and further customize to fit your application's needs. The other alternative is to use Middlegen in a Continuous Integration scenario where you run Middlegen as part of every build and you use its extension mechanisms (as well as those of XDoclet) to obtain the level of customization required for your application's needs.

In this section you'll concentrate on the use of the CMP 2.0 Middlegen plug-in to create all of the domain entities using the TCMS database as the source of the information. Because you're using a fairly small subset of Middlegen's capabilities, it isn't as complicated to implement the previously mentioned Continuous Integration scenario.

Although Middlegen ships with a version of hsqldb, it doesn't work particularly well with the version of hsqldb that comes with the JBoss distributions. Due to this incompatibility, in order to use Middlegen, a file-based mirror image of the TCMS database was created using the version of hsqldb that ships with Middlegen. This was done only for the purposes of keeping the build script independent of the JBoss version being used.

Middlegen and Ant

As with XDoclet, Middlegen works from within the confines of an Ant build. To use Middlegen you'll need Ant version 1.5 or greater. The Ant script for this example builds on the Ant script created previously. The new script will add some new features needed to simplify the TCMS system build process.

The new Ant script will do the following:

- **Init:** Load all the necessary libraries for XDoclet and Middlegen.

- **Db-Setup:** Automate the creation and deletion of all database tables (both for the main TCMS database and for the replica use for Middlegen purposes).

- **Middlegen:** Generate all CMP EJBs using Middlegen.

- **XDoclet:** Run XDoclet on the generated CMP EJBs.

- **Compile:** Compile all Java sources.

- **Package:** Package all CMP EJB in a JAR file.

- **Verify:** Verify the EJB JAR by implicitly using the JBoss verifier. JBoss provides a class that you can use to verify a J2EE module before deployment. This class is actually what JBoss uses during deployment to check a deployed archive against the specification.

- **Deploy:** Deploy the JAR file to the JBoss tcms server.

In order to avoid hard coding specific paths in the Ant script, you'll also make use of a Properties file named tcms.properties, which will reside at the root of the TCMS project directory. For your current configuration, the tcms.properties file is as follows:

```
// app
app.name=tcms
database.type=hsqldb

// jboss specific
jboss.home=c:/java/jboss-3.2.1
jboss.server=tcms
jboss.datasource=java:/tcmsDS
jboss.datasource.mapping=Hypersonic SQL
java.naming.factory.initial=org.jnp.interfaces.NamingContextFactory
java.naming.provider.url=jnp://localhost:1099"

// middlegen
mgen.gui=true

// db properties
global.db.url=jdbc:hsqldb:hsql://localhost:1701
global.db.userid=sa
global.db.password=
global.db.driver=org.hsqldb.jdbcDriver
global.db.driver.file=${jboss.home}/server/tcms/lib/hsqldb.jar

// middlegen db properties
mgen.db.url=jdbc:hsqldb:${build}/hsqldb/tcms
mgen.db.userid=sa
mgen.db.password=
mgen.db.driver=org.hsqldb.jdbcDriver
mgen.db.driver.file=${lib-dev}/middlegen/util/hsqldb.jar

// middlegen CMP properties
mgen.cmp.package=com.ejdoab.tcms.entities
```

The <middlegen> Task

The Ant task that executes Middlegen is the middlegen.MiddlegenTask class. As with XDoclet it needs to be loaded into the context of the executing Ant script using the taskdef task. The attributes of the middlegen task provide relevant high-level information such as application name, where to store user preferences, and details on how to connect to the database. The Middlegen task, as used in the TCMS Ant script, is shown here:

```
<middlegen
    appname="${app.name}"
    prefsdir="${middlegen-prefs}"
    gui="${mgen.gui}"
    databaseurl="${mgen.db.url}"
    providerURL="${java.naming.provider.url}"
    driver="${mgen.db.driver}"
    username="${mgen.db.userid}"
    password="${mgen.db.password}"
    >
...
</middlegen>
```

The attribute gui determines whether Middlegen will show the graphical interface that allows you to visually manipulate the relationships between the tables.

The <cmp20> middlegen Plug-in Subtask

Middlegen plug-ins are specified as nested elements of the <middlegen> task. The cmp20 plug-in subtask dictates how Middlegen will generate CMP Entity Beans from the structure of the source database specified in the <middlegen> task.
The <cmp20> attributes include the following:

- **destination:** Where to place the generated CMP EJB source files.

- **package:** The package where the EJB implementation source files will reside.

- **interfacepackage:** The package where the generated remote and local interfaces will reside.

- **jndiprefix:** The prefix for the generated EJBs relative to the ENC (java:comp/).

- **pkclass:** Whether to instruct XDoclet to generate a Primary Key class.

- **dataobject:** Whether to instruct XDoclet to generate a Data Object class.

- **viewtype:** Passed to the XDoclet view-type parameter in the @ejb.bean view-type attribute.

- **mergeDir:** A directory where snippets of code that will be merged into the generated files are located.

- **readonly:** Whether the generated EJBs are read-only CMP EJBs.

- **fkcmp:** Stands for foreign key CMP. Application servers such as JBoss don't allow a CMP field to also participate in a container-managed relationship. Therefore fkcmp is set to false for JBoss.

- **guid:** Whether to add automatic string GUID generation for fields with string primary keys.

You also make use of the <sequenceblock> nested element for <cmp20>, which enables the usage of the sequence blocks pattern for creating incrementing, integer primary keys using a stateless Session Bean and a CMP Entity Bean. For more information on this primary-key generation strategy see *EJB Design Patterns: Advanced Patterns, Processes, and Idioms* by Floyd Marinescu.[7] The cmp20 subtask is show here:

```
...
<cmp20
    destination="${src-java}"
    package="com.ejdoab.tcms.entities"
    interfacepackage="com.ejdoab.tcms.entities"
    jndiprefix="ejb"
    pkclass="false"
    dataobject="true"
    viewtype="local"
    mergedir="${middlegen-merge}"
    readonly="false"
        fkcmp="false"
        guid="true"
        >
```

---

7. Ibid.

```
            <!-- use The Sequence Block PK generation pattern -->
            <sequenceblock
                blocksize="5"
                retrycount="2"
                table="SEQ_BLOCK"
                />
            <jboss/>
</cmp20>
...
```

The Ant Script

Now that you've set the stage for using Middlegen it's time to introduce the Ant script changes, which will perform the bulk of the work of generating the CMP classes using Middlegen and processing them using XDoclet. The source for the script is shown here (sections of the script already covered in Chapters 3 and 4 are omitted for brevity using ellipses).

```
<?xml version="1.0"?>
<project name="Enterprise Java Development on a Budget" default="all" basedir=".">

...

    <!-- ==================================================================== -->
    <!-- Initialization                                                       -->
    <!-- ==================================================================== -->

    <property name="build" location="build" />
    <property name="lib" location="lib" />
    <property name="lib-dev" location="${lib}/development" />
...
    <property file="build.properties"/>
...
    <property name="src" location="src" />
    <property name="src-java" location="${src}/java" />
    <property name="src-test" location="${src}/test" />
    <property name="src-conf" location="${src}/conf" />
...
    <property name="generated-dir" location="${build}/generated" />
    <property name="generated-ejb" location="${generated-dir}/ejb-src" />
...
    <property name="descriptors-ejb" location="${generated-dir}/ejb-desc" />
...
```

```
    <property name="dist" location="dist" />
    <property name="middlegen" location="${src}/middlegen" />
    <property name="middlegen-merge" location="${middlegen}/merge" />
    <property name="middlegen-prefs" location="${middlegen}" />
...
    <property
        name="server-dir"
        location="${jboss.home}/server/${jboss.server}"
    />
    <property name="server-lib-dir"  location="${server-dir}/lib" />
    <property name="server-conf-dir" location="${server-dir}/conf" />
    <property name="deploy-dir"      location="${server-dir}/deploy" />

...

    <!-- Files -->
    <property name="ear-filename" value="${app.name}.ear" />
    <property name="ear-file" value="${dist}/${ear-filename}" />
    <property name="ejb-jar-filename" value="${app.name}-ejb.jar" />
    <property name="ejb-jar-file" value="${dist}/${ejb-jar-filename}" />
...
    <!-- Paths -->
    <path id="class.path">
        <fileset dir="${lib}">
            <include name="*.jar"/>
        </fileset>
...
    </path>
    <path id="xdoclet.class.path">
        <path refid="class.path"/>
        <fileset dir="${lib-dev}/xdoclet">
            <include name="*.jar"/>
        </fileset>
    </path>
...
    <path id="middlegen.class.path">
        <fileset dir="${lib-dev}/middlegen/util">
            <include name="*.jar"/>
        </fileset>
        <fileset dir="${lib-dev}/middlegen">
            <include name="*.jar"/>
        </fileset>
    </path>
```

```
<path id="verifier.class.path">
    <fileset dir="${server-lib-dir}">
        <include name="*.jar"/>
    </fileset>
    <fileset dir="${jboss.home}/lib">
        <include name="*.jar"/>
    </fileset>
    <pathelement location="${server-conf-dir}"/>
</path>

<path id="app.class.path">
    <pathelement location="${classes}" />
    <path refid="class.path"/>
</path>
...
<path id="jdbc.class.path">
    <pathelement location="${jdbc-driver-jar}" />
</path>
...
<path id="ejb.source.path">
    <pathelement path="${src-java}"/>
    <pathelement path="${generated-ejb}"/>
</path>
...
<path id="all.source.path">
    <path refid="test.source.path" />
    <path refid="ejb.source.path" />
</path>

<!-- Patternsets -->

<patternset id="bean.set">
    <include name="**/*Bean.java" />
</patternset>
...
<patternset id="jar.set">
    <include name="*.jar" />
</patternset>

<patternset id="ear.set">
    <include name="${ejb-jar-filename}" />
    <include name="${war-filename}" />
</patternset>
```

```
    <patternset id="web.classes.set">
        <include name="**/web/**" />
    </patternset>

    <patternset id="ejb.classes.set">
        <exclude name="**/web/**" />
    </patternset>

    <!-- Task Definitions -->

    <!-- XDoclet - www.xdoclet.org -->
    <taskdef
        name="ejbdoclet"
        classname="xdoclet.modules.ejb.EjbDocletTask"
        classpathref="xdoclet.class.path"
        />
...
    <!-- Targets -->

    <!-- ================================================================= -->
    <!-- Middlegen                                                         -->
    <!-- ================================================================= -->

    <target name="middlegen"
        depends-"middlegen-init"
        if="middlegen.required"
        description="Generate CMP Entity Beans."
        >
        <middlegen
            appname="${app.name}"
            prefsdir="${middlegen-prefs}"
            gui="${mgen.gui}"
            databaseurl="${mgen.db.url}"
            providerURL="${java.naming.provider.url}"
            driver="${mgen.db.driver}"
            username="${mgen.db.userid}"
            password="${mgen.db.password}"
            >
```

```
        <cmp20
            destination="${src-java}"
            package="${mgen.cmp.package}"
            interfacepackage="${mgen.cmp.package}"
            jndiprefix="ejb"
            pkclass="false"
            dataobject="false"
            viewtype="local"
            mergedir="${middlegen-merge}"
            readonly="false"
            fkcmp="false"
            guid="true"
            >
            <!-- use The Sequence Block PK generation pattern -->
            <sequenceblock
                blocksize="5"
                retrycount="2"
                table="SEQ_BLOCK"
                />
            <jboss/>
        </cmp20>
    </middlegen>
</target>


<target name="middlegen-init"
        depends="middlegen-check"
        if="middlegen.required">
    <!--
        Typically task definitions are outside the scope of a target and get
        Initialized everytime the script is run. In this case, the middlegen
        tasks generate a lot of unnecessary standard output when initialized.
        So to reduce the amount of output the initialization is place here
        and only called when necessary.
    -->
    <taskdef
        name="middlegen"
        classname="middlegen.MiddlegenTask"
        classpathref="middlegen.class.path"
    />
    <mkdir dir="${build}"/>
</target>
```

```
    <target name="middlegen-check" depends="db-middlegen-setup">
        <condition property="middlegen.required">
            <uptodate>
                <srcfiles dir="${src-java}" includes="**/entities/*.java" />
                <!--fileset-->
                <mapper
                    type="merge"
                    to="${build}/hsqldb/${jboss.server}.script"
                />
            </uptodate>
        </condition>
    </target>


    <!-- ===================================================================== -->
    <!-- Generate EJB glue files using XDoclet's ejbdoclet               -->
    <!-- ===================================================================== -->
...
    <!-- ===================================================================== -->
    <!-- Compiles all the classes                                        -->
    <!-- ===================================================================== -->
...
    <!-- ===================================================================== -->
    <!-- EJB Package                                                     -->
    <!-- ===================================================================== -->

    <target name="ejb"
            depends="ejb-verify"
            description="Creates deployable EJB jar." />

    <target name="ejb-package" depends="compile,dist-init">
      <jar jarfile="${ejb-jar-file}">
        <metainf dir="${descriptors-ejb}" includes="*.xml"/>
        <fileset dir="${classes}">
            <patternset refid="non.test.classes.set"/>
            <patternset refid="ejb.classes.set"/>
        </fileset>
      </jar>
    </target>

    <target name="ejb-package-clean">
        <delete file="${ejb-jar-file}"/>
    </target>
```

```
<target name="ejb-verify" depends="ejb-package">
    <java
        classname="org.jboss.verifier.Main"
        fork="yes"
        failonerror="true"
        classpathref="verifier.class.path"
        >
        <arg value="${ejb-jar-file}"/>
    </java>
</target>
```

...

```
<!-- ==================================================================== -->
<!-- Ear                                                                  -->
<!-- ==================================================================== -->

<target name="ear" depends="war" description="Creates a deployable ear.">
    <ear
        destfile="${ear-file}"
        appxml="${src-conf}/application.xml"
        >
        <fileset dir="${dist}">
            <patternset refid="ear.set"/>
        </fileset>
    </ear>
</target>

<target name="ear-clean">
    <delete file="${ear-file}" />
</target>

<!-- ==================================================================== -->
<!-- Distribution                                                         -->
<!-- ==================================================================== -->

<target
    name="dist"
    depends="dist-init,ear"
    description="Builds distributable versions of the application." />

<target name="dist-init">
    <mkdir dir="${dist}" />
</target>
```

```xml
<target name="dist-clean">
    <delete dir="${dist}" />
</target>


<!-- ==================================================================== -->
<!-- Deploy - Deploys the Application to server                        -->
<!-- ==================================================================== -->

<target name="deploy" depends="ear" description="Deploys EJB Jar.">
    <copy
        file="${ear-file}"
        todir="${deploy-dir}"
        />
</target>

<target name="undeploy" description="Undeploys EJB Jar.">
    <delete file="${deploy-dir}/${ear-filename}" />
</target>


<!-- ==================================================================== -->
<!-- Testing                                                           -->
<!-- ==================================================================== -->

...

<!-- ==================================================================== -->
<!-- Setup the database - file based db for Middlegen Purposes         -->
<!-- ==================================================================== -->

<target name="db-middlegen-setup"
    depends="db-middlegen-check"
    unless="db-middlegen.notRequired"
    description="Sets up database for Middlegen."
    >
    <antcall target="db-setup">
        <param name="db.url" value="${mgen.db.url}"/>
        <param name="db.userid" value="${mgen.db.userid}"/>
        <param name="db.password" value="${mgen.db.password}"/>
        <param name="db.driver" value="${mgen.db.driver}"/>
        <param name="jdbc-driver-jar" value="${mgen.db.driver.file}"/>
    </antcall>
</target>
```

```
<target name="db-middlegen-clean">
    <delete dir="${build}/${database.type}" />
</target>

<target name="db-middlegen-check">
    <uptodate property="db-middlegen.notRequired"
        srcfile="setup/db/${database.type}/${app.name}-create.sql"
        targetfile="${build}/hsqldb/${jboss.server}.script"
        >
    </uptodate>
</target>

<!-- ================================================================ -->
<!-- Setup the database - runtime db under JBoss                      -->
<!-- ================================================================ -->

<target name="db-runtime-setup" description="Sets up runtime database.">
    <antcall target="db-setup">
        <param name="db.url" value="${global.db.url}"/>
        <param name="db.userid" value="${global.db.userid}"/>
        <param name="db.password" value="${global.db.password}"/>
        <param name="db.driver" value="${global.db.driver}"/>
        <param name="jdbc-driver-jar" value="${global.db.driver.file}"/>
    </antcall>
</target>

<!-- ================================================================ -->
<!-- Setup the database                                               -->
<!-- gets called from db-setup-middlegen, db-setup-runtime            -->
<!-- ================================================================ -->

<target name="db-setup">
    <sql
        src="setup/db/${database.type}/${app.name}-drop.sql"
        url="${db.url}"
        userid="${db.userid}"
        password="${db.password}"
        driver="${db.driver}"
        print="yes"
        onerror="continue"
        >
        <classpath>
            <path refid="jdbc.class.path" />
        </classpath>
    </sql>
```

```
        <sql
            src="setup/db/${database.type}/${app.name}-create.sql"
            url="${db.url}"
            userid="${db.userid}"
            password="${db.password}"
            driver="${db.driver}"
            print="yes"
            >
            <classpath>
                <path refid="jdbc.class.path" />
            </classpath>
        </sql>
        <sql
            src="setup/db/${database.type}/${app.name}-populate.sql"
            url="${db.url}"
            userid="${db.userid}"
            password="${db.password}"
            driver="${db.driver}"
            print="yes"
            >
            <classpath>
                <path refid="jdbc.class.path" />
            </classpath>
        </sql>
    </target>


    <!-- ===================================================================== -->
    <!-- JavaDocs                                                          -->
    <!-- ===================================================================== -->

...

    <!-- ===================================================================== -->
    <!-- Formats all non-generated source code                             -->
    <!-- ===================================================================== -->

...

    <!-- ===================================================================== -->
    <!-- Generates browseable source code in HTML format                   -->
    <!-- ===================================================================== -->

...

    <!-- ===================================================================== -->
    <!-- Checks source code for convention violations                      -->
    <!-- ===================================================================== -->

...
```

```
<!-- ======================================================================= -->
<!-- Source Code Metrics                                                     -->
<!-- ======================================================================= -->

...

<!-- ======================================================================= -->
<!-- Cleans everything                                                       -->
<!-- ======================================================================= -->

...

<!-- ======================================================================= -->
<!-- Does it all                                                             -->
<!-- ======================================================================= -->

<target
    name="all"
    depends="dist,deploy"
    description="Generates, compiles, packages and deploys."
    />

</project>
```

As you can see, this script covers every task required. It can initialize the hsqldb database both for your runtime environment under JBoss and for the purposes of Middlegen. The target db-setup is a parameterized target that takes as parameters the details necessary to connect to a database and then executes the tcms-drop.sql, tcms-create.sql, and tcms-populate.sql using the Ant <sql> task. The targets db-setup-middlegen and db-setup-runtime invoke the db-setup target using the <antcall> task and passing the parameters for the Middlegen file-based database and for the JBoss-embedded database.

The verify target uses the JBoss EJB JAR verifier to check the generated JAR file before deployment. It uses the Java task to execute the class org.jboss.verifier.Main on the generated EJB JAR file.

You also want the generated Java source to have a specific JavaDoc comment. To accomplish this you use the mergedir attribute in the cmp20 subtask. The value of the mergedir attribute is set to ${middlegen-merge}, which you defined previously as ${src}/middlegen/merge in the init target of the Ant script. In this directory (/src/middlegen/merge) you place a text file named cmp20-ALL-class-comments.txt with the following contents:

```
* A TCMS domain entity for table: ${table.sqlName}
* Generated by Middlegen CMP2.0 Plugin
*
```

The Middlegen cmp20 plug-in will use the contents of this file in the class-level JavaDoc comment for each generated Bean. For example, for the generated ConferenceBean.java the merging of the comment results is the following code:

```
package com.ejdoab.tcms.entities;

/**
 * A TCMS domain entity for table: CONFERENCES
 * Generated by Middlegen CMP2.0 Plugin
 *
 * @author <a href="http://boss.bekk.no/boss/middlegen/">Middlegen</a>
 *
 *
 * @ejb.bean
 *     type="CMP"
 *     cmp-version="2.x"
 *     name="Conference"
 *     local-jndi-name="ejb.ConferenceLocalHome"
 *     view-type="local"
 *     primkey-field="id"
...
```

Running the Ant Script

You're now finally ready to use the Ant script. First, you want to initialize the databases by running the db-setup-all target from the root of the TCMS project directory type as follows:

```
ant db-setup-runtime
```

You should see output similar to the following:

```
Buildfile: build.xml

init:
     [echo] initializing...

db-setup-runtime:
...

db-setup:
     [echo] setting up the database...
      [sql] Executing file: C:\java\tcms\setup\db\hsqldb\tcms-drop.sql
...
```

```
[sql] 2 of 24 SQL statements executed successfully
[sql] Executing file: C:\java\tcms\setup\db\hsqldb\tcms-create.sql
[sql] 25 of 25 SQL statements executed successfully
[sql] Executing file: C:\java\tcms\setup\db\hsqldb\tcms-populate.sql
[sql] 89 of 89 SQL statements executed successfully
```

```
BUILD SUCCESSFUL
Total time: 1 second
```

Notice that you'll get several Exceptions of type java.sql.SQLException when the tcms-drop.sql script tries to delete any nonexistent tables.

Similarly, running the db-setup-middlegen should produce the following results:

```
Buildfile: build.xml

init:
    [echo] initializing...

db-setup-middlegen:
...

db-setup:
    [echo] setting up the database...
    [sql] Executing file: C:\java\tcms\setup\db\hsqldb\tcms-drop.sql
    [sql] 24 of 24 SQL statements executed successfully
    [sql] Executing file: C:\java\tcms\setup\db\hsqldb\tcms-create.sql
    [sql] 25 of 25 SQL statements executed successfully
    [sql] Executing file: C:\java\tcms\setup\db\hsqldb\tcms-populate.sql
    [sql] 89 of 89 SQL statements executed successfully
```

```
BUILD SUCCESSFUL
Total time: 2 seconds
```

Now that you have both databases created you can run the all target. To do this you can use the ant all or simple ant command (because the all target is the default target for your script). If everything goes according to plan you should see output on the console resembling the following:

```
Buildfile: build.xml

init:
    [echo] initializing...

prepare:
    [echo] preparing...
    [mkdir] Created dir: C:\java\tcms\generated\ejb-src
    [mkdir] Created dir: C:\java\tcms\generated\web-src
    [mkdir] Created dir: C:\java\tcms\generated\descriptors\ejb

middlegen:
...
[middlegen] Database URL:jdbc:hsqldb:C:\java\tcms\build/hsqldb/tcms
[middlegen] (entitybean.CMP20Plugin             ?   ) WARNING: When
fkcmp-"false", you will not be able to use compound primary keys where some of
the columns are also foreign keys. This is because all columns of a primary key
must be CMP fields. See EJB 2.0. spec section 10.8.2
[middlegen] No <table> elements specified. Reading all tables.
    This might take a while...
[middlegen] (middlegen.Middlegen            396 ) Validating cmp20
...
[middlegen] ********************************************************
[middlegen] * CTRL-Click relations to modify their cardinality     *
[middlegen] * SHIFT-Click relations to modify their directionality *
[middlegen] ********************************************************
```

At this point the Middlegen GUI client should appear. The Ant script execution is blocked until the GUI is closed. The GUI enables you to customize the relationships in the generated code. Any changes made with the GUI are reflected in the tcms-prefs.properties (see the prefsdir attribute of the middlegen task in the Ant script). The GUI is shown in Figure 5-12.

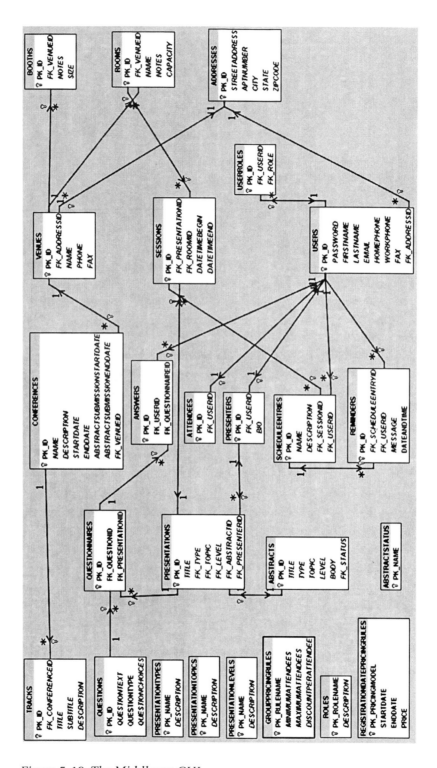

Figure 5-12. The Middlegen GUI

The GUI shows all the relations between the tables in the database, including cardinality and direction. You can change a relationship's cardinality by doing a Ctrl-click closer to the end of the relationship connector between two tables. You can also change the directionality by doing a Shift-click.

Obviously, in a Continuous Integration scenario you wouldn't want the GUI blocking the execution of the script every time that it's run. Once you've refined the relationships you can disable the GUI from appearing by changing the value of the gui attribute of the middlegen task to false. In the Ant script you set that value using the mgen.gui Ant property, which is read from the project's properties file (tcms.properties).

Subsequent runs will use the values in the tcms-prefs.properties file. You can also modify this file manually if needed. For the TCMS project we modified the names of the generated EJBs to names more suitable to our purposes. Middlegen uses an algorithm to take a table name (usually in plural form) and generates a Bean name in singular form. It also keeps the names of the generated EJBs to a certain length, which in this case wasn't long enough for our purposes. The following table highlights the changes made using the Middlegen GUI. For example, because you have a table called Abstracts you need to change the name of the generated Bean to ConferenceAbstractBean as shown in Table 5-4 in order to prevent Middlegen from generating any source using the reserved Java keyword abstract.

Table 5-4. Middlegen Table-to-Bean Mappings

Table	Bean Name	Other Changes
Addresses	AddressBean	None
Answers	AnswerBean	None
Attendees	AttendeeBean	None
Booths	BoothBean	None
Conferences	ConferenceBean	Changed all java.sql.Timestamp to java.util.Dates
Abstracts	ConferenceAbstractBean	Rename Bean
AbstractStatus	ConferenceAbstractStatusBean	None
GroupPricingRules	GroupPricingRuleBean	None
Presentations	PresentationBean	None
PresentationLevels	PresentationLevelBean	None

Table 5-4. Middlegen Table-to-Bean Mappings (Continued)

Table	Bean Name	Other Changes
PresentationTopics	PresentationTopicBean	None
PresentationTypes	PresentationTypeBean	None
Presenters	PresenterBean	None
Questions	QuestionBean	None
Questionnaires	QuestionnaireBean	None
RegistrationDatePricingRules	RegistrationDatePricingRuleBean	Changed all java.sql.Timestamp to java.util.Dates
Reminders	ReminderBean	Changed all java.sql.Dates to java.util.Timestamp
Roles	RoleBean	None
Rooms	RoomBean	None
Sessions	SessionBean	Changed all java.sql.Dates to java.util.Timestamp
ScheduleEntries	ScheduleEntryBean	None
Tracks	TrackBean	None
Users	UserBean	None
UserRoles	UserRoleBean	None
Venues	VenueBean	None

You also changed any java.sql.Timestamp types to java.util.Date. Also, you're going to notice that the positioning of the tables isn't auto-arranged in the GUI. Any changes made to the position of a table on the display are also saved to the properties file. Therefore, if you want to see the tables neatly arranged as in Figure 5-12 you must either arrange them manually or you can just use the tcms-prefs.properties file that's distributed with the example source.

CAUTION As of the time of this writing, the Middlegen team cautions users to use only the local view option when generating interfaces. Apparently, the remote view generation is broken.

Once all customizations to the relationships and the generation parameters are made, press the generate button at the upper-left corner of the application and then simply close the client using the window-closing decoration for whichever operating system you're running.

After closing the GUI you should see the rest of the Ant script execute. The output should resemble the following:

```
(middlegen.Middlegen            414 ) Invoking plugin cmp20
(middlegen.FileProducer         404 ) Generating
C:\java\tcms\src\java\com\ejdoab\tcms\entities\SequenceBean.java
using template from
jar:file:C:\java\tcms\lib\development\middlegen\util\middlegen-entitybean.jar!
/middlegen/plugins/entitybean/sequence-bean.vm
(middlegen.FileProducer         404 ) Generating
C:\java\tcms\src\java\com\ejdoab\tcms\entities\SessionBean.java using
 template from jar:file:C:\java\tcms\lib\development\middlegen\util\middlegen-
entitybean.jar!/middlegen/plugins/entitybean/entity-cmp-20.vm
(middlegen.FileProducer         404 ) Generating
C:\java\tcms\src\java\com\ejdoab\tcms\entities\ConferenceAbstractStatusBean.java
 using template from
 jar:file:C:\java\tcms\lib\development\middlegen\util\middlegen-entitybean.jar!
/middlegen/plugins/entitybean/entity-cmp-20.vm
...
[middlegen] Updated preferences in C:\java\tcms\src\middlegen-prefs\tcms-
prefs.properties

xdoclet:
    [echo] generating...
[ejbdoclet] Running <utilobject/>
[ejbdoclet] Generating Util class for 'com.ejdoab.tcms.entities.AttendeeBean'.
...
[ejbdoclet] Generating Util class for 'com.ejdoab.tcms.entities.QuestionBean'.
[ejbdoclet] Running <remoteinterface/>
[ejbdoclet] Running <localinterface/>
[ejbdoclet] Generating Local interface for
    'com.ejdoab.tcms.entities.AttendeeBean'.
...
```

```
[ejbdoclet] Generating Local interface for
    'com.ejdoab.tcms.entities.QuestionBean'.
[ejbdoclet] Running <homeinterface/>
[ejbdoclet] Running <localhomeinterface/>
[ejbdoclet] Generating Local Home interface for
    'com.ejdoab.tcms.entities.AttendeeBean'.
...
[ejbdoclet] Generating Local Home interface for
    'com.ejdoab.tcms.entities.QuestionBean'.
[ejbdoclet] Running <valueobject/>
[ejbdoclet] Running <entitycmp/>
[ejbdoclet] Generating CMP class for 'com.ejdoab.tcms.entities.AttendeeBean'.
...
[ejbdoclet] Generating CMP class for 'com.ejdoab.tcms.entities.QuestionBean'.
[ejbdoclet] Running <session/>
[ejbdoclet] Generating Session class for
    'com.ejdoab.tcms.entities.SequenceSessionBean'.
[ejbdoclet] Running <entitypk/>
[ejbdoclet] Generating PK class for 'com.ejdoab.tcms.entities.UserRoleBean'.
[ejbdoclet] Running <dataobject/>
[ejbdoclet] Generating Data Object class for
    'com.ejdoab.tcms.entities.AttendeeBean'.
...
[ejbdoclet] Generating Data Object class for
    'com.ejdoab.tcms.entities.QuestionBean'.
[ejbdoclet] Running <utilobject/>
[ejbdoclet] Generating Util class for
    'com.ejdoab.tcms.entities.AttendeeBean'.
...
[ejbdoclet] Generating Util class for 'com.ejdoab.tcms.entities.QuestionBean'.
[ejbdoclet] Running <deploymentdescriptor/>
[ejbdoclet] Generating EJB deployment descriptor (ejb-jar.xml).
[ejbdoclet] Running <jboss/>
[ejbdoclet] Generating jboss.xml.
[ejbdoclet] Generating jbosscmp-jdbc.xml.

compile:
    [echo] compiling...
    [javac] Compiling 162 source files to C:\java\tcms\classes

package:
    [echo] packaging...
     [jar] Building jar: C:\java\tcms\dist\jar\tcms-ejb.jar
```

```
verify:
    [java] Attendee: Verified.
    [java] ScheduleEntry: Verified.
...
    [java] Question: Verified.
    [java] SequenceSession: Verified.

deploy:
    [copy] Copying 1 file to C:\java\jboss-3.2.1\server\tcms\deploy

all:

BUILD SUCCESSFUL
Total time: 23 seconds
```

On the console where JBoss is running you should see the following output:

```
03:02:04,842 INFO  [MainDeployer] Starting deployment of package:
    file:/C:/java/jboss-3.2.1/server/tcms/deploy/tcms-ejb.jar
03:02:05,353 INFO  [EjbModule] Creating
03:02:05,393 INFO  [EjbModule] Deploying UserRole
03:02:05,503 INFO  [EjbModule] Deploying Room
03:02:05,513 INFO  [EjbModule] Deploying Booth
03:02:05,523 INFO  [EjbModule] Deploying Attendee
03:02:05,543 INFO  [EjbModule] Deploying Question
03:02:05,553 INFO  [EjbModule] Deploying User
03:02:05,573 INFO  [EjbModule] Deploying Venue
03:02:05,583 INFO  [EjbModule] Deploying Track
03:02:05,603 INFO  [EjbModule] Deploying ScheduleEntry
03:02:05,613 INFO  [EjbModule] Deploying PresentationTopic
03:02:05,623 INFO  [EjbModule] Deploying Presentation
03:02:05,633 INFO  [EjbModule] Deploying Reminder
03:02:05,643 INFO  [EjbModule] Deploying ConferenceAbstract
03:02:05,653 INFO  [EjbModule] Deploying PresentationLevel
03:02:05,673 INFO  [EjbModule] Deploying Questionnaire
03:02:05,683 INFO  [EjbModule] Deploying Conference
03:02:05,693 INFO  [EjbModule] Deploying RegistrationDatePricingRule
03:02:05,703 INFO  [EjbModule] Deploying Sequence
03:02:05,723 INFO  [EjbModule] Deploying GroupPricingRule
03:02:05,733 INFO  [EjbModule] Deploying ConferenceAbstractStatus
03:02:05,743 INFO  [EjbModule] Deploying PresentationType
03:02:05,753 INFO  [EjbModule] Deploying Role
03:02:05,763 INFO  [EjbModule] Deploying Session
03:02:05,773 INFO  [EjbModule] Deploying Presenter
```

```
03:02:05,783 INFO  [EjbModule] Deploying Answer
03:02:05,793 INFO  [EjbModule] Deploying Address
03:02:05,813 INFO  [EjbModule] Deploying SequenceSession
03:02:06,094 INFO  [EjbModule] Created
03:02:06,094 INFO  [EjbModule] Starting
03:02:07,526 INFO  [Conference] Table 'CONFERENCES' already exists
...
03:02:08,197 INFO  [EjbModule] Started
03:02:08,197 INFO  [MainDeployer] Deployed package:

    file:/C:/java/jboss-3.2.1/server/tcms/deploy/tcms-ejb.jar
```

You can also confirm that the Beans have been deployed correctly by examining the JNDI tree for the JBoss tcms server as shown earlier in the chapter.

Pattern-Driven Development

In this section you're establishing the patterns of communication between the interacting components of a subsystem, and between the subsystems that make up your system. For this you're relying on tried-and-true design and implementation patterns arranged together to fulfill the basic strategy.

- **Facades:** System services are exposed via Session and Message Facades.

- **Service locator:** Clients locate services via a service locator.

- **Data transfer object (aka value objects):** DTOs are responsible for carrying data between processes.

- **Data transfer object factory:** An implementation of the Mapper and Assembler objects used to generate custom DTOs for the presentation layer.

- **Page-by-page iterator/page controller:** A type of DTO that's suited for the transport and manipulation of large sets of tabular data that will be retrieved in an incremental fashion.

- **EJBHomeFactory:** Used for caching of Home Interface objects thereby minimizing JNDI initial context lookups and home lookups.

NOTE We prefer the name "data transfer object" over "value object." For value objects you should follow Fowler's definition instead: "A small simple object, like money or a date range, whose equality isn't based on identity." [8] Value objects are primitive values in the scope of a specific domain or application. For example, in the domain of a banking application, money would be a value object.

TCMS Services

Now that you have a solid EJB-based set of domain entities developed using CMP 2.0 with all the required CMR relationships and support files automated using Middlegen and XDoclet, you can move to the service-oriented part of the system.

The TCMS services, in the form of facades are the main entry point into the EJB-based portion of the application. In the very first examples in this chapter external clients were allowed access to the ConferenceEJB Entity Bean directly. This exposed a lot of intimate knowledge about the persistence and the structure of the database behind the scenes.

Now you're going to expose a set of services via a commonly used pattern in EJB development: the Session Facade. You'll also prevent external clients from accessing the Entity Beans directly. You might be asking yourself, why wrap your Entity Beans with a Session Bean? Aren't Entity Beans legitimate business objects and not just a window into a database table? The answer is yes and no.

The move to a service-oriented architecture places emphasis on applications providing a well-defined set of services to its clients. In the context of a service request, clients will need to have knowledge or certain entities involved in the processing and exchange of information between the client and the applications. If these services are tightly coupled to your Entity Beans then later changes to the database will abruptly cascade all the way out to the application's presentation tier as well as to any other non-HTTP clients.

The facade encapsulates the workflow interactions between the client and the application by presenting clients with a business-driven coarse-grained unified interface to the underlying business components. This has the positive side-effect of reducing the network traffic by minimizing the chattiness over the wire, which is always a great concern when developing distributed applications. Facades also simplify transaction management by removing the need for the client to coordinate transaction boundaries at the component level. Using the facade you minimize the amount of objects exposed to the clients. The communication

---

8.   Fowler. *Patterns of Enterprise Application Architecture* (Addison-Wesley, 2003).

between the facade and other components (other facades and Entity Beans) is performed using EJB local interfaces.

A facade comes in two flavors: Session and Message Facades. For use cases that are synchronous in nature you'll use the Session Facade pattern, though for anything asynchronous you'll use the Message Facade. As mentioned earlier in the chapter, we've opted to keep all facades in the system stateless both for simplicity and performance reasons.

For the TCMS system you'll develop several Stateless Session Facades to fulfill the following subset of the TCMS use cases (as defined in Chapter 2):

- Register

- Authenticate

- View Profile

- Edit Profile

- Browse Sessions

- Browse Presenter Sessions

- Submit Abstract

- Browse Abstracts

- Edit Abstracts

- Browse Schedule

- Add Session to Schedule

- Remove Schedule Entry

- Add Schedule Reminder

- Remove Schedule Reminder

Most of the remaining use cases will be fulfilled in the "Presentation Tier," "Web Services Tier," and "Client Tier." The complete services diagram is shown in Figure 5-13.

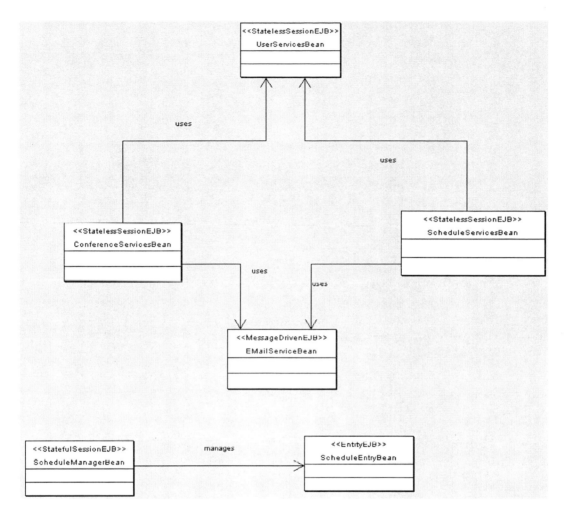

Figure 5-13. TCMS services diagram

From the previous list of use cases you can separate the use cases into Conference, User, and Schedule use cases. This leads naturally to the creation of the following Session Facades:

- **UserServicesBean:** Encapsulates interaction with any attendee and presenters information.

- **ConferenceServicesBean:** Provides general access to conference information.

- **ScheduleServicesBean:** Encapsulates interaction between a user and their conference schedule information.

All three facades will reside under the com.ejdoab.tcms.services package. Let's tackle each facade one at a time and explain in detail the decisions and patterns used.

UserServicesBean.java

You begin by creating a file named UserServicesBean.java in the com.ejdoab.tcms.services package this class should be an abstract class implementing the javax.ejb.SessionBean interface. Next you add class level XDoclet comments to define this Bean as a Stateless Session Bean as follows:

```
/**
 * @ejb.bean
 *       name="UserServices"
 *       type="Stateless"
 *       view-type="both"
 *       jndi-name="ejb.UserServicesHome"
 *       local-jndi-name="ejb.UserServicesLocalHome"
 * @ejb.transaction
 *       type="Required"
 * @ejb.util
 *       generate="physical"
 */
public abstract class UserServicesBean implements SessionBean {
    // add methods here
}
```

By setting the type attribute of the @ejb.bean tag you tell XDoclet to make this a Stateless Session Bean. XDoclet will also make the Bean interface available both locally and remotely as defined in the view-type attribute by setting its value to both.

Also notice that you're setting the transaction type to Required at the class level. The transaction type specifies how the container must manage transaction scopes for the enterprise Bean's method invocations. The value Required specifies that the method is always executed in the context of a transaction. Consequently, if the client invoking the method is making the call in the context of a transaction then that context is used, otherwise the EJB container will execute the method in a newly started global transaction.

TIP Although you've set the default value for the transactions to Required, it's important to note that running a method in the context of a global transaction is much more resource intensive than in a non-transactional scenario. As a rule of thumb, methods that only read data are marked with the NotSupported transaction type. The exception to the rule is when using a CMR collection, which requires that access to the collection (or the iterator for the collection) occur within the transaction in which it was created (this is to guarantee the freshness of the data). Otherwise the familiar java.lang.IllegalStateException is thrown by the container.

Other XDoclet attributes whose default values can be set at the class level include the view-type attribute. In the code for UserServicesBean.java, unless it's specified at the method level, all methods marked with @ejb.interface-method will be available to both remote and local clients.

Now that you have the skeleton for your User Services Facade you can define the operations you wish to make available to the clients. At this point it's relevant to mention that all results to and from our services layer will be handled via DTOs as reflected by the method signatures. You'll delve into the details of DTO layers shortly.

Table 5-5 shows a mapping between the use cases that you're trying to fulfill in this facade and the facade methods implementing them.

Table 5-5. Facade Methods for User Services

Use Case	Method
Register	boolean registerUser(UserProfileDTO up)
Authenticate	boolean authenticate(String email, String password)
View Profile	UserProfileDTO getUserProfile(String email)
Edit Profile	boolean setUserProfile(UserProfileDTO userProfile)

From the use case–method table you can see that the UserProfileDTO is central to delivering and updating data between the application and its clients. For the TCMS system you've implemented a very simple DTO layer. Clients interact with DTOs to get and set values and to create and submit new entities. Your DTOs also simplify the client code needed to manipulate any associated CMR values. In addition, they provide an easy way for clients to validate the contents of a DTO before the contents are sent down the wire to the appropriate facade, thereby reducing the possibility of having to perform multiple network trips.

All DTOs in the system implement a simple interface, com.ejdoab.tcms.services.dto.DTO, which extends the java.io.Serializable interface and provides a single method DTOValidationResults validate() that returns an object, which provides a convenient way to report errors to the user. DTOs are very simple objects that act as envelopes to transport data to and from the client.

On the server side, you have utility objects that correspond to each of the DTO objects in the system and serve as factories for a specific DTO. These factories are an example of the Transfer Object Assembler Pattern,[9] which is a specialized implementation of the Mapper Pattern.[10] The DTO factories can generate a DTO given a Local EJB object and can also update the underlying database when given a DTO. All DTO factories implement the com.ejdoab.tcms.services.dto.DTOFactory interfaces, which defines two methods: getDTO (DTO getDTO(Object obj) throws DTOCreateException) and saveDTO (boolean saveDTO(DTO dto) throws DTOUpdateException).

It's important to note that when using the DTO pattern you effectively couple the clients to the DTO layer. In the TCMS system the DTO layer and the Session Facades define the contract between the clients and the server.

For this implementation you should group both the attendee and presenter information in a single DTO to simplify the code in the clients and reduce the number of dependencies. The UserProfileDTO is an example of a custom data transfer object a common intertier data transfer pattern. For more information on DTOs, custom DTOs, and domain DTO patterns, see Floyd Marinescu's *EJB Design Patterns: Advanced Patterns, Processes, and Idioms.*[11]

One of the drawbacks of the DTO pattern is that although it's relatively easy to create and populate a DTO, the reverse operation, which takes a DTO and updates one or more domain entities, is typically cumbersome, especially if you're dealing with a complicated graph of objects. This is evident in the implementation of the setDTO methods in the DTOFactory classes.

---

9.   Alur, Crupi, Malks. *Core J2EE Patterns: Best Practices and Design Strategies.* 2nd ed. (Upper Saddle River, NJ: Prentice Hall PTR, 2003).

10. Fowler. *Patterns of Enterprise Application Architecture* (Addison-Wesley, 2003).

11. Marinescu, Floyd. *EJB Design Patterns: Advanced Patterns, Processes, and Idioms* (John Wiley & Sons, 2002)

With a clearer picture of the infrastructure needed for your facades, you can now explore the implementation of the UserServicesBean class. Let's begin with the simplest method in the facade, the authenticate method. This method takes as parameters the email and the password of a registered user and determines whether the password matches the password stored in the database. The code for the method is as follows:

```
/**
 * @ejb.interface-method
 * @ejb.transaction
 *      type="NotSupported"
 */
public boolean authenticate(String email, String password)
    throws NoSuchUserException {
    UserLocal user = findUserByEmail(email);
    return (password == null)
        ? (user.getPassword() == null)
        : password.equals(user.getPassword());
}
```

First, note the XDoclet method-level tags. The @ejb.interface tags mark this method as being exposed in the generated interfaces (local and remote as determined by the class-level attribute view-type attribute). Second, you'll override the default transaction type set at the class level with the NotSupported attribute, which will make this method perform faster because it won't be running in the context of a transaction.

Notice that you're making use of the local interface of the UserBean appropriately named UserLocal, which was generated by Middlegen and XDoclet. You'll also create a utility method findUserByEmail that returns a local User object given a user's email. The findUserByEmail method is shown here:

```
/**
 * @ejb.interface-method
 *       view-type="local"
 * @ejb.transaction
 *       type="NotSupported"
 */
public UserLocal findUserByEmail(String email) throws NoSuchUserException {
    try {
        UserLocalHome home = UserUtil.getLocalHome();
        Collection c = home.findByEmail(email);
        if (!c.isEmpty()) {
            UserLocal user = (UserLocal) c.iterator().next();
            return user;
        } else {
            throw new NoSuchUserException(
                "[findUserByEmail] No user with email= " + email);
        }
    } catch (NamingException ne) {
        throw new EJBException(
            "[findUserByEmail] Error retrieving user information",
            ne);
    } catch (FinderException fe) {
        throw new NoSuchUserException(
            "[findUserByEmail] No user with email= " + email);
    }
}
```

Notice that this method is restricted only to the local view as determined by the view-type attribute of the @ejb.interface tag. This is a requirement of the EJB specification because the return value of this method is a local EJB interface. The first line after the opening try statement shows how you obtain the local home interface for the user object using the UserUtil.java object. In the Ant script you instructed XDoclet to create these utility objects for each of the Beans in the TCMS system. The subtask <utilobject kind="physical" includeGUID="true"/> accomplished this. The XDoclet generated util object represents a specific EJB-HomeFactory pattern for a given Bean. Although you provide an implementation of the ServiceLocator pattern that can also cache local home interfaces, you can also use the utility objects for this purpose.

The next method that you want to highlight is the getUserProfile method, which takes as input the email of the user and returns a UserProfileDTO for the user (which includes any attendee- or presenter-specific data also).

```
/**
 * @ejb.interface-method
 * @ejb.transaction
 *      type="NotSupported"
 */
public UserProfileDTO getUserProfile(String email)
    throws NoSuchUserException {
    UserProfileDTO up = null;
    try {
        UserLocalHome home = UserUtil.getLocalHome();
        UserLocal user = findUserByEmail(email);

        if (user != null) {
            Object source = user.getAttendee();
            if (source == null) {
                source = user.getPresenter();
            }

            if (source != null) {
                UserProfileDTOFactory builder =
                    (UserProfileDTOFactory) DTOAbstractFactory
                        .getInstance()
                        .getDTOBuilder(
                        UserProfileDTO.class);
                try {

                    up = (UserProfileDTO) builder.getDTO(source);
                } catch (DTOCreateException dce) {
                    dce.printStackTrace();
                }
            } else {
                new EJBException("no role found");
            }

        } else {
            throw new NoSuchUserException(
                "[getUserProfile] No user with email= " + email);
        }

    } catch (NamingException ne) {
        new EJBException("Error accessing User Information", ne);
    }
```

Notice the use of the DTOAbstractFactory class, which is a simple abstract factory for DTOFactory objects. To obtain a DTOFactory, uses the singleton instance of the abstract factory and calls the getDTOBuilder method by passing the class object of the desired DTO for which a factory is required. Once you have a DTOFactory, you can invoke the getDTO method to obtain a DTO from a Local EJB object or you can call the setDTO method to reflect the changes in the DTO to the database.

ConferenceServicesBean.java

Similarly to the UserServicesBean the ConferenceServicesBean provides a simple interface to the access conference data such as session and abstract information. Table 5-6 maps the use cases fulfilled to the methods in the Bean.

Table 5-6. Facade Methods for Conference Services

Use Case	Method
Browse Sessions	Page getSessions(int start, int size)
Browse Presenter Sessions	Page getSessionsByPresenter(String email, int start, int size)
Submit Abstract	boolean submitAbstract(ConferenceAbstractDTO dto)
Browse Abstracts	Page getAbstracts(int start, int size)
Browse Presenter Abstracts	Page getAbstractsByPresenter(String email, int start, int size)

The method getSession implements a rather simple (and at this point inefficient) version of the page-by-page iterator without doing any caching of the obtained result set. The page-by-page iterator design pattern breaks up a larger result set into smaller pages that can be handled one page at a time by the receiving clients. In the TCMS system the number of sessions can be rather large, depending on the size of the conference, and a client might only want to see a smaller set of sessions to be shown on a web page. The code for the getSessions method is shown here:

```
/**
 * @ejb.interface-method
 * @ejb.transaction
 *        type="NotSupported"
 */
public Page getSessions(int start, int size) {
    SessionLocalHome slh;
    Page page = Page.EMPTY_PAGE;
    Collection c = null;

    try {
        slh = SessionUtil.getLocalHome();
        c = slh.findAll();
    } catch (NamingException ne) {
        throw new EJBException("Error accessing Session Information", ne);
    } catch (FinderException fe) {
        throw new EJBException("Error accessing Session Information", fe);
    }

    SessionDTOFactory dtoFactory =
        (SessionDTOFactory) DTOAbstractFactory.getInstance().getDTOBuilder(
            SessionDTO.class);
    if (c != null) {
        try {
            page - PageFactory.buildPage(c, start, size, dtoFactory);
        } catch (DTOCreateException dce) {
            throw new EJBException("Error building page", dce);
        }
    }

    return page;
}
```

Notice that as part of your DTO layer you have a Page and a PageFactory class. The Page represents a subset of a larger result set and the PageFactory builds Pages containing DTOs by using as input a collection of Local EJB interfaces and a DTOFactory. It then uses the DTOFactory to build the DTOs out of the Local EJB objects and returns them as part of the Page object.

The next method of interest in this facade is getSessionByPresenter. In this method you're using a ServiceLocator to access the UserServices Bean findPresenterByEmail method, and the page-by-page iterator to return a constrained result set. It also makes extensive use of CMR collection fields (consequently this method is forced to run within a transaction).

```
/**
 * @ejb.interface-method
 */
public Page getSessionsByPresenter(String email, int start, int size)
    throws NoSuchUserException {
    UserLocalHome ulh = null;
    UserServicesLocal us = null;
    Page page = Page.EMPTY_PAGE;

    ServiceLocator sl;
    try {
        sl = ServiceLocator.getInstance();
        UserServicesLocalHome usHome =
                (UserServicesLocalHome) sl.getLocalHome(
                "ejb.UserServicesLocalHome");
        us = usHome.create();
    } catch (ServiceLocatorException e) {
        new EJBException("could not access user services", e);
    } catch (CreateException e) {
        new EJBException("could not access user services", e);
    }

    Collection c = new ArrayList();
    PresenterLocal presenter = us.findPresenterByEmail(email);
    Collection abstracts = presenter.getConferenceAbstracts();

    Iterator i = abstracts.iterator();
    for (int index = 0, n = abstracts.size(); index < n; index++) {
        PresentationLocal presentation =
            ((ConferenceAbstractLocal) i.next()).getPresentation();
        if (presentation != null) {
            Collection sessions = presentation.getSessions();
            c.addAll(sessions);
        }
    }
```

```
    SessionDTOFactory dtoBuilder =
        (SessionDTOFactory) DTOAbstractFactory.getInstance().getDTOBuilder(
            SessionDTO.class);
    if (c != null) {
        try {
            page = PageFactory.buildPage(c, start, size, dtoBuilder);
        } catch (DTOCreateException dce) {
            throw new EJBException("Error building page", dce);
        }
    }
    return page;
}
```

The ServiceLocator provides a way for objects in the system to look up components (both local and remote) and other resources that the application might need such as datasources, connections, and connection factories. By centralizing lookups the ServiceLocator pattern simplifies lookup code in the application and it can also serve as a per-JVM cache that eliminates redundant lookups, which in turn improve application performance.

The ServiceLocator is implemented as a singleton, although it isn't a truly "distributed" singleton, the ServiceLocator is a per-JVM singleton (or per-class loader). Contrary to popular belief it's safe to use the singleton pattern in J2EE development as long as the singleton is implemented in a stateless read-only fashion. That is, there's no need for a user of the singleton to be associated with a particular instance of it.

 NOTE   The classic notion of a singleton cannot be achieved with plain Java classes in J2EE. Application servers have fairly complex class-loading behaviors. It's typical for each ejb-jar and/or each EAR file to have its own class loader, in which case it would have its own class instance of a singleton. Therefore if the singleton's state is modified, your code will only see changes to the instance that was loaded in your application's class loader. You can achieve a truly distributed singleton in J2EE by using Entity Beans or JNDI, but that could potentially introduce a single point of failure for your application, or a performance bottleneck.

ScheduleServicesBean.java

The schedule services are provided by the ScheduleServicesBean, which provides the following two methods for accessing and updating schedule information:

- ScheduleDTO getUserSchedule(String email)

- boolean setUserSchedule(ScheduleDTO dto)

These two methods are used to satisfy all of the use cases shown in Table 5-7.

Table 5-7. Facade Methods for Schedule Services

Use Case	Method
Browse Schedule	ScheduleDTO getUserSchedule(...)
Add Sessions to Schedule	getUserSchedule(...) + setUserSchedule(...)
Remove Schedule Entry	getUserSchedule(...) + setUserSchedule(...)
Add Schedule Reminder	getUserSchedule(...) + setUserSchedule(...)
Remove Schedule Reminder	getUserSchedule(...) + setUserSchedule(...)

The ScheduleServicesBean depends heavily on the ScheduleDTO, which in turn uses the ScheduleEntryDTO and the ScheduleReminderDTO. The schedule hierarchy of objects represents a fairly complex object graph, and as we mentioned before, one of the disadvantages of the DTO pattern comes when you try to update or create an interrelated set of domain entities with a compound DTO.

The following code for the updateSchedule method should give you an idea of the issues:

```
private boolean updateSchedule(ScheduleDTO dto) throws DTOUpdateException {
    boolean retValue = true;
    UserLocal user = null;
    UserLocalHome ulh = null;
    UserServicesLocal us = null;
    ServiceLocator sl;
    try {
        sl = ServiceLocator.getInstance();
        UserServicesLocalHome usHome =
            (UserServicesLocalHome) sl.getLocalHome(
                "ejb.UserServicesLocalHome");
```

```
        us = usHome.create();

    } catch (ServiceLocatorException e) {
        new EJBException("could not access user services", e);
    } catch (CreateException e) {
        new EJBException("could not access user services", e);
    }


    // find the user
    String email = dto.getUserEmail();
    try {
        user = us.findUserByEmail(email);
    } catch (NoSuchUserException nsue) {
        throw new DTOUpdateException(
            "There is no user with email " + email,
            nsue);
    }


    ScheduleEntryDTOFactory dtoBuilder =
        (ScheduleEntryDTOFactory) DTOAbstractFactory
            .getInstance()
            .getDTOBuilder(
            ScheduleEntryDTO.class);


    if (user != null) {
        // you need to do a comparison of the items in the schedule and those
        // in the database and remove any items that are in the database but
        // not in the schedule
        Collection c = user.getScheduleEntries();
        Iterator items = c.iterator();
        for (int index = 0; index < c.size(); index++) {
            ScheduleEntryLocal se = (ScheduleEntryLocal) items.next();
            int seId = se.getId().intValue();
            if (!dto.hasEntry(seId)) {
                try {
                    se.remove();
                } catch (RemoveException re) {
                    throw new DTOUpdateException(
                        "Could not remove schedule item with id" + seId,
                        re);
                }
            }
        }
    }
```

```
        // loop through the schedule items
        Iterator dtos = dto.getEntries();
        for (int index = 0; index < dto.getEntryCount(); index++) {
            DTO item = (DTO) dtos.next();
            retValue = retValue && dtoBuilder.setDTO(item);
        }
    }
    return retValue;
}
```

Summary

From the development of the business tier of the TCMS system you've learned that CMP 2.0 Entity Beans are much better suited to represent a fairly complex database schema that their 1.X counterparts. You also learned how two very powerful Open Source tools, XDoclet and Middlegen, can drastically reduce the amount of work needed to get an EJB-based project up and running. By using these tools in conjuction with your well-crafted Ant buildfile and some well-known design and implementation patterns and strategies, you've taken the TCMS business tier from specification to development.

Throughout the chapter you've learned about JBoss and how to configure and deploy an EJB-based application and you briefly delved into the world of J2EE management with Java Management Extensions.

Earlier in the chapter you also learned about the different choices developers, designers, and architects face when creating an enterprise application, and you learned that using J2EE doesn't equate to using EJBs. You learned that EJBs offer a good solution to a wide range of problems, but there are many factors that you should weigh when making the decision to go with EJBs.

You also learned about CMP 2.0 and CMR relationships, which formed the basis for the domain entities of the TCMS system. J2EE is a deep and wide technology stack, and experience will teach you, as quoted at the beginning of the chapter, when to "chop off whatever you don't need."

CHAPTER 6

Data Storage Options

The best way to have a good idea is to have a lot of ideas.[1]

—Linus C. Pauling

DATABASES ARE EVERYWHERE in modern society and represent the backbone of the information age. In a J2EE application, choosing the right database platform can mean the difference between a successful application and a failed one.

How do you go about choosing where to put your data? The criteria for choosing a database are as complex as those for choosing an application server or an operating system. The fact that the largest percent of applications end up using a relational database doesn't automatically mean that it's the best solution to your particular problem. For the majority of corporate applications the data that will be manipulated is already living in a relational database, therefore the choice has already been made for you. But for those applications that you're starting from scratch, there are a lot of ideas you can try. Some of the issues that you should weigh before making a decision about which database to choose for your next J2EE application include the following:

- **Cost:** Proprietary or Open Source? The total cost of ownership (TCO) is what determines the impact on the bottom line. Hidden costs can, depending on your application needs, surpass the initial price tag. Sorting through the licensing and support schemes for proprietary databases can be a daunting experience. Proprietary database vendors have artfully devised myriad schemes based on developer seats, CPUs, concurrent users, and connection modes (intranet and/or Internet) to get the most money out of their customers.

- **Maintenance/Administration:** From installation to day-to-day maintenance, a database administrator (DBA) needs tools to ease the tasks of administration, including security, auditing, backup/restore, replication, recovery, and remote databases. Documentation and support, both traditional and online are important for the daily work of a DBA.

---

1. Safire, William and Leonard Safir. *Leadership: A Treasury of Great Quotations for Those Who Aspire to Lead* (Galahad Books: September 2000).

- **Performance/Scalability:** Although many performance problems attributed to the database are usually caused by poor database design, poorly structured queries and a lack of indexing (in the case of relational databases), relative database performance is usually more a factor of the architecture and real-time demands of an application. Understanding how your application works with data is the first step toward performance analysis. Scalability on the other hand is a more concrete and quantifiable feature. Do the things that work for a few users work for many? How do you respond to an increase in the demand for resources? Can your database support intelligent partitioning or clustering?

- **Features:** Database vendors compete based on a value-added market for features such as multiuser access, storage transparency, query optimization, transactions and concurrency (locking) controls, stored procedures, XML support, and others.

- **Standards:** Whether you're planning to use a relational database or an object database, a basic adherence to standards can mean the difference between the portability of both data and the code that's manipulating the data. For relational databases and Java the question is to what version of the Structured Query Language (SQL) standard does the database adhere? Is the compliance only for a subset of the SQL features? For object databases, do they follow the Object Data Management Group (ODMG) standards?

- **Channels:** Who is consuming the application's information? Are the target clients web-based, wireless handheld devices, or rich GUI clients? What about connectivity? Are they connected continuously or are their connections intermittent?

- **Productivity:** How would choosing a particular database affect your application development? What's the impact on existing code? What's the learning curve for the technology like? Development man hours can quickly surpass the cost of runtime resources. The combination of documentation, development tools, and an adherence to standards can minimize the risk of switching database technology.

Figure 6-1 shows some of the options available when storing and retrieving data in J2EE.

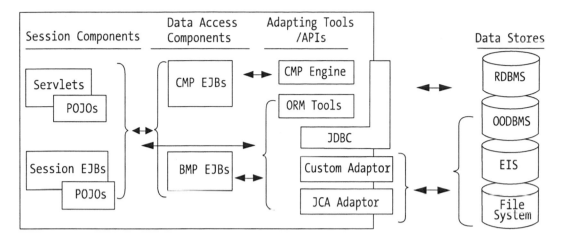

Figure 6-1. Java/J2EE and data storage

Understanding the strengths and weakness of the various choices is a very application-specific task. As you learned in Chapter 2, a solid application design and an understanding of the domain that the data belongs to and the context in which it will be used are the most accurate ways to find requirements for a data-storage technology.

In this chapter some of the open-sourced choices for data storage are covered. In Chapter 7 you'll learn about object-relational mapping (ORM) tools, which can be used to implement your persistence layer when your J2EE applications are confined to work with relational databases.

This chapter begins with some of the pros and cons between choosing a relational or an object database and then moves on to show you some of the choices available from the Open Source community. We use the following four categories of technologies when it comes to storing data:

- Java (embedded) relational database management system (RDBMS)

- Java object-oriented database management system (OODBMS)

- Java XML DBMS (XDBMS)

- Object serialization (including Java Prevalence/Prevayler)

This chapter isn't an attempt to cover all the choices listed in depth, but it's intended as an introduction that should help you gain an understanding of some of the differences between the storage technologies at the conceptual and practical levels, as they apply to the J2EE platform. In particular, this chapter concentrates on the installation, configuration, and usage issues for each tool as they apply to the JBoss application server.

Choosing Between Object and Relational Databases

The relational model proposed by E. F. Codd and the subsequent SQL standard are based on an abstracted model of the data based on the mathematical principles of set theory. In the relational model, data is decoupled from the application logic that uses it. Relational databases provide optimized storage and retrieval of data at the expense of "flattening" the richer semantical connections that the data might have when it's coupled with behavior in the realm of objects. Relational databases are designed with the concept of normalization in mind. Normalization is based on the simple idea that it's more efficient and safer to keep a piece of data in one place only, as proposed by Codd's "Information Rule."

Part of the success of the relational database is due to the SQL standard (an ANSI/ISO standard), which is to an extent the only reason that makes porting an application from one relational database to another a feasible endeavor. Of course, database vendors deviate from the standard in the race to provide market differentiators and value-added features, or when they're simply trying to cover holes left in the standard (such as stored procedures and database triggers).

Comparison of Terms

In the relational model, a relation (a table) is a concept similar to that of an object's class, yet classes can support inheritance and complex composition with statically and dynamically defined datatypes, although, in the relational model, relationships are based on foreign keys. The concept of a tuple (a table row) can be contrasted with an instance of an object, but, although a tuple is a set of values, an object encompasses any type of data and the operations to manipulate it. A column in a database is similar to an object's attribute, but again, in the case of an object, the possible datatypes are only restricted by the programming language base types and the user-defined types.

Relational databases go hand in hand with procedural languages and have been proven to work particularly well when dealing with complex queries, when adding or modifying large volumes of data, or when working with data for which only simple datatypes are required. Relational databases are an obvious choice for data warehousing, and high-volume Online Transaction Processing (OLTP), in which the data is combined and queried in very predictable ways.

Yet for certain domains it has been proven that the relational model falls short, especially when data needs to be manipulated and analyzed in highly complex ways. This is clearly seen in the fields of financial analysis and forecasting, in the chemical and biological sciences, in game theory, network management, process control, computer-aided design/manufacturing (CAD/CAM), and multimedia storage and analysis, among many others. Generally speaking, object-oriented databases are better suited for storing data with complex datatypes and numerous relationships. The differences between the two models are brought to light when you try to use the relational model to store medium to complex object hierarchies given that the concepts of data abstraction, inheritance, and encapsulation can't be easily represented using the relational model.

These differences are the root of the object-relational impedance mismatch that you'll learn how to deal with in Chapter 7. With an object database there's no need for any kind of "mapping" between your objects and their storage format.

The answers to the following questions can guide you in the decision between a relational database and an object-oriented database:

- **Simple data:** If your data has a natural tendency to be organized in table form, then use a relational database.

- **Complex data:** If your data is highly complex and it makes little sense to manipulate it outside of the realm of an object, then use an object database.

- **Transactions:** If you have a high number of concurrent users performing short-lived transactions, then use a relational database.

- **Volume of data:** If you're dealing with large volumes of data that need to be queried in complex ways—often to provide specific pieces of information—and the manipulation of the data is left to the client, then use a relational database.

- **Reporting:** Reporting tools in general use SQL to gather data to produce reports. Ad hoc query tools expose SQL-like constructs so that users can create their own customized reports. Data stored in relational databases is usually easier to manipulate in order to produce tabular reports, therefore, if your business depends on reporting, use a relational database.

- **Legacy concerns:** If your company already has a heavy investment in relational technology, legacy data, legacy applications, and in-house expertise, it's very likely that unless your application can work in isolation you'll have to use a relational database.

NOTE   If you're working with an already-designed object model and you're now faced with the decision of what database technology to use, it's important to understand what the guiding forces where when the model was created. You can usually tell this by the granularity of the objects in the model. Typically with data-driven models, you tend to have large, coarse-grained objects that reflect the "normalized" nature of relational databases and look very much like an Entity Relation Diagram (ERD) that has been infused with behavior by the addition of methods. On the other hand, an object-driven model tends to have smaller, finer-grained, more reusable objects that are the result of the process of object-oriented analysis and design (OOAD), as you learned in Chapter 2.

Figure 6-2 shows the relationship between data and query complexity and the choice between a relational and an object database. In Figure 6-2 you can see that as query complexity increases you're better served by a relational database, although increased object model or data complexity calls for an object database. The problem arises when you need a combination of both; for those situations, the safest bet is to use a relational database couple with a strong ORM tool.

There are, however, applications that can benefit from using a combination of both technologies. For example, for data that's only manipulated as objects you can use an object database, though for data used in ad hoc queries, or data that's purely descriptive and doesn't represent the state of an object or for data that is used in objects that are simple data wrappers you can use a relational database. Caching is another area where an in-memory object-database in the middle tier can improve performance without introducing a great deal of complexity. Of course, using both technologies together in certain scenarios requires a tight integration between the relational and object systems, especially if there's a need to share data stored using both technologies. In such cases, issues such as data synchronization and replication become relevant.

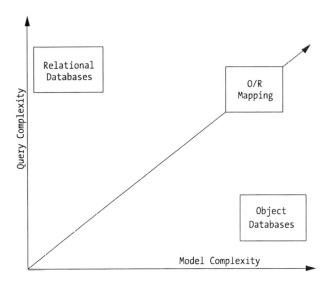

Figure 6-2. Trade-offs between relational and object databases

Relational Database Choices

The relational database is the standard for data storage in the enterprise. Regardless of its advantages or disadvantages, there's a great deal invested in the technology, and products have attained levels of maturity that are deemed to be at the enterprise level. Relational-database technology has proven itself in countless fields. The fact that it's decoupled from the applications has proven to be a blessing when it comes to adapting itself to the changing needs and trends of enterprise computing. From the mainframe, through the client-server, to the world of web services and service-oriented architectures, there's a good chance that you'll be using a relational database in your next project.

When choosing a relational database, take into account the following factors:

- **SQL:** What level of the SQL standard (SQL-92/SQL-99) does it support?

- **Features:** Store procedures, triggers, clustering, and replication available.

- **Optimizations:** Dynamic query optimization, caching.

- **Connectivity:** Level (type) of JDBC driver supported. See sidebar on JDBC drivers.

- **Datatypes:** Are special or custom datatypes supported?

Also, there are other choices that come into play when you use a relational database, because you need to take data from the relational world of tables to the Java world of objects. The strategies available for enterprise applications are as follows:

- **ORM:** Uses a relational database adapted with an ORM tool to turn relational data into objects and back (bridging the so called object-relational impedance mismatch), as shown in Chapter 7.

- **CMP:** Uses a coarser-grained component-based approach, as shown in Chapter 5.

- **JDBC:** Uses the JDBC API in either Session Beans or BMP Entity Beans.

BEST PRACTICE   When using a relational database, regardless of the method of access (ORM, CMP) it's a good idea to test, with handwritten JDBC, the queries that will be the bread and butter of your application against several different databases, using different drivers with the help of a qualified DBA. If performance is a concern these numbers can give you a baseline for choosing your database, driver, and mapping/access strategy. Also, by comparing any generated SQL against the hand-optimized queries you can judge the relative efficiency of a tool.

JDBC Drivers

The quality of the connectivity solution you choose can have dramatic effects on application performance, scalability, and reliability. Most database vendors bundle a JDBC driver with their products, and experience has demonstrated that frequently they are subpar to both commercial and open-sourced third-party drivers.

The type of the driver supported by the database is also important. The JDBC specification mandates a set of interfaces to be implemented. How they are implemented is left to the vendors. The different types of implementation are officially categorized as follows:

- **Type 1:** Uses a call to native libraries typically written in a lower-level language like C.

- **Type 2:** Uses a hybrid approach of Java code and native libraries.

- **Type 3:** Uses only Java, but it has to map SQL calls to a vendor-specific protocol using an adaptor on the server side.

- **Type 4:** Pure client-side Java implementation that requires no mapping adaptors.

JDBC Type 4 drivers are typically recommended because they are usually more efficient, more portable, require less maintenance, and have easier installation procedures (no client-side binaries, no server-side adaptors, just put it in the classpath).

Pure Java Databases

Most J2EE servers come with an integrated/embedded pure-Java database. An embedded Java database is normally running in the same Java Virtual Machine (JVM) as the processes using it, therefore it gets a boost in performance by avoiding interprocess communication. Also, most of the time the JDBC driver can intelligently talk to the database without incurring any network overhead. The pure Java databases that are currently available provide a lightweight solution that's SQL compliant and requires a minimal amount of administration. There are a few pure Java-embedded SQL databases that have gained acceptance, among them hsqldb, McKoi SQL, and Axion DB. Table 6-1 shows a comparison of features in all three open-sourced databases.

 NOTE This section covers hsqldb and McKoi SQL databases. The Axion DB product is, at the time of this writing, not ready to be used with JBoss.

Table 6-1. Pure Java Databases Feature Matrix

Database	URL	SQL Level
hsqldb	`http://hsqldb.sourceforge.net`	SQL-92 subset
McKoi SQL	`http://mckoi.com/database`	SQL-92 subset
Axion DB	`http://axion.tigris.org/`	SQL-92 subset

hsqldb

The hsqldb database engine is the successor to the now-closed Hypersonic SQL project, and it's the most-used open-sourced Java RDBMS. It's bundled with many Open Source and commercial projects and distributed under an Apache/BSD-like license. It's a fairly fast and small database.

In Chapter 5 you learned how to set up a JBoss datasource using the embedded version of hsqldb in Server mode. The original version of the TCMS case study system was developed using hsqldb given its availability and its support for a large percent of the SQL-92 standard.

hsqldb Operating Modes

hsqldb can operate in several modes:

- **In-memory:** In this mode hsqldb keeps data in memory only and serves as a relational application cache. The data is never saved to disk, therefore this option is useful for testing scenarios where you would normally need to flush the database after each test. It's also useful for applications that don't need persistent data but want the advantages of SQL in order to manipulate transient data.

- **In-process:** Also referred to as stand-alone mode. In this mode hsqldb writes data to the file system once as part of its shutdown sequence.

Multithreaded	Transactions	JDBC License	Client/Server Mode
No	Yes	HSQL Development Group License (include copyright/ no implied endorsements)	Yes
Yes	Yes	GPL	Yes
No	Yes	Axion License (include copyright/ no implied endorsements)	No

- **Client/Server:** Supports server, web server, and servlet modes. The server mode allows TCP/IP connections to the database and it's the preferred mode for "production" applications using hsqldb in JBoss. The web server mode uses HTTP, effectively serving as a proxy/gateway to go through firewalls or for general connections over the Internet. The servlet mode is similar to the web server mode, but it's encapsulated in a Java servlet (and isn't meant to be used by servlet-based applications necessarily, but it can be deployed in a web container).

By creating appropriate hsqldb datasources in JBoss you can use a combination of the modes to cover your application needs. For example for volatile session information you can use the in-memory mode in combination with the server mode for your enterprise data.

 TIP   In the JBoss configuration file hsqldb-ds.xml (as well as in the file tcms-ds.xml created in Chapter 5), the hsqldb operating mode is defined by the connection-url element of the local-tx-datasource element. Setting the value to "jdbc:hsqldb:." uses the in-memory mode or a value in the form "jdbc:hsqldb:database" where "database" is the name of the database file for in-process mode.

hsqldb Database Manager

The hsqldb distribution includes a database manager that's a Swing-based application that let's you administer to your databases. Typically, you can start this application by using the following command line (assuming that hsqldb.jar is in your classpath):

```
java org.hsqldb.util.DatabaseManager
```

But because you're running hsqldb embedded in JBoss, you can use the JBoss JMX Admin console to take advantage of the hsqldb MBean integration to launch the application. To accomplish this from the JBoss console (`http://localhost:8080/jmx-console`) find the service named "Hypersonic" as shown in Figure 6-3.

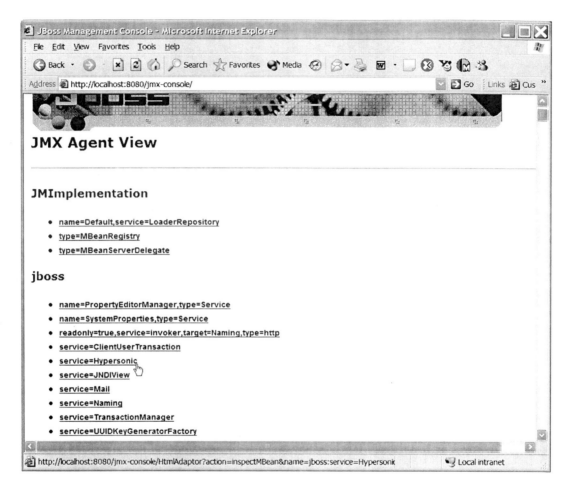

Figure 6-3. JBoss JMX Admin console

Next, click the link that will take you to the MBean view for the Hypersonic service. Here you can invoke the startDatabaseManager() MBean operation as shown in Figure 6-4.

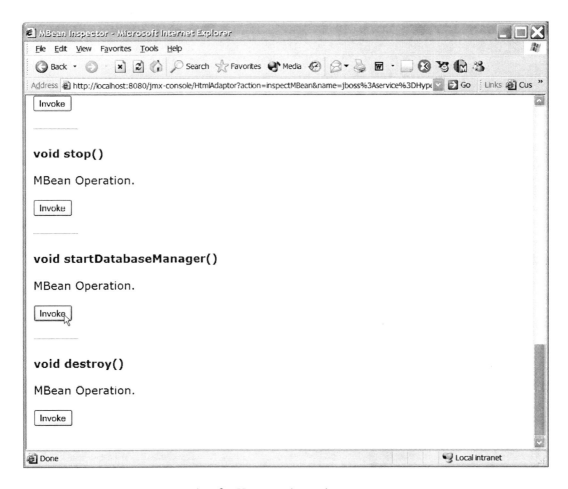

Figure 6-4. JBoss JMX MBean view for Hypersonic service

Invoking the method should launch the HSQLDB Database Manager, as shown in Figure 6-5, in which a typical SQL query is shown against one of the TCMS tables.

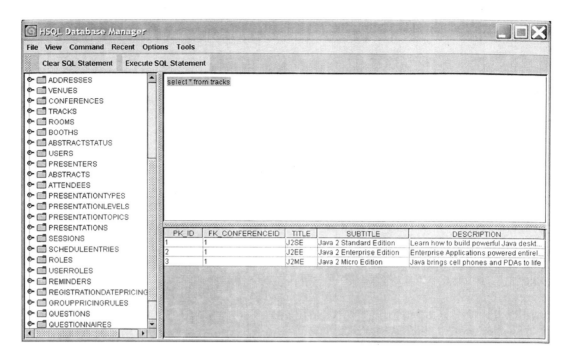

Figure 6-5. HSQLDB Database Manager

CAUTION When launching the HSQLDB Manager from the JMX Admin console the Database Manager executes in the server process and if the MBean method is invoked several times then there will be as many instances of the Database Manager as the number of times the startDatabaseManager() method was invoked. Therefore it's important to secure the JBoss console because a simple script could easily compromise your server.

McKoi SQL

The McKoi SQL database is another pure-Java RDBMS that, like hsqldb, can be used in embedded stand-alone mode or in client/server mode. One of the features that make the McKoi SQL database more suited for an enterprise production system is that it offers support for the highest level of transaction isolation (TRANSACTION_SERIALIZABLE). Although not as popular as hsqldb, the McKoi database is informally reported to be a stronger database platform both in performance and scalability.

CAUTION Before you consider embedding a Java database such as the McKoi SQL database in your product, it would be wise to seek legal counsel (at least informal) on the intricacies of the GPL and LGPL licenses when it comes to Java applications. This is especially important if you're planning to use the software in a commercial fashion or are planning to distribute it outside of your organization.

Creating a McKoi JBoss Datasource

Datasource deployments in JBoss are handled by the JBoss JCA implementation. Most databases, especially those that are open-sourced, include a custom JCA adapter in the form of a configuration file and one or more MBeans (for other databases you can use one the two generic JDBC JCA adaptors for regular "local" drivers and for XA (2PC) drivers). McKoi DB ships with a JBoss JCA MBean adaptor contributed by Howard Lewis Ship (creator of the Tapestry web framework).

The rest of this section shows you how to configure and deploy the McKoi DB in JBoss.

Make the McKoi JAR File Available to JBoss

The first step is to copy the mckoidb.jar to the tcms/lib directory (or the lib directory of the JBoss server that you're using).

Create a Database

To create a database, change directories to the location of the McKoi distribution and on the command line enter the following command:

```
java -jar mckoidb.jar -create "sa" "admin"
```

This will create a database with the username sa and the password admin. The console output should look like this:

```
Mckoi SQL Database ( 1.0.2 )
Copyright (C) 2000, 2001, 2002, 2003 Diehl and Associates, Inc.  All rights
reserved.
Use: -h for help.

  Mckoi SQL Database comes with ABSOLUTELY NO WARRANTY.
  This is free software, and you are welcome to redistribute it
  under certain conditions.  See LICENSE.txt for details of the
  GPL License.
```

Under the McKoi distribution directory you should now have a subdirectory named data, which contains the newly generated database files. Create a new directory under the tcms/data directory and name it mckoi (you should see an hsqldb directory at that level also). Copy the data directory under the newly created mckoi directory. The resulting directory structure is shown in Figure 6-6. It isn't necessary to copy the log directory because this directory is automatically created.

Figure 6-6. McKoi directory in JBoss

The McKoi database uses a properties file called db.conf to control the runtime behavior of the database engine. In the mckoi directory created in the previous step, create a new text file and name it db.conf. The sample db.conf provided here should suffice (notice that the standard port is 9157, if you use any other port number you would have to specify it in the connection URL used in your code or connection configuration files):

```
############################################################
#
# Configuration options for the Mckoi SQL Database.
#
############################################################

database_path=./data
log_path=./log
root_path=configuration
jdbc_server_port=9157
ignore_case_for_identifiers=disabled
regex_library=gnu.regexp
data_cache_size=4194304
max_cache_entry_size=8192
maximum_worker_threads=4
debug_log_file=debug.log
debug_level=20
```

Create the Datasource File

The McKoi JCA adaptor is contained in the package net.sf.tapestry.contrib.mckoi, which is part of the current McKoi distribution. This package contains the MBean used to interact with the database.

An XML descriptor with the -ds.xml suffix is needed for deployment so that the JBoss JCA deployer can recognize it. Next, create a file with the contents as shown here and save it as mckoi-ds.xml in any directory. Notice that the connection-url element doesn't specify a port because you're using the default port 9157.

```xml
<?xml version="1.0" encoding="UTF-8"?>
<datasources>
    <local-tx-datasource>
        <depends>jboss:service=McKoi</depends>
        <jndi-name>mckoiDS</jndi-name>
        <connection url>jdbc:mckoi://localhost</connection-url>
        <driver-class>com.mckoi.JDBCDriver</driver-class>
        <user-name/>
        <password/>
        <min-pool-size>5</min-pool-size>
    </local-tx-datasource>
    <mbean code="net.sf.tapestry.contrib.mckoi.McKoiDB"
           name="jboss:service=McKoi">
        <!--
        ConfigPath attribute is relative to the current working directory which
        is the %JBOSS_HOME%/bin directory
        -->
        <attribute name="ConfigPath">../server/tcms/data/mckoi/db.conf</attribute>
    </mbean>
</datasources>
```

Deploy the Datasource

To deploy the datasource simply copy the mckoi-ds.xml file to the tcms/deploy directory. The output on the JBoss console should resemble the following:

```
01:01:21,314 INFO  [MainDeployer] Starting deployment of package:
file:/C:/java/jboss/jboss-3.2.1/server/tcms/deploy/mckoi-ds.xml
01:01:21,344 INFO  [XSLSubDeployer] transformed into doc: [#document: null]
01:01:21,374 INFO  [McKoiDB] Creating
01:01:21,384 INFO  [McKoiDB] Created
01:01:21,384 INFO  [RARDeployment] Creating
01:01:21,384 INFO  [RARDeployment] Created
```

```
01:01:21,384 INFO  [JBossManagedConnectionPool] Creating
01:01:21,384 INFO  [JBossManagedConnectionPool] Created
01:01:21,384 INFO  [TxConnectionManager] Creating
01:01:21,384 INFO  [TxConnectionManager] Created
01:01:21,384 INFO  [McKoiDB] Starting
01:01:21,454 INFO  [McKoiDB] TCP JDBC Server (multi_threaded) on port: 9157
01:01:21,454 INFO  [McKoiDB] Started
01:01:21,454 INFO  [RARDeployment] Starting
01:01:21,464 INFO  [RARDeployment] Started
01:01:21,464 INFO  [JBossManagedConnectionPool] Starting
01:01:21,464 INFO  [JBossManagedConnectionPool] Started
01:01:21,464 INFO  [TxConnectionManager] Starting
01:01:21,474 INFO  [mckoiDS] Bound connection factory for resource adapter for
ConnectionManager 'jboss.jca:service=LocalTxCM
,name=mckoiDS to JNDI name 'java:/mckoiDS'
01:01:21,474 INFO  [TxConnectionManager] Started
01:01:21,474 INFO  [MainDeployer] Deployed package: file:/C:/java/jboss/jboss-
       3.2.1/server/tcms/deploy/mckoi-ds.xml
```

Now you can use the McKoi database in JBoss by using the datasource with the JNDI name mckoiDS. The McKoi JDBC driver is contained in both the mckoidb.jar (along with the database engine), and individually in the mkjdbc.jar, which would be suitable for distribution to external clients.

The McKoi Query Tool

The McKoi query tool is a simple Swing-based tool that manipulates the database. It's included as part of the mckoidb.jar file. To launch the Query Tool type (with JBoss started and the McKoi datasource deployed), enter the following:

```
java -cp mckoidb.jar com.mckoi.tools.JDBCQueryTool
    —url "jdbc:mckoi://localhost" -u "sa" -p "admin"
```

The console will display a short message showing the JDBC driver being used and the URL of the database, as shown here:

```
Using JDBC Driver: com.mckoi.JDBCDriver
Connection established to: jdbc:mckoi:
```

Figure 6-7 shows the McKoi query tool in action.

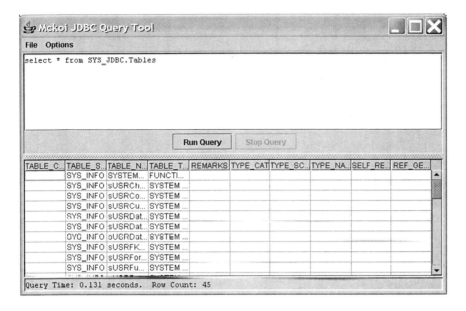

Figure 6-7. McKoi query tool

 NOTE There are other up-and-coming, open-sourced, pure-Java databases, many of which came out of the original Hypersonic project created by Thomas Mueller (like hsqldb). The Axion database, hosted at http://axion.tigris.org, doesn't have a formal 1.0 release yet, but it's one project to keep in mind in the near future.

Non-Java Relational Databases and Java

Typically, after the prototyping and development stages of a project you'll have to move to a non-Java database to handle the increasing loads. Many Internet sites looking for an open-sourced alternative have settled on using MySQL (http://www.mysql.com) including Yahoo! and NASA. Following behind MySQL is PostgreSQL (http://www.postgresql.org), Firebird (http://firebird.sourceforge.net), which is a fork of Borland's Interbase 6.0 during its short stint as an open-sourced database. MaxDB (http://www.mysql.com/products/maxdb) is an enhanced version of the former SAP DB (SAP AG's Open Source database).

PostgreSQL, Firebird, and MaxDB all cover a broader portion of the SQL-92 standard than MySQL does, and they offer more enterprise features such as stored procedures, triggers, distributed 2-phase commit (2PC) support, among other features. MySQL offers great speed (provides RAM tables), which makes it suitable for e-commerce websites, where most data is read. All four databases are supported by JBoss and provided under the docs/examples/jca directory of the JBoss distribution (3.2.X), where you'll find -ds.xml files for each of them. The procedure for using these databases is similar to the steps taken to enable the use of the McKoi and hsqldb databases.

For a fine-grained, feature-by-feature comparison you can use the MySQL online tool located at http://www.mysql.com/information/crash-me.php.

Java Object-Oriented Database Management System

In Chapter 7 we cover some of the intricacies of object-relational mapping. If you work with objects and are using a relational database you'll have to deal with mapping sooner or later. The more complex and rich your object model becomes, the more complex the mapping between it and a relational database will be. The ORM tools covered in Chapter 7, as an implied goal, have to sit between your object model and a relational database by providing your objects with an interface for persistence that, for all intents and purposes, isn't any different from an OODBMS.

In Chapter 7 you'll also read about orthogonal persistence (also called transparent persistence), which is the idea that at the code level, you deal with a system that knows objects only, and that you shouldn't need to be very aware of the fact that some objects are persistent and some others are transient. Although this isn't completely the case with either OODBMS or ORM tools, their APIs provide a natural extension for persistence in an object-oriented environment. ORM tools ease the object-relational impedance mismatch although OODBMS completely make it disappear. Without the layer of convoluted JDBC code embedded in your object models, or the maintenance of OR mappings required for ORM tools you gain the following:

- **Ease of development:** A reduction of complexity in your development process by making object persistence a natural feature of the system.

- **Performance:** A common misconception is that OODBMSs are naturally slower and less scalable that RDBMSs. In reality, given the right application, an OODBMS can be much more efficient than an RDBMS.

- **Integration:** Just like a CORBA ORB can provide access to remote objects, an OODBMS can serve as a repository of active objects in a system composed of many applications.

- **Simplicity:** Complex data is better handled by an object database. Many-to-many relationships are dealt with naturally, without normalization. Traversing an object hierarchy is much easier and efficient than in the relational model.

The relational model is simple and elegant but it's fundamentally different from the object model. As the complexity of applications increase, a good object model calls for fine-grained objects. For such highly complex object models, an OODBMS can provide ease of development (no data mapping), better performance, and scalability. OODBMS can provide features such as fast navigation and retrieval of information, versioning, and support for long transactions.

The ODMG Standard

Interest in OODBMS prompted the formation in 1991 of the Object Database Management Group (ODMG), which comprised most major OODBMS vendors at the time. The last version of the standard was specified in 1999 and it's referred to as ODMG 3.0. The ODMG standard defines an Object Definition Language (ODL), an Object Query Language (OQL), and language mappings. The JDO specification is the replacement or continuation for the Java language mappings work started by the ODMG.

TIP A possible low-risk entry point for an OODBMS in your enterprise application is the storage of session state information. Object databases make excellent middle-tier databases for use by EJBs or servlets. An e-commerce architecture using an object database for session state will likely provide better performance and reliability than if no database or a relational database was used instead.

Ozone Object-Oriented Database

The Ozone Database project (http://www.ozone-db.org) is a pure-Java OODBMS distributed under the GNU GPL/LGPL licenses (GPL for the core database engine and LGPL for the access API). The Ozone Database project started as a research project by Falko Braeutigam and is rapidly evolving into a full-fledged OODBMS. Ozone provides a multithreaded, multiuser, transactional, cached and clustered database environment that provides both an ODMG 3.0 interface as well as a native API to store and retrieve Java objects, binary large objects (BLOBs), and XML documents. Ozone integrates with J2EE environments by providing JTA/XA support and JMX-based management of services. It provides fine-grained access rights (at the object level), deadlock recognition, garbage collection, and an advanced collections API with support for lazy loading using dynamic proxies.

Ozone uses a central activation architecture in which objects never physically leave the database but are manipulated by reference with proxy objects using Ozone RMI (Ozone's version of Remote Method Invocation) in conjunction with Java serialization and runtime reflection, which makes persistence as transparent as possible. This architecture is better suited for application where the state of the objects is constantly being modified by client applications because only the data for the specific mutating operation needs to be transported over the wire.

Ozone works by storing the root object (referred to as "named objects") of an object graph, from which you can, by using normal Java constructs, navigate and retrieve related objects. Because Ozone uses Java serialization and RMI, your objects (at least the Ozone-aware implementations) need to implement and extend certain Ozone classes and interfaces. Ozone promotes that persistence logic should be executed in the database server to reduce the network overhead, which is similar to Entity Beans being fronted by a Session Facade. For an object to be stored in Ozone it must provide an interface that extends the Ozone remote interface (org.ozoneDB.OzoneRemote) and an implementation of said interface that extends the Ozone remote object (org.ozoneDB.OzoneObject, which implements java.io.Serializable). After compiling your classes, the Ozone Post Processor (OPP) is used to create stubs for the remote objects. Ozone RMI uses a remote object's stub class as a proxy in clients so that clients can manipulate a particular database object. By working with the remote interface, the code that's manipulating an Ozone object is unaware that it's dealing with a persistent object.

Download Ozone

In this chapter you'll be using version 1.2-alpha of the Ozone DB, which can be obtained from the project's download page at http://sourceforge.net/projects/ozone (at the SourceForge project page). The Ozone distribution is available in both source and binary forms. For the JBoss examples in this chapter you'll need the binary distribution contained in the ozone-1.2-alpha-bin.zip file. Download the file and unzip the contents to a suitable location such as c:\java\ozone-1.2.

Embedding Ozone DB as a JBoss Service

For Ozone to work inside of JBoss you need to compile the provided Ozone MBean (org.ozoneDB.embed.jboss.OzoneService) and deploy it as a JBoss service archive (SAR). A JBoss SAR file contains a JBoss service definition (jboss-service.xml) and its associated files.

 NOTE   A SAR file is a JAR archive with the extension .sar. They are specific to JBoss and aren't part of the J2EE specification.

The Ozone distribution provides a complete Java project that packages and deploys the SAR file to your local JBoss server. This project is contained under the thirdparty\jboss directory of the Ozone distribution.

 TIP   Under the Ozone JBoss MBean project directory (thirdparty\jboss) the Ozone project distributes some of the JBoss JARs that are needed to compile the MBean. These JARs are located under the thirdparty\jboss\lib directory. We recommend that you overwrite these JARs with the JARs from your JBoss distribution to avoid any class incompatibilities. The JARs that need to be updated are jboss-system.jar, jboss-common.jar, jboss-jmx.jar, and jboss.jar. The first three can be found under the lib directory of the JBoss distribution, and jboss.jar is found in the server/{JBOSS_SERVER}/lib directory (in the case of the TCMS system that directory resolves to server/tcms/lib).

At the root of the thirdparty\jboss directory you'll find an Ant build script. On the command line, use the now familiar projecthelp Ant command-line switch to discover the available Targets, as follows:

```
ant -projecthelp
```

This should produce output similar to the following:

```
Buildfile: build.xml

Main targets:

Other targets:

 compile
 deploy
 package
 prepare
Default target: deploy
```

 CAUTION The Ant script for the Ozone JBoss integration assumes that you're using the source distribution of OZONE and therefore looks for the OZONE libraries in the server/build/lib directory. In the binary distribution these files are located under the lib directory at the root of the distribution. Therefore, for the Ant build to work you would need to change the value of the Ant property server.lib.dir from ../../ server/build/lib to ../../lib.

As you can see from the output of the Ant projecthelp command the default target is deployed, which on further examination of the Ant script, uses the JBOSS_HOME environment property to deploy the packaged file to the deploy directory of the "default" JBoss server. If you're using the tcms server (or any server besides "default") you'll have to execute the package target instead and manually copy the file to the deploy directory of the tcms server (or you can change the Ant script to use the "tcms" server rather than the default). To package the OZONE JBoss SAR file type, enter the following:

```
ant package
```

The output of the Ant script should resemble the following:

```
Buildfile: build.xml

prepare:
   [delete] Deleting directory C:\java\ozone-1.2-alpha\thirdparty\jboss\dist
    [mkdir] Created dir: C:\java\ozone-1.2-alpha\thirdparty\jboss\dist
```

```
compile:
    [javac] Compiling 2 source files to C:\java\ozone-1.2-
alpha\thirdparty\jboss\build

package:
     [jar] Building jar: C:\java\ozone-1.2-
alpha\thirdparty\jboss\dist\ozoneService.sar

BUILD SUCCESSFUL
Total time: 5 seconds
```

After running the Ant script, a directory named dist under the thirdparty\jboss is created. In this directory you'll find the SAR file ozoneService.sar. To deploy the service simply copy the file to the deploy directory of the tcms JBoss server. The output of the deployment should resemble the following:

```
00:59:45,914 INFO  [MainDeployer] Starting deployment of package:
    file:/C:/java/jboss/jboss-3.2.1/server/tcms/deploy/ozoneService.sar
...
00:59:50,070 INFO  [OzoneService] Creating
00:59:50,070 INFO  [OzoneService] Created
00:59:50,120 INFO  [OzoneService] Starting
00:59:50,120 INFO  [OzoneService] Ozone ObjectServer - Starting up...
00:59:50,120 INFO  [OzoneService]
    ** Starting Database in C:\java\jboss\jboss-3.2.1\server\tcms/db/OzoneDB **
00:59:50,320 INFO  [OzoneService]        No DB found, creating new Database...
...
00:59:50,671 INFO  [Env] Ozone version 1.2-alpha
...
00:59:53,765 INFO  [GarbageCollector] startup...
...
00:59:53,765 INFO  [KeyGenerator] startup...
...
00:59:53,785 INFO  [ClassManager] startup...
...
00:59:53,795 INFO  [UserManager] startup...
00:59:53,795 INFO  [UserManager] admin user: Brian Sam-Bodden
...
00:59:53,925 INFO  [TransactionManager] startup...
...
00:59:54,086 INFO  [WizardStore] startup...
...
00:59:54,086 INFO  [WizardStore] checking for pending shadow clusters...
...
```

```
00:59:54,166 INFO  [AdminManager] startup...
...
00:59:54,196 INFO  [AdminManager] No admin object found. Initializing...
...
00:59:54,396 INFO  [OzoneService] ** Database ready **
...
00:59:54,406 INFO  [OzoneService] Started
00:59:54,426 INFO  [MainDeployer] Deployed package:
    file:/C:/java/jboss/jboss-3.2.1/server/tcms/deploy/ozoneService.sar
```

You can check the deployment of the Ozone service by using the JBoss JMX console Agent view as shown in Figure 6-8.

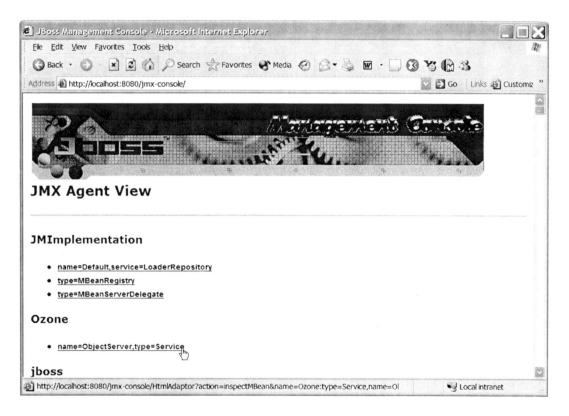

Figure 6-8. The Ozone service in the JBoss console

Clicking the hyperlink name=ObjectServer,type=Service will take you to the MBean view where you can start and stop the Ozone service as shown in Figure 6-9, which might come in handy during the testing stages of your application.

Figure 6-9. The Ozone service MBean view

Exploring the Database with the Ozone AdminGui

Now that you have an Ozone database running you can use the included
AdminGui to manage and browse the contents of the database. The AdminGui
application is contained in the ozoneAdminGui-0.1.jar JAR file, which is located
in the lib directory of the Ozone distribution. A Windows batch file as well as a

UNIX shell script is provided in the bin directory. To launch the application (in Windows) change directories to the Ozone bin directory and enter the following:

```
ozoneAdminGui
```

On the console you should see the following message:

```
Starting AdminGui ....
```

The AdminGui application should now be running, as shown in Figure 6-10.

 CAUTION In the 1.2-alpha distribution of the Ozone DB the batch file AdminGui.bat doesn't work. Instead you can use the following command line at the root of the Ozone distribution directory: java -cp "lib/ozoneAdminGui-0.1.jar;lib/ozoneServer-1.2-alpha.jar;lib/ log4j-1.2.jar" org.ozoneDB.adminGui.main.AdminGui.

Figure 6-10. The Ozone DB AdminGui tool

The AdminGui connect dialog box has a field where you must enter the database URL, which defaults to a remote Ozone DB running on the local host at the default port (ozonedb:remote://localhost:3333). Because the Ozone DB running under JBoss is running in local mode you would need to change the URL to point to the directory where the DB is running. In the case of the tcms JBoss server at C:/java/jboss/jboss-3.2.1/server/tcms/ the correct local URL would be ozonedb:local://C:/java/jboss/jboss-3.2.1/server/tcms/db/OzoneDB.

From the AdminGui you have three main areas of functionality:

- **Accounts:** Allows you to create database accounts as well as list database groups and database users.

- **Server:** Allows you to monitor transactions on the server, force the Ozone garbage collector, or shut down the database server.

- **Data:** Allows you see a list of all named (root) objects, and provides functions to back up and restore a database to and from a file.

At startup on an empty database, the only named object you should see (by selecting Data ➤ named objects) is the ozonedb.admin object as shown in Figure 6-11.

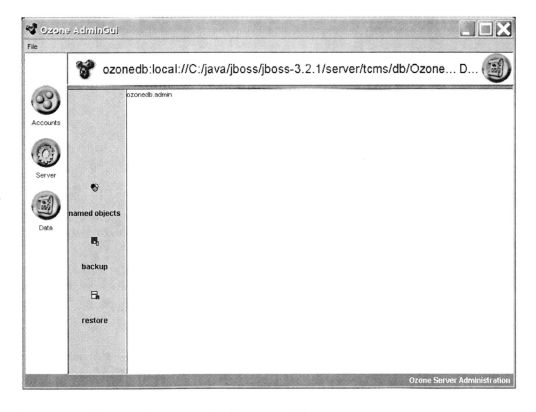

Figure 6-11. Ozone DB named object in an empty database

Session Bean Ozone Project

Now that you have the Ozone DB integrated and deployed as a JBoss service, it's time to write a J2EE application to use with the database. As you did in Chapter 5, you'll use the domain objects Conference and ConferenceTrack. You'll create two plain old Java objects (POJOs), one for Conference and one for Tracks and use Ozone to store them.

Before coding begins you need a suitable project structure. Like the EJB CMP examples shown in Chapter 5, Figure 6.12 shows the directory structure of the Ozone/JBoss project (the complete project is available from the download site).

Figure 6-12. Ozone/JBoss project directory structure

The steps to create a typical Ozone/JBoss application are as follows:

- **Remote interfaces:** Create the remote interfaces for each one of your business objects (which the POJOs will implement). This interface needs to extend the org.ozoneDB.OzoneRemote interface.

- **POJOs:** For each remote interface, create a POJO that implements the remote interface and extends the org.ozoneDB.OzoneObject class.

- **DTOs:** Data transfer objects are a flexible way to provide a "client" view of the database. Well-designed DTOs can provide semantically rich objects as return types for a service, and they can minimize network round-trips and provide client-side validation.

- **DatabaseManager:** The DatabaseManager class represents your persistence logic. It's the only class that will directly deal with Ozone persistence APIs. This class will represent the root of your application's object hierarchy as well as the facade for all database operations.

- **Session Facade:** A stateless Session Bean will provide business logic and will become the database client (just like a CMP EJB is the client to a relational database). All J2EE clients interact with your database objects through the Session Bean Facade, thereby isolating your data and providing a deterministic point of control.

The next few sections will walk you through the development of an Ozone/JBoss sample application.

Creating the Remote Interfaces

For the example you'll create two interfaces in the package com.ejdoab.pojos: Conference and Track. A Conference can contain a collection of Track objects.

The code for the Conference class is shown here:

```
package com.ejdoab.pojos;

import java.util.Date;
import java.util.List;

import org.ozoneDB.OzoneRemote;

public interface Conference extends OzoneRemote {
    // getters
    public String getName();
    public String getDescription();
    public Date getStartDate();
    public Date getEndDate();
    public Date getAbstractSubmissionStartDate();
    public Date getAbstractSubmissionEndDate();
    public List getTracks();
    // setters / mutators
    public void setName(String value); /*update*/
    public void setDescription(String value); /*update*/
    public void setStartDate(Date value); /*update*/
    public void setEndDate(Date value); /*update*/
    public void setAbstractSubmissionStartDate(Date value); /*update*/
    public void setAbstractSubmissionEndDate(Date value); /*update*/
    public void addTrack(Track track); /*update*/
    public void deleteTrack(String name); /*update*/
}
```

The first thing to notice is that every method signature of a method that changes the object is followed by the comment /*update*/. These comments are used by the OPP tool to determine which methods in the generated proxies need to be part of a transaction.

The code for the Track interface is similar to that of the Conference interface, as shown here:

```
package com.ejdoab.pojos;

import org.ozoneDB.OzoneRemote;

public interface Track extends OzoneRemote {
    // getters
    public String getDescription();
    public String getSubTitle();
    public String getTitle();
    // setters
    public void setDescription(String value); /*update*/
    public void setSubTitle(String value); /*update*/
    public void setTitle(String value); /*update*/
}
```

Creating Data Transfer Objects

DTOs will be used as the transport mechanism for data in and out of a Session Facade. Typically, your DTOs will represent a "client" view of the data, which is structured in a way to make the client's work easier and more efficient. In the case of the example at hand the DTOs are merely POJOs with identical method signatures, as the remote interfaces previously defined.

All DTOs for the sample application will be placed in the com.ejdoab.dto package. The code for ConferenceDTO is shown here:

```
package com.ejdoab.dto;

import java.io.Serializable;
import java.util.ArrayList;
import java.util.Date;
import java.util.Iterator;
import java.util.List;

import com.ejdoab.pojos.Conference;
import com.ejdoab.pojos.Track;
```

```
public class ConferenceDTO implements Serializable {
    protected String _name;
    protected String _description;
    protected Date _startDate;
    protected Date _endDate;
    protected Date _abstractSubmissionStartDate;
    protected Date _abstractSubmissionEndDate;
    protected List _tracks;

    //
    // constructors
    //

    private ConferenceDTO() {
        _tracks = new ArrayList();
    }

    public ConferenceDTO(
        String name,
        String description,
        Date startDate,
        Date endDate,
        Date abstractSubmissionStartDate,
        Date abstractSubmissionEndDate) {
        this();
        _name = name;
        _description = description;
        _startDate = startDate;
        _endDate = endDate;
        _abstractSubmissionStartDate = abstractSubmissionStartDate;
        _abstractSubmissionEndDate = abstractSubmissionEndDate;
    }

    public ConferenceDTO(Conference conference) {
        this();
        _name = conference.getName();
        _description = conference.getDescription();
        _startDate = conference.getStartDate();
        _endDate = conference.getEndDate();
        _abstractSubmissionStartDate =
conference.getAbstractSubmissionStartDate();
        _abstractSubmissionEndDate = conference.getAbstractSubmissionEndDate();
```

```java
        for (Iterator i = conference.getTracks().iterator(); i.hasNext();) {
            Track track = (Track) i.next();
            _tracks.add(new TrackDTO(track));
        }
    }

    //
    // getters
    //

    public String getName() {
        return _name;
    }

    public String getDescription() {
        return _description;
    }

    public Date getStartDate() {
        return _startDate;
    }

    public Date getEndDate() {
        return _endDate;
    }

    public Date getAbstractSubmissionStartDate() {
        return _abstractSubmissionStartDate;
    }

    public Date getAbstractSubmissionEndDate() {
        return _abstractSubmissionEndDate;
    }

    public List getTracks() {
        return _tracks;
    }

    //
    // setters
    //
```

```java
public void setName(String value) {
    _name = value;
}

public void setDescription(String value) {
    _description = value;
}

public void setStartDate(Date value) {
    _startDate = value;
}

public void setEndDate(Date value) {
    _endDate = value;
}

public void setAbstractSubmissionStartDate(Date value) {
    _abstractSubmissionStartDate = value;
}

public void setAbstractSubmissionEndDate(Date value) {
    _abstractSubmissionEndDate = value;
}

public void addTrack(TrackDTO track) {
    _tracks.add(track);
}

public void deleteTrack(String name) {
    if (_tracks != null) {
        for (Iterator i = _tracks.iterator(); i.hasNext();) {
            Conference old = (Conference) i.next();
            if (old.getName().equalsIgnoreCase(name)) {
                _tracks.remove(old);
            }
        }
    }
}

//
// utility
//
```

```
        public String toString() {
            return new StringBuffer()
                .append("[Conference] name = ")
                .append(_name != null ? _name : "n/a")
                .append(", description = ")
                .append(_description != null ? _description : "n/a")
                .append(", start date = ")
                .append(_startDate != null ? _startDate.toString() : "n/a")
                .append(", end date = ")
                .append(_endDate != null ? _endDate.toString() : "n/a")
                .append(", # tracks = ")
                .append(_tracks != null ? _tracks.size() : 0)
                .toString();
        }
}
```

As you can see, the signature of ConferenceDTO is identical to that of the remote interface Conference. The DTO also provides a constructor that takes an instance of Conference to populate itself. This is an alternative approach to the one taken in Chapter 5 when you used a DTOFactory to create DTOs from business objects and vice versa. Notice that the ConferenceDTO contains a list of TrackDTOs, thereby mimicking the structure in Conference (and ConferenceImpl, which you'll see in the next section).

The code shown here for the TrackDTO is equally simple:

```
package com.ejdoab.dto;

import java.io.Serializable;

import com.ejdoab.pojos.Track;

public class TrackDTO implements Serializable {

    protected String _title;
    protected String _subTitle;
    protected String _description;
    protected Integer _conferenceId;

    //
    // constructors
    //
```

```
public TrackDTO(String title, String subTitle, String description) {
    _title = title;
    _subTitle = subTitle;
    _description = description;
}

public TrackDTO(Track track) {
    _title = track.getTitle();
    _subTitle = track.getSubTitle();
    _description = track.getDescription();
}

//
// getters
//

public String getDescription() {
    return _description;
}

public String getSubTitle() {
    return _subTitle;
}

public String getTitle() {
    return _title;
}

//
// setters
//

public void setDescription(String value) {
    _description = value;
}

public void setSubTitle(String value) {
    _subTitle = value;
}

public void setTitle(String value) {
    _title = value;
}
```

```
        public String toString() {
            return new StringBuffer()
                        .append("[Track] title = ")
                        .append(_title != null ? _title : "n/a")
                        .append(", subTitle = ")
                        .append(_subTitle != null ? _subTitle : "n/a")
                        .append(", description = ")
                        .append(_description != null ? _description : "n/a")
                        .toString();
        }
}
```

NOTE Notice that the DTO doesn't directly implement the remote interface because that would introduce dependencies on Ozone in the client side and it wouldn't work in the case of using an Ozone LocalDatabase as in the JBoss example. This is because proxies cannot be passed from a LocalDatabase environment to an external client.

Creating the POJOs

The Ozone-ready implementations of the business interfaces extend the org.ozoneDB.OzoneObject class, which makes them database (server-side, persistent) objects. The OzoneObject class provides a default implementation of the OzoneCompatible interface, which binds the object to the database for life-cycle management.

The code for the ConferenceImpl is shown here:

```
package com.ejdoab.pojos;

import java.util.ArrayList;
import java.util.Date;
import java.util.Iterator;
import java.util.List;

import org.ozoneDB.OzoneObject;

import com.ejdoab.dto.*;
```

```
public class ConferenceImpl extends OzoneObject implements Conference {
    /**
     * set the serialization version to make it compatible
     * with new class versions
     */
    public static final long serialVersionUID = 1L;

    protected String _name;
    protected String _description;
    protected Date _startDate;
    protected Date _endDate;
    protected Date _abstractSubmissionStartDate;
    protected Date _abstractSubmissionEndDate;
    protected List _tracks;

    //
    // constructors
    //

    public ConferenceImpl() {
        _tracks = new ArrayList();
    }

    public ConferenceImpl(
        String name,
        String description,
        Date startDate,
        Date endDate,
        Date abstractSubmissionStartDate,
        Date abstractSubmissionEndDate) {
        this();
        ...
    }

    public ConferenceImpl(ConferenceDTO conference) {
        this();
        _name = conference.getName();
        _description = conference.getDescription();
        _startDate = conference.getStartDate();
        _endDate = conference.getEndDate();
        _abstractSubmissionStartDate =
            conference.getAbstractSubmissionStartDate();
        _abstractSubmissionEndDate = conference.getAbstractSubmissionEndDate();
```

```
        for (Iterator i = conference.getTracks().iterator(); i.hasNext();) {
            TrackDTO track = (TrackDTO) i.next();
            _tracks.add(new TrackImpl(track));
        }
    }

    //
    // getters
    //

    ...

    //
    // setters
    //

    ...

    public void addTrack(Track track) {
        _tracks.add(track);
    }

    public void deleteTrack(String name) {
        if (_tracks != null) {
            for (Iterator i = _tracks.iterator(); i.hasNext();) {
                Conference old = (Conference) i.next();
                if (old.getName().equalsIgnoreCase(name)) {
                    _tracks.remove(old);
                }
            }
        }
    }

    //
    // utility
    //

    public String toString() {
        ...
    }
}
```

Notice that at the beginning of the class serialVersionUID is set to the value 1L. Because Ozone uses Java serialization, it's important to set the serialVersionUID to a unique value so that the objects stored in the server and those that are being manipulated in the client are compatible (because compiling a Java class generates a new serialVersionUID if one isn't explicitly set).

The addTrack and deleteTrack methods are provided to add and remove a Track object from a given Conference object. Also, a constructor is provided to create a ConferenceImpl, given a ConferenceDTO. The TrackImpl class implementing the Track interface follows the same pattern, except that because it doesn't hold any depended objects it's actually simpler than the ConferenceImpl class, as shown here:

```
package com.ejdoab.pojos;

import org.ozoneDB.OzoneObject;

import com.ejdoab.dto.TrackDTO;

public class TrackImpl extends OzoneObject implements Track {
    /**
     * set the serialization version to make it compatible
     * with new class versions
     */
    public static final long serialVersionUID = 1L;

    protected String _title;
    protected String _subTitle;
    protected String _description;
    protected Integer _conferenceId;

    //
    // constructors
    //

    public TrackImpl() {
    }

    public TrackImpl(String title, String subTitle, String description) {
        ...
    }
```

```
public TrackImpl(TrackDTO track) {
    _title = track.getTitle();
    _subTitle = track.getSubTitle();
    _description = track.getDescription();
}

//
// getters
//
...

//
// setters
//
...

//
// utility
//

public String toString() {
    ...
}
}
```

Persistence Logic

To manage a collection of Conferences and provide create, read, update, and delete (CRUD) operations you'll need a database object to serve as the entry point for your persistence-logic operations. This object will become the root object of your hierarchy of objects in Ozone (a named object).

Like the two previous database objects (Conference and Track) the ConferencesManager provides a remote interface and an implementation. Because it's a good idea to separate the persistence logic from the business logic, the ConferencesManager interface and implementation are placed in the com.ejdoab.db package. The ConferencesManager will provide the entry point into the database for the Session Facade, as follows:

```
package com.ejdoab.db;

import java.util.Collection;
import org.ozoneDB.OzoneRemote;
import com.ejdoab.dto.ConferenceDTO;

public interface ConferencesManager extends OzoneRemote {
    // getters
    public ConferenceDTO getConferenceByName(String name);
    public Collection getAllConferences();

    // setters / mutators
    public void addOrUpdateConference(ConferenceDTO conference); /*update*/
    public boolean deleteConference(String name), /*update*/
    public boolean deleteAllConferences(); /*update*/
}
```

The ConferencesManager provides several methods for retrieving one or more Conference objects as well as methods for adding and deleting one or all Conferences. Internally, the list of Conferences is kept in a Java List. Notice that the implementation of the ConferencesManager interface enforces a persistence-logic rule by enabling only uniquely named Conferences to be stored. The implementation of the ConferencesManager is shown here:

```
package com.ejdoab.db;

import java.util.ArrayList;
import java.util.Collection;
import java.util.Iterator;
import java.util.List;

import org.ozoneDB.OzoneInterface;
import org.ozoneDB.OzoneObject;

import com.ejdoab.dto.ConferenceDTO;
import com.ejdoab.pojos.Conference;
import com.ejdoab.pojos.ConferenceImpl;

public class ConferencesManagerImpl
    extends OzoneObject
    implements ConferencesManager {
```

```
/**
 * set the serialization version to make it compatible
 * with new class versions
 */
public static final long serialVersionUID = 1L;

private List conferences;

//
// factory method
// (to avoid the chicken-egg problem when building the app)
//
public static ConferencesManager create(OzoneInterface db) {
    return (ConferencesManager) db.createObject(
                                ConferencesManagerImpl.class,
                                OzoneInterface.Public,
                                ConferencesManager.class.getName()
                            );
}

//
// constructors
//
public ConferencesManagerImpl() {
    conferences = new ArrayList();
}

//
// getters
//

public ConferenceDTO getConferenceByName(String name) {
    ConferenceDTO result = null;

    for (Iterator i = conferences.iterator(); i.hasNext();) {
        Conference conference = (Conference) i.next();
        if (conference.getName().equalsIgnoreCase(name)) {
            result = new ConferenceDTO(conference);
        }
    }

    return result;
}
```

```java
    public Collection getAllConferences() {
        return conferences;
    }


    //
    // setters
    //
    public void addOrUpdateConference(ConferenceDTO conference) {
        if (conference.getName() != null) {
            for (Iterator i = conferences.iterator(); i.hasNext();) {
                Conference old = (Conference) i.next();
                if (old.getName().equalsIgnoreCase(conference.getName())) {
                    conferences.remove(old);
                }
            }
            conferences.add(new ConferenceImpl(conference));
        }
    }


    public void removeConferences() {
        conferences.clear();
    }


    public boolean deleteConference(String name) {
        Conference target = null;
        for (Iterator i = conferences.iterator(); i.hasNext();) {
            Conference conference = (Conference) i.next();
            if (conference.getName().equalsIgnoreCase(name)) {
                target = conference;
            }
        }
        return conferences.remove(target);
    }


    public boolean deleteAllConferences() {
        conferences.clear();
        return conferences.isEmpty();
    }
}
```

The only method of particular interest is the static factory create method, which takes an instance of an OzoneInterface as a parameter. This method's purpose is to construct a ConferencesManager object, which is bound to the database. As mentioned before, the OPP generates a comprehensive factory class, so technically this method isn't required, but in order for the application build process to have a single compilation target, this method should be added here because it will be used in the Session Facade. Otherwise the Session Facade would have to be compiled after the OPP target, which needs to happen before compilation of the classes in the pojos and dto packages.

Creating the Session Facade

To work with the Ozone database you'll use a stateless Session Bean that will provide services to manipulate the Conferences and Track objects in the database using their peer DTOs. The com.ejdoab.beans.ConferenceOzoneFacadeBean will provide the following methods:

- ConferenceDTO getConferenceByName(String name)

- Collection getAllConferences

- void addOrUpdateConference(ConferenceDTO dto)

- boolean deleteConference(String name)

- boolean deleteAllConferences()

As you learned in Chapter 5, you'll use XDoclet to automate the creation of the EJB glue files. A private field will hold an instance of OzoneInterface, which is looked up using JNDI in the Bean's ejbCreate method. The OzoneInterface is then used to find (or create if it doesn't exist) the named object stored under the com.ejdoab.db.ConferencesManager name, as shown here:

```
package com.ejdoab.beans;

import java.util.ArrayList;
import java.util.Collection;
import java.util.Collections;
import java.util.Iterator;
import java.util.List;

import javax.ejb.CreateException;
import javax.ejb.EJBException;
import javax.ejb.SessionBean;
import javax.naming.Context;
import javax.naming.InitialContext;
import javax.naming.NamingException;
```

```
import org.ozoneDB.OzoneInterface;

import com.ejdoab.db.ConferencesManager;
import com.ejdoab.db.ConferencesManagerImpl;
import com.ejdoab.dto.ConferenceDTO;
import com.ejdoab.pojos.Conference;

/**
 * @ejb.bean
 *      name="ConferenceOzoneFacade"
 *      type="Stateless"
 *      view-type="both"
 *      jndi-name="ejb.ConferenceOzoneFacadeHome"
 *      local-jndi-name="ejb.ConferenceOzoneFacadeLocalHome"
 * @ejb.transaction
 *      type="Required"
 * @ejb.util
 *      generate="physical"
 */
public abstract class ConferenceOzoneFacadeBean implements SessionBean {

    private OzoneInterface db;
    private ConferencesManager conferencesManager;

    //
    // business methods
    //

    /**
     * @ejb.interface-method
     * @ejb.transaction
     *      type="NotSupported"
     */
    public ConferenceDTO getConferenceByName(String name) {
        ConferenceDTO result = null;
        if (conferencesManager != null) {
            result = conferencesManager.getConferenceByName(name);
        }
        return result;
    }
```

```
/**
 * @ejb.interface-method
 * @ejb.transaction
 *      type="NotSupported"
 */
public Collection getAllConferences() {
    List results = Collections.EMPTY_LIST;
    if (conferencesManager != null) {
        Collection allConferences = conferencesManager.getAllConferences();
        if (!allConferences.isEmpty()) {
            results = new ArrayList(allConferences.size());
            for (Iterator iter = allConferences.iterator();
                iter.hasNext();
                ) {
                Conference conference = (Conference) iter.next();
                // return a DTO instead of a proxy object,
                // we don't want clients to have
                // direct access to the database objects
                results.add(new ConferenceDTO(conference));
            }
        }
    }
    return results;
}


/**
 * @ejb.interface-method
 * @ejb.transaction
 *      type="NotSupported"
 */
public void addOrUpdateConference(ConferenceDTO dto) {
    if (conferencesManager != null) {
        conferencesManager.addOrUpdateConference(dto);
    }
}


/**
 * @ejb.interface-method
 * @ejb.transaction
 *      type="NotSupported"
 */
```

```java
public boolean deleteConference(String name) {
    boolean result = false;
    if (conferencesManager != null) {
        result = conferencesManager.deleteConference(name);
    }
    return result;
}


/**
 * @ejb.interface-method
 * @ejb.transaction
 *       type="NotSupported"
 */
public boolean deleteAllConferences() {
    boolean result = false;
    if (conferencesManager != null) {
        result = conferencesManager.deleteAllConferences();
    }
    return result;
}


//==========================================
//  EJB callbacks
//==========================================


/**
 * @ejb.create-method
 */
public void ejbCreate() throws CreateException {
    Context context = null;
    // Lookup the Ozone DB Interface
    try
    {
        context = new InitialContext();
        db = (OzoneInterface) new InitialContext()
            .lookup(OzoneInterface.class.getName());
        conferencesManager = (ConferencesManager) db
            .objectForName(ConferencesManager.class.getName());
        if (conferencesManager == null) {
            conferencesManager = ConferencesManagerImpl.create(db);
        }
```

```
        } catch (NamingException e) {
            throw new EJBException(e);
        } catch (Exception e) {
            throw new EJBException(e);
        }
    }


    public void ejbActivate() {
        try {
            db = (OzoneInterface) new InitialContext()
                .lookup(OzoneInterface.class.getName());
            db.reloadClasses();
        } catch (Exception e) {
            throw new EJBException(e);
        }
    }


    public void ejbPassivate() {
        db = null;
    }


    public void ejbPostCreate() throws CreateException {}
}
```

Notice that the connection to the database is managed via the EJB callback methods ejbCreate, ejbActivate, and ejbPassivate. In ejbCreate an OzoneInterface (to the database) is looked up using JNDI. The OzoneInterface is used to locate the instance of ConferencesManager, which is bound to the database under the name com.ejdoab.db.ConferencesManager (the result of using ConferencesManager.class.getName method). If the object isn't found then it's created using the factory method in ConferencesManagerImpl. In ejbActivate the ConferenceManager is retrieved again and the classes are reloaded using the reloadClasses method.

The Session Bean business methods in turn use the instance of ConferencesManager to perform their functions.

Putting It All Together with Ant

Let's walk through the Ant build script that will accomplish the build tasks required for the example. The build script is located at the root of the project directory. A sample of the build.properties file shown here has a section that defines the ejb-jar that will be generated. It also has a section for the JBoss-specific settings (refer to Chapter 5 for JBoss configuration instructions), and finally, it has a section that defines the location of the Ozone distribution.

```
// app
jar-name=ozone-jboss-test.jar

// jboss specific
jboss.home=c:/java/jboss/jboss-3.2.1
jboss.server=tcms
java.naming.factory.initial=org.jnp.interfaces.NamingContextFactory
java.naming.provider.url=jnp://localhost:1099

// OZONE specific
OZONE_HOME=c:/java/ozone-1.2-alpha
```

The first section of the script deals with loading and configuring the build properties:

```xml
<?xml version="1.0"?>
<project name="ozone-jboss" default="all" basedir=".">

    <!-- ================================================================= -->
    <!-- Configures Project's Properties                                   -->
    <!-- ================================================================= -->
    <property file="build.properties"/>
    <property name="server-dir"
              location="${jboss.home}/server/${jboss.server}" />
    <property name="server-lib-dir"  location="${server-dir}/lib" />
    <property name="server-conf-dir" location="${server-dir}/conf" />
    <property name="server-client-dir"  location="${jboss.home}/client" />
    <property name="deploy-dir"      location="${server-dir}/deploy" />

    <property name="root" location="${basedir}" />
    <property name="src" location="${root}/src/java" />
    <property name="classes" location="${root}/classes" />
    <property name="generated" location="${root}/generated" />
    <property name="generated-ejb" location="${generated}/ejb-src" />
    <property name="generated-ozone" location="${generated}/ozone-src" />
    <property name="descriptors-ejb" location="${generated}/descriptors/ejb" />
    <property name="dist" location="${root}/dist" />
    <property name="conf" location="${root}/conf" />
    <property name="build" location="${root}/build" />

    <property name="lib" location="lib" />
    <property name="lib-dev" location="${lib}/development" />
```

Next, several path elements are created for all the project dependencies, including Ozone, JBoss, and XDoclet. Notice that throughout the build you make use of the ${jboss.home} and ${OZONE _HOME} properties. Both of these properties are defined in the build.properties file.

```
<!-- ================================================================= -->
<!-- Configures the ClassPath                                          -->
<!-- ================================================================= -->
<path id="class.path">
    <fileset dir="lib">
        <include name="*.jar"/>
    </fileset>
    <fileset dir="${server-lib-dir}">
        <include name="*servlet.jar"/>
    </fileset>
    <fileset dir="${server-client-dir}">
        <include name="jbossall-client.jar"/>
    </fileset>
    <pathelement location="${classes}" />
</path>

<path id="xdoclet.class.path">
    <path refid="class.path"/>
    <fileset dir="${lib-dev}/xdoclet">
        <include name="*.jar"/>
    </fileset>
</path>

<path id="ozone.class.path">
    <path refid="xdoclet.class.path"/>
    <fileset dir="${OZONE_HOME}/lib">
        <include name="*.jar"/>
    </fileset>
</path>
```

The taskdefs for the XDoclet ejbdoclet are loaded and the tasks for preparing and cleaning the project directories are provided. The Ozone distribution provides an Ant task to execute OPP. The task class is OPPTask and it's contained in the org.ozoneDB.tools.OPP directory. In the script you'll load the task under the name oppdoclet, as shown here:

```
<!-- ================================================================= -->
<!-- Declare taskdefs                                                  -->
<!-- ================================================================= -->
<taskdef
    name="ejbdoclet"
    classname="xdoclet.modules.ejb.EjbDocletTask"
    classpathref="xdoclet.class.path"
    />

<taskdef
    name="oppdoclet"
    classname="org.ozoneDB.tools.OPP.OPPTask"
    classpathref="ozone.class.path"
    />


<!-- ================================================================= -->
<!-- Prepares the directory structure                                  -->
<!-- ================================================================= -->
<target name="prepare" description="prepares the project's directories">
    <echo>preparing project's directories...</echo>
    <mkdir dir="${classes}"/>
    <mkdir dir="${generated-ejb}"/>
    <mkdir dir="${generated-ozone}"/>
    <mkdir dir="${descriptors-ejb}"/>
    <mkdir dir="${build}"/>
    <mkdir dir="${dist}"/>
</target>


<!-- ================================================================= -->
<!-- Cleans the directory structure                                    -->
<!-- ================================================================= -->
<target name="clean" description="removes all build products">
    <echo>cleaning...</echo>
    <delete dir="${classes}"/>
    <delete dir="${generated}"/>
    <delete dir="${build}"/>
    <delete dir="${dist}"/>
</target>
```

The generate task uses the loaded XDoclet ejbdoclet to generate the required EJB files from the annotated ConferenceOzoneFacadeBean, as shown here:

```
<!-- ================================================================ -->
<!-- Generate EJB glue files using XDoclet's ejbdoclet               -->
<!-- ================================================================ -->
<target name="generate" description="uses XDoclet to generate EJB files">
    <echo>generating ejbs glue...</echo>
    <ejbdoclet
        destdir="${generated-ejb}"
        excludedtags="@version,@author,@todo"
        ejbspec="2.0"
        force="true"
        >
        <fileset dir="${src}">
            <include name="**/*Bean.java"/>
        </fileset>

        <utilobject kind="physical" includeGUID="true"/>
        <remoteinterface/>
        <localinterface/>
        <homeinterface/>
        <localhomeinterface/>
        <valueobject/>
        <entitycmp/>
        <session/>
        <entitypk/>
        <utilobject cacheHomes="true" includeGUID="true"/>
        <deploymentdescriptor
            destdir="${descriptors-ejb}"
            validatexml="true"
            />
        <jboss
            version="3.0"
            unauthenticatedPrincipal="nobody"
            xmlencoding="UTF-8"
            destdir="${descriptors-ejb}"
            validatexml="true"
            />
    </ejbdoclet>
</target>
```

The compile target depends on the generate task and it compiles both the files in the ${src} directory as well as the generated EJB files in the directory ${generated-ejb}, as shown here:

```
<!-- ===================================================================== -->
<!-- Compiles all the classes                                              -->
<!-- ===================================================================== -->
<target name="compile" depends="generate"
    description="compiles all sources">
    <echo>compiling...</echo>
    <javac
        destdir="${classes}"
        classpathref="ozone.class.path"
        debug="on"
        deprecation="on"
        optimize="off"
        >
        <src path="${src}"/>
        <src path="${generated-ejb}"/>
    </javac>
</target>
```

Generating the Proxies with the Ozone Post Processor

The OPP is a postprocessor that creates the actual proxy classes, as well as factory classes, which the database direct clients manipulate. OPP is a code generator and it doesn't perform any kind of bytecode manipulation. OPP inspects your Ozone implementation classes (those extending OzoneObject) and creates a proxy peer class, which is actually what the clients interact with. The methods in these proxy classes invoke the server-side object using Ozone RMI.

The target OPP, which depends on the compile target, uses the oppdoclet task to invoke the OPP processor executable, which is contained in the org.ozoneDB.tools.OPP.OPP class. To learn about the command-line options for OPP at the Ozone distribution bin directory, enter the following:

```
opp
```

This should produce the OPP command-line help as shown here:

```
Ozone Post Processor
usage: opp [-ks] [-st] [-p<pattern>] [-ni] [-nf] [-nc] [-q] [-h] [-o<directory>]
[-odmg] [-ip] class [class]*
    -ks       save the generated resolver files
    -KS       save the generated resolver files; do not invoke compiler
    -st       print stack trace
    -p        regular expression to specify update methods
    -ni       do not search interface code for update methods
    -nf       do not create a Factory class
    -q        supress output of any messages
    -o        output directory
    -s        resolver directory
    -odmg     create proxies for the ozone ODMG interface
    -ip       ignore package names
    -nc       do not create code needed for direct invokes and ClientCacheDatabase
    -version  shows version information
    -h        shows this help
```

The OPP target executes OPP using the loaded task. The cache attribute tells OPP to keep the generated source files, the equivalent of using the –KS switch, as shown in the command-line help. The source element tells OPP where the Java source tree containing the implementation files are located; in this case, it's in the ${src} directory. The output attribute option determines where the generated files are to be placed; in this case, they go in the ${generated-ozone} directory.

```xml
<!-- ===================================================================== -->
<!-- Builds the proxies                                                    -->
<!-- ===================================================================== -->
<target name="OPP" depends="compile">
    <oppdoclet output="${generated-ozone}" cache="true">
        <source dir="${src}">
            <include name="**/*Impl.java"/>
        </source>
        <classpath refid="ozone.class.path"/>
    </oppdoclet>
</target>
```

The ejb-jar uses the jar task to create a JAR file that can be deployed to JBoss, as follows:

```
<!-- ================================================================= -->
<!-- Package the EJB JAR                                               -->
<!-- ================================================================= -->
<target name="ejb-jar" depends="OPP"
    description="packages the ejb-jar file">
    <echo>packaging ejb-jar...</echo>
    <jar jarfile="${dist}/${jar-name}">
    <metainf dir="${descriptors-ejb}" includes="*.xml"/>
    <fileset dir="${classes}">
        <include name="com/ejdoab/**/*.class" />
        <exclude name="com/ejdoab/client/*" />
    </fileset>
  </jar>
</target>
```

Finally, a convenience target called deploy is added to perform all of the build tasks and to copy the resulting ejb-jar file to the JBoss deploy directory, as shown here:

```
<!-- ================================================================= -->
<!-- Deploys EJB-JAR                                                   -->
<!-- ================================================================= -->
<target name="deploy" depends="clean,prepare,ejb-jar"
    description="deploys the EJB-JAR file to JBoss">
    <copy file-"${dist}/${jar-name}" todir-"${deploy-dir}"/>
</target>
```

To execute the build file on a command line, type the following:

```
ant deploy
```

This should produce output similar to what's shown here:

```
Buildfile: build.xml

clean:
    [echo] cleaning...
...
prepare:
    [echo] preparing project's directories...
...
generate:
    [echo] generating ejbs glue...
...
```

```
compile:
    [echo] compiling...
...
OPP:
[oppdoclet] Loader is set
[oppdoclet] Begin build
[oppdoclet] Begin Processing com.ejdoab.db.ConferencesManagerImpl...
[oppdoclet]     Begin Resolving update methods...
[oppdoclet]         No ocd was found!
[oppdoclet]     End Resolving update methods
[oppdoclet]     update method [4]: addOrUpdateConference
[oppdoclet]     update method [4]: deleteAllConferences
[oppdoclet]     update method [4]: deleteConference
[oppdoclet]     Begin Generating factory for:
    com.ejdoab.db.ConferencesManagerImpl...
[oppdoclet]     End Generating factory for: com.ejdoab.db.ConferencesManagerImpl
[oppdoclet]     Begin Generating proxy for:
    com.ejdoab.db.ConferencesManagerImpl...
[oppdoclet]     End Generating proxy for: com.ejdoab.db.ConferencesManagerImpl
[oppdoclet] End Processing com.ejdoab.db.ConferencesManagerImpl
    generated in 0.17 seconds.
[oppdoclet] Generation completed with 0 warnings and 0 errors
[oppdoclet] End build
[oppdoclet] Loader is set
[oppdoclet] Begin build
[oppdoclet] Begin Processing com.ejdoab.pojos.ConferenceImpl...
[oppdoclet]     Begin Resolving update methods...
[oppdoclet]         No ocd was found!
[oppdoclet]     End Resolving update methods
[oppdoclet]     update method [4]: setName
[oppdoclet]     update method [4]: setDescription
[oppdoclet]     update method [4]: setStartDate
[oppdoclet]     update method [4]: setEndDate
[oppdoclet]     update method [4]: setAbstractSubmissionStartDate
[oppdoclet]     update method [4]: setAbstractSubmissionEndDate
[oppdoclet]     update method [4]: addTrack
[oppdoclet]     update method [4]: deleteTrack
[oppdoclet]     Begin Generating factory for: com.ejdoab.pojos.ConferenceImpl...
[oppdoclet]     End Generating factory for: com.ejdoab.pojos.ConferenceImpl
[oppdoclet]     Begin Generating proxy for: com.ejdoab.pojos.ConferenceImpl...
[oppdoclet]     End Generating proxy for: com.ejdoab.pojos.ConferenceImpl
[oppdoclet] End Processing com.ejdoab.pojos.ConferenceImpl
    generated in 0.14 seconds.
[oppdoclet] Generation completed with 0 warnings and 0 errors
```

```
[oppdoclet] End build
[oppdoclet] Loader is set
[oppdoclet] Begin build
[oppdoclet] Begin Processing com.ejdoab.pojos.TrackImpl...
[oppdoclet]    Begin Resolving update methods...
[oppdoclet]       No ocd was found!
[oppdoclet]    End Resolving update methods
[oppdoclet]    update method [4]: setDescription
[oppdoclet]    update method [4]: setSubTitle
[oppdoclet]    update method [4]: setTitle
[oppdoclet]    Begin Generating factory for: com.ejdoab.pojos.TrackImpl...
[oppdoclet]    End Generating factory for: com.ejdoab.pojos.TrackImpl
[oppdoclet]    Begin Generating proxy for: com.ejdoab.pojos.TrackImpl...
[oppdoclet]    End Generating proxy for: com.ejdoab.pojos.TrackImpl
[oppdoclet] End Processing com.ejdoab.pojos.TrackImpl generated in 0.121 seconds.
[oppdoclet] Generation completed with 0 warnings and 0 errors
[oppdoclet] End build

ejb-jar:
    [echo] packaging ejb-jar...
...
deploy:
    [copy] Copying 1 file to C:\java\jboss\jboss-3.2.1\server\tcms\deploy


BUILD SUCCESSFUL
Total time: 11 seconds
```

On the JBoss console you should see the archive being deployed with output similar to the following:

```
...
13:39:50,387 INFO  [MainDeployer] Starting deployment of package:
    file:/C:/java/jboss/jboss-3.2.1/server/tcms/deploy/ozone-jboss-test.jar
13:39:51,038 INFO  [EjbModule] Creating
13:39:51,048 INFO  [EjbModule] Deploying ConferenceOzoneFacade
13:39:51,058 INFO  [StatelessSessionContainer] Creating
13:39:51,068 INFO  [StatelessSessionInstancePool] Creating
13:39:51,068 INFO  [StatelessSessionInstancePool] Created
13:39:51,068 INFO  [StatelessSessionContainer] Created
13:39:51,068 INFO  [EjbModule] Created
13:39:51,078 INFO  [EjbModule] Starting
13:39:51,078 INFO  [StatelessSessionContainer] Starting
13:39:51,118 INFO  [StatelessSessionInstancePool] Starting
13:39:51,118 INFO  [StatelessSessionInstancePool] Started
```

```
13:39:51,118 INFO  [StatelessSessionContainer] Started
13:39:51,118 INFO  [EjbModule] Started
13:39:51,118 INFO  [EJBDeployer] Deployed:
    file:/C:/java/jboss/jboss-3.2.1/server/tcms/deploy/ozone-jboss-test.jar
13:39:51,128 INFO  [MainDeployer] Deployed package:
    file:/C:/java/jboss/jboss-3.2.1/server/tcms/deploy/ozone-jboss-test.jar
...
```

Test Client

Finally, you'll need a test client similar to the one used in Chapter 5. In this client you'll look up the ConferenceOzoneFacade Session Bean and manipulate the Conference objects stored in the database. First, you'll retrieve all existing conferences. Next, you'll search for a Conference object by its name. If it isn't found, then you'll create the Conference object and store it in the database, as follows:

```java
package com.ejdoab.client;

...

import com.ejdoab.beans.ConferenceOzoneFacade;
import com.ejdoab.beans.ConferenceOzoneFacadeHome;
import com.ejdoab.dto.ConferenceDTO;
import com.ejdoab.dto.TrackDTO;

/**
 * Simple EJB Test — ConferenceOzoneFacade Test
 */
public class Client {
    private static final String ICF = "org.jnp.interfaces.NamingContextFactory";
    private static final String SERVER_URI = "localhost:1099";
    private static final String PKG_PREFIXES =
        "org.jboss.naming:org.jnp.interfaces";

    public static void main(String args[]) {
        Context ctx;
        ConferenceOzoneFacadeHome confHome;
        ConferenceOzoneFacade conf;
```

```
// initial context JBossNS configuration
Hashtable env = new Hashtable();
env.put(Context.INITIAL_CONTEXT_FACTORY, ICF);
env.put(Context.PROVIDER_URL, SERVER_URI);
env.put(Context.URL_PKG_PREFIXES, PKG_PREFIXES);

try {

    // ----------
    // JNDI Stuff
    // ----------

    ctx = new InitialContext(env);
    // look up the home interface
    System.out.println(
        "[jndi lookup] Looking Up ConferenceOzoneFacade" +
        " Remote Home Interface" );
    Object obj = ctx.lookup("ejb.ConferenceOzoneFacadeHome");
    // cast and narrow
    confHome = (ConferenceOzoneFacadeHome) PortableRemoteObject
        .narrow( obj, ConferenceOzoneFacadeHome.class);
    conf = confHome.create();

    // ----------
    // Tests
    // ----------

    //
    // getAllConferences
    //
    Collection c = conf.getAllConferences();
    if (!c.isEmpty()) {
        Iterator i - c.iterator();
        System.out.println(
            "[getAllConferences] listing conferences in the database:");
        while (i.hasNext()) {
            ConferenceDTO conference = (ConferenceDTO) i.next();
            System.out.println(conference.toString());
        }
    }
```

```
    else {
        System.out.println(
            "[getAllConferences] there are no conferences "
            + "in the database");
    }

    //
    // Find Conference by Name
    //
    String confName = "Apress OSC";
    System.out.println("[getConferenceByName] searching with "
        + confName);

    ConferenceDTO conference = null;
    try {
        conference = conf.getConferenceByName(confName);
    } catch (Exception e) {
        e.printStackTrace();
    }

    Date today = new Date();

    if (conference == null) {
        System.out.println(
            "[getConferenceByName] Conference was not found"
            + ", creating it");
        ConferenceDTO newConf =
            new ConferenceDTO(
                "Apress OSC",
                "Apress Open Source Conference",
                today,
                today,
                today,
                today);
        newConf.addTrack(
            new TrackDTO(
                "J2SE",
                "Java 2 Standard Edition",
                "Learn how to build powerful Java desktop applications"));
```

```
                  newConf.addTrack(
                      new TrackDTO(
                        "J2EE",
                        "Java 2 Enterprise Edition",
                       "Enterprise Applications powered entirely by Open Source"));
                  newConf.addTrack(
                      new TrackDTO(
                          "J2ME",
                          "Java 2 Micro Edition",
                          "Java brings cell phones and PDAs to life"));

                  conf.addOrUpdateConference(newConf);
              }
              else {
                  System.out.println(
                      "[getConferenceByName] Conference was found\n" +
                      conference + "\n");
                  System.out.println("Here are the tracks:\n");
                  Collection tracks = conference.getTracks();
                  for (Iterator iter = tracks.iterator(); iter.hasNext();) {
                      TrackDTO track = (TrackDTO) iter.next();
                      System.out.println(track);
                  }
              }
          }
          catch (RemoteException re) {
              System.out.println("[rmi] remote exception: " + re.getMessage());
          }
          catch (NamingException ne) {
              System.out.println("[naming] naming exception: " + ne.getMessage());
          }
          catch (CreateException ce) {
              System.out.println("[ejb] create exception: " + ce.getMessage());
          }
      }
}
```

Results

To run the test, as you've done previously with all JBoss test clients, you'll need the jbossall-client.jar in the classpath. Compile the test client class (the included Ant build script should have already compiled the class) and execute it by issuing the following command:

```
java –cp classes;%JBOSS_HOME%\client\jbossall-➥
client.jar;%OZONE_HOME%\lib\ozoneServer-1.2-➥
alpha.jar com.ejdoab.client.Client
```

where JBOSS_HOME refers to the JBoss distribution and OZONE_HOME refers to the Ozone distribution. The results of running the test-client application for the first time are shown here:

```
[jndi lookup] Looking Up ConferenceOzoneFacade Remote Home Interface
[getAllConferences] there are no conferences in the database
[getConferenceByName] searching for Apress OSC
[getConferenceByName] Conference was not found, creating it
```

As you can see on the first run, the Conference object isn't found by either of the methods selected, so it's created. On the second run, as you can see in the following output, the newly created Conference object is now found along with its associated Tracks:

```
[jndi lookup] Looking Up ConferenceOzoneFacade Remote Home Interface
[getAllConferences] listing conferences in the database:
[Conference] name = Apress OSC,
            description = Apress Open Source Conference,
            start date = Sun Feb 01 05:34:03 EST 2004,
            end date = Sun Feb 01 05:34:03 EST 2004,
            # tracks = 3
[getConferenceByName] searching with Apress OSC
[getConferenceByName] Conference was found
[Conference] name = Apress OSC,
            description = Apress Open Source Conference,
            start date = Sun Feb 01 05:34:03 EST 2004,
            end date = Sun Feb 01 05:34:03 EST 2004,
            # tracks = 3
```

Here are the tracks:

```
[Track] title = J2SE,
        subTitle = Java 2 Standard Edition,
        description = Learn how to build powerful Java desktop applications
[Track] title = J2EE,
        subTitle = Java 2 Enterprise Edition,
        description = Enterprise Applications powered entirely by Open Source
[Track] title = J2ME,
        subTitle = Java 2 Micro Edition,
        description = Java brings cell phones and PDAs to life
```

You can now use the Ozone AdminGUI tool to browse the database. Figure 6-13 shows the newly created named object ConferencesManager.

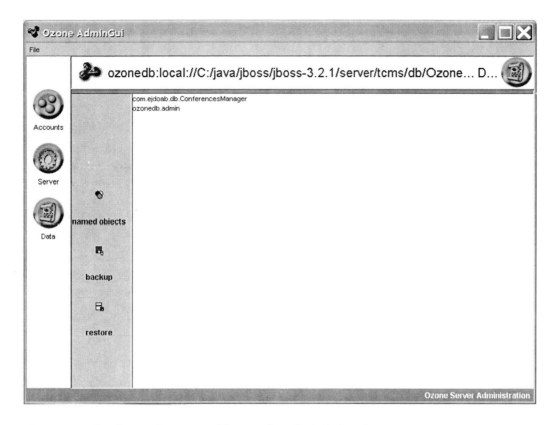

Figure 6-13. ConferenceManager object on the AdminGui tool

An object-oriented alternative to a relational database, the Ozone DB can handle the complexities of a rich object model. If you're accustomed to working with RMI or EJBs, the Ozone DB will make you feel at home. We expect that in the near future the creation of the remote interface, implementation classes, and OCD files will be automated further with the use of an attribute-oriented programming (AOP) tool such as XDoclet. There are, of course, countless features of the Ozone DB that aren't covered in this chapter. You can learn more about them by visiting the Ozone website (http:// http://www.ozone-db.org) or reading through the posts in the Ozone user newsgroup (comp.java.ozone.user).

Other Data-Storage Technologies

There are other data-storage technologies worthy of mention that this chapter doesn't cover. This section briefly mentions the choices available and points you to the right places to gather more information.

Java Prevalence

Java Prevalence, as embodied by the Prevayler project (http://www.prevayler.org), is a new take on the idea of a totally in-memory database that provides transparent persistence, fault-tolerance, and load-balancing capabilities. The Prevayler project was started by Klaus Wuestefeld, and it's rapidly gaining both supporters and detractors at a very high rate. Prevayler works on the assumption that the available amount of physical memory is sufficient to keep all objects in the system in memory.

Prevayler uses object serialization at set intervals (or on demand) to produce a snapshot of the system. Atomic changes to the state of the working memory are logged as serialized "transactions" before they're applied to the system. If the system crashes, the last snapshot is loaded and any commands logged after the time of the snapshot creation are executed against the snapshot in order to bring the system to its last known state.

For usage purposes, Prevayler works like an object-oriented database except that if you want to mutate the data in a Prevayler system (similar to a named object in Ozone) you must encapsulate the operations that perform the changes in a transaction, which in Prevayler is a serializable class that represents a command object. Each command is applied in a serialized fashion to the system. A Prevayler transaction must be deterministic, meaning that it should always produce the same final state when applied to a Prevayler system in certain state.

Prevayler is a very simple, robust, and fast system that can be used to provide transparent persistence in a J2EE system in certain scenarios. It shares the advantages of object-databases in that it let's you work with POJOs (it's actually one of the least intrusive tools we tested). It can be a great choice for a fault-tolerant in-memory solution or for an object graph that doesn't grow wildly. As mentioned previously the only imposition on the development is in the semantics of the interactions that mutate your prevalent system.

Prevayler can be a great way to prototype your system and gain a baseline for what the performance could be with a complete in-memory solution. Development is fairly simple, it doesn't require any pre- or postprocessing of your classes, bytecode manipulation, or the need to inherit or implement any proprietary classes or interfaces (except for the marker interface java.io.Serializable).

The semantics of a Prevayler transaction are easily applied to a service-oriented architecture.

So, if all of the criteria for using an object-oriented database apply to your system, your object graph can comfortably fit in memory, and if your system has no distribution requirements then Prevayler can be a great choice to provide unparalleled performance to your users.

Native XML Databases

XML is rapidly become the lingua franca for business-to-business transactions, and a new breed of database that's tailored for the efficient storage, retrieval, and management of XML is surfacing. Just as object and relational systems have impedance mismatches, XML, with its document-centric hierarchical paradigm, also has incompatibilities at certain levels with object systems and relational databases. XML databases provide a way to store XML in its natural state. These databases typically create indexes for each document stored, which eases the task of querying and aggregating data.

The XML:DB initiative for XML databases (http://www.xmldb.org/) is a group that's looking to standardize the definition of an XML database. It identifies the following areas as examples of applications that could benefit from using a native XML database:

- Corporate information portals

- Membership databases

- Product catalogs

- Parts databases

- Patient-information tracking

- Business-to-business document exchange

A native XML database will ideally enable you to work with native XML technologies and tools such as (in the case of Java) XSLT, XPath, XQuery, JAXP, Xerces/Xalan, JDOM, and XOM. Currently two Open Source implementations exist. They are mature enough (there are many mature commercial XML database such as Software AG's Tamino) and are close to being ready for use in production environments. These are as follows:

- **Xindice** (`http://xml.apache.org/xindice`): The Xindice native XML database (formerly dbXML) is an Apache project that provides a pure-Java XML database that supports the XML:DB API. It uses the XML:DB XUpdate for updates and the W3C's XPath for queries.

- **eXist** (`http://exist.sourceforge.net`): The eXist project provides a native XML database that supports XQuery, autoindexing, and extensions for full-text searching. An XQuery processing servlet (XQueryServlet) can be used in combination with XSLT to generate content such as HTML with simple XQuery files.

XML provides a way for modeling document-based unstructured or semi-structured data that's sometimes difficult to model in the object and relational models. A native XML database can ease the complexity of working with XML by offering a native way to store and work with your XML documents.

Conclusion

In this chapter you've learned that deciding where and how to store your data can be a daunting decision. The storage mechanism you choose will have a deep impact in the way you develop your applications. Although not an in-depth treatise on Java data-storage choices, this chapter should have given you a place to start the quest for the right database for your application.

The lesson of this chapter is that you should understand your application's needs when it comes to storing and manipulating data, and the best way to do this is to prototype and test the main features of your application by using different approaches including CMP EJBs, ORM tools, embedded in-memory SQL databases, OODBMS, and XDBMS.

CHAPTER 7

Object-Relational Mapping

In theory, there is no difference between theory and practice.
In practice, there is.

—Jan L.A. van de Snepscheut[1]

TODAY, OBJECT AND COMPONENT technologies are the reigning programming paradigms. They give you the ability to build understandable, maintainable, and scalable systems. The early 1990s saw the emergence of object databases as an ideal counterpart for the up-and-coming object-oriented and object-based languages. In theory, it seemed like a no-brainer because object-oriented languages create and manipulate objects; what better place to store those objects' states than in a database that's specialized for that purpose?

Several problems soon became apparent for those early pioneers that decided to forego their relational database management systems (RDBMS) in favor of an object-oriented database management system (OODBMS). The lesson is that for data that's heterogeneous and hierarchical or for highly complex structured data (think a 3D scene or a molecular structure) an OODBMS (or a native XML database) is a perfect fit. But for the majority of the data that drives corporate systems, the only feasible storage option is an RDBMS. OODBMS have poor query support, are still relatively young, and the data stored in them tends to be tightly coupled to a specific application. The normalized, tabular nature of the data stored in relational systems enables it to efficiently perform the most common operations needed for enterprise-level systems, and at the same time it ensures the integrity of the data.

As a Java developer it's very likely that you'll find yourself retrieving data from a relational database and you'll want to look at ways to move that data to and from your objects and components. There's also a very high probability that you'll be working with an existing database schema that might predate any sort of object-oriented system. The question is how to approach the problem of storing your objects' state in an RDBMS. In Chapter 5 you explored in detail the use of J2EE

---

1. van de Snepscheut, Jan L.A. "What Computing Is All About (Texts & Monographs in Computer Science S.)" (Springer-Verlag Berlin and Heidelberg GmbH & Co. KG, July 31, 1993).

CMP EJBs as a persistence solution for the state of the TCMS domain model that you designed in Chapter 2. CMP EJBs provide a coarse-grain component-oriented approach to persistence.

In this chapter you'll explore some of the alternatives to EJB CMPs using more fine-grained approaches and receive some guidance on how to choose between the technologies and tools available.

The Object-Relational Impedance Mismatch

As the title of this section points out, there's a certain amount of work that needs to happen for your objects to be stored and retrieved from a relational database. The problems that arise during this process are the result of several factors, and incredibly, one of the greatest roadblocks is of a cultural nature. In many a project, object technologists seem to take the database for granted and database professionals end up designing relational schemas in a vacuum. Although a proper separation of concerns will lead you to the conclusion that this is acceptable, in reality however, for an object-oriented system to work efficiently with a relational database these two groups most work together. As pointed out by Scott Ambler, there's certain amount of predisposition from the part of both camps. The typical objection from "object developers that claim relational technology either shouldn't or can't be used to store objects" and their counterparts the "data professionals that claim that your object/component models must be driven by their data models."[2]

Aside from the cultural impedance mismatch there are some very real technical issues to consider, as you learned in Chapter 6. At the root of the problem you have the two paradigms that are focused on very different goals. An object system focuses on providing the best representation of the problem in terms of objects in order to solve a set of business requirements. But with relational technologies, schemas are created to provide a normalized and "flattened" set of data that can be efficiently stored and accessed. Relational databases work on the mathematical principle of relations, in which you work with a matrix of tuples (rows) and domains (columns), but in object-oriented systems you work by traversing relationships that interconnect objects producing an object graph. With relational technology you work with relations between types, but in the object world you work with relations between entities. Objects are encapsulated entities and it's this encapsulation that sometimes causes havoc on performance when objects are mapped to relational databases.

Object technologists know well that data models tend to be very poor drivers for an object model, because an object model not only deals with data but also

---

2. Ambler, Scott. *Agile Database Techniques: Effective Strategies for the Agile Software Developer* (John Wiley & Sons, 2003).

behavior, and the relationships between data tend to be semantically shallower than the relationships encountered when modeling behavior. This makes the impedance between a data model and an object model a matter of fidelity. It's possible in the early stages of design for an object model and a relational model to look very similar, but as the system matures these similarities become only superficial.

Object-Relational Mapping

Object-Relational mapping (ORM) is the name given to the technologies, tools, and techniques used to bridge the divide between objects and relational databases. ORM tools allow you to declaratively map data objects to data and relations in a relational database. This breed of tools generates all of the SQL code needed to interact with the database. Developers work at the object level and the concept of queries and transactions are applied to the objects rather than database objects.

Although under the same umbrella the tools can vary greatly in the way they work, from the level of "transparency" to whether they work by generating code, modifying bytecode, or using runtime inspection. Some of the tools covered in this chapter adhere to committee-based standards like JDO though others have their own nonstandard APIs.

NOTE   The concept of transparency as applied to ORM tools is still very vague in the industry. Persistence transparency or orthogonality implies that objects are treated without any implicit notion of persistence. Most of the existing tools aren't truly transparent yet they provide a good separation of concerns by isolating the persistence of objects behind very simple object-oriented constructs.

Also worthy of consideration is how to fit the way a certain tool works with the rest of your development process. With some tools, you start with an object model and derive a relational persistence model; with others, you start with a relational model and derive an object model. Most of the time you'll find that you have both an existing object model and a relational model, in which case most tools fall short of expectations and most of the mapping work will be done manually. Sometimes it's impossible to avoid the situation when trade-offs need to be made between your object model and the database schema. It's important that both models are developed in cooperation. An ORM tool can help this collaborative work but it's the human factor that plays the larger role.

The Open Source ORM tool market has evolved considerably. At the time of this writing the following ORM tools listed in Table 7-1 were available.

Table 7-1. Open-Sourced ORM Tools

Tool	URL	JDO
OJB	http://db.apache.org/ojb	Partial
Hibernate	http://hibernate.org	No
Castor	http://www.castor.org	No
Torque	http://db.apache.org/torque	No
Cayenne	http://objectstyle.org/cayenne	No
Jaxor	http://jaxor.sourceforge.net	No
iBATIS SQL Maps	http://www.ibatis.com	No
TJDO	http://tjdo.sourceforge.net	Yes
XORM	http://xorm.org	Yes

Using JDBC

At both ends of the spectrum; for extremely simple object models and for extremely complex object models, there's the choice of going with lower-level, fine-grained control provided by using straight SQL through JDBC. Sometimes your application's success might hinge on its performance and that performance might depend on a proprietary database feature. JDBC will let you tap into features like stored procedures and other database functions. We recommend that you take this approach only as a last resort because embedding SQL into Java code leads to code that's very hard to maintain and the quality of the SQL is most of the time very questionable.

In case you decide to use straight JDBC for your enterprise application we recommend that you follow these guidelines to ensure that your JDBC code is efficient and maintainable:

- Understand how the data is to be used by the most critical parts of the application. Use the 80-20 rule as it applies to code optimizations, whereby 80 percent of the time a system is being used is spent on 20 percent of the code.

- Use parameterized queries with prepared statements. This can keep your code cleaner and can help you handle other nuances of regular statements such as escaping quotes and dates.

- Use a database-connection pool package. Database connections are an expensive resource to create; by pooling connections you can give your applications a performance boost.

Table 7-1. Open-Sourced ORM Tools

ODMG	J2EE	Style	Query Language
Yes	Yes	Runtime	OQL (partial)
Partial	Yes	Runtime	Proprietary (SQL-like/SQL)
No	Yes	Runtime	OQL (ODMG 3.0 subset)
No	Yes	Code Generator	Proprietary
No	Yes	Runtime/Code Generator	Proprietary
No	Yes	Code Generator	SQL
No	Yes	Runtime	SQL
Yes	Yes	Bytecode Enhancer	JDOQL
Yes	Yes	Runtime	JDOQL

- Use well-known patterns to isolate persistence logic from business logic. Decoupling persistence logic from business logic will make your applications maintainable and flexible to change.

- Test several different database drivers, preferably type 4 JDBC drivers. JDBC driver compliance varies widely from driver to driver.

- Turn off the JDBC connection Auto-Commit option and plan transaction boundaries and levels carefully.

- Never allow a database transaction to span multiple user requests. Whenever possible make a long transactional operation asynchronous and provide a notification mechanism.

- Use optimistic locking whenever possible. With optimistic locking, database rows and objects are never actually locked. If a retrieved record is to be changed and the underlying database data has changed, the update will fail. An advantage of optimistic locking is that it's easy to use and it doesn't require any extra database resources.

- Avoid distributed transactions whenever possible. Distributed database transactions are complex and expensive.

- Minimize database round-trips by batching your queries. As with learned with EJBs it's cheaper to get a lot of data once than getting small chunks at a time.

- Don't be afraid of using store procedures if they prove to provide a significant performance gain. Well-written store procedures usually outperform SQL queries and, if written by a well-seasoned DBA, they can guarantee a higher level of data integrity.

Regardless of the tool chosen they all have to deal with several technical questions. Object persistence is, like most hard problems, all about the trade-offs. The theme with Java persistence is about choices, as with many things in Java. No tool is perfect for every persistence scenario. Some tools trade transparency for performance or simplicity for capabilities. Some of the questions that arise during the selection (or creation) of an object-relational tool include the following:

- How to convert column values to Java objects and primitives. For example, a Java Date object can be mapped to many database types.

- How to model object relationships (such as inheritance, aggregation, and composition) on a database schema or how to model relations between tables in an object or group of objects.

- How to deal with database keys and object identity, which might not exist in the object model.

- How to optimize the resultant SQL calls.

- How to take advantage of proprietary database features such as updateable views and stored procedures.

- How to guarantee referential integrity without limiting the behavioral expressiveness of the object model.

- How to deal with transactions when the database is accessed concurrently from multiple sources. From a relational point of view, an object is nothing but an in-memory cache of the database data that must be invalidated and refreshed when appropriate.

- How to deal with expensive operations like loading many child objects in a one-to-many relationship (lazy loading or proxy objects or caching).

Obviously, as the object graphs get more complex the tools have to be more "intelligent." You've seen countless companies that start with a very simple system for which they write their own persistence layer from the ground up. We equate this to writing your own application server. Sooner or later you'll run into some of technical questions pondered previously by others and discover that you're spending most of your time "fine tuning" your persistence framework. ORM tools take away the complexity of mapping classes in memory to databases. They provide interfaces that automatically select, insert, update, and delete tables in the database in order to reflect changes made to an object model.

Therefore we recommend that you choose a mapping tool earlier rather than later before any "temporary" persistence logic in your application starts to look like a homemade framework. Using an ORM layer has proven to increase productivity by moving developer focus away from figuring out how to store objects (a nonfunctional concern) to solving the real business problems. Another positive side-effect of using an ORM tool is that, like JDBC, it provides an isolating layer between the database and the application by providing an objectified view of the database. In a better case, it completely makes persistence "transparent," without the complexity of writing and maintaining straight JDBC code.

ORM tools also have drawbacks, including performance, portability (does the tool implement any of the known standards?), and the initial learning curve. If performance is of paramount importance in your application, isolate the key components of your application and test them against a significant amount of data.

Apache DB Project's Object Relational Bridge

OJB is an Open Source object-relational mapping tool that allows for transparent persistence of Java objects using relational databases. OJB works using runtime reflection and therefore doesn't need to generate code or modify bytecode at compile time. OJB allows you to use plain old Java objects (POJO) by transparently mapping them to the underlying data store.

OJB started as the brainchild of Thomas Mahler in mid-2000 after discovering how much easier database access was while using ODMG-compliant object databases (Poet and Objectivity). OJB eventually became part of Apache's DB project, which is an effort to group all database-related work under Apache (http://db.apache.org).

At its heart an OJB mapping relies on an XML metadata file that details how to map objects to tables. This file is referred to as the "repository" and it's equivalent to the ejb-jar.xml files you worked with in Chapter 5. OJB provides value-added features besides O/R mapping such as object caching, lazy loading using virtual proxies, and distributed lock management.

As with many of the well-architected Apache projects, OJB provides many plug-in and extensibility points that make it an ideal platform to build more complex transactional object brokers. OJB uses a microkernel architecture that allows it to support multiple "personalities" or database APIs. You can use OJB in three different modes supported by the following four different APIs:

- **PersistenceBroker:** The PersistenceBroker (PB) is the simplest and most straightforward. This API is at a lower level than the ODMG and JDO APIs and provides the foundation for higher-level APIs to be implemented.

- **ODMG implementation:** Implements the ODMG 3.0 object persistence API, which is a portability specification designed to allow for portable applications. It provides a higher-level API build on top of the Persistence-Broker API.

- **JDO RI plug-in:** The OjbStore StoreManager is a plug-in to the JDO reference implementation that makes OJB a fully JDO 1.0–compliant solution for stand-alone applications (nonmanaged). Currently, you cannot use the JDO features from within an application server. OJB 2.0 will provide a fully compliant JDO solution. For more information on the JDO RI see `http://jcp.org/en/jsr/detail?id=12`.

- **OTM:** The OTM is an abstracted object-level transaction API used by both the ODMG and JDO implementation. This API will be exposed as an officially supported API in the near future.

Figure 7-1 shows a simplified view of the OJB architecture.

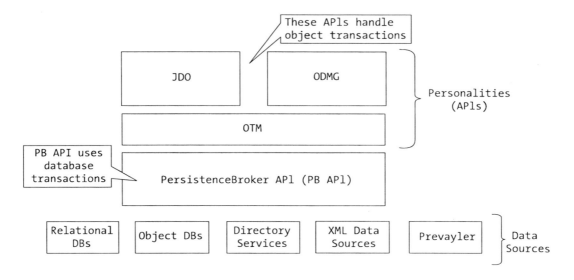

Figure 7-1. OJB architecture

OJB provides other features such as the following:

- **Object cache:** An object caching facility

- **Sequence manager:** Pluggable primary key generation

- **Complex object graphs:** Automatic persistence of dependent or "children" objects

- **Locking:** Support for multiple locking strategies

- **J2EE integration:** Easy integration with managed environments (J2EE)

Creating an OJB Distribution

You can obtain OJB from the Apache DB project website at http://db.apache.org/ojb in both binary and source distributions. For stand-alone applications OJB installation is very simple, because it only requires a few JARs and the XML configuration files, which define the database(s) being used and the mappings between your objects and the tables.

We recommend that you use the source distribution because It wlll allow you to build a distribution tailored to your needs. For the examples in this section we obtained the 1.0 version candidate release 5 (db-ojb-1.0.rc5-src.zip), which is the last candidate release before the highly anticipated 1.0 release. Simply unzip the file to a suitable location, for example c:\java\ojb. To build a binary distribution you need a working version of Ant.

For an enterprise example you'll need OJB working within the confines of a J2EE application server. Fortunately, OJB integrates with most application servers. It fully supports JNDI lookup of data sources and it provides JTA and JCA integration. For the purpose of this chapter you'll build a distribution that will contain the needed JBoss MBeans, which will allow for using OJB as a JBoss service. JBoss's JMX microkernel allows for pretty much any kind of Java code to be wrapped with an MBean, thereby making integration a snap.

As with any Ant-based Java project we recommend that you first run Ant with the -projecthelp switch to learn about the options available in the build. Doing so will also help you discover other features that are sometimes packaged as part of the build such as unit tests, performance tests, and targets that can help you get started with your own projects.

At a command prompt, change directories to the OJB directory and type the following:

```
ant -projecthelp
```

The output should resemble the following (targets that aren't relevant to the example have been omitted and output has been formatted for readability):

```
Buildfile: build.xml
Main targets:

all                  rebuild all sources (incl. preprocessing)
clean                Cleans the build and distribution directories.
ejb-examples         Generate the sample session bean ejb-app jar
jar                  Builds the binary ojb-xxx.jar in the dist directory.
junit                Performs all JUnit regression tests.
main                 Compile all Java sources with debugging on.
main-opt             Same as main, but with debugging off and
                     optimizations on.
ojb-blank            Build a sample project
perf-test            Simple performance benchmark and stress test
                     for PB- and ODMG api
performance          Performance benchmark, compare the PB-api/ODMG-api
                      with direct JDBC calls
performance2         Performance benchmark and stress test for PB-
                     and ODMG-api
performance3         Stress test for PB- and ODMG-api using multiple
                     databases
prepare-jboss        Copy jboss mbeans to code base
rar                  Builds the RAR for the OTM in optimized mode
reverse-db           Starts the OJB RDBMS reverse engineering tool
reverse-db2          Starts the next generation OJB RDBMS reverse
                     engineering tool
war                  Builds a sample war-file for deployment in tomcat
with-jdori           Compile OJB JDORI

Default target: all
```

Of significance to getting started with OJB is the ojb-blank task, which will create a blank stand-alone Java OJB project including an Ant build script and all required libraries. If you're evaluating OJB and performance is one of your considerations you can run the performance targets to get an idea of how the OJB's APIs compare against using direct JDBC calls and also how they compare to each other. For more information on the performance targets see http://db.apache.org/ojb/performance.html.

For the purposes of this chapter you need to get OJB working from within JBoss. To accomplish this, you'll need to run the OJB Ant build script with the targets prepare-jboss and jar. The prepare-jboss target copies the code for the PB and ODMG APIs JBoss MBeans to the code base for compilation, while the jar target invokes all the needed targets to compile and package the OJB distribution JARs.

Before executing the Ant targets you need to determine what target database you'll be using. OJB doesn't impose any restrictions on the target database other than a compliant JDBC driver, but for certain functions OJB uses several internal database tables that need to be created. These internal tables are used for sequencing (autoincrementing primary keys), locking, and several ODMG-specific structures. The schema for these tables varies slightly from database platform to platform, therefore OJB uses a profile to define the target database (which is defined by a build property, which in turn enables the selection of a profile file from the directory named profile under the OJB distribution). In the case of the TCMS samples that will be created, the target database is HSQLDB, which happens to be the default as defined in the build.properties file located at the root of the OJB directory.

OJB also needs to know the location of certain JAR files that aren't distributed as part of OJB such as the J2EE API JARs, which are needed for compiling the MBeans and the JDO reference implementation JARs if you decide to use JDO. For the TCMS examples you'll be using the JBoss J2EE JAR file jboss-j2ee.jar, which is located in the JBOSS_HOME/client directory. Copy this file to the OJB lib directory. To instruct OJB to use this JAR file change the value of the property j2ee.jars in the build.properties to jboss-j2ee.jar.

You'll also need to copy to the OJB lib directory, the following files, which are located in the JBOSS_HOME/lib directory:

- jboss-common.jar

- jboss-jmx.jar

- jboss-system.jar

With these preliminary configuration tasks finished you can now run Ant with the appropriate targets to build the OJB distribution JARs. At the command prompt type the following:

```
ant prepare jboss jar
```

The output should resemble the following:

```
Buildfile: build.xml

prepare-jboss:
prepare-jboss:
jar:
...
main-opt:
    [javac] Compiling 600 source files to C:\java\ojb\target\classes
    [javac] Note: Some input files use or override a deprecated API.
    [javac] Note: Recompile with -deprecation for details.
    [javac] Compiling 242 source files to C:\java\ojb\target\classestest
...
init:

jar-internal:
    [delete] Deleting: C:\java\ojb\dist\db-ojb-1.0.rc5.jar
    [delete] Deleting: C:\java\ojb\dist\db-ojb-1.0.rc5-junit.jar
    [delete] Deleting: C:\java\ojb\dist\db-ojb-1.0.rc5-src.jar
    [delete] Deleting: C:\java\ojb\dist\db-ojb-1.0.rc5-tools.jar
    [delete] Deleting: C:\java\ojb\dist\db-ojb-1.0.rc5-tutorial.jar
    [delete] Deleting: C:\java\ojb\target\classes\MANIFEST.MF
      [copy] Copying 1 file to C:\java\ojb\target\classes
       [jar] Building jar: C:\java\ojb\dist\db-ojb-1.0.rc5.jar
       [jar] Building jar: C:\java\ojb\dist\db-ojb-1.0.rc5-tools.jar
       [jar] Building jar: C:\java\ojb\dist\db-ojb-1.0.rc5-tutorial.jar
       [jar] Building jar: C:\java\ojb\dist\db-ojb-1.0.rc5-junit.jar
       [jar] Building jar: C:\java\ojb\dist\db-ojb-1.0.rc5-src.jar

BUILD SUCCESSFUL
Total time: 1 minute 40 seconds
```

As a result of the build, you'll end up with several JAR files in the OJB dist directory. The main JAR needed for the examples is (in the case of the rc5 distribution) db-ojb-1.0.rc5.jar.

One-to-Many Example with OJB and JBoss

As you did in Chapter 5 you'll use the domain objects Conference and Conference-enceTrack. But instead of using CMP Entity EJBs, you'll create POJOs and use OJB to persist them to the underlying TCMS database. As seen before, these two classes share a one-to-many relationship in which a Conference can have many associated Tracks. The table schema for the two existing tables is shown here (the relationship to the Venue table, via the foreign key fk_VenueId is ignored for the purpose of this example):

```
CREATE TABLE Conferences (
  pk_Id INTEGER NOT NULL PRIMARY KEY,
  Name varchar(64),
  Description LONGVARCHAR,
  StartDate DATETIME,
  EndDate DATETIME,
  AbstractSubmissionStartDate DATETIME,
  AbstractSubmissionEndDate DATETIME,
  fk_VenueId int NULL,
  CONSTRAINT ConferencesVenuesFK FOREIGN KEY(fk_VenueId) REFERENCES Venues(pk_Id)
);

CREATE TABLE Tracks (
  pk_Id INTEGER NOT NULL PRIMARY KEY,
  fk_ConferenceId INTEGER,
  Title VARCHAR(32),
  Subtitle VARCHAR(32),
  Description LONGVARCHAR,
  CONSTRAINT TracksConferencesFK FOREIGN KEY(fk_ConferenceId) REFERENCES
    Conferences(pk_Id)
);
```

Before coding begins you need a suitable project structure. Similar to the EJB CMP examples in Chapter 5, Figure 7.2 shows the directory structure of the OJB/JBoss project.

Figure 7-2. OJB and JBoss project directory structure

The basic premise of the example is to map two POJOs, one for the table Conferences and one for the table Tracks and perform some create, read, update, and delete (CRUD) operations. For this you'll use a simple stateless Session Bean, which in turn will use OJB's PersistenceBroker API to manipulate the objects. Figure 7-3 shows a sequence diagram with the interactions between the classes.

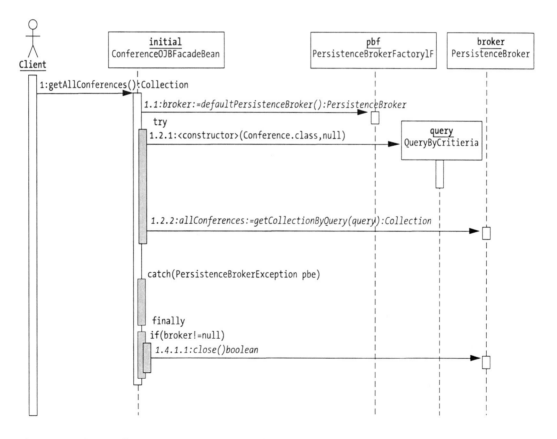

Figure 7-3. OJB and JBoss project sequence diagram

In this example you'll use OJB to map one table per class. Each table closely aligns with the EJB CMP solution previously implemented and could ease the transition from one to the other. As with the generation of EJB's glue files, you'll use XDoclet with the ojbdoclet module, which will enable you to mark up the POJOs with JavaDoc comments, which will drive the generation of the OJB mappings.

Creating the Plain Old Java Objects

The first class to be created is the Conference class, which will be part of the com.ejdoab.pojos package. This simple class contains several fields that will be mapped to the CONFERENCES database table, which was shown previously. Notice the addition of a field named tracks, which is a vector that will contain a collection of Track objects associated with the Conference. Also notice that this class is made to implement the serializable interface so that you can use it remotely. The only requirement for a class to be made persistence-aware in OJB is to provide a no-args constructor. To make the classes more usable and to make object creation simpler add an all-args constructor as well as JavaBeans-style getters and setters.

OJB can access data from a class by using reflection to access a class member or using the object's getters and setters methods. OJB doesn't need getters and setters to work; it can actually work directly on the class members regardless of their visibility. Direct field access is the fastest way for OJB to access an object. Use getter and setter if you need to abstract how the data is actually handled, and need to do some precomputation with the values from the database or for any other required side effects.

 TIP You configure how OJB handles reading and writing to and from a Java class with the PersistentFieldClass attribute in OJB.properties. The default value is the PersistentFieldDefaultImpl class, which is located in the org.apache.ojb.broker.metadata package. This class uses Java reflection. To use the object's getters and setters set this value to org.apache.ojb.broker.metadata.PersistentFieldPropertyImpl.

The code for the Conference class is shown here:

```
package com.ejdoab.pojos;

import java.io.Serializable;
import java.util.*;

public class Conference implements Serializable {
    protected int id;
    protected String name;
    protected String description;
    protected Date startDate;
    protected Date endDate;
    protected Date abstractSubmissionStartDate;
    protected Date abstractSubmissionEndDate;
    protected Vector tracks;

    public Conference() {}
...
    public List getTracks() {
        return tracks;
    }
...
    public void addTrack(Track track) {
        if (tracks == null) {
            tracks = new Vector();
        }
        tracks.add(track);
    }

    public void deleteTrack(int trackId) {
        if (tracks != null) {
            boolean found = false;
            Iterator i = tracks.iterator();
            Track trackToRemove = null;
            while ((!found) && (i.hasNext())) {
                Track t = (Track) i.next();
                if (t.id == trackId) {
                    trackToRemove = t;
                    found = true;
                }
            }
```

```
            if (trackToRemove != null) {
                tracks.remove(trackToRemove);
            }
        }
    }
}
```

Similarly, the Track class provides an object-oriented view of the TRACKS table, as follows:

```
package com.ejdoab.pojos;

import java.io.Serializable;

public class Track implements Serializable {

    protected int id;
    protected String title;
    protected String subTitle;
    protected String description;
    protected int conferenceId;
    protected Conference conference;

    public Track() {}

    //
    // getters
    //
...
    //
    // setters
    //
...
}
```

O/R Mapping: The OJB Repository File

In order to map both the Conference.java and Track.java classes to their respective tables, you need to provide OJB with a descriptor of how the object's fields map to the table columns. OJB looks for this information on the repository.xml file, which is defined by the document type declaration (DTD) repository.dtd. The repository.xml file also contains information about JDBC connections and OJB's mappings for internal tables. For the purposes of using OJB in the context of a JBoss application the repository.xml file is packaged in as part of a JBoss service archive (SAR) as explained later in the chapter.

 TIP   The OJB repository file is very well documented at
http://db.apache.org/ojb/repository.html.

In order to simplify the configuration file, you include XML fragments using entity references as shown in this sample repository.xml:

```xml
<?xml version="1.0" encoding="UTF-8"?>
<!DOCTYPE descriptor-repository PUBLIC
    "-//Apache Software Foundation//DTD OJB Repository//EN"
    "repository.dtd"
[
<!ENTITY database SYSTEM "repository_database.xml">
<!ENTITY internal SYSTEM "repository_internal.xml">
<!ENTITY user SYSTEM "repository_user.xml">
]>

<descriptor-repository
    version="1.0"
    isolation-level="read-uncommitted"
    proxy-prefetching-limit="50"
    >
    <!-- include all used database connections -->
    &database;
    <!-- include ojb internal mappings here -->
    &internal;
    <!-- include user defined mappings here -->
    &user;
</descriptor-repository>
```

Notice that there are three fragments included: database (which maps to repository_database.xml), internal (repository_internal.xml), and user (repository_user.xml). As you can probably guess, repository_user.xml contains the object-relational mappings for the POJOs. For the Conference-Track example the repository_user.xml file is made up of two class-descriptor elements, one for each of the classes.

For a concrete class, the class-descriptor element defines a mapping between a Java class and a database table. Each class-descriptor can contain several different types of elements, including the following:

- **field-descriptor:** Represents a mapping of a class field to a table column.

- **collection-descriptor:** Represents a mapping of a collectionlike field to a set of records in a table referenced by a foreign key.

- **reference-descriptor:** Represents a mapping from a field in the current class to another OJB mapped class.

- **extent-class:** Used to model object inheritance. OJB is flexible enough to allow for a multiple approach to mapping inheritance relationships including one table per class and one table per class hierarchy.

The basic skeleton for the class-descriptor element for the Conference class shown here, tells you that the com.ejdoab.pojos.Conference class is to be mapped to the table conferences:

```
<class-descriptor
    class="com.ejdoab.pojos.Conference"
    table="conferences"
>
    <field-descriptor>...</field-descriptor>
...
</class-descriptor>
```

Table 7-2 provides the specifics of mapping Conference.java to the Conferences table. For most Java-type to JDBC-type conversions, OJB guesses the correct transformation. For more complex types that require explicit transformation, OJB provides the ability to use conversion classes. An OJB conversion class implements the org.apache.ojb.broker.accesslayer.conversions.FieldConversion, which declares the javaToSql and sqlToJava methods.

Table 7-2. Object Fields to Table Column Mappings for Conference.java

Object Field	Java Type	Table Column
id	int	PK_ID
name	String	NAME
description	String	DESCRIPTION
startDate	Date	STARTDATE
endDate	Date	ENDDATE
abstractSubmissionStartDate	Date	ABSTRACTSUBMISSIONSTARTDATE
abstractSubmissionEndDate	Date	ABSTRACTSUBMISSIONENDDATE
tracks	Vector	TRACKSCONFERENCESFK (TRACKS Table)

The PK_ID field is the primary key for the table conferences. It's declared NOT NULL in the table schema. In order to map the Java field ID to the column PK_ID you need a field-descriptor element as shown here:

```
<field-descriptor
    name="id"
    column="PK_ID"
    jdbc-type="INTEGER"
    primarykey="true"
    nullable="false"
    autoincrement="true"
/>
```

Notice that a field-descriptor element enables you to define the name of the Java field, the table column it maps to, and whether it's a primary key and nullable. The last attribute is especially important because it tells OJB to generate the value for the primary key for new objects being persisted. This value gets automatically incremented as new objects are persisted to the database. Later in this section you'll learn how to configure OJB's autoincrement feature.

Table 7-2. Object Fields to Table Column Mappings for Conference.java

JDBC Type	Special Processing
INTEGER	None
VARCHAR(64)	None
LONGVARCHAR	None
TIMESTAMP	Java Date >> SQL Timestamp
TIMESTAMP	Java Date >> SQL Timestamp
TIMESTAMP	Java Date >> SQL Timestamp
TIMESTAMP	Java Date >> SQL Timestamp
INTEGER	One-to-many mapping

BEST PRACTICE   When choosing a primary key for a new table, especially if you know that the table will be used in an object-oriented system by an ORM tool, use surrogate primary keys whenever possible. Surrogate primary keys are small, simple keys that have no business meaning and are normally not updated or even seen by end users. They provide an audit trail, result in small indexes, make joins easier to write and faster to execute, are more resilient to business changes (because they have no business meaning), and make referential integrity easier to maintain. An example of dangerous business-key usage as a primary key would be using telephone numbers as account identifiers. Because telephone numbers can and do change, maintenance or some sort of mapping would be required when a customer's telephone number changes.

Characterlike JDBC types like VARCHAR and LONGVARCHAR map directly to Java Strings as shown in the field-descriptor elements for the name and description columns. Notice that the lengths are specified using the length attribute. If no length is specified OJB will assign a default value, as follows:

```
<field-descriptor
    name="name"
    column="NAME"
    jdbc-type="VARCHAR"
    length="64"
/>
<field-descriptor
    name="description"
    column="DESCRIPTION"
    jdbc-type="LONGVARCHAR"
    length="255"
/>
```

For the Java fields of java.util.Date type a conversion from the SQL type TIMESTAMP is required. If you examine the OJB JavaDocs under the org.apache.ojb.broker.accesslayer.conversions package you'll find the JavaDate2SqlTimestampFieldConversion class. As the name implies this class can convert between java.util.Date and SQL TIMESTAMP. To use the OJB's conversion feature you need to use the conversion attribute as shown in the descriptor of the field startDate, as follows:

```
<field-descriptor
    name="startDate"
    column="STARTDATE"
    jdbc-type="TIMESTAMP"
    conversion="(...).JavaDate2SqlTimestampFieldConversion"
/>
```

To map the one-to-many relationship between Conference and Track you use a collection-descriptor element, as shown here:

```
<collection-descriptor
    name="tracks"
    element-class-ref="com.ejdoab.pojos.Track"
    auto-retrieve="true"
    auto-update="true"
    auto-delete="true"
    >
    <orderby name="pk_Id" sort="ASC"/>
    <inverse-foreignkey field-ref="conferenceId"/>
</collection-descriptor>
```

The collection-descriptor element maps the tracks field of type Vector to a collection of objects of com.ejdoab.pojos.Track type, for which the conferenceId field matches the value of the Conference object primary key (the ID field). Under the covers, the collection-descriptor is a specialized type of reference-descriptor for working with collections of related objects such as the case of the one-to-many relationship in the example.

Most of the fields in the Track object are mapped in similar fashion, with the only special case being the mapping of the field conference, which should return the object of type Conference to which a given Track object belongs. For this you'll use a reference-descriptor that maps the field conference to the object of the Conference class for which the primary key matches the conferenceId foreign key as shown here:

```
<class-descriptor
    class="com.ejdoab.pojos.Track"
    table="tracks"
>
...
    <field-descriptor
        name="conferenceId"
        column="fk_ConferenceId"
        jdbc-type="INTEGER"
    />
...
    <reference-descriptor
        name="conference"
        class-ref="com.ejdoab.pojos.Conference"
    >
        <foreignkey field-ref="conferenceId"/>
    </reference-descriptor>
</class-descriptor>
```

The mappings shown in this example are a very simple example of the mapping capabilities of OJB. For example, when mapping inheritance you can use the extent-class element with different mapping strategies such as one class per table, one class per hierarchy, and one class per table with foreign keys. Lazy loading and proxy classes are some of the advanced concepts not covered in this chapter that you might want to investigate at the OJB website.

Generating OJB Mappings with XDoclet

OJB provides a faster and more streamlined way to generate the repository_user.xml file by using the OJB XDoclet module, which ships as part of the OJB distribution. By using XDoclet attributes on the POJOs you only need to maintain the mappings at the place that's most likely to change often, the source code. As with EJBs, XDoclet lets you stay true to XP's "Once and Only Once" rule by eliminating the work of manually maintaining the XML mapping file.

The module is contained in the xdoclet-ojb-module-1.2.jar file and provides you with the ojbdoclet Ant task. Place this file in the lib/development/xdoclet directory of the sample project along with the base XDoclet JARs (you can just copy all of the files under the XDoclet distribution lib directory) as follows:

- commons-collections-2.0.jar

- commons-logging.jar

- log4j.jar

- xdoclet-1.2.jar

- xdoclet-ejb-module-1.2.jar

- xdoclet-java-module-1.2.jar

- xdoclet-jboss-module-1.2.jar

- xdoclet-web-module-1.2.jar

- xdoclet-xdoclet-module-1.2.jar

- xjavadoc-1.0.2.jar

For the sample project, you can use the path declaration shown to gain access to all the necessary OJB JARs from within Ant. Notice the use of the ${OJB_HOME} property, as follows:

```
<path id="ojb.class.path">
    <path refid="xdoclet.class.path"/>
    <fileset dir="${OJB_HOME}/lib">
        <include name="*.jar"/>
    </fileset>
    <fileset dir="${OJB_HOME}/dist">
        <include name="*.jar"/>
    </fileset>
</path>
```

Load the Doclets

```
<!-- ====================================================================== -->
<!-- Declare taskdefs                                                       -->
<!-- ====================================================================== -->
<taskdef
    name="ejbdoclet"
    classname="xdoclet.modules.ejb.EjbDocletTask"
    classpathref="xdoclet.class.path"
    />

<taskdef
    name="ojbdoclet"
    classname="xdoclet.modules.ojb.OjbDocletTask"
    classpathref="ojb.class.path"
    />
```

To use the ojbdoclet task in your Ant script to create the OJB mappings file repository_user.xml, you use the Ant target shown here. The ojbdoclet task has two subtasks: ojbrepository and torqueschema. For the examples in this chapter you'll only need the ojbrepository subtask, which creates the XML fragment containing the user descriptors. The torqueschema subtask creates Torque XML schemas, which can be transformed into SQL statements for a particular database.

NOTE Torque is also a persistence layer that can generate code to map an object model to a set of databases. Torque, which came from the Apache Turbine framework, is a less flexible O/R mapping technology than OJB. It uses an XML file that describes the object model and generates both Java classes and SQL scripts. It can operate with many databases and it's used by OJB to generate database-specific SQL scripts. Torque can also reverse engineer existing database schemas into a Java object model.

Similar to the previously used ejbdoclet, ojbdoclet requires a set of source files so that you can scan for XDoclet tags. It also requires the name and destination of the generated XML fragment, as shown here:

```
<!-- ================================================================== -->
<!-- Generates OJB repository_user.xml using OJB XDoclet's Task        -->
<!-- ================================================================== -->
<target name="ojb-mapping" depends="clean,prepare"
    description="generates OJB repository file using ojbdoclet task">
    <echo>generating repository_user.xml...</echo>
    <ojbdoclet destdir="${descriptors-ojb}">
        <fileset dir="${src}"/>
        <ojbrepository destinationFile="repository_user.xml"/>
    </ojbdoclet>
</target>
```

Finally, all you have to do now is annotate your POJOs with XDoclet tags. Most attributes map directly to the attributes found in the OJB repository file. To generate an OJB class-descriptor element simply add a class-scoped xdoclet comment using the @ojb.class tag. Similarly, for field-descriptor elements, use @ojb.field; for collection-descriptor use @ojb.collection, and so forth.

```
...
/**
 * @ojb.class
 *     generate-table-info="true"
 *     table="conferences"
 */
```

```
public class Conference implements Serializable {

    /**
     * @ojb.field
     *     column="PK_ID"
     *     jdbc-type="INTEGER"
     *     primarykey="true"
     *     autoincrement="true"
     *     nullable="false"
     *     id="0"
     */
    protected int id;

    /**
     * @ojb.field
     *     column="NAME"
     *     jdbc-type="VARCHAR"
     *     length="64"
     *     id="1"
     */
    protected String name;
...
    /**
     * @ojb.field
     *     column="STARTDATE"
     *     jdbc-type="TIMESTAMP"
     *     id="3"
     *     conversion="org.apache.ojb.broker.accesslayer➥
                       .conversions.JavaDate2SqlTimestampFieldConversion"
     */
    protected Date startDate;
...
    /**
     * @ojb.collection
     *     element-class-ref="com.ejdoab.pojos.Track"
     *     foreignkey="conferenceId"
     *     auto-retrieve="true"
     *     auto-update="true"
     *     auto-delete="true"
     *     orderby="pk_Id"
     */
    protected Vector tracks;

...
}
```

TIP Before the 1.0 release of OJB, the XDoclet module documentation wasn't available on the OJB site. To obtain the module documentation run the doc target of the OJB build script. The xdoclet-module.html file should now be in the doc directory of your OJB distribution.

Putting It All Together with Ant

Let's walk through the Ant build script that will accomplish the build tasks required for the example. The build script is located at the root of the project directory. A sample of the build.properties file shown here has a section that defines the ejb-jar to be generated, a section for the database type (hsqldb in our case), a section for the JBoss-specific settings (refer to Chapter 5 for JBoss configuration instructions), and finally a section that defines the location of the OJB distribution.

```
// app
jar-name=ojb-jboss-test.jar

// database (for OJB profile)
database.type=hsqldb

// jboss specific
jboss.home=C:/java/jboss-3.2.1
jboss.server=${app.name}
jboss.datasource=java:/tcmsDS
jboss.datasource.mapping=Hypersonic SQL
java.naming.factory.initial=org.jnp.interfaces.NamingContextFactory
java.naming.provider.url=jnp://localhost:1099

// db properties
global.db.url=jdbc:hsqldb:hsql://localhost:1701
global.db.userid=sa
global.db.password=
global.db.driver=org.hsqldb.jdbcDriver
global.db.driver.file=${jboss.home}/server/${jboss.server}/lib/hsqldb.jar

// OJB specific
OJB_HOME=C:/java/ojb
```

The first section of the script deals with loading and configuring the build properties, as follows:

```
<?xml version="1.0"?>
<project name="ojb-jboss" default="all" basedir=".">

    <!-- ==================================================================== -->
    <!-- Configures Project's Properties                                      -->
    <!-- ==================================================================== -->
    <property file="build.properties"/>
    <property name="server-dir"
              location="${jboss.home}/server/${jboss.server}" />
    <property name="server-lib-dir"  location="${server-dir}/lib" />
    <property name="server-conf-dir" location="${server-dir}/conf" />
    <property name="server-client-dir"  location="${jboss.home}/client" />
    <property name="deploy-dir"        location="${server-dir}/deploy" />

    <property name="root" location="${basedir}" />
    <property name="src" location="${root}/src/java" />
    <property name="classes" location="${root}/classes" />
    <property name="generated" location="${root}/generated" />
    <property name="generated-ejb" location="${generated}/ejb-src" />
    <property name="descriptors-ejb" location="${generated}/descriptors/ejb" />
    <property name="descriptors-ojb" location="${generated}/descriptors/ojb" />
    <property name="generated-sql" location="${root}/generated/sql" />
    <property name="dist" location="${root}/dist" />
    <property name="conf" location="${root}/conf" />
    <property name="build" location="${root}/build" />

    <property name="lib" location="lib" />
    <property name="lib-dev" location="${lib}/development" />
```

Next, several path elements are created for all the project dependencies, including OJB, JBoss, and XDoclet. Notice that throughout the build you make use of the ${jboss.home} and ${OJB_HOME} properties. Both of these properties are defined in the build.properties file.

```xml
<!-- ======================================================================= -->
<!-- Configures the ClassPath                                                -->
<!-- ======================================================================= -->
<path id="class.path">
    <fileset dir="lib">
        <include name="*.jar"/>
    </fileset>
    <fileset dir="${server-lib-dir}">
        <include name="*servlet.jar"/>
    </fileset>
    <fileset dir="${server-client-dir}">
        <include name="jbossall-client.jar"/>
    </fileset>
    <pathelement location="${classes}" />
</path>

<path id="jdbc.class.path">
    <pathelement location="${global.db.driver.file}" />
</path>

<path id="xdoclet.class.path">
    <path refid="class.path"/>
    <fileset dir="${lib-dev}/xdoclet">
        <include name="*.jar"/>
    </fileset>
</path>
```

The jdbc.class.path path element points to the location of the hsqldb JDBC drivers.

OJB Internal Tables

For the JBoss and OJB example you'll be using the PersistenceBroker API, and because you'll be using OJB's autoincrement feature you'll need to have the certain OJB internal tables in your database. The autoincrement feature automatically creates primary keys (object identifier from the object's point of view) for new objects being persisted. OJB will detect that the object field that represents the primary key isn't assigned (typically by checking for null) and assign a new primary key based on the selected policy. The O/R mappings for these tables are contained in the XML repository_internal.xml fragment. Instead of re-creating a lot of the work performed by the OJB build script (build-torque.xml) you can use the Ant task to invoke the OJB build and generate the needed tables.

NOTE The PersistenceBroker API only requires the OJB_HL_SEQ table. Because you're calling the OJB build script you'll actually end up with all of OJB internal tables, including those for APIs that aren't used in the examples.

The Ant target shown here invokes the OJB build-torque.xml build script and executes the project-sql-classpath target. This will generate a SQL script in the target/src/sql directory of the OJB distribution, which you'll then run against your database using the SQL Ant task. All Torque-related OJB targets use the value of the profile property (hsqldb for this example) to generate the database-specific SQL, therefore you load the OJB property file for the selected profile before invoking the targets, as shown here:

```xml
<!-- ===================================================================== -->
<!-- Create OJB Internal Tables                                       -->
<!-- ===================================================================== -->

<target name="ojb-internal-tables"
    description="uses the OJB build to generate the OJB's internal tables">
    <property file="${OJB_HOME}/build.properties"/>

    <!-- load the profile set in build.properties -->
    <property file="${OJB_HOME}/profile/${profile}.profile"/>

    <ant dir="${OJB_HOME}"
        antfile="build-torque.xml"
        target="project-sql-classpath"
    />
    <!-- use the sql task to execute the ojbcore-schema.sql file -->
    <sql
        driver="${global.db.driver}"
        url="${global.db.url}"
        userid="${global.db.userid}"
        password="${global.db.password}"
        src="${OJB_HOME}/target/src/sql/ojbcore-schema.sql"
        autocommit="true"
        onerror="continue">
        <classpath refid="jdbc.class.path"/>
    </sql>
</target>
```

OJB SAR File

For OJB to work inside of JBoss you need to deploy the following OJB MBeans:

- **PBFactoryMBean:** If you're using the PB API

- **ODMGFactoryMBean:** If you're using the ODMG API

Both classes are part of the org.apache.ojb.jboss package and are located in the src/connector directory of the OJB distribution. The OJB distribution created previously contains both of these MBeans.

To deploy OJB as a JBoss service you need to create an OJB SAR file. A JBoss SAR file contains a JBoss service definition (jboss-service.xml) and its associated files.

 NOTE A SAR file is a JAR archive with the extension .sar. SAR files are specific to JBoss and aren't part of the J2EE specification.

Figure 7-4 shows the structure of the OJB service SAR file. As you can see, it contains the service definition jboss-service.xml along with a simple manifest in the META-INF directory. In the root directory you'll find the OJB distribution files (previously created) and their dependencies and configuration files.

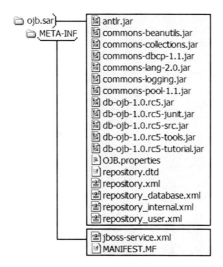

Figure 7-4. OJB JBoss service archive

Table 7-3 provides a brief explanation of the configuration files needed for OJB to work correctly.

Table 7-3. OJB JBoss SAR Configuration Files

File	Purpose	Where to Find It
OJB.properties	OJB runtime environment configuration	doc directory (under the name OJB.properties.txt)
repository.xml	Used to generate the metadata layer using by OJB at runtime	doc directory
repository_database.xml	XML fragment included in repository.xml, contains JDBC connection information	doc directory
repository_internal.xml	XML fragment included in repository.xml, contains O/R mappings for OJB internal tables	
repository_user.xml	XML fragment containing application-specific O/R mappings	Generated by Ant script
jboss-service.xml	JBoss service configuration file	Hand-coded

OJB.properties

The OJB.properties file handles runtime environment configuration items such as execution mode (single instance vs. client-server), the initial size of the PersistenceBroker, locking, caching, and logging. In the OJB.properties file you'll need to set the value of the ConnectionFactoryClass property to the org.apache.ojb.broker.accesslayer.-ConnectionFactoryManagedImpl class. The connection factory is used to obtain a database connection in a managed environment like JBoss through the JBoss data source that was created previously for the TCMS application in Chapter 5 (tcmsDS). Also, for OJB to integrate with the JBoss transaction manager you'll need to set the value of the OJBTxManagerClass property to org.apache.ojb.odmg.JTATxManager. Finally, to enable OJB to obtain a transaction manager, a factory class is defined in the JTATransactionManagerClass property by setting its value to org.apache.ojb.odmg.transaction.JBossTransactionManagerFactory.

To make your life easier during deployment of the OJB and JBoss application an Ant target is provided that will take care of creating and deploying the OJB SAR. In order to generate the SAR archive you'll need to place the OJB.properties files, repository.xml, repository_database.xml, and jboss-service.xml in the conf directory of the application.

repository_database.xml

The repository_database.xml file contains information about the databases, which OJB will interact with. For the example, you'll be using the tcmsDS data source created in Chapter 5. As mentioned earlier in the chapter you'll be using OJB's autoincrement feature.

 NOTE HSQLDB doesn't support database-based key generation so a sequence manager such as SequenceManagerHighLowImpl or SequenceManagerInMemoryImpl is required. For more information on OJB sequence managers see http://db.apache.org/ojb/ sequencemanager.html.

This feature requires you to configure a specific sequence manager class. You'll be using the SequenceManagerHighLowImpl, which uses the OJB_HL_SEQ table.

```
<jdbc-connection-descriptor
    jcd-alias="tcms"
    default-connection="true"
    platform="Hsqldb"
    driver="org.hsqldb.jdbcDriver"
    jdbc-level="2.0"
    jndi-datasource-name="java:tcmsDS"
    username="sa"
    password=""
    eager-release="true"
    batch-mode="false"
    useAutoCommit="0"
    ignoreAutoCommitExceptions="false"
>
    <sequence-manager
        className=
            "org.apache.ojb.broker.util.sequence.SequenceManagerHighLowImpl"
    />
</jdbc-connection-descriptor>
```

jboss-service.xml

The jboss-service.xml file defines the MBeans that will be deployed. For the example you'll need to deploy the PBFactory MBean, which will be used to obtain an instance of a PBBroker. This PBFactory is bound to the JNDI name obj/PBAPI, as follows:

```xml
<?xml version="1.0" encoding="UTF-8"?>
<server>
  <mbean code="org.apache.ojb.jboss.PBFactory"
         name="DefaultDomain:service=PBAPI,name=ojb/PBAPI">
    <depends>jboss.jca:service=RARDeployer</depends>
    <attribute name="JndiName">ojb/PBAPI</attribute>
  </mbean>
</server>
```

Packaging the SAR File

Once all the configuration files have been modified, generating the SAR file is as simple as invoking the Ant target, which simply uses the jar task to create a JAR file with the .sar extension, as shown here:

```xml
<!-- ===================================================================== -->
<!-- Package the SAR                                                       -->
<!-- ===================================================================== -->
<target name="sar" depends="ojb-mapping"
    description="packages a jboss SAR file for OJB deployment">
    <echo>packaging sar...</echo>
    <jar jarfile="${dist}/ojb.sar">
    <metainf dir="${conf}" includes="jboss-service.xml"/>
    <fileset dir="${OJB_HOME}/lib">
        <include name="commons-*.jar" />
        <include name="antlr.jar" />
    </fileset>
    <fileset dir="${OJB_HOME}/dist">
        <include name="db-ojb-1.0*.jar" />
    </fileset>
    <fileset dir="${conf}">
        <include name="repository*.xml" />
        <include name="repository.dtd" />
        <include name="OJB.properties" />
    </fileset>
```

```
        <fileset dir="${descriptors-ojb}">
            <include name="repository_user.xml" />
        </fileset>
    </jar>
</target>
```

Deploying the SAR File to JBoss

To deploy the SAR file to JBoss you simply need to copy it to the tcms deploy
directory. The Ant target shown takes care of deploying both the SAR file and the
generated EJB-JAR file.

```
<!-- =================================================================== -->
<!-- Deploys SAR and EJB-JAR                                             -->
<!-- =================================================================== -->
<target name="deploy" depends="sar,ejb-jar"
    description="deploys both the SAR and EJB-JAR files to JBoss">
    <copy file="${dist}/ojb.sar" todir="${deploy-dir}"/>
    <!-- give JBoss time to deploy the SAR -->
    <sleep seconds="5"/>
    <copy file="${dist}/${jar-name}" todir="${deploy-dir}"/>
</target>
```

After copying the SAR file to the JBoss deploy directory the console will show
the PBFactory being created and started as follows:

```
...
00:12:22,277 INFO  [MainDeployer] Starting deployment of package:
    file:/C:/java/jboss/ /server/tcms/deploy/ojb.sar
00:12:22,327 INFO  [SARDeployer] nested deployment: file:...
...
00:12:24,079 INFO  [PBFactory] Creating
00:12:24,079 INFO  [PBFactory] Created
00:12:24,089 INFO  [PBFactory] Starting
00:12:24,099 INFO  [PBFactory] PBFactory: org.apache.ojb.jboss.PBFactory /
DefaultDomain:service=PBAPI,name=ojb/PBAPI
00:12:24,109 INFO  [PBFactory] Lookup PBFactory via 'java:/ojb/PBAPI'
00:12:24,109 INFO  [PBFactory] Started
00:12:24,109 INFO  [MainDeployer] Deployed package: file:/C:/java/jboss/jboss-
3.2.1/server/tcms/deploy/ojb.sar
...
```

Session Bean

To work with the PersistenceBroker API you'll use a stateless Session Bean that will provide services to manipulate the Conferences and Track objects. The com.ejdoab.beans.ConferenceOJBFacadeBean will provide the following methods:

- Collection getAllConferences

- Conference findConferenceMatching(Conference searchTemplate)

- Conference findConferenceByCriteria(Criteria criteria)

- boolean saveConference(Conference conference)

- boolean deleteConference(Conference conference)

The first step is to create a skeleton for the Session Bean, as you did in Chapter 5. You'll use XDoclet to automate the creation of the EJB glue files. A private field will hold an instance of PersistenceBrokerFactoryIF which is looked up using JNDI in the Bean's ejbCreate method. Notice that the PBFactoryIF class provides a static public field PBFACTORY_JNDI_NAME that contains the JNDI name, as shown:

```
package com.ejdoab.beans;

import org.apache.ojb.broker.PersistenceBroker;
import org.apache.ojb.broker.PersistenceBrokerException;
import org.apache.ojb.broker.core.PBFactoryIF;
import org.apache.ojb.broker.core.PersistenceBrokerFactoryIF;
import org.apache.ojb.broker.query.Criteria;
import org.apache.ojb.broker.query.Query;
import org.apache.ojb.broker.query.QueryByCriteria;

import com.ejdoab.pojos.Conference;
import com.ejdoab.pojos.Track;
```

```
/**
 * @ejb.bean
 *      name="ConferenceOJBFacade"
 *      type="Stateless"
 *      view-type="both"
 *      jndi-name="ejb.ConferenceOJBFacadeHome"
 *      local-jndi-name="ejb.ConferenceOJBFacadeLocalHome"
 * @ejb.transaction
 *      type="Required"
 * @ejb.util
 *      generate="physical"
 */
public abstract class ConferenceOJBFacadeBean implements SessionBean {

    private PersistenceBrokerFactoryIF pbf;

    //=========================================
    //  EJB callbacks
    //=========================================

    /**
     * @ejb.create-method
     */
    public void ejbCreate() throws CreateException {
        Context context = null;
        // Lookup the PBF implementation
        try {
            context = new InitialContext();
            pbf = ((PBFactoryIF)context
                    .lookup(PBFactoryIF.PBFACTORY_JNDI_NAME))
                    .getInstance();
        }
        catch (NamingException e) {
            throw new EJBException(new PersistenceBrokerException(e));
        }
    }
}
```

Retrieving a Collection of Objects

The getAllConference method instantiates a PersistenceBroker by calling the defaultPersistenceBroker method of the PersistenceBroker factory. To retrieve a collection of all conferences an org.apache.ojb.broker.query.QueryByCriteria is constructed using the Conference class as the target class and null for the criteria, which will return all available Conference objects. Notice that all PersistenceBroker methods throw a PersistenceBrokerException, which is a runtime exception and the base class for all OJB exceptions, as follows:

```
/**
 * @ejb.interface-method
 * @ejb.transaction
 *      type="NotSupported"
 *
 * @return a Collection of all Conferences in the database
 */
public Collection getAllConferences() {
    PersistenceBroker broker = pbf.defaultPersistenceBroker();
    Collection allConferences = Collections.EMPTY_LIST;

    try {
        Query query = new QueryByCriteria(Conference.class, null);
        allConferences = broker.getCollectionByQuery(query);
    } catch (PersistenceBrokerException pbe) {
        throw new EJBException("Could not retrieve list of conferences", pbe);
    } finally {
        if (broker != null)
            broker.close();
    }

    return allConferences;
}
```

Finding an Object Using a Template

The findConferenceMatching method takes a Conference object, which is created by the client code and partially populated with the values that are being searched for. The Conference object is then passed as a parameter, which is used to create a QueryByCriteria that's passed to the getObjectByQuery, which will return the first object in the database that matches the field values set on the searchTemplate Conference object, as follows:

```
/**
 * @ejb.interface-method
 * @ejb.transaction
 *       type="NotSupported"
 *
 * @return a Conference object matching the
 *         searchTemplate or null if none is found
 */
public Conference findConferenceMatching(Conference searchTemplate) {
    PersistenceBroker broker = pbf.defaultPersistenceBroker();
    Conference conference;
    try {
        Query query = new QueryByCriteria(searchTemplate);
        conference = (Conference) broker.getObjectByQuery(query);
    } catch (PersistenceBrokerException pbe) {
        throw new EJBException("Could not retrieve list of conferences", pbe);
    } finally {
        if (broker != null)
            broker.close();
    }

    return conference;
}
```

Find an Object by Criteria

Similar to the findConferenceMatching method, the findConferenceByCriteria method takes an object of type org.apache.ojb.broker.query.Criteria and uses it to construct a QueryByCriteria object, which will be used in the getObjectByQuery call. The Criteria object represents search attributes that are linked using logic operators (like AND and OR) and can be precompiled for efficient searching (instead of having to parse a string query). The code for the findConferenceBy-Criteria method is shown here.

 NOTE The OJB distribution doesn't intend for the Criteria object to be passed as a remote parameter, and doing so couples your client code to an OJB-specific class. A more reasonable choice would be to accept an application-specific Criteria-like object and use this to create an OJB criteria object on the server side.

```
/**
 * @ejb.interface-method
 * @ejb.transaction
 *       type="NotSupported"
 *
 * @return
 */
public Conference findConferenceByCriteria(Criteria criteria) {
    PersistenceBroker broker = pbf.defaultPersistenceBroker();
    Conference conference;
    try {
        Query query = new QueryByCriteria(Conference.class, criteria);
        conference = (Conference) broker.getObjectByQuery(query);
    } catch (PersistenceBrokerException pbe) {
        throw new EJBException("Could not retrieve list of conferences", pbe);
    } finally {
        if (broker != null)
            broker.close();
    }

    return conference;
}
```

Saving an Object

So far you've seen how to retrieve an object from the database using OJB. But to get those objects to the database in the first place is even simpler—all you need to do is invoke the PersistenceBroker store method. If an object's primary key attribute isn't set, OJB will detect this and autogenerate a primary key for the object, which makes the underlying operation an INSERT. If the primary key is set then the operation becomes an UPDATE if the object exists, and an INSERT if it doesn't, as shown here:

```
/**
 * @ejb.interface-method
 * @ejb.transaction
 *       type="NotSupported"
 *
 * @return
 */
```

```
public boolean saveConference(Conference conference) {
    PersistenceBroker broker = pbf.defaultPersistenceBroker();
    boolean result = true;

    try {
        broker.store(conference);
    } catch (PersistenceBrokerException pbe) {
        result = false;
    } finally {
        if (broker != null) broker.close();
    }

    return result;
}
```

Deleting an Object

Deleting a persistent object in OJB is as simple as invoking the PersistenceBroker delete(Object object) method. Dependent object deletion, such as in the case of the collection of Tracks belonging to a Conference depends on the value of the auto-delete attribute in the reference-descriptor element or the collection-descriptor elements of the class-descriptor.

You can tell OJB what to do with object references by setting retrieve (auto-retrieve), update (auto-update), and delete (auto-delete) attributes in the reference and collection descriptors. For deletion in a one-to-many scenario, you need to take into account the nature of the relationship. For example, in the Conference-Track case you don't want a Track to exist without a corresponding Conference so the auto-delete attribute is set to true. In the case where the related objects aren't going to be deleted, like in a Department-Employee scenario, you would want the Employee objects to be deleted when the Department object is deleted (although you probably would want to reassign them to another Department object or a "dummy" Department object that represents the state when an Employee doesn't officially belong to any department). The code for the deleteConference method is shown here:

```
/**
 * @ejb.interface-method
 * @ejb.transaction
 *       type="NotSupported"
 *
 * @return
 */
```

```
    public boolean deleteConference(Conference conference) {
        PersistenceBroker broker = pbf.defaultPersistenceBroker();
        boolean result = true;

        try {
            broker.delete(conference);
        } catch (PersistenceBrokerException pbe) {
            result = false;
        } finally {
            if (broker != null) broker.close();
        }

        return result;
    }
```

Test Client

Finally, you'll need a test client similar to the one used in Chapter 5. In this client you'll look up the ConferenceOJBFacade Session Bean and invoke the exposed methods. First, you'll retrieve all existing conferences. If you ran the SQL scripts provided in Chapter 5 you should have one Conference object and three associated Tracks in the database. Next you'll search for a Conference object using the two different methods provided and create the Conference object if it doesn't exist, as shown here:

```
package com.ejdoab.client;

import org.apache.ojb.broker.query.Criteria;
import com.ejdoab.beans.ConferenceOJBFacade;
import com.ejdoab.beans.ConferenceOJBFacadeHome;
import com.ejdoab.pojos.Conference;
import com.ejdoab.pojos.Track;

/**
 * Simple OJB/JBoss Test Client
 */
public class Client {
    private static final String ICF = "org.jnp.interfaces.NamingContextFactory";
    private static final String SERVER_URI = "localhost:1099";
    private static final String PKG_PREFIXES =
        "org.jboss.naming:org.jnp.interfaces";
```

```
public static void main(String args[]) {
    Context ctx;
    ConferenceOJBFacadeHome facadeHome;
    ConferenceOJBFacade facade;

    // initial context JBossNS configuration
    Hashtable env = new Hashtable();
    env.put(Context.INITIAL_CONTEXT_FACTORY, ICF);
    env.put(Context.PROVIDER_URL, SERVER_URI);
    env.put(Context.URL_PKG_PREFIXES, PKG_PREFIXES);
    ...
}
```

The first step is to locate the Facade Session Bean using JNDI, as follows:

```
...
try {
    // ----------
    // JNDI Stuff
    // ----------
    ctx = new InitialContext(env);
    // look up the home interface
    System.out.println(
        "[jndi lookup] Looking Up ConferenceOJBFacade " +
        "Remote Home Interface" );
    Object obj = ctx.lookup("ejb.ConferenceOJBFacadeHome");
    // cast and narrow
    facadeHome = (ConferenceOJBFacadeHome) PortableRemoteObject
        .narrow( obj, ConferenceOJBFacadeHome.class);
    // create the facade
    facade = facadeHome.create();
    ...
```

Now you use the ConferenceOJBFacade Session Bean to retrieve a list of all conferences:

```
// ----------
// Tests
// ----------
System.out.println("[retrieving all conferences]");
Collection c = facade.getAllConferences();
Iterator i = c.iterator();
while (i.hasNext()) {
    Conference conference = (Conference)i.next();
    System.out.println(conference.toString());
}
```

To find a conference using a search template you simply need to construct a Conference object, set some of its values, and invoke the findConferenceMatching method:

```
//
// Find using a search template
//
System.out.println("[searching using template object]");
Conference searchTemplate = new Conference();
searchTemplate.setId(1);
// searchTemplate.setName("Apress OSC"); <-- can search on any field
Conference conference = facade.findConferenceMatching(searchTemplate);

if (conference != null) {
    System.out.println(conference);
}
else {
    System.out.println("could not find a conference matching = "
        + searchTemplate);
}
```

For more control over the search results you can use the OJB Criteria object. In the code snippet shown here, a Conference is searched for by name:

```
//
// Find by criteria
//
System.out.println("[searching using criteria]");
Criteria criteria = new Criteria();
criteria.addEqualTo("name", "Apress OSC");
conference = facade.findConferenceByCriteria(criteria);
```

If the object is found then it's displayed, along with any associated Track object, as follows:

```
if (conference != null) {
    //
    // Conference found, displaying it
    //
    System.out.println("Conference was found\n" + conference + "\n");
    System.out.println("Here are the tracks:\n");
    Vector tracks = (Vector) conference.getTracks();
    for (Iterator iter = tracks.iterator(); iter.hasNext();) {
        Track track = (Track) iter.next();
        System.out.println(track);
        System.out.println("This track belongs to conference " +
            track.getConference().getName());
    }
}
```

If the object isn't found then you can create it. The code snippet adds three new tracks to the newly created Conference object and it then invokes the saveConference method to persist the object, as shown:

```
...
else {
    Date today = new Date();
      //
      // Conference not found, creating it
      //
    System.out.println("Conference was not found, creating it");

    // create the new conference object
    Conference newConf =
        new Conference("Apress OSC", "Apress Open Source Conference",
                        today, today, today, today);
    // add some tracks
    newConf.addTrack(
        new Track("J2SE",
                    "Java 2 Standard Edition",
                "Learn how to build powerful Java desktop applications"));
    newConf.addTrack(
        new Track(
            "J2EE",
            "Java 2 Enterprise Edition",
          "Enterprise Applications powered entirely by Open Source"));
```

```
                    newConf.addTrack(
                        new Track(
                            "J2ME",
                            "Java 2 Micro Edition",
                            "Java brings cell phones and PDAs to life"));

                    // invoke the session bean to save the conference
                    boolean result = facade.saveConference(newConf);
                    System.out.println(
                        "The conference was " + (result ? "saved" : "NOT saved"));
                }
            }
            catch (RemoteException re) {
                System.out.println("[rmi] remote exception: " + re.getMessage());
            }
            catch (NamingException ne) {
                System.out.println("[naming] naming exception: " + ne.getMessage());
            }
            catch (CreateException ce) {
                System.out.println("[ejb] create exception: " + ce.getMessage());
            }
        }
}
```

Results

The results of running the test client application for the first time are shown here:

```
[jndi lookup] Looking Up ConferenceOJBFacade Remote Home Interface
[retrieving all conferences]

[searching using template object]
could not find a conference with id = 1

[searching using criteria]
Conference was not found, creating it
The conference was saved
```

As you can see, on the first run the Conference object isn't found by either of the methods selected so it's created. On the second run you can see that the newly created Conference object is now found along with its associated Tracks:

```
[jndi lookup] Looking Up ConferenceOJBFacade Remote Home Interface
[retrieving all conferences]
[Conference] id = 1,
            name = Apress OSC,
            description = Apress Open Source Conference,
            start date = Wed Jan 07 16:53:15 EST 2004,
            end date = Wed Jan 07 16:53:15 EST 2004,
            tracks = 3

[searching using template object]
Conference was found
[Conference] id = 1,
            name = Apress OSC,
            description = Apress Open Source Conference,
            start date = Wed Jan 07 16:53:15 EST 2004,
            end date = Wed Jan 07 16:53:15 EST 2004,
            tracks = 3

Here are the tracks:

[Track] id = 1,
        title = J2SE,
        subTitle = Java 2 Standard Edition,
        description = Come and learn how to build powerful
                      Java desktop applications
This track belongs to conference Apress OSC
[Track] id = 2,
        title = J2EE,
        subTitle = Java 2 Enterprise Edition,
        description = Enterprise Applications powered entirely by Open Source
This track belongs to conference Apress OSC
[Track] id = 3,
        title = J2ME,
        subTitle = Java 2 Micro Edition,
        description = Java brings cell phones and PDAs to life
This track belongs to conference Apress OSC
```

As you can see, OJB covers most of the needs of an enterprise application when it comes to persistence. There are features of OJB that aren't covered in this chapter and you can learn more about them by visiting the OJB website (http://db.apache.org/ojb) or reading through the post in the OJB user newsgroup (comp.jakarta.ojb.user). Among these features are proxy classes which enable lazy loading for performance purposes.

Hibernate

Hibernate is an ORM tool billed as a "relational persistence for idiomatic Java," which can be translated as a way of saying "object-oriented transparent persistence mechanism for Java." Hibernate provides both persistence and object-querying capabilities that allow you to work in a fine-grained fashion with rich object models. It provides an object-oriented declarative programming model that doesn't depend on code generation or bytecode modification (). Like OJB, Hibernate uses runtime reflection and its O/R mappings are XML documents. (Hibernate also provides the ability to define the mappings in the Java code, which can be useful for tool automation or query building tools.) Hibernate works equally well in stand-alone applications or in managed environments such as a J2EE server.

The Hibernate project got started by Gavin King in late 2001 as the result of his experiences working with the earlier versions of CMP EJBs. Hibernate's easy-to-use SQL-like query language makes it easier for developers who are accustomed to writing SQL to make the transition from either CMP EJBs or straight JDBC. Hibernate has become a successful example of an Open Source project because it provides a large, clean amount of documentation, and has very responsive community support. In late 2003, Hibernate became part of the JBoss project and will be used as the foundation for JBoss' CMP engine.

As opposed to OJB, Hibernate doesn't support multiple personalities or APIs. Hibernate provides a single, simple API that strives for familiarity (to SQL) rather than standards compliance. Figure 7-5 shows a simplified view of Hibernate's architecture.

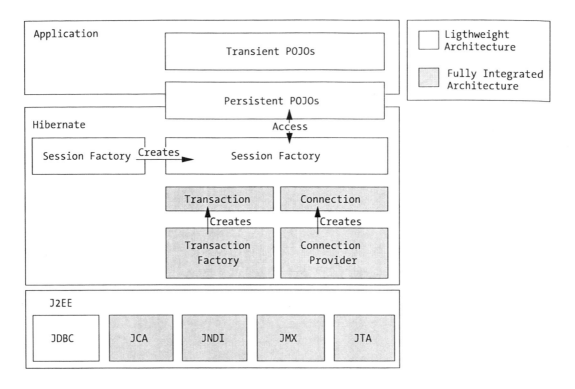

Figure 7-5. Hibernate architecture

In Hibernate, O/R mappings are compiled and cached by the Session factory, which is used to retrieve Hibernate Sessions. A Session's role is similar to a stateless Session Bean in that it's a short-lived object used as a bridge between an application and the underlying data storage (similar to OJB's PersistenceBroker). The Hibernate Session embodies the concept of a persistence service that can be used to insert, update, and delete operations on instances of a class mapped by Hibernate.

As you can see from Figure 7-5, however much you use Hibernate depends on your needs. At its simplest level Hibernate provides a lightweight architecture that only deals with ORM. Although a full-blown Hibernate architecture fully abstracts most aspects of persistence such as transaction, caching, and connection pooling. To learn more about Hibernate's architecture go to http://www.hibernate.org/hib_docs/reference/html/architecture.html or get *Hibernate in Action: Practical Object/Relational Mapping* by Christian Bauer and Gavin King.[3]

---

3. Bauer, Christian and Gavin King. *Hibernate in Action, Practical Object/Relational Mapping* (Greenwich, CT: Manning, 2004).

Obtaining Hibernate

You can download Hibernate (version 2.1.1) from http://www.hibernate.org in both binary and source distributions. For the examples, you'll need the binary distribution file hibernate-2.1.1.zip, which you can unzip and save to any location, for example c:\java\hibernate.

Configuring the Sample Project

For the Hibernate example you'll mimic the directory structure created for the OJB example shown in Figure 7-2. Hibernate's dependencies are all contained in the lib directory under the Hibernate distribution. As you did in the OJB example, you'll now access the required Hibernate libraries with an Ant script that will do most of the work of copying and configuring your Hibernate and JBoss project.

 NOTE For stand-alone Hibernate applications you need to configure the file hibernate.properties, which controls the runtime behavior of Hibernate and must be found in the classpath. In the case of the JBoss examples there's no need to do so because most runtime parameters are defined at the JBoss service level or are dynamically guessed by Hibernate.

There are also some minor changes required to the POJOs used in this example. In the OJB example, you used the int primitive Java type for the object's IDs. With Hibernate's way of detecting whether an object has been saved or not, nonprimitive nullable IDs result in easier configuration of the mappings. Therefore you'll need to change the int fields in favor of Integer fields for the Conference.java and Track.java as shown here:

```
...
public class Conference implements Serializable {
    protected Integer id;
        ...
    public Integer getId() {
        return id;
    }
...
    public void setId(Integer value) {
        id = value;
    }
...
```

NOTE   Hibernate doesn't require the use of object identifiers, if one isn't provided Hibernate will keep track of the objects internally. However, as pointed out in the Hibernate online documentation, having a simple and consistent object identifier per class is a good practice, and some of Hibernate's optional optimizations, such as cascaded updates and dynamic "save or update" functionality, might require them.

Hibernate O/R Mappings

Let's take a brief look at the Hibernate mappings needed for the Conference and Track objects. Hibernate strives for simplicity of the metadata. If something is missing in a mapping, Hibernate attempts to guess the appropriate values or defaults using reflection. This makes the Hibernate mapping process more forgiving than most other ORM tools.

Remember with the Conference and Tracks classes you have a bidirectional one-to-many association, therefore you need a way to get all Tracks for an associated Conference and the associated Conference for a given Track.

The Hibernate mappings are very similar to the OJB mappings, with the exception that Hibernate promotes the use on one mapping file per class, which eases collaborative work, especially in the early stages of ORM process. This effectively changes the way you work with the persistence framework, thereby giving you a class-driven view of the system as opposed to a database-driven one.

The skeleton for the Conference.hbm.xml file (all Hibernate mappings have the hbm prefix before the .xml extension) should resemble the following:

```xml
<?xml version="1.0"?>

<!DOCTYPE hibernate-mapping PUBLIC
    "-//Hibernate/Hibernate Mapping DTD 2.0//EN"
    "http://hibernate.sourceforge.net/hibernate-mapping-2.0.dtd">

<hibernate-mapping>
    <class
        name="com.ejdoab.pojos.Conference"
        table="conferences"
        dynamic-update="false"
        dynamic-insert="false"
    >
        <!-- field mappings go here -->
    </class>
</hibernate-mapping>
```

The root element is named hibernate-mapping and for each mapped class you'll have a class element. The main properties to notice in the class element are the fully qualified name of the class that will be mapped under the name property, and the table that will be used to map the said class.

To map the individual fields of an object to columns in a table there are several elements that you can use depending on the function of the given field. Table 7-4 shows the field mapping elements that you'll use in the example.

Table 7-4. Hibernate Mapping Elements Used in the Example

Element	Purpose
id	Defines a mapping between an object identity property and a primary key column in the database
property	Defines a mapping between an object property and a column in the database
set	One of the many collection mapping elements that include list, map, bag, array, and primitive-array
many-to-one	Defines a simple object reference in a many-to-one relationship

Mapping Identity Columns

For the Conferences class the id field is of type Integer. Hibernate provides a flexible framework for unique identifier generation. The element generator determines the class used to generate unique identifiers.

Table 7-5 shows a quick summary of the generator strategies provided by Hibernate.

Table 7-5. Hibernate's Identifier Generation Strategies

Strategy	Description
increment	identity
identity	Uses database identity columns for those databases that support it. Use it with an integer-type object property.
sequence	Uses a database sequence or internal database generator for those databases that support these features.

Table 7-5. Hibernate's Identifier Generation Strategies (Continued)

Strategy	Description
hilo	Uses an algorithm to determine the next value based on a column in a given table.
seqhilo	Uses a named database sequence and the hilo algorithm.
uuid.hex	Uses a pseudo globally unique identifier algorithm and returns a hex encoded 32 digit number
uuid.string	Uses a pseudo globally unique identifier algorithm and returns a 16-character string.
foreign	Uses the identifier of an associated object.
native	Intelligently chooses the appropriate strategy. It's the recommended strategy for maximum portability.
assigned	Used for applications that use provided business unique keys.

In the case of the Conference class the "increment" generator class is chosen, primarily for ease of use because it doesn't require the creation of any Hibernate-specific tables.

 CAUTION   There seems to be a bug with the HSQLDB database version and the use of IDENTITY columns of type BIGINT that shipped with JBoss 3.0.x and 3.2.x. If the generation strategy chosen is "identity" or "native" you'll experience SQL errors. Because the TCMS schema is designed for maximum portability IDENTITY columns aren't used.

The id element for the Conference table is shown here:

```
<id
    name="id"
    column="PK_ID"
    type="java.lang.Integer"
>
    <generator class="increment">
    </generator>
</id>
```

Mapping Field to Columns

The mapping of regular (nonidentity) field-to-database columns is very straight-forward in Hibernate. Hibernate handles most types of conversions automatically. The following example shows the mappings of some Conference.java fields as well as the name field of type String, and the startDate field, which is a java.util.Date. These two fields map respectively to VARCHAR(64) and DATETIME SQL types, as shown:

```
<property
    name="name"
    type="java.lang.String"
    update="true"
    insert="true"
    column="name"
    length="64"
/>

...

<property
    name="startDate"
    type="java.util.Date"
    update="true"
    insert="true"
    column="startDate"
/>
```

If you remember, with OJB you had to specify a conversion class between the java.util.Date fields and the DATETIME (or TIMESTAMP) fields. Hibernate takes care of this conversion automatically.

One-to-Many Mapping Using the set Element

To map the one-to-many relationship between the Conference and Track objects, you use a set element, as shown here:

```
<set
    name="tracks"
    table="tracks"
    lazy="false"
    inverse="false"
    cascade="all"
    sort="unsorted"
    >
    <key
        column="fk_ConferenceId"
    />
    <one-to-many
        class="com.ejdoab.pojos.Track"
    />
</set>
```

Different from OJB, the foreign key that's used is the actual database foreign key column and not an object field mapped to the foreign key column. This is an example of one of the core differences in approaches between these two ORM tools. OJB takes more of a purist-object approach, though Hibernate embraces SQL as a side-by-side complement to your object's model.

Many-to-One Mapping

To retrieve a given Track object associated with the Conference object, you need an object reference that will return the Conference object. The object's identity should match the value of the column fk_ConferenceId. The many-to-one element provides such a link. Notice the hybrid nature of this declaration. On the one hand you refer to a class that will be linked but you'll use a table column value to determine the lookup, as follows:

```
<many-to-one
    name="conference"
    class="com.ejdoab.pojos.Conference"
    cascade="none"
    outer-join="auto"
    update="true"
    insert="true"
    column="fk_ConferenceId"
/>
```

NOTE   To decide whether to use outer-join fetching see section 3.5.2 of the Hibernate2 Reference Documentation (http://www.hibernate.org/hib_docs/) and section 20 for related Best Practices. Outer joins can significantly reduce the amount of calls against the database but it can possibly increase the server load. A decision to use outer joins should be based on the particular tables, how they're configured, and how they're related.

Hibernate and XDoclet

As for many of the projects covered in this book, there's a Hibernate XDoclet module that's shipped with the XDoclet distribution. The Hibernate doclet simplifies the creation and maintenance of Hibernate mapping files (hbm.xml files) as well as the deployment of Hibernate on JBoss. The Ant script is this section is based on the build used in the OJB examples. For the sake of brevity, only the portions that need to be changed are shown.

NOTE   You can find the documentation for both the Hibernate XDoclet task and the Hibernate tags at the XDoclet website at http://xdoclet.sourceforge.net. The first is under /ant/xdoclet/ modules/hibernate/HibernateDocletTask.html and the latter is under /tags/hibernate-tags.html.

XDoclet JARs

The project's directory contains a lib/development/xdoclet directory under which you need to copy the following the xdoclet-hibernate-module-1.2.jar file (for version 1.2 of XDoclet), in addition to the base XDoclet files used in the OJB example.

Annotating the Plain Old Java Objects

Adding Hibernate XDoclet tags to the Conference and Track classes is very similar to the work you did previously with OJB. The most noticeable difference between the OJB and Hibernate XDoclet mappings is the default data-access method used. In OJB, direct field access is the default, but in Hibernate, access with getters and setters is the default, as shown here:

```
...
/**
 * @hibernate.class
 *     table="conferences"
 */
public class Conference implements Serializable {
...
    //
    // getters
    //

    /**
     * @hibernate.id
     *     column="PK_ID"
     *     generator-class="increment"
     */
    public Integer getId() {
        return id;
    }
```

Hibernate's intelligent guessing of the default attributes makes it easy to keep XDoclet tags to a minimum. In some cases, as shown next in the hibernate.property tag, it's all that's required:

```
/**
 * @hibernate.property
 *     length="64"
 */
public String getName() {
    return name;
}
...

/**
 * @hibernate.property
 */
public Date getStartDate() {
    return startDate;
}
```

The XDoclet tag for the mapping of the Tracks collection that belongs to a Conference is the most complex. The cascade attribute enables operations such as updates and deletes to "cascade" appropriately to child objects.

```
...

    /**
     * @hibernate.set
     *      role="tracks"
     *      table="tracks"
     *      cascade="all"
     *      inverse="true"
     * @hibernate.collection-key
     *      column="fk_ConferenceId"
     * @hibernate.collection-one-to-many
     *      class="com.ejdoab.pojos.Track"
     */
    public Collection getTracks() {
        return tracks;
    }
```

Finally, to make the addition of Tracks to a Conference object simple, you can provide an addTrack method as shown:

```
    ...

    public void addTrack(Track track) {
        if (tracks == null) {
            tracks = new HashSet();
        }
        track.setConference(this);
        tracks.add(track);
    }
}
```

Ant Script

The first item that needs to be addressed is the project's properties. A sample of the relevant entries in the build.properties is shown. See the OJB example for the jboss and db properties section.

```
// app
jar-name=hibernate-jboss-test.jar

// jboss specific
...
```

```
// db properties
...

// hibernate properties
HIBERNATE_HOME=C:/java/hibernate-2.1
hibernate.dialect=net.sf.hibernate.dialect.HSQLDialect
hibernate.service.jndi.name=java:/hibernate/HibernateFactory
```

In the Ant script, replace the ${descriptors-ojb} property, which indicates where the generated O/R mappings are to be placed with the ${descriptors-hibernate} property, as shown here:

```
<?xml version="1.0"?>
<project name="hibernate-jboss" default="all" basedir=".">

    <!-- ================================================================= -->
    <!-- Configures Project's Properties                                   -->
    <!-- ================================================================= -->
...
    <property name="descriptors-hibernate"

            location="${generated}/descriptors/hibernate" />
```

To be able to use the hibernatedoclet you need to first load the task using Ant's taskdef task as shown here:

```
    <!-- ================================================================= -->
    <!-- Declare taskdefs                                                  -->
    <!-- ================================================================= -->
...
    <taskdef
        name="hibernatedoclet"
        classname="xdoclet.modules.hibernate.HibernateDocletTask"
        classpathref="hibernate.class.path"
        />
```

Generating the Mappings and the JBoss Service Definition

The following Ant target uses the hibernatedoclet to generate the O/R mappings using the annotated POJO classes. The hibernatedoclet task is very simple to use, and only requires that you point it to the location where you want to place the generated mappings and the location that contains the annotated Java classes. The nested fileset element, further qualifies the files that will be processed to be the source files located in the pojos directory under the directory specified by ${src}.

 NOTE For the hibernatedoclet to work correctly you'll need to specify the Hibernate version in a nested element as shown here:

```
<!-- =================================================================== -->
<!-- Generates Hibernate's HBM.XML files using Hibernate XDoclet's Task -->
<!-- =================================================================== -->
<target name="hibernate-mapping"
    description=
        "generates Hibernate repository file using hibernatedoclet task">
    <echo>
    generating hibernate mappings and JBoss service descriptor...
    </echo>
    <hibernatedoclet
        destdir="${descriptors-hibernate}"
        excludedtags="@version,@author,@todo,@see,@desc"
        addedtags="@xdoclet-generated at ${TODAY}"
        force="${xdoclet.force}"
        mergedir="${conf}"
        verbose="false"
    >
        <fileset dir="${src}">
            <include name="**/pojos/*.java"/>
        </fileset>

        <hibernate version="2.0"/>
        ...
```

The rest of the Target uses the jbossservice nested element to create the jboss-service.xml file, which is used to deploy Hibernate as a JBoss, as follows:

```
...
<jbossservice
    destdir="${descriptors-hibernate}"
    serviceName="Hibernate"
    jndiName="${hibernate.service.jndi.name}"
    dataSource="${jboss.datasource}"
    dialect="${hibernate.dialect}"
    useOuterJoin="true"
    showSql="true"
    transactionManagerStrategy
        ="net.sf.hibernate.transaction.JBossTransactionManagerLookup"
    transactionStrategy
        ="net.sf.hibernate.transaction.JTATransactionFactory"
    userTransactionName="UserTransaction"
/>
</hibernatedoclet>
</target>
```

TIP   For debugging purposes the jbossservice nested tag provides an attribute that tells Hibernate to show the SQL statements generated for every operation. This is an invaluable feature when debugging and profiling your application.

Deployment on JBoss

With the O/R mappings generated now all you need is a way to make Hibernate available in your J2EE environment. There are several options for how to deploy Hibernate on JBoss:

- **JCA adaptor:** An archive with a .rar extension that implements the Java Connector Architecture

- **SAR archive:** A JBoss-specific service archive

In this example you'll use the SAR deployment. As you did previously with OJB, the jar task is used to generate the SAR file. In the SAR file you'll need the following:

- **hibernate2.jar:** The Hibernate JAR file.

- **commons-collections.jar:** Provides replacements and enhancements to the core Java collections classes.

- **commons-logging.jar:** A thin API that abstracts logging implementations.

- **cglib2.jar:** Used to enhance classes at runtime in combination with Java reflection.

- **jcs.jar:** JCS cache implementation.

- **odmg.jar:** ODMG 3.0 API. ODMG semantics are used to map collections.

- **dom4j.jar:** Used to parse the XML configuration and mapping files.

- **ehcache.jar:** EHCache cache implementation.

- **jboss-service.xml:** The generated JBoss service definition.

- **hbm.xml files:** The generated hibernate mapping XML files.

All the needed JAR files are part of the Hibernate distribution. The hibernate2.jar file is located at the root of the distribution, but all other JARs are found in the lib directory. The Ant target will take care of copying the appropriate files from the Hibernate distribution directory, as long as you've set the ${HIBERNATE_HOME} property.

```
<!-- ===================================================================== -->
<!-- Package the SAR                                                       -->
<!-- ===================================================================== -->
<target name="sar" depends="hibernate-mapping"
    description="packages a jboss SAR file for Hibernate deployment">
    <echo>packaging sar...</echo>
    <jar jarfile="${dist}/hibernate.sar">
    <metainf dir="${descriptors-hibernate}" includes="jboss-service.xml"/>
    <fileset dir="${HIBERNATE_HOME}/lib">
        <include name="commons-collections.jar" />
        <include name="commons-logging.jar" />
        <include name="cglib2.jar" />
        <include name="jcs.jar" />
        <include name="odmg.jar" />
        <include name="dom4j.jar" />
        <include name="ehcache.jar" />
```

```
            </fileset>
            <fileset dir="${HIBERNATE_HOME}">
                <include name="hibernate2.jar" />
            </fileset>
            <fileset dir="${descriptors-hibernate}">
                <include name="**/*.hbm.xml" />
            </fileset>
        </jar>
    </target>
```

There are several ways to deploy the SAR archive. The Hibernate mappings are compiled during deployment (although you can precompile them). Therefore the classes that they map must be available in the classpath. Because these classes are contained in the ejb-jar as part of the application, the ejb-jar should be deployed first. Note that the SAR archive can also be deployed as part of an EAR archive, as shown here:

Deploying the hibernate.sar on JBoss results in output similar to the following:

```
2004-01-18 15:16:37,346 INFO  [org.jboss.deployment.MainDeployer]
    Starting deployment of package:
    file:/C:/java/jboss/jboss-3.2.1/server/tcms/deploy/hibernate.sar
2004-01-18 15:16:37,416 INFO  [org.jboss.deployment.SARDeployer]
    nested deployment:
    file:/C:/java/jboss/jboss-3.2.1/server/tcms/tmp/deploy/server/tcms/deploy/
        hibernate.sar/2.hibernate.sar-contents/cglib2.jar
...
2004-01-18 15:16:37,506 INFO  [org.jboss.deployment.SARDeployer]
    nested deployment:
    file:/C:/java/jboss/jboss-3.2.1/server/tcms/tmp/deploy/server/tcms/deploy/
        hibernate.sar/2.hibernate.sar-contents/odmg.jar
2004-01-18 15:16:37,556 INFO  [org.jboss.deployment.SARDeployer]
    nested deployment:
    file:/C:/java/jboss/jboss-3.2.1/server/tcms/tmp/deploy/server/tcms/deploy/
        hibernate.sar/2.hibernate.sar-contents/hibernate2.jar
2004-01-18 15:16:38,207 INFO  [org.jboss.deployment.MainDeployer]
    Deployed package:
    file:/C:/java/jboss/jboss-3.2.1/server/tcms/deploy/hibernate.sar
```

Session Bean

The com.ejdoab.beans.ConferenceHibernateFacadeBean will provide capabilities similar to the OJB facade that you created for the OJB example. The Hibernate stateless Session Bean will provide the following methods to manipulate the Conferences and Track objects:

- Collection getAllConferences

- Conference findConferenceMatching(Conference searchTemplate)

- boolean saveConference(Conference conference)

- boolean deleteConference(Conference conference)

First, you'll create a skeleton for the Session Bean and use XDoclet to automate the creation of the EJB glue files. A private field will hold an instance of SessionFactory, which is looked up using JNDI in the Bean's ejbCreate method. The hibernate.service.jndi.name property defined in the build.properties with the value java:/hibernate/HibernateFactory determines the jndi name of the Hibernate JBoss service. As you can probably guess, the SessionFactory is a factory for Hibernate Session objects, as follows:

```
package com.ejdoab.beans;

import java.util.Collection;
import java.util.Collections;

import javax.ejb.CreateException;
import javax.ejb.EJBException;
import javax.ejb.SessionBean;
import javax.naming.Context;
import javax.naming.InitialContext;
import javax.naming.NamingException;

import net.sf.hibernate.Criteria;
import net.sf.hibernate.HibernateException;
import net.sf.hibernate.Session;
import net.sf.hibernate.SessionFactory;
import net.sf.hibernate.expression.Example;

import com.ejdoab.pojos.Conference;
```

```
/**
 * @ejb.bean
 *      name="ConferenceHibernateFacade"
 *      type="Stateless"
 *      view-type="both"
 *      jndi-name="ejb.ConferenceHibernateFacadeHome"
 *      local-jndi-name="ejb.ConferenceHibernateFacadeLocalHome"
 * @ejb.transaction
 *      type="Required"
 * @ejb.util
 *      generate="physical"
 */
public abstract class ConferenceHibernateFacadeBean implements SessionBean {

    private SessionFactory sessionFactory;

    //==========================================
    //  EJB callbacks
    //==========================================

    /**
     * @ejb.create-method
     */
    public void ejbCreate() throws CreateException {
        Context context = null;
        // Lookup the SessionFactory implementation
        try {
            context = new InitialContext();
            sessionFactory =
              (SessionFactory)context.lookup("java:/hibernate/HibernateFactory");
        }
        catch (NamingException e)
        {
            throw new EJBException(e);
        }
    }
    ...
}
```

Retrieving a Collection of Objects

The getAllConference method instantiates a Session method by calling the openSession method of the Session factory. Figure 7-6 shows how the Session bean interacts with the SessionFactory to retrieve a Session and perform its work.

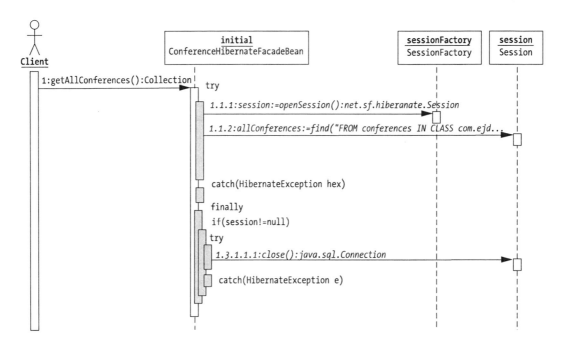

Figure 7-6. The getAllconference Sequence diagram

To retrieve a Collection of all Conferences the find method is used, which can take a String containing a Hibernate object-oriented query, which is syntactically similar to a regular SQL query. Notice that all Session methods throw a HibernateException, which is a Checked Exception as opposed to OJBs use of Runtime Exceptions.

```
/**
 * @ejb.interface-method
 * @ejb.transaction
 *       type="NotSupported"
 *
 * @return
 */
public Collection getAllConferences() {
    Collection allConferences = Collections.EMPTY_LIST;

    Session session = null;
    try {
        session = sessionFactory.openSession();
        allConferences =
            session.find(
                "FROM conferences IN CLASS com.ejdoab.pojos.Conference"
            );
    } catch (HibernateException hex) {
        throw new EJBException("Could not retrieve the list of conferences",
hex);
    } finally {
        if (session != null) {
            try {
                session.close();
            } catch (HibernateException e) {
                // do nothing, just log it
            }
        }
    }

    return allConferences;
}
```

Finding an Object Using a Template

Hibernate provides an API query that supports both string-based queries as well as objectified-aggregate query expressions. String queries as defined by the Hibernate Query Language (HQL). The Criteria is built by aggregating Criterion object which are clauses defining the query.

The findConferenceMatching method takes a Conference object as a parameter that's used to create an Example object, which is a type of Criterion that you can add to an object of type Criteria to perform a search. The uniqueResult

method will return the first object in the database that matches the field values
set on the searchTemplate Conference object, as shown:

```
/**
 * @ejb.interface-method
 * @ejb.transaction
 *       type="NotSupported"
 *
 * @return
 */
public Conference findConferenceMatching(Conference searchTemplate) {
    Conference conference = null;

    Session session = null;
    try {
        session = sessionFactory.openSession();
        Example example = Example.create(searchTemplate);
        Criteria criteria = session.createCriteria(Conference.class);
        criteria.add(example);
        conference = (Conference) criteria.uniqueResult();
    } catch (HibernateException hex) {
        throw new EJBException("Could not find the object", hex);
    } finally {
        if (session != null) {
            try {
                session.close();
            } catch (HibernateException e) {
                // do nothing, just log it
            }
        }
    }

    return conference;
}
```

Saving an Object

Hibernate's Session object provides several methods that persist the state of an
object to the database, including save, update, and saveOrUpdate. If an object's
primary key attribute isn't set, Hibernate will detect this and autogenerate a
primary key for the object based on the strategy selected on the id element. This
will make the underlying operation an INSERT.

NOTE Hibernate detects that an object hasn't been saved by checking the primary key value for null, which is the default of the unsaved-value attribute. If your class required a value other than null, set this value in the unsaved-value attribute.

If the primary key is set then the operation becomes an UPDATE if the object exists, and an INSERT if it doesn't, as shown here:

```
/**
 * @ejb.interface-method
 * @ejb.transaction
 *        type="NotSupported"
 * @return
 */
public boolean saveConference(Conference conference) {
    boolean result = true;

    Session session = null;
    try {
        session = sessionFactory.openSession();
        session.saveOrUpdate(conference);
        session.flush();
    } catch (HibernateException hex) {
        result = false;
        throw new EJBException("Could not save the conference", hex);
    } finally {
        if (session != null) {
            try {
                session.close();
            } catch (HibernateException e) {
                // do nothing, just log it
            }
        }
    }

    return result;
}
```

Notice that for any methods that modify the database, the flush method of the Session object has to be called in order for the transaction to be committed.

Flush synchronizes the state of any of the objects in the Session cache that are being modified with the state of the underlying database.

Deleting an Object

To delete an object in Hibernate the Session object provides a delete method. Dependent object deletion, such as in the case of the collection of Tracks belonging to a Conference object, depends on the nature of the relationship. In this case the Conference-Track represents a parent-child relationship so it would be expected that if the Conference is to be deleted the Tracks associated with it will be deleted as well.

```java
/**
 * @ejb.interface-method
 * @ejb.transaction
 *      type="NotSupported"
 *
 * @return
 */
public boolean deleteConference(Conference conference) {
    boolean result = true;

    Session session = null;
    try {
        session = sessionFactory.openSession();
        session.delete(conference);
        session.flush();
    } catch (HibernateException hex) {
        result = false;
        throw new EJBException("Could not delete the conference", hex);
    } finally {
        if (session != null) {
            try {
                session.close();
            } catch (HibernateException e) {
                // do nothing, just log it
            }
        }
    }

    return result;
}
```

Testing

The test client used in the OJB example needs very little modification to work with the Hibernate Session Facade Bean. Simply change the name of the Bean classes and replace the JNDI lookup string with that of the Hibernate Session Bean. The results should match the results obtained previously with OJB.

Where Are the Java Data Object Tools and Examples?

The marketing around the JDO specification makes it sound like it could become one of the main alternatives to CMP EJBs for those who are looking for a portable persistence solution. JDO is a standard specification of a generic API for transparent and store-neutral persistence of Java objects that's brought together in an effort to simplify Java. The JDO initiative came out of the early Java persistence work done by the Object Data Management Group (ODMG), and continued with the creation of Java specification request 12 (JSR 12), which is overseen by the Java Community Process (JCP). The current version of the specification is the 1.0.1 maintenance release, which you can find at http://www.jcp.org. Behind-the-scenes JDO works with existing objects by using bytecode manipulation or runtime reflection to "enhance" Java classes with persistence capability.

We gathered opinions from those in the know. People who work with persistence frameworks, like TopLink and Cocobase, or the open-sourced OJB and Hibernate, every day, feel that JDO isn't ready for prime time. The main concern from many is that as a committee-driven standard it will take some time to evolve. This is one of the drawbacks of committee-driven standards.

The JDO 2.0 is expected to cover some of shortcomings of the current 1.0.1 release. Yet, the opinion of most is that the missing features are already present in many commercial and open-sourced offerings. OJB is already planning a full JDO implementation in the future and the Hibernate team would consider an implementation, if most of the limitations of the specification are overcome in the new release.

Although Open Source projects that cover the JDO specifications, including JORM, TJDO, XORM, OJB, and now JBossDO are emerging, their usability in an enterprise environment does warrant their inclusion as a practical alternative to other persistence solutions if most of the limitations are overcome in newer releases.

Conclusions

In this chapter you learned about some of the problems you'll encounter when objects and relational databases come together. Nowadays an unacceptably large amount of time is spent by developers tweaking and "hacking" the data-access tier of their applications. Architects and developers can avoid most of these problems if they understand early in the process how the data is used by their applications. There truly isn't a one-size-fits-all solution.

The Open Source community has two powerful tools in OJB and Hibernate, both of which deal with the object-relational impedance mismatch. OJB and Hibernate are the two leading open-sourced ORM tools. The best way to make an informed decision about which of the two might be better suited for your project is to do a small prototype by mapping the classes and tables that are the bread and butter of your application. To get you started, the following guidelines can help you with the decision:

- **Configuration:** Both OJB and Hibernate are relatively easy to configure.

- **Performance:** With ORM tools, performance is usually in direct correlation to the SQL generated by the tool. Although you have no concrete testing numbers the SQL generated by both tools is more or less the same.

- **License:** OJB is an Apache project and therefore has the more business-friendly Apache license. Hibernate is licensed under the LGPL.

- **JDO:** OJB is designed to support multiple "personalities," with JDO being one of them. In contrast, the Hibernate project doesn't support or plan to support JDO (unless the specification is significantly improved).

- **ODMG:** Both OJB and Hibernate to some extent support the ODMG standard.

- **Querying capabilities:** HQL provides for a smoother transition for programmers who are already accustomed to SQL.

- **Tools:** Both OJB and Hibernate provide several tools for facilitating the creation of mapping files, schemas, and complete object models.

For a feature comparison of several ORM tools (both commercial and open-sourced) see the Portland Pattern Repository's Wiki ORM tool-comparison page at `http://c2.com/cgi/wiki?ObjectRelationalToolComparison`, where you'll see that both tools offer similar capabilities. Therefore, for most projects, you can use either OJB or Hibernate in conjunction with Session Beans and seamlessly integrate them into your J2EE applications so that you can replace or complement an EJB CMP-based architecture.

CHAPTER 8

MVC Frameworks and the Presentation Tier

That was a surprise to me—that people were prepared to painstakingly write HTML.[1]

—Tim Berners-Lee

MANY ENTERPRISE APPLICATIONS support large numbers of users. Rather than manage the complexities of client-application installation and upgrades, organizations have opted for web-based applications. For this reason, Java Server Pages (JSP) and servlets are key components of the J2EE specification.

Many organizations start developing the web tier using JSP or servlets. Organizations that start by developing servlets quickly learn that it's difficult to create and even more difficult to change the look and feel of the application. Often developers receive mocked-up HTML pages from designers. Then the developer has to decompose the HTML and put them in out.println() statements and escape common HTML characters like double quotes. Add the deployment cycle and developing or changing a servlet-based application to this, and you'll see that it can take a long time or require a complete rewrite. When JSPs were released, they changed the way web applications were developed in Java. Instead of embedding HTML in Java, the metaphor changed to embedding Java into HTML. Productivity increased because there was no longer a need to redeploy and because JSPs are dynamically compiled to a servlet when they're requested after a modification. However, using JSPs leads to bad practices such as putting business logic in the presentation tier. In addition, JSPs don't provide any good means of reusing code that's often placed in scriptlets. This can lead to duplicate code and dual maintenance.

To reduce the problems of developing web applications with JSPs and servlets, developers started applying the model-view-controller (MVC) design pattern. This design pattern separates the data (model) from the presentation (view) and the workflow (controller). Unfortunately, without careful design, this practice can also turn into a difficult-to-manage web application. Servlets become large nested if/else

---

1. Berners-Lee, Tim. *World Wide Web Journal (W3J)*, vol. 1, issue 3, Summer 1996.

statements that are difficult to read and maintain. Many Open Source MVC frameworks have been developed to minimize bad practices that were initially introduced by JSPs and servlets. This chapter will introduce some popular MVC frameworks and then focus on the popular de facto standard Struts framework.

Model-View-Controller Frameworks

MVC frameworks have changed the way web applications are developed. Separating an application into models, views, and controllers enables a separation of responsibility. Developers are able to focus on writing Java code while designers focus on the look and feel.

Many Open Source MVC frameworks have been developed to fill the gap left open by commercial software vendors. Table 8-1 contains a list of just some of the popular frameworks.

Table 8-1. Popular Open Source MVC Frameworks

Framework	Struts	Turbine	WebWork
Model	Action Forms, JavaBeans	JavaBeans	Java Objects
View	JSP, Velocity	JSP, Velocity	JSP, Velocity
Controller	ActionServlet, Action mapping	TurbineServlet	Actions, Dispatcher
URL	jakarta.apache.org/ struts/	jakarta.apache.org/ turbine/	www.opensymphony.com/ webwork/

Most of the MVC frameworks use a similar approach, as shown in Figure 8-1. The controller is implemented as a servlet. The controller implementation is extended to perform application-specific functionality by creating custom classes usually called actions. A configuration file read by the controller servlet is used to configure how a request is redirected to the application-specific functionality, which is responsible for looking up information from a data source such as a relational database through JDBC, EJB, and/or data-access objects. The results are then placed into a model, which is implemented as a JavaBean or plain old Java object (POJO). The model is passed to the view layer as an attribute of the request object. The view is commonly implemented as JSP or Velocity templates. The view gets the model out of the request attribute and displays it appropriately. The view should never contain any business logic, so it should contain mostly HTML and simple Java constructs such as loops and calls to the model accessors.

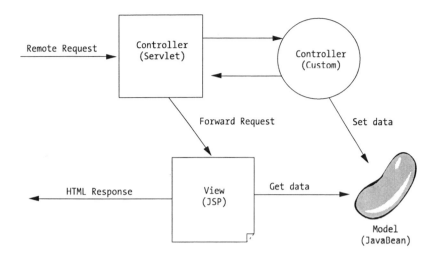

Figure 8-1. MVC pattern

Most of the MVC frameworks don't just provide an implementation of MVC; they also provide value-added services. Some of the services include validation, templating, web services, security, localization, pooling, caching, and scheduling.

Struts Overview

Although Apache Struts isn't a Java standard technology, it has become the de facto standard MVC implementation for Java web application. Struts is even singled out in Sun's J2EE BluePrints as a best practice. It's likely that Struts will continue to lead the MVC pack until the long-anticipated standard JavaServer Faces specification is completed.

Struts Components

As discussed earlier and depicted in Figure 8-2, Struts implements MVC patterns by using the standard servlet, JavaBean, and JSP technologies. To be specific, Struts includes an ActionServlet that uses a standard servlet configuration in the web.xml file to receive requests. The ActionServlet uses the configuration loaded from the struts-config.xml file at startup to determine how to route requests to application-specific classes called Actions. The Action class may use a combination of JDBC, EJBs, or data-access objects to perform application-specific functionality. The Action class may take the results of JDBC, EJB, or data-access object calls and in turn create JavaBeans that contain the results. Struts also contains a special JavaBean called an ActionForm, which is used to encapsulate the data on an HTML form. ActionForms will be discussed in greater detail later in the chapter. When an Action class finishes, it returns a forward, which is used to determine the View page or template to use. The ActionServlet receives the forward and, again using the struts-config.xml file, determines which view component to forward the request to. Typically the view is a JSP, but you can use other view technologies such as Velocity or XSLT.

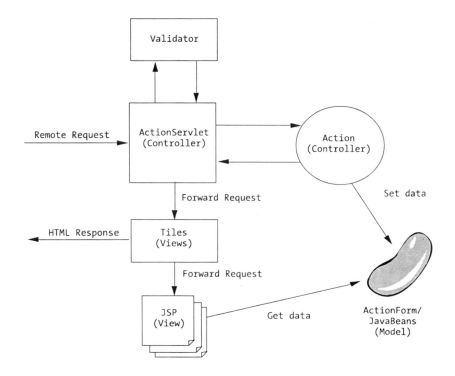

Figure 8-2. Struts MVC implementation

 NOTE Struts provides a number of components, thus it can initially seem difficult and overwhelming. However, once the initial learning curve is overcome, Struts becomes an easy-to-use, flexible, and predictable framework.

Struts includes some important value-added features that make web development easier, including the validator service, Tiles framework, and tag libraries. The Struts validator service, which as of Struts 1.1 is based on another Open Source framework, Jakarta Commons Validator, which makes simple HTML form validation simple and requires no coding. The validator framework uses XML to describe validation rules. The ActionServlet can automatically call the validator service prior to invoking the Action class. This prevents the Action class from ever being called if data in an HTML form is invalid. The framework can also automatically repopulate the HTML form and display validation errors.

As of Struts 1.1 the template framework has been replaced by the more flexible Tiles framework. The Tiles framework helps you create layouts with placeholders for elements such as headers, footers, menus, and content. At runtime a tiles definition file is used to determine which component referred to as tiles belongs in each placeholder. A tile is commonly a reusable JSP. So the Tiles framework is really just a more flexible way of doing JSP includes.

In an effort to remove as much Java code as possible from JSPs and to automate some of the more mundane code, Struts includes several tag libraries: bean, html, logic, nested, and tiles. The html and tiles libraries will be discussed later in the chapter. Some of the tags in the Struts bean and logic libraries will become deprecated and replaced by functionality provided by the JSP Standard Tag Library (JSTL). So whenever possible use the JSTL tags over the Struts tags. The Apache Taglibs project includes an Open Source implementation of the JSTL.

For applications requiring multiple language support, Struts also includes a Message Resource framework for looking up text based on the language choice of a specific user.

Setting Up a Web Application with Struts and the Java Standard Tag Library

Setting up a web application involves creating a proper directory structure and configuring a web.xml file. Adding Struts and JSTL involves updating the web.xml and gathering configuration and JAR files. To wrap up the setup an ant target should be included so that you can package the necessary files into the standard web archive file (WAR), which you can also include in a deployable enterprise archive (EAR) if it's a part of a larger enterprise application.

You should keep the Java code and web files separate, so the first step in creating a directory structure is to create a web directory under the src directory. All web-related files such as HTMLs, JSPs, images, and configuration files belong here. The Java files related to a web application like the custom Action classes discussed later still belong in the src/java directory structure. These files will later be packaged in a JAR file and included in the web application. You can also add common web application directories such as images, style, and scripts to the web directory. Lastly, there is an important Java web application directory, the WEB-INF.

According to the servlet spec, the WEB-INF directory isn't addressable with an HTTP request. Therefore this directory is the primary place for configuration files such as the web.xml and tag library definition files. However, due to the behavior of the ANT War task, which will be discussed later, the web.xml file must be in a separate location at development time. At build time the ANT War task will place the web.xml file in the WAR file under the WEB-INF directory. A common place to put configuration files such as the web.xml file until build time is in a src/conf directory. Figure 8-3 illustrates a web-application directory structure.

```
□ 🗀 src
      🗀 conf
      🗀 java
□ 🗀 web
      🗀 images
      🗀 scripts
      🗀 style
   □ 🗀 WEB-INF
         🗀 jsp
```

Figure 8-3. Common web-application directory structure

NOTE   You can use XDoclet to generate a web.xml.

The next step is configuring the web application. Web-application configurations reside in a web.xml deployment descriptor. This file is stored in a src/conf directory, then at build time the ANT War task includes the file in the WAR file's WEB-INF directory. Initially, this file may not include anything but the standard doctype reference and an empty web-app tag. Listing 8-1 shows an example of a simple web.xml file with an optional display name of the web application.

Listing 8-1. Original web.xml File

```
<?xml version="1.0" encoding="UTF-8"?>
<!DOCTYPE web-app PUBLIC "-//Sun Microsystems, Inc.//DTD Web Application 2.2//EN"
  "http://java.sun.com/j2ee/dtds/web-app_2_2.dtd">

<web-app id="WebApp">
  <display-name>TCMS Web Application</display-name>
</web-app>
```

The display name element of the web.xml file is primarily used by development and deployment tools. However in some versions of JBoss, if a context isn't provided when making an HTTP request, JBoss uses the display name, if provided, when listing all the installed web applications and their contexts. See Figure 8-4 for an example of the TCMS web-application display name.

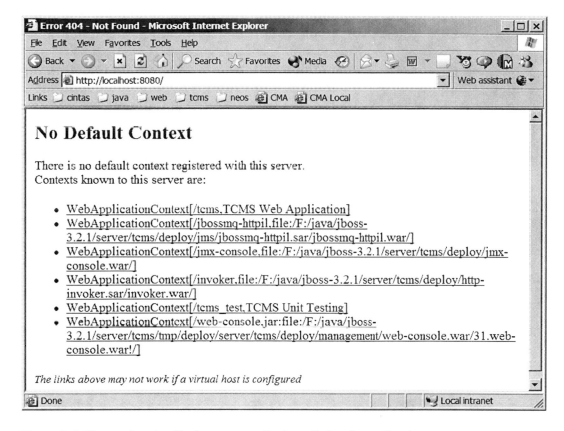

Figure 8-4. JBoss using the display name to list installed web-application contexts

The Struts and JSTL configuration requires that their JAR files be included in the WEB-INF/lib directory. The WEB-INF/lib directory is a special directory in which the application server automatically appends the JAR files to the web application's class loader. The Ant task discussed later will automatically include the required JAR files at build time. The required JAR files for Struts 1.1 are commons-beanutils.jar, commons-collections.jar, commons-digester.jar, commons-fileupload.jar, commons-lang.jar, commons-logging.jar, commons-validator.jar, jakarta-oro.jar, and struts.jar. Jakarta's JSTL 1.1 implementation only requires that jstl.jar and standard.jar be included.

To use the tag libraries found in Struts and JSTL, the associated tag-library definition (TLD) files must be included in the WEB-INF directory. The TLD files are basically tag-library deployment descriptors that tell the application server about the tags and tag attributes. Depending on the application, it may not be necessary to include all the TLDs if only certain libraries are being used. For example, in the TCMS application, not all the JSTL libraries are being used. TCMS only uses the core and format libraries. Therefore, only the c.tld and fmt.tld files are copied to the WEB-INF directory.

Continuing the Struts and JSTL configuration the web.xml file must be updated to include a servlet mapping for the Struts ActionServlet and tag-library declarations. The ActionServlet is the primary controller for Struts. It must be configured to do three things. The ActionServlet must load on startup, read a Struts configuration file, and be configured to direct requests to it. Listing 8-2 shows a portion of the web.xml file that contains a typical configuration for the Struts ActionServlet.

Listing 8-2. ActionServlet Mapping in the web.xml.

```
<!-- Servlet definitions -->
<servlet>
  <servlet-name>action</servlet-name>
  <servlet-class>org.apache.struts.action.ActionServlet</servlet-class>
  <init-param>
    <param-name>config</param-name>
    <param-value>/WEB-INF/struts-config.xml</param-value>
  </init-param>
  <load-on-startup>1</load-on-startup>
</servlet>
<servlet-mapping>
  <servlet-name>action</servlet-name>
  <url-pattern>*.do</url-pattern>
</servlet-mapping>
```

Listing 8-2 shows the ActionServlet being defined with the name action. The ActionServlet is also passed an initialization parameter named config, which points to the Struts configuration file. The Struts config file contains, among other things, a mapping between virtual URLs and Action classes. The Struts config file will be discussed in detail later in the chapter. Notice that the Struts config file is placed in the WEB-INF directory so that it can't be externally addressed. In addition, the file is named struts-config.xml. Although this name isn't a requirement, it's a common practice. As mentioned earlier, the ActionServlet must be started as soon as the application is started. The load-on-startup element takes an ordinal value that tells the application server the order in which to load servlets. Without a load-on-startup a servlet isn't loaded until the first time it's requested.

The last step in configuring the ActionServlet is to map requests to it. The servlet-mapping in Listing 8-2 shows that any request ending in a .do extension is passed to the ActionServlet. Any extension or URL pattern can work but .do is the standard Struts convention.

The tag libraries must also be declared in the web.xml to be available to the JSPs. Tag-Library declarations are found after servlet mappings in the web.xml file. The declaration includes a taglib element that contains taglib-uri and taglib-location elements. The taglib-uri is a name used by taglib directives in the JSP. Basically, the taglib-uri is a dereference of the taglib-location so the location can be changed without requiring a change to every JSP using the tag library. The taglib-location is the location of the TLD file associated with the tag library. The TLD files are often placed in the WEB-INF directory with other configuration files so they aren't externally addressable. Listing 8-3 shows the tab library declarations from the TCMS project.

Listing 8-3. The Tag-Library Declaration Found in the web.xml File

```
<!-- Tag libraries declarations -->
<taglib>
  <taglib-uri>struts-html</taglib-uri>
  <taglib-location>/WEB-INF/struts-html.tld</taglib-location>
</taglib>
<taglib>
  <taglib-uri>struts-tiles</taglib-uri>
  <taglib-location>/WEB-INF/struts-tiles.tld</taglib-location>
</taglib>
<taglib>
  <taglib-uri>struts-bean</taglib-uri>
  <taglib-location>/WEB-INF/struts-bean.tld</taglib-location>
</taglib>
<taglib>
  <taglib-uri>struts-logic</taglib-uri>
  <taglib-location>/WEB-INF/struts-logic.tld</taglib-location>
</taglib>
<taglib>
  <taglib-uri>jstl-core</taglib-uri>
  <taglib-location>/WEB-INF/c.tld</taglib-location>
</taglib>
<taglib>
  <taglib-uri>jstl-format</taglib-uri>
  <taglib-location>/WEB-INF/fmt.tld</taglib-location>
</taglib>
```

Ultimately the web application has to be packaged in a WAR file. For true enterprise applications it's likely the WAR file will be included in an EAR file. You can use an Ant target to automate the packaging activity. Listing 8-4 shows the war target from the TCMS project.

Listing 8-4. Ant Target Responsible for Packaging the Web Application

```
<patternset id="jar.set">
  <include name="*.jar" />
</patternset>
<patternset id="web.classes.set">
  <include name="**/web/**" />
</patternset>

<target name="war"
        depends="ejb,war-jar"
        description="Creates a deployable war.">
  <war destfile="${war-file}" webxml="${src-conf}/web.xml">
    <lib dir="${struts-lib}">
      <patternset refid="jar.set"/>
    </lib>
    <lib dir="${dist}">
      <include name="${war-jar-filename}"/>
    </lib>
    <fileset dir="${src-web}"/>
  </war>
</target>

<target name="war-jar">
  <jar jarfile="${war-jar-file}">
    <fileset dir="${classes}">
      <patternset refid="web.classes.set"/>
    </fileset>
  </jar>
</target>
```

The example in Listing 8-4 shows a war target that's dependent on ejb and war-jar targets. The ejb target builds an EJB JAR file that's also packaged in the EAR file. The WAR-JAR file builds a JAR file containing all the classes from the web package and subpackages. It uses a patternset with an include filter of **/web/** to the JAR of the classes. This is necessary because depending on the application server Struts isn't always able to find classes in other class loaders. To create this special web JAR file put the necessary Action classes in the same class loader as Struts. After all the dependencies have been completed, the War task builds the WAR file. The war target requires the destfile attribute to identify the output of the task. The webxml attribute identifies where to find the web.xml. Next, the lib element is used to include the JAR files in the WEB-INF/lib directory. The first lib gets all the Struts and JSTL JAR files. The second includes the JAR file created in the dependant war-jar target. The fileset includes all the files found in the src/web directory.

Tiles

Many websites have comment elements on every page such as the header, footer, and menu. Figure 8-5 is an example from the TCMS application that includes a common header, footer, and menu. JSP applications commonly use include directives or actions to include common elements. Unfortunately, the include technique requires includes and sometimes even layout information on every page. Depending on how the pages are organized, adding or removing elements can require updating every page.

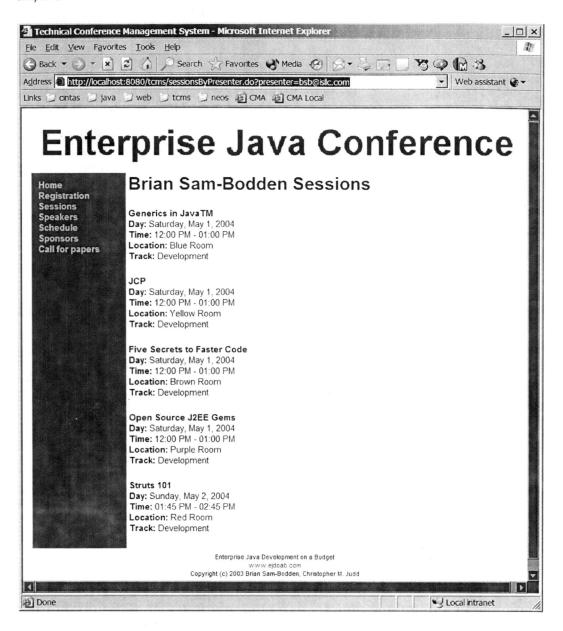

Figure 8-5. TCMS page containing common header, footer, and menu elements

The Struts Tiles framework simplifies common elements and page layouts. Using Tiles, a separate JSP is created that contains the layout information of all the pages. The layout JSP contains placeholders identified with tags from the Tiles tag library. An XML-based tiles definition file is used to determine which components are placed in which placeholder. Therefore, when elements are added or removed, you only have to update the layout JSP.

Tiles Layout

Creating a tiles layout first involves some planning. A layout diagram like the one shown in Figure 8-6 should be used to get feedback from all the stakeholders of a project. Using the layout diagram, a web designer can create a template containing the reusable elements and example content.

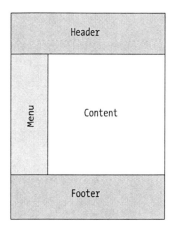

Figure 8-6. TCMS layout diagram

Once the designer is finished with the template, a developer can decompose the template into the common components and master layout. The master layout contains the look and feel of the application with the placeholders. Listing 8-5 is an example of a master layout from the TCMS application.

Listing 8-5. TCMS Master Layout

```
<%@ taglib uri="struts-tiles" prefix="tiles" %>

<html>
  <head>
    <title><tiles:getAsString name="title"/></title>
    <meta http-equiv="Content-Type" content="text/html; charset=iso-8859-1">
    <link href="style/default.css" rel="stylesheet" type="text/css">
  </head>

  <body>
    <table width="660">
      <tr>
       <td>
         <tiles:insert attribute='header'/>
       </td>
      </tr>
    </table>
    <table width="660">
      <tr>
        <td width="120" class="menu">
          <!-- menu begin -->
          <tiles:insert attribute='menu'/>
          <!-- menu end -->
        </td>
        <td width="540" class="content">
        <!-- content begin -->
          <tiles:insert attribute='body' />
        <!-- content end -->
      </tr>
    </table>
    <table width="660">
      <tr>
        <td>
          <tiles:insert attribute='footer'/>
        </td>
      </tr>
    </table>
  </body>
</html>
```

Notice that Listing 8-5 looks like a typical HTML page that uses a table to layout the header, footer, and menu. A couple of noticeable differences are that the page begins with a taglib directive and includes some JSP tags from the Tiles tag library. The directive tells the application server that this page is using JSP tags from the Struts Tiles tag library. In particular, this page uses two Tiles tags as placeholders. The first is the getAsString tag in the HTML title. This tag gets a string value from the Tiles definition file, which will be displayed in the browsers caption bar. The page also includes four insert tags identified with an attribute of the four primary parts of the layout diagram. These insert tags represent the placeholders that will be filled by other JSP pages. The particular page that will be used is defined in the tiles definition file.

Depending on the size of the web application there may be a large number of JSP files. Keeping them well organized makes maintenance easier. It's a good idea to name the main layout page masterLayout.jsp and place it in a src/web/WEB-INF/jsp/layout/ directory. You should place other common elements such as headers, footers, and the menu in a src/web/WEB-INF/jsp/tiles/ or src/web/WEB-INF/jsp/commons/ directory.

 BEST PRACTICE   It's a good idea to put JSP pages related to Struts applications in a directory under the WEB-INF directory. This is because most pages will require you to call Actions first. If the JSP pages are in the WEB-INF directory, you cannot access them directly, which would present the user with errors.

After the master layout is complete you can place each of the common elements in their own file. Most of these will look very simple like the footer found in Listing 8-6.

Listing 8-6. TCMS Footer

```
<div class="copyright">
  Enterprise Java Development on a Budget<br>
  <a href="http://www.ejdoab.com" target="_blank">www.ejdoab.com</a><br>
  Copyright (c) 2003 Brian Sam-Bodden, Christopher M. Judd
</div>
```

Tile Definitions

Tiles uses a definition file to configure the elements used by the getAsString and insert tags in the master layout, as discussed in the previous section. The definition file is an XML file with a root element of tiles-definition; it contains zero or more definitions. Basically each definition represents a page a user would see. Listing 8-7 is an example of the tiles-defs.xml file from the TCMS application.

Listing 8-7. TCMS Tiles Definition File

```
<!DOCTYPE tiles-definitions PUBLIC
    "-//Apache Software Foundation//DTD Tiles Configuration 1.1//EN"
    "http://jakarta.apache.org/struts/dtds/tiles-config_1_1.dtd">

<tiles-definitions>

  <!-- ======================================= -->
  <!-- Master definition                       -->
  <!-- ======================================= -->

  <!-- Master index page description  -->

  <definition name="master" path="/WEB-INF/jsp/layout/masterLayout.jsp">
    <put name="title" value="Technical Conference Management System" />
    <put name="header" value="/WEB-INF/jsp/tiles/header.jsp" />
    <put name="menu" value="/WEB-INF/jsp/tiles/menu.jsp" />
    <put name="footer" value="/WEB-INF/jsp/tiles/footer.jsp" />
    <put name="body" value="" />
  </definition>

  <!-- Page Descriptions -->

  <definition name="index" extends="master">
    <put name="body" value="/WEB-INF/jsp/index.jsp" />
  </definition>

  <definition name="sessions" extends="master">
    <put name="body" value="/WEB-INF/jsp/sessions.jsp" />
  </definition>

  <definition name="speakers" extends="master">
    <put name="body" value="/WEB-INF/jsp/speakers.jsp" />
  </definition>
```

```
<definition name="call" extends="master">
  <put name="body" value="/WEB-INF/jsp/call.jsp" />
</definition>

<definition name="registration" extends="master">
  <put name="body" value="/WEB-INF/jsp/registration.jsp" />
</definition>

<definition name="registrationThanks" extends="master">
  <put name="body" value="/WEB-INF/jsp/speakerThanks.jsp" />
</definition>

<definition name="speakerThanks" extends="master">
  <put name="body" value="/WEB-INF/jsp/speakerThanks.jsp" />
</definition>

<definition name="sessionsByPresenter" extends="master">
  <put name="body" value="/WEB-INF/jsp/sessionsByPresenters.jsp" />
</definition>

</tiles-definitions>
```

Listing 8-7 contains nine definitions. One of the definitions is a master definition that defines all the default elements. Just like Java objects, tile definitions can be inherited. The remaining eight definitions extend the master definition by using the extends attribute.

The master definition declares a path equal to the masterLayout.jsp, as described earlier. In addition, it uses put elements to put values into the Tiles tags of the masterLayout.jsp. The put with the name title contains a string value that replaces the getAsString tag. The header, menu, and footer puts have values equal to JSP pages that contain the appropriate content. The body put is associated with the content of a page. Because each page has different content the body has a value of nothing. Definitions that extend the master layout will override the empty body with a specific JSP.

 CAUTION   If an insert tag renders content on some pages but not on others the put value in the master layout should point to an empty JSP rather than an empty value. Otherwise an error finding the page can occur. The actual error differs according to application server.

The remaining definitions like index and sessions have a name attribute referenced in the Struts configuration file mapping, which is discussed later in this chapter. As discussed in the previous paragraph the extends attribute contains the name of another definition that contains the default puts. A definition may override any put from the super definition. In Listing 8-7 each of the definitions only overrides the body to display the appropriate content.

Setting Up Tiles

Most of the Tiles setup was actually accomplished by setting the web application up with Struts. By making the Struts JAR files available to the web application class loader, declaring the Tiles tag library in the web.xml, and placing its TLD file in the WEB-INF directory, most of the work is done. One additional step is required. The Tiles plug-in must be defined in the struts-config.xml file. The struts-config.xml file will be discussed later in the chapter but an example of the plug-in declaration is shown in Listing 8-8.

Listing 8-8. Tiles Plug-in Definition Found in struts-config.xml

```
<plug-in className="org.apache.struts.tiles.TilesPlugin">
  <set-property property="definitions-config"
              value="/WEB-INF/tiles-defs.xml" />
</plug-in>
```

The Tiles plug-in declaration in Listing 8-8 tells Struts to load Tiles. This is necessary when using Tiles definitions like the ones described earlier. The Tiles plug-in has a required definitions-config property. The property value is the name of the XML file or comma-delimited list of XML files that contain the Tiles definitions.

Struts

The remainder of this chapter focuses on becoming productive with Struts. Entire books have been dedicated to the subject so one chapter cannot possibly be a definitive guide. Definitive Struts books are likely to cover alternative configurations, details of additional Struts JSP tags, and alternative view technologies such as Velocity. To make Struts easier to digest, you'll examine the process behind three different page requests. You'll begin by requesting a page that contains nothing but HTML so the focus is on the mapping aspect of Struts. Next, a page displaying information will be requested to emphasize Action classes and JSTL's role. Lastly, a page containing an HTML form will explain ActionForms and validation. Of course all of the pages will contain the common header, footer, and menu elements provided by Tiles.

Struts Mapping

Many web applications contain pages with content that is static HTML. Examples might include an index or confirmation page. These types of pages are a great place to start. They enable you to focus on how Struts performs simple mapping. They also allow you to start looking at the struts-config.xml.

The struts-config.xml file is an XML file used by the Struts ActionServlet, among other things, to map virtual URLs that typically end in a .do extension to Struts components such as an Action class, JSP page, or Tiles definition. Listing 8-9 shows an entire struts-config.xml file used in the TCMS project. Every aspect of Listing 8-9 will be explained throughout the remainder of this chapter.

Listing 8-9. TCMS's struts-config.xml File

```xml
<!DOCTYPE struts-config PUBLIC
"-//Apache Software Foundation//DTD Struts Configuration 1.1//EN"
"http://jakarta.apache.org/struts/dtds/struts-config_1_1.dtd">
<struts-config>

  <form-beans>
   <form-bean name="attendeeForm"
              type="org.apache.struts.validator.DynaValidatorForm">
    <form-property name="firstname" type="java.lang.String"/>
    <form-property name="lastname"  type="java.lang.String"/>
    <form-property name="email"     type="java.lang.String"/>
    <form-property name="password"  type="java.lang.String"/>
    <form-property name="homephone" type="java.lang.String"/>
    <form-property name="workphone" type="java.lang.String"/>
    <form-property name="fax"       type="java.lang.String"/>
    <form-property name="street"    type="java.lang.String"/>
    <form-property name="city"      type="java.lang.String"/>
    <form-property name="state"     type="java.lang.String"/>
    <form-property name="zip"       type="java.lang.String"/>
   </form-bean>
   <form-bean name="registrationForm"
              type="com.ejdoab.tcms.web.forms.RegistrationForm" />
  </form-beans>
```

```
<action-mappings>

 <action path="/index" forward="index" />

 <action path="/speakers"
         type="com.ejdoab.tcms.web.actions.ListSpeakersAction">
  <forward name="success" path="speakers" />
 </action>

 <action path="/sessions"
         type="com.ejdoab.tcms.web.actions.ListSessionsAction">
  <forward name="success" path="sessions" />
 </action>

 <action path="/sessionsByPresenter"
         type="com.ejdoab.tcms.web.actions.SessionByPresenterAction">
  <forward name="success" path="sessionsByPresenter" />
 </action>

 <action path="/registration" forward="registration" />

 <action path="/submitRegistration"
         type="com.ejdoab.tcms.web.actions.SubmitRegistrationAction"
         name="registrationForm"
         scope="request"
         input="registration"
         validate="true"
 >
  <forward name="success" path="registrationThanks" redirect="true" />
  <forward name="failure" path="registration" redirect="true" />
 </action>

 <action path="/call" forward="call" />

 <action path="/submitPresenter"
   type="com.ejdoab.tcms.web.actions.SubmitPresenterAction"
   name="attendeeForm"
   scope="request"
   input="call"
   validate="true"
 >
  <forward name="success" path="speakerThanks" redirect="true" />
  <forward name="failure" path="call" redirect="true" />
 </action>
```

```
</action-mappings>

<message-resources parameter="com.ejdoab.tcms.web.ApplicationResources"/>

<!-- Plug ins -->
<plug-in className="org.apache.struts.tiles.TilesPlugin">
 <set-property property="definitions-config"
               value="/WEB-INF/tiles-defs.xml" />
</plug-in>
<plug-in className="org.apache.struts.validator.ValidatorPlugIn">
 <set-property property="pathnames"
               value="/WEB-INF/validator-rules.xml,/WEB-INF/validation.xml"/>
</plug-in>

</struts-config>
```

Initially, Listing 8-9 may seem overwhelming so you should focus on mapping a single index.do request that contains nothing but static HTML in the content area. The resulting page will look like Figure 8-7.

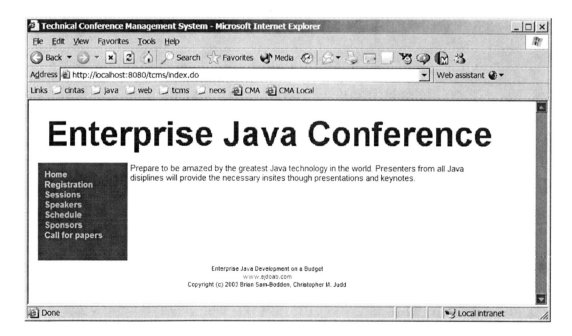

Figure 8-7. TCMS index page

Listing 8-10 shows the action element found in the action-mappings element of the struts-config.xml file that's responsible for mapping the incoming index.do request to a Tiles definition. For simple HTML pages like this one, the action element will contain a path and forward attribute. The path represents the incoming request. Notice that the path doesn't include the .do extension. This is because the .do extension is already assumed because of the discussed web.xml servlet mapping. The forward attribute contains the name of the Struts component to forward the request to. This can be either a JSP page or a Tile definition. In this case the forward is to the index Tile definition shown in Listing 8-7.

Listing 8-10. index.do Action Mapping

```
<action path="/index" forward="index" />
```

NOTE The web.xml's welcome-file-list doesn't appear to work in all versions of JBoss. Therefore, Listing 8-11 shows a simple index.html file that uses JavaScript to redirect a directory request to index.do.

Listing 8-11. index.html Page to Redirect Directory Requests to index.do

```
<html>
<head>
  <script type="text/javascript">
    function redirect() {
        location.replace("index.do");
        return true;
    }
  </script>
</head>
<body onload="setTimeout('redirect()', 0);" >
</html>
```

Actions and the JSP Standard Tag Library

Most pages in an enterprise web application aren't going to contain static HTML. Instead, many pages will interact with a data source or service such as a database or EJB. The simplest example would be a page that displays data. For example, Figure 8-5 displays conference sessions in the TCMS application. Displaying a listing of sessions requires code that will retrieve and display the list. Instead of directly accessing the data model that's holding the sessions information in the JSP, you're going to use Struts actions to put the data into the request scope. You're also going to simplify the JSP pages by using the JSTL instead of writing scriptlets of JSP code in the JSP. An Action class will contain the necessary information to get the data and build a model. The Action class then puts the collection of models in the request attribute list. The Action class also determines which JSP page to use by returning a forward. Once the ActionServlet gets the forward from the Action class and forwards the request to the view, the JSTL in the JSP page is able to get the collection from the request attributes and iterate through it appropriately.

An Action class must extend org.apache.struts.action.Action or one of its descendants. The Action should override one of the two execute methods to implement the application-specific functionality. The only difference between the execute methods is that one passes a ServletRequest and ServletResponse parameter and the other passes an HttpServletRequest and HttpServletReponse parameter. Typically, most Struts applications are HTTP based and the latter is appropriate. The execute method is also passed an ActionMapping and ActionForm parameter. The ActionMapping parameter represents the information about the mapping found in the struts-config.xml file. The ActionForm is a specialized Bean representing data from an HTML form. The ActionForm classes will be discussed later in the chapter. Actions can perform any application-specific functionality that's necessary. Actions commonly use values from the request parameters to determine behavior and the request attributes are used to pass models to the view. Actions can also get to the HTTP session attributes by calling the request's getSession() method. Listing 8-12 is an example of an Action class from the TCMS application that builds a model of conference sessions.

Listing 8-12. Action That Lists the First 1000 Sessions

```
package com.ejdoab.tcms.web.actions;

import com.ejdoab.tcms.services.ConferenceServicesLocal;
import com.ejdoab.tcms.services.ConferenceServicesLocalHome;
import com.ejdoab.tcms.services.ConferenceServicesUtil;
import com.ejdoab.tcms.services.dto.page.Page;

import org.apache.struts.action.Action;
import org.apache.struts.action.ActionForm;
import org.apache.struts.action.ActionForward;
import org.apache.struts.action.ActionMapping;

import java.util.ArrayList;
import java.util.List;

import javax.servlet.http.HttpServletRequest;
import javax.servlet.http.HttpServletResponse;
```

```
/**
 * List conference sessions.
 * @author cjudd
 */
public class ListSessionsAction extends Action {

    public ActionForward execute(ActionMapping mapping, ActionForm form,
        HttpServletRequest request, HttpServletResponse response)
        throws Exception {
        ConferenceServicesLocalHome csHome =
            ConferenceServicesUtil.getLocalHome();
        ConferenceServicesLocal cs = csHome.create();

        Page page = cs.getSessions(0, 1000);
        List sessions = new ArrayList();

        while (page.hasNext()) {
            sessions.add(page.next());
        }

        request.setAttribute("sessions", sessions);

        return (mapping.findForward("success"));
    }
}
```

In Listing 8-12, the ListSessionAction extends Action and overrides the execute method in order to access a stateless session Bean, which in turn is used to get a collection of conference sessions. Once the collection is received as a Page, an ArrayList is created and each conference session in the page is added to the ArrayList. The ArrayList is added to the request attributes so that it can be used later by the view. The execute method concludes by looking up a success forward in the struts-config.xml file. The success forward represents a view based on the mapping shown in Listing 8-13.

Listing 8-13. Sessions Action Mapping from the struts-config.xml File

```
<action path="/sessions"
        type="com.ejdoab.tcms.web.actions.ListSessionsAction">
  <forward name="success" path="sessions" />
</action>
```

Listing 8-13 shows the mapping for an HTTP request of sessions.do. When the ActionServlet receives a request for sessions.do it forwards the request to the

ListSessionsAction, which is presented in Listing 8-12 based on the type attribute. When the ListSessionsAction returns a forward of success, the ActionMapping object maps to a forward element with the name of success. The path attribute represents a view that may be either a JSP page or, as in this example, a Tiles definition.

The Tiles definitions in Listing 8-7 shows that the sessions definition extends the master layout and overrides the body with a sessions.jsp page. Listing 8-14 is the sessions.jsp, which uses the JSTL to render session information.

Listing 8-14. sessions.jsp View Using the JSTL

```
<%@ taglib uri="jstl-core" prefix="c" %>
<%@ taglib uri="jstl-format" prefix="fmt" %>

<h2>Sessions</h2>

<c:forEach var="session" items="${sessions}">
  <b><c:out value="${session.title}"/></b><br>
  <b>Presenter:</b>
    <a href="sessionsByPresenter.do?presenter=
        <c:out value="${session.presenterId}"/>">
      <c:out value="${session.presenter}"/>
    </a>
    <br>
  <b>Day:</b>
    <fmt:formatDate value="${session.dtBegin}" type="date" dateStyle="full"/>
    <br>
  <b>Time:</b>
    <fmt:formatDate value="${session.dtBegin}" pattern="hh:mm a"/>
    - <fmt:formatDate value="${session.dtEnd}" pattern="hh:mm a"/>
    <br>
  <b>Location:</b> <c:out value="${session.where}"/><br>
  <b>Track:</b> <c:out value="${session.topic}"/><br>
  <p>
</c:forEach>
```

In Listing 8-14, the JSP begins by defining taglib directives for the JSTL core and format tag libraries. After the sessions heading, the JSP uses the core's forEach tag to iterate though the sessions list from the request attributes. Remember that the sessions list was added to the request attributes at the end of the ListSession-sAction in Listing 8-12. Each iteration of a session instance is put in a session variable, which can be used by other JSTL tags such as the core's out tag. The first item displayed is a bolded session title. Next a presenter name is listed in a hyperlink. A hyperlink is built using the core's out tag to add the presenters id as a presenter parameter value. This way, when the hyperlink is clicked by a user, another Action can build a list of sessions based on a particular presenter. Other information about the session is presented including dates and times that use the formatDate tags from the format library to properly format them.

Struts Forms

Getting information from a user requires the use of an HTML form like the TCMS registration form shown in Figure 8-8. In a typical web application, JSPs or servlets must get the values of a form from the request parameter list. Because each of the values from the parameter list is returned as a String, you must take care to convert the values to another type if something other then a String is required.

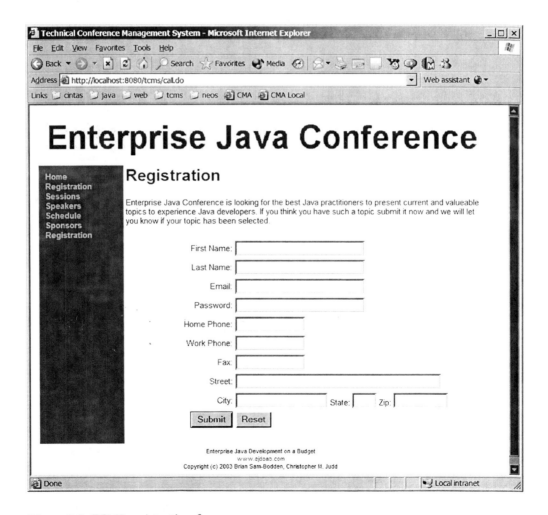

Figure 8-8. TCMS registration form

Struts makes working with forms more object oriented by introducing a concept of an ActionForm. The ActionForm is JavaBean with properties that relate to each of the form fields. Struts takes care of calling the ActionForm mutators with form values from the parameter list, and it even converts the values if necessary. The instance of the ActionForm is passed to the Action execute method as a parameter. Listing 8-15 shows an example of the TCMS RegistrationForm.

Listing 8-15. TCMS RegistrationForm

```
package com.ejdoab.tcms.web.forms;

import org.apache.struts.action.*;

import javax.servlet.http.*;

/**
 * Registration Form
 *
 * @author cjudd
 */
public class RegistrationForm extends ActionForm {
    private String city;
    private String email;
    private String fax;
    private String firstname;
    private String homephone;
    private String lastname;
    private String password;
    private String state;
    private String street;
    private String workphone;
    private String zip;

    public String getCity() {
        return city;
    }

    public void setCity(String city) {
        this.city = city;
    }
```

```java
public String getEmail() {
    return email;
}

public void setEmail(String email) {
    this.email = email;
}

public String getFax() {
    return fax;
}

public void setFax(String fax) {
    this.fax = fax;
}

public String getFirstname() {
    return firstname;
}

public void setFirstname(String firstname) {
    this.firstname = firstname;
}

public String getHomephone() {
    return homephone;
}

public void setHomephone(String homephone) {
    this.homephone = homephone;
}

public String getLastname() {
    return lastname;
}

public void setLastname(String lastname) {
    this.lastname = lastname;
}

public String getPassword() {
    return password;
}
```

```java
    public void setPassword(String password) {
        this.password = password;
    }

    public String getState() {
        return state;
    }

    public void setState(String state) {
        this.state = state;
    }

    public String getStreet() {
        return street;
    }

    public void setStreet(String street) {
        this.street = street;
    }

    public String getWorkphone() {
        return workphone;
    }

    public void setWorkphone(String workphone) {
        this.workphone = workphone;
    }

    public String getZip() {
        return zip;
    }

    public void setZip(String zip) {
        this.zip = zip;
    }

    public ActionErrors validate(ActionMapping actionMapping,
        HttpServletRequest httpServletRequest) {
        /**@todo: finish this method, this is just the skeleton.*/
        return null;
    }

}
```

In Listing 8-15, the RegistrationForm is a JavaBean that contains getters and setters for each of the form fields in the HTML form. Struts forms must also extend ActionForm or one of its descendants as the RegistrationForm does. You can put validation code into the optional validate method, which is called before the Action execute method. If the validate method returns ActionErrors then the Action execute method is never called. An alternative to putting validation code in the validate method is to extend the form class from ValidatorForm. The implementation of the validate method in the ValidatorForm knows how to validate against rules in an XML file. Validation will be covered in more detail later in this chapter.

Once the form class is created, it must be declared in the form-beans section of the struts-config.xml file. Listing 8-16 shows an example of the declaration of the RegistrationForm. The form Bean name will be used by action mappings and validation. The type is the fully qualified class name.

Listing 8-16. RegistrationForm Declaration in struts-config.xml

```
<form-beans>
 <form-bean name="registrationForm"
          type="com.ejdoab.tcms.web.forms.RegistrationForm" />
</form-beans>
```

Using an ActionForm in the Action class is easy. In the execute method the ActionForm must be typecast to the specific ActionForm descendant in order to have access to the bean properties. Listing 8-17 shows the SubmitRegistrationAction, which uses the RegistrationForm.

NOTE   You can also use XDoclet to generate the form Bean declaration, action mappings, and form validation.

Listing 8-17. SubmitRegistrationAction, Which Uses the RegistrationForm

```
package com.ejdoab.tcms.web.actions;

import com.ejdoab.tcms.services.*;
import com.ejdoab.tcms.services.dto.*;
import com.ejdoab.tcms.services.exceptions.*;
import com.ejdoab.tcms.web.forms.*;
```

```
import org.apache.struts.Globals;
import org.apache.struts.action.Action;
import org.apache.struts.action.ActionError;
import org.apache.struts.action.ActionErrors;
import org.apache.struts.action.ActionForm;
import org.apache.struts.action.ActionForward;
import org.apache.struts.action.ActionMapping;

import javax.servlet.http.HttpServletRequest;
import javax.servlet.http.HttpServletResponse;

/**
 * @author cjudd
 */
public class SubmitRegistrationAction extends Action {

    public ActionForward execute(ActionMapping mapping, ActionForm form,
        HttpServletRequest request, HttpServletResponse response)
        throws Exception {
        ActionErrors errors = new ActionErrors();
        RegistrationForm rf = (RegistrationForm) form;

        UserServicesHome uslh = UserServicesUtil.getHome();
        UserServices us = uslh.create();

        UserProfileDTO attendee = new UserProfileDTO();

        try {
            attendee.setUserType(UserProfileDTO.UserType.ATTENDEE);
            attendee.setPassword(rf.getPassword());
            attendee.setFirstName(rf.getFirstname());
            attendee.setLastName(rf.getLastname());
            attendee.setEmail(rf.getEmail());
            attendee.setHomePhone(rf.getHomephone());
            attendee.setWorkPhone(rf.getWorkphone());
            attendee.setFax(rf.getFax());

            attendee.setAddressStreet(rf.getStreet());
            attendee.setAddressCity(rf.getCity());
            attendee.setAddressState(rf.getState());
            attendee.setAddressZipCode(rf.getZip());
```

```
            us.registerUser(attendee);
        } catch (DuplicateEmailException ex) {
            errors.add(ActionErrors.GLOBAL_ERROR,
                new ActionError("error.register.duplicate"));
        }

        if (errors.isEmpty()) {
            return (mapping.findForward("success"));
        } else {
            request.setAttribute(Globals.ERROR_KEY, errors);

            return (mapping.findForward("failure"));
        }
    }
}
```

In Listing 8-17, the execute method typecasts the form reference from an ActionForm to a RegistrationForm. The rf instance of the registration form is used to map the form fields to an attendee data transfer object before it's registered with the UserService stateless session bean.

To make all the magic work in the JSP, tags from the Struts html tag library must be used rather then the standard HTML form input elements. There is almost a one to one correlation between the Struts html tags and the HTML form tags. Listing 8-18 shows the JSP code for the registration form.

Listing 8-18. registration.jsp, Which Uses the RegistrationForm

```
<%@ taglib uri="struts-html" prefix="html" %>
<%@ taglib uri="struts-bean" prefix="bean" %>
<%@ taglib uri="struts-logic" prefix="logic" %>

<h2>Registration</h2>
<p>Join us at the Enterprise Java Conference.
</p>

<logic:messagesPresent>
   <bean:message key="errors.header"/>
   <ul>
   <html:messages id="error">
      <li><bean:write name="error"/></li>
   </html:messages>
   </ul><hr>
</logic:messagesPresent>
```

```
<html:form action="submitRegistration.do">

 <table border="0" width="100%">
  <tr>
   <td align="right" width="30%">First Name:</td>
   <td align="left"><html:text property="firstname" size="30"/></td>
  </tr>
  <tr>
   <td align="right" width="30%">Last Name:</td>
   <td align="left"><html:text property="lastname" size="30"/></td>
  </tr>
  <tr>
   <td align="right" width="30%">Email:</td>
   <td align="left"><html:text property="email" size="30"/></td>
  </tr>
  <tr>
   <td align="right" width="30%">Password:</td>
   <td align="left"><html:text property="password" size="30"/></td>
  </tr>
  <tr>
   <td align="right" width="30%">Home Phone:</td>
   <td align="left"><html:text property="homephone" size="14"/></td>
  </tr>
  <tr>
   <td align="right" width="30%">Work Phone:</td>
   <td align="left"><html:text property="workphone" size="14"/></td>
  </tr>
  <tr>
   <td align="right" width="30%">Fax:</td>
   <td align="left"><html:text property="fax" size="14"/></td>
  </tr>
  <tr>
   <td align="right" width="30%">Street:</td>
   <td align="left"><html:text property="street" size="50"/></td>
  </tr>
  <tr>
   <td align="right" width="30%">City:</td>
   <td align="left">
    <html:text property="city" size="20"/>
    State: <html:text property="state" size="2"/>
    Zip: <html:text property="zip" size="10"/>
   </td>
  </tr>
```

```
<tr>
 <td align="right">
  <html:submit>Submit</html:submit>
 </td>
 <td align="left">
  <html:reset>Reset</html:reset>
 </td>
</tr>
</table>

</html:form>
```

Notice that in Listing 8-18, registration.jsp begins by declaring the Struts html, bean, and logic tag libraries. The bean and logic tag libraries will be used to display validation errors. The html library will be used to get the properties values out of the ActionForm and generate standard HTML form tags. After a page title and message, the logic tags are used to display validation errors—more on this in the validation session of this chapter.

Just like HTML forms, which must be surrounded by an HTML form tag, a Struts form must be surrounded by a Struts form tag. The Struts form tag like the HTML form tag contains an action that tells the browser the URL to submit the form to. Within the Struts form tag, other Struts html tags can be used such as the text, password, textarea, checkbox, hidden, and radio tags. These tags generate standard HTML input tags with the value of the property if there is any. At the bottom of most forms the submit and reset tags can be used to generate HTML input types of submit and reset.

The struts-config action mapping ties the Action class, ActionForm class, and Tiles definition together. Listing 8-19 shows an example of a mapping that ties the SubmitRegistrationAction and RegistrationForm together with the post from the registration.jsp.

Listing 8-19. submitRegistration Mapping

```
<action path="/submitRegistration"
        type="com.ejdoab.tcms.web.actions.SubmitRegistrationAction"
        name="registrationForm"
        scope="request"
        input="registration"
        validate="true"
>
 <forward name="success" path="registrationThanks" redirect="true" />
 <forward name="failure" path="registration" redirect="true" />
</action>
```

Validation

Giving feedback about invalid form data early in the process provides a better user experience. Users can be given an opportunity to correct the data before the database becomes corrupt. Implementing such a feedback loop is a lot of effort. On every form field a check has to be made to determine if a previous value had been entered, and if so, it needs to be redisplayed. In addition, it's often difficult to determine where validation code belongs and how to make it easily reusable. Fortunately, Struts already includes a validation framework that takes the complexity out of validating HTML forms. The Struts validation framework is a reusable XML-based framework that extends the Jakarta Commons Validator project.

NOTE   Originally, the Jakarta Commons Validator project came from Struts 1.0 as many of the other Jakarta Commons projects did.

Struts already contains a number of built-in validation rules, including required, minlength, maxlength, mask, and many more. These built-in rules are defined in the validator-rules.xml file that's found in the Struts lib directory. These rules are a great place to start. However, with little effort you can add other rules easily.

The framework has to be told how to validate specific forms. This is typically done in a separate XML file called validation.xml. Separating the files for each form make them easier to work with, but it's possible to combine them into a single file. The validation.xml file contains a root tag of form-validation and an element of formset. The form set is a collection of form elements. Each form element represents a form Bean. The name of the form element should match the name of the Bean declared in the struts-config.xml. Listing 8-20 shows an example of the validation.xml file that contains the registrationForm.

Listing 8-20. RegistrationForm Validation

```
<?xml version="1.0" encoding="ISO-8859-1" ?>

<!DOCTYPE form-validation PUBLIC
    "-//Apache Software Foundation//
        DTD Commons Validator Rules Configuration 1.0//EN"
    "http://jakarta.apache.org/commons/dtds/validator_1_0.dtd">
```

```
<form-validation>
  <formset>
    <form name="registrationForm">
      <field property="firstname"
             depends="required">
        <arg0 key="firstname.label"/>
      </field>
      <field property="lastname"
             depends="required">
        <arg0 key="lastname.label"/>
      </field>
      <field property="email"
             depends="required,email">
        <arg0 key="email.label"/>
      </field>
      <field property="password"
             depends="required">
        <arg0 key="password.label"/>
      </field>
      <field property="street"
             depends="required">
        <arg0 key="street.label"/>
      </field>
      <field property="city"
             depends="required">
        <arg0 key="city.label"/>
      </field>
      <field property="state"
             depends="required">
        <arg0 key="state.label"/>
      </field>
      <field property="zip"
             depends="required">
        <arg0 key="zip.label"/>
      </field>
    </form>
    </formset>
</form-validation>
```

Listing 8-20 contains a registrationForm with validation rules for the regis-trationForm that's declared in the struts-config.xml file. For each property of the RegistrationForm that requires validation, there's a field element. The field element contains the property name and the validation rule. In the case of the firstName property, it depends on passing the required rule. If the required rule fails, it uses the arg0 element to help build the validation error message. The firstName key of firstname.label is a property name found in the Struts message resource.

NOTE The message resources is a property file declared in the message-resource element of the struts-config.xml file as shown in Listing 8-9.

To make a form automatically validate against the validation.xml file the ActionForm must extend ValidatorForm rather than ActionForm. Listing 8-21 shows an updated RegistrationForm that extends the ValidatorForm class.

CAUTION ValidatorForm descendants must not include a validate method unless it calls the super validate method.

Listing 8-21. Validating RegistrationForm

```
package com.ejdoab.tcms.web.forms;

import org.apache.struts.validator.*;

/**
 * Registration Form
 *
 * @author cjudd
 */
public class RegistrationForm extends ValidatorForm {
    private String city;
    private String email;
    private String fax;
    private String firstname;
    private String homephone;
    private String lastname;
    private String password;
    private String state;
    private String street;
    private String workphone;
    private String zip;
```

```java
    public String getCity() {
        return city;
    }

    public void setCity(String city) {
        this.city = city;
    }

    public String getEmail() {
        return email;
    }

    public void setEmail(String email) {
        this.email = email;
    }

    public String getFax() {
        return fax;
    }

    public void setFax(String fax) {
        this.fax = fax;
    }

    public String getFirstname() {
        return firstname;
    }

    public void setFirstname(String firstname) {
        this.firstname = firstname;
    }

    public String getHomephone() {
        return homephone;
    }

    public void setHomephone(String homephone) {
        this.homephone = homephone;
    }

    public String getLastname() {
        return lastname;
    }
```

```
    public void setLastname(String lastname) {
        this.lastname = lastname;
    }

    public String getPassword() {
        return password;
    }

    public void setPassword(String password) {
        this.password = password;
    }

    public String getState() {
        return state;
    }

    public void setState(String state) {
        this.state = state;
    }

    public String getStreet() {
        return street;
    }

    public void setStreet(String street) {
        this.street = street;
    }

    public String getWorkphone() {
        return workphone;
    }

    public void setWorkphone(String workphone) {
        this.workphone = workphone;
    }

    public String getZip() {
        return zip;
    }

    public void setZip(String zip) {
        this.zip = zip;
    }
}
```

The validation framework is called before the Action class. If the validation fails the page is redirected to the input attribute of the action mapping. In most cases, this is probably the same Tiles mapping as the submitted form. The form should repopulate the fields with the previous values and display the validation errors. When you use the Struts tag libraries, this work is already handled. The Struts html tags take care of repopulating the fields. You can use the Struts logic and bean tags to display the validation errors. Listing 8-22 is a snippet from registration.jsp that shows a common example of displaying the validation errors.

Listing 8-22. Displaying Validation Errors

```
<logic:messagesPresent>
   <bean:message key="errors.header"/>
   <ul>
   <html:messages id="error">
      <li><bean:write name="error"/></li>
   </html:messages>
   </ul><hr>
</logic:messagesPresent>
```

Listing 8-22 uses the Struts logic tag libraries messagesPresent tag to determine if any messages or errors need to be displayed. If there are any messages or errors, the body of the tag is executed, otherwise nothing is rendered. The Struts bean tag is used to display a property value from the message resources property file. Then the Struts html messages tag is used to iterate through all the messages or errors. The Struts bean write tag is used to actually render the message.

 NOTE   The validation error presentation logic in Listing 8-22 would make a great reusable tile.

Setting Up Validation

To use the validation framework, you must configure a plug-in in the struts-config.xml file just like the Tiles plug-in. Listing 8-23 shows an example of configuring the validator plug-in. The primary purpose of configuring the validator plug-in is to tell the Struts where to find the validation rules and form validations.

Listing 8-23. struts-config.xml Validator Plug-in Configuration

```
<plug-in className="org.apache.struts.validator.ValidatorPlugIn">
  <set-property property="pathnames"
    value="/WEB-INF/validator-rules.xml,/WEB-INF/validation.xml"/>
</plug-in>
```

The only other requirement for the validation is to provide the validation rules. As mentioned earlier, the easiest way to start is by copying the validator-rules.xml from the Struts lib directory to the location defined in the validator plug-in configuration, which is commonly the WEB-INF directory.

Conclusion

Without a good model-view-controller framework, the presentation tier can become impossible to maintain. There are many good MVC frameworks to choose from. Struts is the most-common and possibly most-documented framework, but choose the one that meets your needs and stick with it.

CHAPTER 9

Web Services and Mobile Clients

Web services is the best way we know to create a service-oriented architecture.[1]

—Bob Sutor

MANY ORGANIZATIONS ARE now developing service-oriented architectures (SOA) or exposing parts of their applications as services. Web services are often used to expose services and the most popular form of web services is the W3C standard Simple Object Access Protocol (SOAP). SOAP is a messaging framework that uses XML and Internet standard transfer protocols such as HTTP to make remote procedure calls or transfer data rather than language-proprietary mechanisms. Rather than explain all the nuances and formats of a SOAP message in this chapter, we'll focus on how to expose parts of a J2EE-based application as web services and how to consume web services using the Open Source Apache Axis framework. The chapter concludes by developing a J2ME/MIDP web services consumer.

Web Services and Axis

In the TCMS application parts of the application lend itself very well to being exposed as a service. Imagine being able to expose news or attendees' schedules as web services. Attendees could write consumers to notify them of new news regarding the conference rather than forcing them to view the conference website on a daily basis. Also, imagine a web services consumer who could take attendees' individual online schedules and update their PDA or Outlook calendars with them. Web services could also be used to expose the same information to cell phones so that attendees could easily determine the next room or get updated on session cancellations and room changes.

Figure 9-1 illustrates the web services model. Producers expose services, for example the TCMS application exposes the service getNews, which returns the

---

1. Sutor, Bob. "A Web Services Wish List" (CNET News.com, January 14, 2004). See http://news.com.com/2010-7345-5139148.html.

current news items. The consumer can make requests of the producer. The producer fulfills the request and response with the appropriate answer such as a collection of new items. This is the traditional client/server model. One advantage of using SOAP is that the requests and responses are both implemented as XML-based SOAP messages, and the communication between the consumer and producer occurs because of HTTP. The combination of XML and HTTP allows web services to be language independent. In addition, web services doesn't rely on commercial products or frameworks. For these reasons, web services are ideal for integrating Java with non-Java systems such as .NET.

Figure 9-1. Web services model

SOAP uses an XML file called a web service description language (WSDL) to define a set of abstract operations that are tied to a concrete set of endpoints, which in turn, are deployed as a web service. The WSDL can also describe complex datatypes that are similar to structures or data transfer objects (DTOs). Listing 9-1 shows the WSDL of the News service, which will be used later in the chapter.

Listing 9-1. News Service WSDL

```
<?xml version="1.0" encoding="UTF-8"?>
<wsdl:definitions targetNamespace="http://localhost:8080/tcms/services/News"
    xmlns="http://schemas.xmlsoap.org/wsdl/"
    xmlns:apachesoap="http://xml.apache.org/xml-soap"
    xmlns:impl="http://localhost:8080/tcms/services/News"
    xmlns:intf="http://localhost:8080/tcms/services/News"
    xmlns:soapenc="http://schemas.xmlsoap.org/soap/encoding/"
    xmlns:tns1="services.tcms.ejdoab.com"
    xmlns:wsdl="http://schemas.xmlsoap.org/wsdl/"
    xmlns:wsdlsoap="http://schemas.xmlsoap.org/wsdl/soap/"
    xmlns:xsd="http://www.w3.org/2001/XMLSchema">
```

```
<wsdl:types>
 <schema targetNamespace="services.tcms.ejdoab.com"
     xmlns="http://www.w3.org/2001/XMLSchema">
   <import namespace="http://schemas.xmlsoap.org/soap/encoding/"/>
   <complexType name="NewsItemDTO">
     <sequence>
       <element name="body" nillable="true" type="xsd:string"/>
       <element name="creationDate" nillable="true" type="xsd:dateTime"/>
       <element name="creationdate" nillable="true" type="xsd:dateTime"/>
       <element name="date" nillable="true" type="xsd:dateTime"/>
       <element name="newsItemId" type="xsd:int"/>
       <element name="published" type="xsd:boolean"/>
       <element name="removeDate" nillable="true" type="xsd:dateTime"/>
       <element name="removedate" nillable="true" type="xsd:dateTime"/>
       <element name="title" nillable="true" type="xsd:string"/>
     </sequence>
   </complexType>
 </schema>
 <schema targetNamespace="http://localhost:8080/tcms/services/News"
     xmlns="http://www.w3.org/2001/XMLSchema">
   <import namespace="http://schemas.xmlsoap.org/soap/encoding/"/>
   <complexType name="ArrayOf_tns1_NewsItemDTO">
     <complexContent>
       <restriction base="soapenc:Array">
         <attribute ref="soapenc:arrayType"
             wsdl:arrayType="tns1:NewsItemDTO[]"/>
       </restriction>
     </complexContent>
   </complexType>
 </schema>
</wsdl:types>
<wsdl:message name="getNewsResponse">
  <wsdl:part name="getNewsReturn" type="impl:ArrayOf_tns1_NewsItemDTO"/>
</wsdl:message>
<wsdl:message name="getNewsRequest">
</wsdl:message>
```

```
<wsdl:portType name="News">
  <wsdl:operation name="getNews">
    <wsdl:input message="impl:getNewsRequest" name="getNewsRequest"/>
    <wsdl:output message="impl:getNewsResponse" name="getNewsResponse"/>
  </wsdl:operation>
</wsdl:portType>
<wsdl:binding name="NewsSoapBinding" type="impl:News">
  <wsdlsoap:binding style="rpc"
      transport="http://schemas.xmlsoap.org/soap/http"/>
  <wsdl:operation name="getNews">
    <wsdlsoap:operation soapAction=""/>
    <wsdl:input name="getNewsRequest">
      <wsdlsoap:body encodingStyle="http://schemas.xmlsoap.org/soap/encoding/"
          namespace="http://ws.tcms.ejdoab.com" use="encoded"/>
    </wsdl:input>
    <wsdl:output name="getNewsResponse">
      <wsdlsoap:body encodingStyle="http://schemas.xmlsoap.org/soap/encoding/"
          namespace="http://localhost:8080/tcms/services/News"
          use="encoded"/>
    </wsdl:output>
  </wsdl:operation>
</wsdl:binding>
<wsdl:service name="NewsService">
  <wsdl:port binding="impl:NewsSoapBinding" name="News">
    <wsdlsoap:address location="http://localhost:8080/tcms/services/News"/>
  </wsdl:port>
</wsdl:service>
</wsdl:definitions>
```

Listing 9-1 was generated using the AxisServlet, which will be discussed later in the chapter. The wsdl:service element at the bottom of the WSDL file identifies the service you're exposing as the NewsService. SOAP clients can bind to the NewsService to access the TCMS application using the URL http://localhost:8080/tcms/services/News/ in the wsdlsoap:address element. wsdl:operation elements identify the exposed methods. In this example there's a single getNews method. The getNews on the NewsService doesn't except any parameters but does return an array of NewsItemDTO. NewsItemDTO is a complex type described by the complexType elements. The NewsItem object contains the properties you might expect—body, title, date, and so on.

Axis is an Open Source SOAP framework that's available as a part of the Web Services project at Apache (http://ws.apache.org/axis/). Axis can be used by either the producer or consumer. Axis can use WSDL to generate skeletons and stubs, which are responsible for making what appears to be local method calls from SOAP requests and responses. Axis accomplishes this by marshaling the Java objects to XML before the message is sent. When Axis receives SOAP messages it unmarshals the XML and turns them into Java objects or primitive datatypes.

Producing Services

Axis can be used to expose plain old Java objects (POJOs) or EJBs as SOAP producers. Axis requires an HTTP server. Axis includes an internal HTTP server but a web container such as Tomcat or the web container in a J2EE application server is commonly used. If a web container is used, two servlets are used. One of the servlets responds to SOAP requests and the other manages Axis. The servlets are org.apache.axis.transport.http.AxisServlet and org.apache.axis.transport.http.AdminServlet.

Setting Up Axis

Setting up Axis 1.1 and deploying it in a web container such as JBoss involves creating a web application or adding the Axis servlet definitions to an existing web application. Chapter 8 already describes how to create a web application so the discussion will be expanded in this chapter to support web services.

Like other servlet-based frameworks, Axis involves installing the required JAR files in the WEB-INF/lib directory so that they become a part of the web application class loader. Then the servlet or servlets must be configured in the web.xml file. Axis is no different. Axis requires the axis.jar, jaxrpc.jar, saaj.jr, commons-logging.jar, commons-discovery.jar, wsdl4j.jar, and an XML parser. Listing 9-2 shows the common web.xml configuration for the AxisServlet and AdminServlet.

Listing 9-2. Axis web.xml Configuration

```xml
<?xml version="1.0" encoding="UTF-8"?>
<!DOCTYPE web-app PUBLIC
  "-//Sun Microsystems, Inc.//DTD Web Application 2.2//EN"
  "http://java.sun.com/j2ee/dtds/web-app_2_2.dtd">

<web-app id="WebApp">

  <display-name>TCMS Web Application</display-name>

  <!-- Servlet definitions -->
  <servlet>
    <servlet-name>action</servlet-name>
    <servlet-class>org.apache.struts.action.ActionServlet</servlet-class>
    <init-param>
      <param-name>config</param-name>
      <param-value>/WEB-INF/struts-config.xml</param-value>
    </init-param>
    <init-param>
      <param-name>application</param-name>
      <param-value>com.ejdoab.tcms.web.ApplicationResources</param-value>
    </init-param>
    <load-on-startup>1</load-on-startup>
  </servlet>

  <servlet>
    <servlet-name>AxisServlet</servlet-name>
    <display-name>Apache-Axis Servlet</display-name>
    <servlet-class>org.apache.axis.transport.http.AxisServlet</servlet-class>
  </servlet>

  <servlet>
    <servlet-name>AdminServlet</servlet-name>
    <display-name>Axis Admin Servlet</display-name>
    <servlet-class>org.apache.axis.transport.http.AdminServlet</servlet-class>
    <load-on-startup>100</load-on-startup>
  </servlet>

  <servlet-mapping>
    <servlet-name>action</servlet-name>
    <url-pattern>*.do</url-pattern>
  </servlet-mapping>
```

```xml
  <servlet-mapping>
    <servlet-name>AxisServlet</servlet-name>
    <url-pattern>/services/*</url-pattern>
  </servlet-mapping>

  <servlet-mapping>
    <servlet-name>AdminServlet</servlet-name>
    <url-pattern>/servlet/AdminServlet</url-pattern>
  </servlet-mapping>

  <mime-mapping>
    <extension>wsdl</extension>
     <mime-type>text/xml</mime-type>
  </mime-mapping>

  <!-- Tag libraries declarations -->
  <taglib>
    <taglib-uri>struts-html</taglib-uri>
    <taglib-location>/WEB-INF/struts-html.tld</taglib-location>
  </taglib>
  <taglib>
    <taglib-uri>struts-tiles</taglib-uri>
    <taglib-location>/WEB-INF/struts-tiles.tld</taglib-location>
  </taglib>
  <taglib>
    <taglib-uri>struts-bean</taglib-uri>
    <taglib-location>/WEB-INF/struts-bean.tld</taglib-location>
  </taglib>
  <taglib>
    <taglib-uri>struts-logic</taglib-uri>
    <taglib-location>/WEB-INF/struts-logic.tld</taglib-location>
  </taglib>
  <taglib>
    <taglib-uri>jstl-core</taglib-uri>
    <taglib-location>/WEB-INF/c.tld</taglib-location>
  </taglib>
  <taglib>
    <taglib-uri>jstl-format</taglib-uri>
    <taglib-location>/WEB-INF/fmt.tld</taglib-location>
  </taglib>
</web-app>
```

The common configuration in Listing 9-2 shows that the AxisServlet is mapped to the /services/* URL. The AdminServlet is mapped to the /servlet/AdminServlet URL. In addition, there is mime typing of wsdl to text/xml in case the web container doesn't already have the mapping.

To ensure that the web application has been configured correctly and that all the JAR files are located in the class loader, Axis provides a happyaxis.jsp file. If everything is configured correctly, accessing http://localhost:8080/tcms/happyaxis.jsp should look like Figure 9-2.

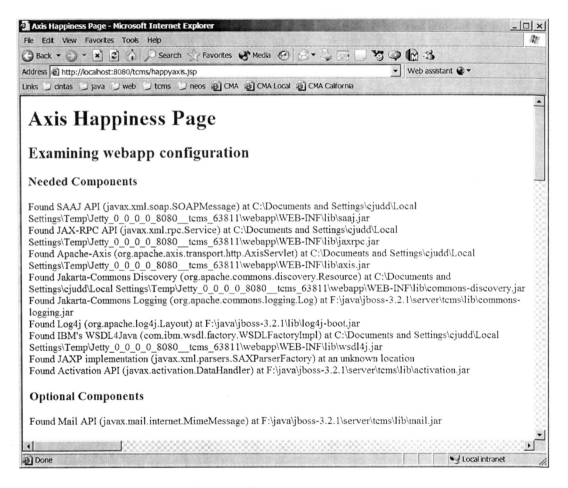

Figure 9-2. Correctly configured Axis application

Exposing Services

Assuming Axis has been deployed correctly in an existing application with either POJOs or EJBs, there's only one step that will expose the functionality as a SOAP service. An Axis proprietary web services deployment descriptor or deploy.wsdd file must be created in any directory. The WSDD file tells the Axis engine what services to expose and how to expose them. Using an admin client tool this file can be sent to the Axis engine to enable the service. Likewise an undeploy.wsdd file can be used to disable the service. However, this enabling is only a runtime enabling. If the application is redeployed or the application server restarted, the service will have to be re-enabled. So the deploy.wsdd method is only practical for testing or temporary purposes. The WSDD file can be used as input to another admin tool to generate a server-config.wsdd. When placed in the WEB-INF directory, the server-config.wsdd autostarts a service when the application is started.

The deploy.wsdd file is an XML file that contains the service and possible Bean mappings. The service describes the service name and provider. The provider may be either java:RPC for POJOs or java:EJB for EJBs. The service also contains parameters describing which class to expose and which methods should be exposed. The Bean mapping is used to describe complex web service types. Listing 9-3 illustrates the news service deploy.wsdd from the TCMS project.

Listing 9-3. News service deploy.wsdd.

```
<deployment xmlns="http://xml.apache.org/axis/wsdd/"
            xmlns:java="http://xml.apache.org/axis/wsdd/providers/java">
 <service name="News" provider="java:RPC">
  <parameter name="className" value="com.ejdoab.tcms.ws.News"/>
  <parameter name="allowedMethods" value="*"/>
 </service>
 <beanMapping qname="ns:NewsItemDTO"
     xmlns:ns="services.tcms.ejdoab.com"
     languageSpecificType="java:com.ejdoab.tcms.services.dto.NewsItemDTO"/>
</deployment>
```

Notice that in Listing 9-3, the news service is indicated to be a POJO because it uses the java:RPC provider. You may be asking yourself why use a POJO when the system has EJBs that implement the functionality? Well, the answer is type conversions. SOAP doesn't have all the rich datatypes that Java offers due to its language neutrality. The com.ejdoab.tcms.services.ConferenceServices Bean returns a collection of NewsItemDTOs as a Page collection. Interoperability with SOAP is easier when a collection is an array. Therefore, a com.ejdoab.tcms.ws.News class was created to convert the NewsItemDTO in the Page collection to an array of NewsItemDTOs. Notice that the new class is specified in the className parameter. Listing 9-4 contains the source code for the News class.

Listing 9-4. News Class That Converts NewsItemDTOs from a Page to an Array

```
package com.ejdoab.tcms.ws;

import com.ejdoab.tcms.services.*;
import com.ejdoab.tcms.services.dto.*;
import com.ejdoab.tcms.services.dto.page.*;
import java.rmi.*;
import java.util.*;

/**
 * Web service for getting news.
 */
public class News {
  /**
   * Gets all current news items
   *
   * @return An array of news items
   *
   * @throws RemoteException Any possible exception.
   */
  public NewsItemDTO[] getNews() throws RemoteException {
    try {
      Calendar currentCalendar = Calendar.getInstance();
      Calendar newsCalendar = Calendar.getInstance();
      List currentNews = new ArrayList();
      ConferenceServicesLocalHome cslh = ConferenceServicesUtil.getLocalHome();
      ConferenceServicesLocal csl = cslh.create();
      Page page = csl.getNews(0, csl.getNewsCount());

      while (page.hasNext()) {
        NewsItemDTO item = (NewsItemDTO) page.next();

        newsCalendar.setTime(item.getRemovedate());
```

```
        if (item.isPublished() && currentCalendar.before(newsCalendar)) {
          currentNews.add(item);
        }
      }

      NewsItemDTO[] items = new NewsItemDTO[currentNews.size()];
      int i = 0;

      for (Iterator iter = currentNews.iterator(); iter.hasNext(); i++) {
        items[i] = (NewsItemDTO) iter.next();
      }

      return items;
    } catch (Exception ex) {
      throw new RemoteException(ex.getMessage(), ex);
    }
  }
}
```

Listing 9-4 also shows the Bean mapping, which enables access to turn the com.ejdoab.tcms.services.NewsItemDTO class into a complex type. Axis uses introspection to get the properties of the class to build element sequences in the WSDL file.

Once this deploy.wsdd file has been created you can invoke the org.apache.axis.client.AdminClient on the command line by passing the deploy.wsdd file to it. Listing 9-5 shows an example of running the utility.

Listing 9-5. Deploying the deploy.wsdd File

```
java org.apache.axis.client.AdminClient deploy.wsdd
```

Once the web service has been deployed, you verify that it was enabled by using Axis's AxisServlet. Use the http://localhost:8080/tcms/servlet/AxisServlet URL to see all enabled services. Figure 9-3 shows the News service with the exposed getNews method that was deployed along with the Axis AdminService and Version services.

Figure 9-3. List of enabled services

In Figure 9-3, notice that next to each of the service names is a wsdl link. The link displays the corresponding wsdl, which describes the service. Clicking the News wsdl will present the wsdl found in Listing 9-1. In the next section, when the consumer is created you'll see how the URL to the wsdl can be used to generate the necessary classes that make requests to the service.

Now that the service has been verified it can be invoked with a web browser. Axis enables its services to be invoked by an HTTP get method, not just a traditional post method. To invoke the News with a browser enter the http://localhost:8080/tcms/services/News?method=getNews URL. The services path indicates that the AxisServlet receives the request. The following News path is the exposed service and getNews is the method or operation on the News service that will be invoked. The results should be similar to Listing 9-6.

Listing 9-6. Response from the News Service's getNews

```
<?xml version="1.0" encoding="UTF-8"?>
<soapenv:Envelope
    xmlns:soapenv="http://schemas.xmlsoap.org/soap/envelope/"
    xmlns:xsd="http://www.w3.org/2001/XMLSchema"
    xmlns:xsi="http://www.w3.org/2001/XMLSchema-instance">
```

```
<soapenv:Body>
 <getNewsResponse
     soapenv:encodingStyle="http://schemas.xmlsoap.org/soap/encoding/">
  <getNewsReturn
      xsi:type="soapenc:Array"
      soapenc:arrayType="ns1:NewsItemDTO[4]"
      xmlns:soapenc="http://schemas.xmlsoap.org/soap/encoding/"
      xmlns:ns1="services.tcms.ejdoab.com">
   <item href="#id0"/>
   <item href="#id1"/>
   <item href="#id2"/>
   <item href="#id3"/>
  </getNewsReturn>
 </getNewsResponse>
 <multiRef id="id1" soapenc:root="0"
     soapenv:encodingStyle="http://schemas.xmlsoap.org/soap/encoding/"
     xsi:type="ns2:NewsItemDTO"
     xmlns:soapenc="http://schemas.xmlsoap.org/soap/encoding/"
     xmlns:ns2="services.tcms.ejdoab.com">
  <body xsi:type="xsd:string">Cancelled</body>
  <creationdate xsi:type="xsd:dateTime">2004-06-02T05:00:00.000Z</creationdate>
  <date xsi:type="xsd:dateTime">2004-06-03T05:00:00.000Z</date>
  <newsItemId xsi:type="xsd:int">1</newsItemId>
  <published xsi:type="xsd:boolean">true</published>
  <removedate xsi:type="xsd:dateTime">2004-06-02T05:00:00.000Z</removedate>
  <title xsi:type="xsd:string">Session 12</title>
 </multiRef>
 <multiRef id="id3" soapenc:root="0"
     soapenv:encodingStyle="http://schemas.xmlsoap.org/soap/encoding/"
     xsi:type="ns3:NewsItemDTO"
     xmlns:ns3="services.tcms.ejdoab.com"
     xmlns:soapenc="http://schemas.xmlsoap.org/soap/encoding/">
  <body xsi:type="xsd:string">
   Brian and Chris will be signing books in the vendor area at 12:00 noon.
  </body>
  <creationdate xsi:type="xsd:dateTime">2004-06-02T05:00:00.000Z</creationdate>
  <date xsi:type="xsd:dateTime">2004-06-05T05:00:00.000Z</date>
  <newsItemId xsi:type="xsd:int">4</newsItemId>
  <published xsi:type="xsd:boolean">true</published>
  <removedate xsi:type="xsd:dateTime">2004-06-02T05:00:00.000Z</removedate>
  <title xsi:type="xsd:string">Book signing</title>
```

```
    </multiRef>
    <multiRef id="id2" soapenc:root="0"
        soapenv:encodingStyle="http://schemas.xmlsoap.org/soap/encoding/"
        xsi:type="ns4:NewsItemDTO"
        xmlns:ns4="services.tcms.ejdoab.com"
        xmlns:soapenc="http://schemas.xmlsoap.org/soap/encoding/">
      <body xsi:type="xsd:string">
       Keep a close eye on your laptops.
       Several have been stolen thoughout the conference.
      </body>
      <creationdate xsi:type="xsd:dateTime">2004-06-02T05:00:00.000Z</creationdate>
      <date xsi:type="xsd:dateTime">2004-06-04T05:00:00.000Z</date>
      <newsItemId xsi:type="xsd:int">3</newsItemId>
      <published xsi:type="xsd:boolean">true</published>
      <removedate xsi:type="xsd:dateTime">2004-06-02T05:00:00.000Z</removedate>
      <title xsi:type="xsd:string">Caution with laptops</title>
    </multiRef>
    <multiRef id="id0" soapenc:root="0"
        soapenv:encodingStyle="http://schemas.xmlsoap.org/soap/encoding/"
        xsi:type="ns5:NewsItemDTO"
        xmlns:ns5="services.tcms.ejdoab.com"
        xmlns:soapenc="http://schemas.xmlsoap.org/soap/encoding/">
      <body xsi:type="xsd:string">
       Lunch will be box lunches in the main lobby at 12:00 noon
      </body>
      <creationdate xsi:type="xsd:dateTime">2004-06-02T05:00:00.000Z</creationdate>
      <date xsi:type="xsd:dateTime">2004-06-02T05:00:00.000Z</date>
      <newsItemId xsi:type="xsd:int">0</newsItemId>
      <published xsi:type="xsd:boolean">true</published>
      <removedate xsi:type="xsd:dateTime">2004-06-02T05:00:00.000Z</removedate>
      <title xsi:type="xsd:string">Lunch</title>
    </multiRef>
   </soapenv:Body>
  </soapenv:Envelope>
```

Listing 9-6 shows the results of invoking the getNews method of the News service. These results include four news items. Each news item contains an ID, title, body, date, creation date, expiration date, and published status.

As mentioned earlier, using the deploy.wsdd isn't the most efficient or effective way to enable a web service because it must be re-enabled each time the application is redeployed or the web container is restarted. Instead, the admin utility can be used to convert the deploy.wsdd into a server-config.wsdd, which is read by the AxisServlet at runtime to determine which services to autostart. Listing 9-7 shows the command line for running the admin utility.

Listing 9-7. Command-line Admin Utility for Generating the server-config.wsdd

```
java org.apache.axis.utils.Admin server deploy.wsdd
```

The admin utility takes two parameters. The first parameter indicates that the configuration file is read by the server at startup. The second parameter is the input deploy file, which is used to determine the services and operations to expose at startup. The resulting server-config.wsdd should be placed in the WEB-INF directory of the web application. The next time the application is redeployed the services will automatically be enabled.

TCP Monitor

Axis includes a great utility for debugging SOAP communications called TCP Monitor, which acts as a proxy by capturing the requests and the responses between a consumer and producer. TCP Monitor isn't limited to SOAP applications. It can be helpful in any TCP-based application, including standard web applications. To run TCP Monitor type **java org.apache.axis.utils.tcpmon 8082 localhost 8080** on the command line. The tcpmon takes three parameters. The first parameter is the port requested in the browser. The second and third parameters are the server name and port to redirect the request to. To demonstrate this, hit http://localhost:8082/tcms/happyaxis.jsp and you'll see the HTTP request and response.

Consuming Services

Axis makes consuming a SOAP service really easy, and it isn't for just another Axis service, but any service that follows the standard SOAP Protocol. Just execute the WSDL2Java utility and tell it where to find a local or remote wsdl. Axis will generate all the necessary stub classes. Axis will even turn the complex types into JavaBeans.

To generate the client side classes for the News service type **java org.apache. axis.wsdl.WSDL2Java –p com.ejdoab.tcms.services http://localhost:8080/tcms/ services/News?wsdl**. The –p option identifies the package in which to place the generated classes. The second parameter can either be a local or remote WSDL file. Axis will generate a remote interface for the service, a remote procedure call interface, a service locator, and a SOAP-binding stub along with any necessary JavaBean that represents complex SOAP types. The generated classes can be used to create any type of client necessary to interact with the web service. Listing 9-8 shows a simple client that gets the news and prints the results of the title and body to standard out.

Listing 9-8. Simple Web Servcies Client

```
package com.ejdoab.tcms;

import com.ejdoab.tcms.services.*;

/**
 * Simple News Web Services Client
 */
public class NewsClient {

  public static void main(String[] args) throws Exception {
    NewsServiceLocator locator = new NewsServiceLocator();
    News news = locator.getNews();
    NewsItemDTO[] items = news.getNews();

    System.out.println("Conference News");

    for(int i = 0; i < items.length; i++) {
      System.out.println("*** " + items[i].getTitle() + " ***");
      System.out.println(items[i].getBody());
    }
  }
}
```

The client in Listing 9-8 starts by using the NewsServiceLocator to look up the remote web service. By using getter methods, it gets a reference to the News service. Once it has a reference to the service it can invoke the methods of that service. In this case, the getNews() operation is called and the method returns a collection of NewsItemDTOs. The NewsItemsDTO is a JavaBean created to represent the complex type defined in the WSDL file. In the previous example the collection is iterated through and printed out, but the results could have been used on another web page, put in a database, or used for any other necessary behavior.

JBoss.NET

JBoss 3.0 provides an optional plug-in called JBoss.NET, which wraps Apache Axis as an alternative way of deploying web services. JBoss.NET uses web service archives (WSR) to deploy web services.

Mobile Consumer

As society and devices become more mobile, there's a push to provide more functionality to users on the go. Applications are being extended for use on devices such as PDAs and phones. Java's micro edition (J2ME) combined with web services is a great way to solve the mobile problem.

J2ME Overview

J2ME is a scaled-down version of Java that runs on consumer devices. J2ME is divided into profiles that target specific types of devices. The mobile information device profile (MIDP) targets cell phones and PDAs such as the Palm. J2ME has many advantages over the alternative web-based Wireless Access Protocol (WAP), including the following:

- Offline capability

- Performance

- Reduces air time

- Reduces service charges

- Richer user experience

J2ME has an internal data store that can be used to hold data, thereby allowing the device to be used when a service is unavailable. Because the application executes in the memory of the device and doesn't need to make a round-trip to the server for every request, J2ME performs better and saves money by reducing the amount of used airtime. In addition, J2ME provides access to the canvas so that custom components, screen, and functionality can be developed. WAP is limited to a small number of HTML components and a simple scripting language.

To develop MIDP applications you'll need to install the J2ME Wireless Toolkit 1.0.4, which contains the J2ME API and emulators. The Wireless toolkit isn't Open Source but is freely available at `http://java.sun.com/products/j2mewtoolkit/`. If you want your J2ME application to be a SOAP consumer, you'll also need kSOAP and kXML from `http://ksoap.enhydra.org` and `http://kxml.enhydra.org`. There are version 2 releases of these frameworks developed by a separate group at `http://www.kobjects.org`, but they don't appear to work in all emulators and may not work on all devices.

Unit Testing J2ME

As discussed in Chapter 4, unit testing is an important part of developing quality applications. Therefore, it only makes sense that you would want to create unit tests for mobile applications as well. However, due to the limited J2ME API, JUnit can't be run in a J2ME environment. So instead of bring JUnit to a J2ME environment, how about bringing the J2ME environment to JUnit. An Open Source framework called ME4SE does just that. ME4SE is available at `http://www.kobjects.org` and it makes the J2ME API available on the J2SE platform. This enables developers to continue using JUnit to develop unit tests for the J2ME platform. ME4SE, combined with Personal Java can also be used to port J2ME applications to the Pocket PC. However, the results aren't as aesthetically pleasing as if the application was directly developed for the Pocket PC using Personal Java.

J2ME applications are deployed as two files, a JAR and a Java Application Descriptor (JAD). Like other Java applications the JAR file contains Java classes and related files such as images. The JAD file is basically a deployment descriptor in a property file format with attributes that describe things about the application such as its name, vendor, version, URL location, and size. See Listing 9-9 for the example from the TCMS application.

Listing 9-9. TCMS JAD file

```
MIDlet-Name: tcms
MIDlet-Vendor: tcms
MIDlet-Version: 1.0
MIDlet-1: tcms, , com.ejboab.tcms.midp.TCMSMidlet
MIDlet-Jar-URL: tcms-midp.jar
MIDlet-Jar-Size: 76701
```

The JAD file in Listing 9-9 shows a JAD file describing a MIDlet, a J2ME application with a name of tcms, and a vendor of tcms. The version of this application is 1.0. A JAD file can have a collection of MIDlets referred to as a MIDlet suite. In this case there's only one MIDlet. If there were multiple MIDlets, there would be more MIDlet-# attributes. The MIDlet-# attributes contain three characteristics. The first characteristic is the title that will be displayed in the list of available applications. Each device might present the list differently. The second is an image that will be displayed next to the name and the third is the class to invoke when the application is executed. In this example the title is tcms and the class to invoke is com.ejboad.tcms.midp.TCMSMidlet. The image characteristic is left blank, and therefore the default device icon will be displayed. The MIDlet-Jar-URL is a URL to the JAR file that contains the MIDlet. This may either be a local or remote URL, depending on the device installation, which can vary from Over-the-Air (OTA) to serial connection with a proprietary application. See the phone instructions for specific information. The last required attribute is the MIDlet-Jar-Size. This is the size in bytes of the JAR file. Some devices use this size to determine whether the application can be installed before it's even downloaded. If it's over the minimum limit, an error message will be displayed. In addition, if the size attribute doesn't match the size of the JAR file, an error message may also be displayed.

Application Size

Due to the limited amount of space on J2ME devices, many of them have a limit of how large the application can be. Phones often have a 100 kb limit. On some devices this limit is only for the class files. On other devices it's size is determined by the size of the JAR file, which might also contain images and other resources. Either way, size is a concern. Reducing the size of the class files can increase the amount of functionality that can be deployed to the device. Using an obfuscator can reduce the size of class files by 30 to 40 percent. Obfuscators are often used to name mangled classes to make them more difficult to reverse engineer. As a side-effect they reduce class-file sizes by changing variable and method names from a human-readable name to names such as A and AA. Because all the references are changed, the application still works like it should. Using an obfuscator is critical to J2ME development. Two commonly used Open Source obfuscators are ProGuard and RetroGuard, which can be found at http://proguard. sourceforge.net and http/www.retrologic.com, respectively.

Building a deployable MIDP application involves additional build steps not required by standard J2SE applications. For example, a preverification process, which verifies the application, is secure from the standpoint of not accessing resources it doesn't have access to, such as pointers. J2SE applications are verified at runtime, but due to the limited nature of J2ME devices, preverification must occur as part of the build. Rather than manually performing all the build details, it's recommended that you use the Ant Antenna extension. Antenna provides tasks for building, packaging, creating a JAD, running the application in an emulator, preverifying, obfuscating, and creating a Palm application. Antenna can be downloaded from http://antenna.sourceforge.net. Listing 9-10 shows the use of Antenna in the TCMS application.

Listing 9-10. MIDP Targets

```
<!-- Antenna - antenna.sourceforge.net -->
<taskdef name="wtkjad" classname="de.pleumann.antenna.WtkJad"/>
<taskdef name="wtkbuild" classname="de.pleumann.antenna.WtkBuild"/>
<taskdef name="wtkpackage" classname="de.pleumann.antenna.WtkPackage"/>
<taskdef name="wtkmakeprc" classname="de.pleumann.antenna.WtkMakePrc"/>
<taskdef name="wtkrun" classname="de.pleumann.antenna.WtkRun"/>
<taskdef name="wtkpreverify" classname="de.pleumann.antenna.WtkPreverify"/>
<taskdef name="wtkobfuscate" classname="de.pleumann.antenna.WtkObfuscate"/>
<taskdef name="wtksmartlink" classname="de.pleumann.antenna.WtkSmartLink"/>
<taskdef name="wtkpreprocess" classname="de.pleumann.antenna.WtkPreprocess"/>


<!-- ================================================================ -->
<!-- MIDP Client                                                      -->
<!-- ================================================================ -->

<target name="midp" depends="jar-midp"
    description="Creates a deployable MIDP application" />

<target name="compile-midp" depends="compile-init-midp">
 <wtkbuild srcdir="${src-midp}"
           destdir="${build-midp}"
           preverify="false"/>
  <copy todir="${build-midp}">
   <fileset dir="${src-midp}">
    <patternset refid="non.source.set"/>
   </fileset>
  </copy>
</target>
```

```
<target name="jad">
 <wtkjad jadfile="${jad}"
         name="${app.name}"
         vendor="${app.name}"
         version="1.0">
  <midlet name="${app.name}"
          icon=""
          class="${midlet-class}"/>
 </wtkjad>
</target>

<target name="jar-midp" depends="compile-midp,jad">
 <wtkpackage jarfile="${midp-jar}"
             jadfile="${jad}"
             obfuscate="${midp-obfuscate}"
             autoversion-"false">
  <fileset dir="${build-midp}"/>
 </wtkpackage>
 <wtkpreverify jarfile="${midp-jar}"
               jadfile="${jad}"/>
</target>

<target name="compile-init-midp">
 <mkdir dir="${build-midp}" />
</target>
```

Listing 9-10 begins by defining all the Antenna targets followed by the MIDP-specific targets. The midp target is the overall target that builds the entire application. The compile-midp target compiles the classes and copies all related material to the build directory. The jad target uses the application name property to build a JAD file. The jar-midp target packages the classes and related files into a JAR file and obfuscates the JAR. It then performs the necessary preverification process.

 NOTE   Due to the difference in APIs, J2SE and J2ME source code and classes should remain in separate source and build directories.

The resulting JAR and JAD files can be deployed to a multitude of J2ME-enabled devices or emulators.

kSOAP

The TCMS J2ME application enables attendees to get current news items about the conference they're attending by using their cell phones. The application uses the web service described earlier to get the current news items. The application then lists the news titles as shown in Figure 9-4.

Figure 9-4. List of current news titles

To view the details of a news item, the attendee can select a title. Figure 9-5 shows what a detailed news item looks like.

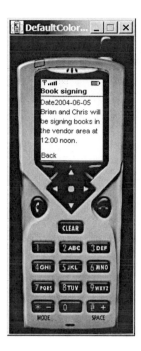

Figure 9-5. News details

To begin using kSOAP and kXML, the Java source code in those packages should be copied to the MIDP application source directory. It's advisable to use the source directly because these packages are rather large and can take advantage of source compression through obfuscation (see the "Application Size" sidebar).

A MIDP application requires a MIDlet class. This class is similar to the main class of a J2SE application. The MIDlet class is the starting point of the application and contains several life-cycle methods including startApp, pauseApp, and destroyApp. Listing 9-11 contains the source code for the TCMSMidlet class.

Listing 9-11. TCMSMidlet Class

```
package com.ejboab.tcms.midp;

import javax.microedition.midlet.*;
import javax.microedition.lcdui.*;

public class TCMSMidlet extends MIDlet {
  private static TCMSMidlet instance;
  private NewsDisplayable displayable = new NewsDisplayable();

  public TCMSMidlet() {
    instance = this;
  }

  /** Start method */
  public void startApp() {
    setCurrent(displayable);
  }

  /** Handle pausing */
  public void pauseApp() {
  }

  /** Clean up */
  public void destroyApp(boolean unconditional) {
  }

  /** Exit */
  public static void quitApp() {
    instance.destroyApp(true);
    instance.notifyDestroyed();
    instance = null;
  }

  public static void setCurrent(Displayable next) {
    Display.getDisplay(instance).setCurrent(next);
  }

  public static void setCurrent(Alert alert, Displayable next) {
    Display.getDisplay(instance).setCurrent(alert, next);
  }
}
```

The TCMSMidlet class in Listing 9-11 is a very basic MIDlet. As a matter of fact, most of the life-cycle methods are empty so they don't even do anything. This class does provide a couple of convenient methods. The first is quitApp. It provides a lean way of exiting the application. The second two are mechanisms for setting the current screen. A screen in MIDP is referred to as a Displayable. Only one Displayable can be visible at a time and it takes up the entire screen. MIDP includes two descendants of Displayable. The first is the Canvas, which provides the most freedom but also requires the most implementation. The second is the Screen, which is further subclassed into the Form, List, and TextBox for developing business-oriented applications. The setCurrent method, which takes a single Displayable parameter, simply sets the current screen. The second one accepts an alert, which is basically a message dialog box that briefly shows and then displays the Displayable, which is passed as the second parameter.

The TCMS application uses a NewsDisplayable screen to display all the news titles. See Figure 9-4 to see what this screen looks like. The source code for NewsDisplayable is listed in Listing 9-12.

Listing 9-12. NewsDisplayable Class

```
package com.ejboab.tcms.midp;

import javax.microedition.lcdui.*;
import java.util.*;

/**
 * Displays a list of news items
 */
public class NewsDisplayable extends List implements CommandListener {

  public static Command getCommand = new Command("Get", Command.SCREEN, 1);
  public static Command selectCommand = new Command("Select", Command.ITEM, 1);
  public static Command exitCommand = new Command("Exit", Command.EXIT, 3);

  private Vector news = null;

  /** Constructor */
  public NewsDisplayable() {
    super("Conference News", List.IMPLICIT);
    try {
      init();
    }
```

```
      catch(Exception e) {
        e.printStackTrace();
      }
    }

    private void init() throws Exception {
      setCommandListener(this);
      addCommand(getCommand);
      addCommand(selectCommand);
      addCommand(exitCommand);
      listNews();
    }

    /** Handle events*/
    public void commandAction(Command command, Displayable displayable) {
      if (command == exitCommand) {
        TCMSMidlet.quitApp();
      } else if (command == getCommand) {
        news = SyncAgent.getAgent().getNews();
        listNews();
      } else if (command == selectCommand) {
        if(news != null) {
          Hashtable item = (Hashtable)news.elementAt(getSelectedIndex());
          NewsItemDisplayable nid = new NewsItemDisplayable(item, this);
          TCMSMidlet.setCurrent(nid);
        }
      }
    }

    private void listNews() {
      Hashtable item = null;
      if(news != null) {
        for (Enumeration e = news.elements() ; e.hasMoreElements() ;) {
          item = (Hashtable)e.nextElement();
          append((String)item.get("title"), null);
        }
      }
    }
}
```

The NewsDisplayable in Listing 9-12 extends javax.microedition.lcdui.List, which is similar to a javax.swing.JList component except that it fills the entire screen because it extends Displayable. In this example each item in the list is a news title. This Displayable also contains three commands. Commands create menu items and events in a MIDP application. So in this case there's a getCommand that downloads all the news items from the web service using a SyncAgent class. There is also a selectCommand that displays the details of the currently selected news item title, and lastly, there's an exitCommand, which exits the application by calling the TCMSMidlet's quitApp method. When this class is created, it sets the title of the application to be ConferenceNews and adds all the commands. This class also uses the commandAction method to handle each of the commands/events. The method uses the command parameter to determine which command was executed and then performs the appropriate action. The class ends by including a method to iterate through all the news items on the device and appends or adds the title to the displayed list.

The TCMS MIDlet also contains a NewsItemDisplayable to view the details of the selected news item. Listing 9-13 contains the source code for the NewsItemDisplayable.

Listing 9-13. NewsItemDisplayable

```
package com.ejboab.tcms.midp;

import java.util.*;
import javax.microedition.lcdui.*;

/** Displays an individual News Item */
public class NewsItemDisplayable extends Form implements CommandListener {
  StringItem date;
  StringItem body;
  Displayable returnTo;
  Hashtable item = null;

  /**
   * Display a news item
   * @param item News Item to display.
   */
  public NewsItemDisplayable(Hashtable item, Displayable prev) {
    super((String)item.get("title"));

    this.item = item;
    returnTo = prev;

    try {
      init();
    }
```

```
      catch(Exception e) {
        e.printStackTrace();
      }
    }

    private void init() throws Exception {

      String sDate = ((String)item.get("date")).substring(0,10);

      date = new StringItem("Date:", sDate);
      body = new StringItem("", (String)item.get("body"));
      date.setLabel("Date");
      setCommandListener(this);
      addCommand(new Command("Back", Command.BACK, 1));
      this.append(date);
      this.append(body);
    }

    /**Handle events*/
    public void commandAction(Command command, Displayable displayable) {
      if(command.getCommandType() == Command.BACK) {
        TCMSMidlet.setCurrent(returnTo);
      }
    }
  }
```

The NewsItemDisplayable in Listing 9-13 extends the javax.microedition.lcdui.Form. The Form class is able to include form elements such as text fields and radio buttons for import, or in this example, just StringItems for displaying content. This Displayable sets the form title to the title of the news item and adds the date and body to string items. The only command this Displayable contains is the back command, which returns to the NewsDisplayable to display the list of news-item titles.

All the web services' work is contained within the SyncAgent class in Listing 9-14.

Listing 9-14. SyncAgent Class

```java
package com.ejboab.tcms.midp;

import java.util.*;

import org.ksoap.SoapObject;
import org.ksoap.SoapFault;
import org.ksoap.transport.HttpTransport;
import org.kobjects.serialization.*;
import org.ksoap.ClassMap;
import org.ksoap.*;

/**
 * Wraps SOAP calls
 */
public class SyncAgent {

  private static SyncAgent agent = null;

  private static final String SERVER = "localhost:8080";

  private SyncAgent() {}

  public static SyncAgent getAgent() {
    if(agent == null) {
      agent = new SyncAgent();
    }
    return agent;
  }

  /**
   * Retrieves Current News Items
   * @return Collection of news items as a Hashtable
   */
  public Vector getNews() {

    HttpTransport ht = null;
    String method = "getNews";
    Vector requests = null;
```

```
    try {
      ht = createTransport(method);

      SoapObject request = createObject(method);
      Vector result = (Vector)ht.call(request);

      requests = mapSoapToHash(result);
    } catch (SoapFault sf) {
      System.out.println(sf.faultcode + " - " + sf.faultstring);
    } catch (Exception ex) {
      System.out.println(ex.getMessage());
    }

  return requests;
}


/**
 * Converts Soap objects to Hashtables
 * @param requests Collection of soap objects to convert
 * @return Collection of objects as a Hashtable
 */
private Vector mapSoapToHash (Vector requests) {

  Vector v = new Vector(requests.size());
  Hashtable ht = null;
  Object value = null;
  PropertyInfo pi = new PropertyInfo();

  for (Enumeration e = requests.elements(); e.hasMoreElements();) {
    Object item = e.nextElement();
    if(item instanceof SoapObject) {
      SoapObject so = (SoapObject)item;
      ht = new Hashtable();

      ht.put("class", so.getName());

      for (int i = 0; i < so.getPropertyCount(); i++) {
        so.getPropertyInfo(i, pi);
        value = so.getProperty(i);
        if(value instanceof SoapPrimitive) {
          value = ((SoapPrimitive)value).toString();
        }
```

```
        ht.put(pi.name, value);
      }

      v.addElement(ht);
    }
  }
  return v;

}


/** Factory method for creating new HttpTransport intances
  * with url to prefered server.
  * @param action SOAP action placed in
  *                 HTTP header (typically remote method name)
 * @return new HttpTransport instance
 * @throws Exception Unable to determine server from preferences
 */
private static HttpTransport createTransport(String action) throws Exception {
  HttpTransport ht;

  ht = new HttpTransport("http://" + SERVER + "/tcms/services/News", action);
  ht.debug = true;
  return ht;
}

/** Factory method for creating new SoapObjects with the appropriate user name
 * and password.
 * @return new SoapObject instance
 * @param name name of soap object
 * @throws Exception
 */
private static SoapObject createObject(String name) throws Exception {
  SoapObject so = new SoapObject("", name);
  return so;
}
}
```

The SyncAgent in Listing 9-14 uses the kSOAP framework directly, and the kXML framework indirectly in order to communicate over HTTP with web services with the server. The SyncAgent is a singleton, so only one instance of it can reside in memory at any one time. To get a reference to the instance, use the getAgent method. The SyncAgent contains a getNews() convenience method that can be called by the rest of the application to the current news. The getNews() method wraps the complexities of using kSOAP. The getNews() method gets a org.ksoap.transport.HttpTransport instance by calling a factory method on the SyncAgent. The HttpTransport represents the connection to the News web service. The action parameter represents the method on the service that will be called. In this case the getNews method. The method then creates a SoapObject to pass to the web service when it's called. A SoapObject is basically a set of name/value pairs. The call method on the HttpTransport object is used to invoke the web service using the request SoapObject. The call method creates a SOAP request and sends it by HTTP to the web service. The web service builds a SOAP response and sends it back. The call method then turns the SOAP response into one of several object types and returns the result as an object. Depending on the SOAP response, the returned object may be a SoapObject (name/value pair), String, or Vector of SoapObjects for complex types. In this case, the result is a Vector of SoapObjects representing a news item complex type. The mapSoapToHash method is used to convert the Vector of SoapObjects to a Vector of HashTables, so the values of the news items can be easily used by the Displayables.

NOTE All MIDP 1.0 devices are required to support HTTP but don't all support HTTPS. In MIDP 2.0 HTTPS becomes a requirement. You should consider the HTTPS capability of the device when selecting devices and when tight security is required.

To run the application in the emulator, you can either select Run MIDP Application in the Start menu or execute emulatorw –gui –Xdescriptor: from the toolkits bin directory. A dialog box will prompt you for a JAD file. Once the JAD file is selected the emulator will start the application specified in the JAD file. The toolkit comes with multiple emulators. To switch emulators, use either the –Xdevice: option on the command line or select Default Device Selection from the Start menu.

Conclusion

Environments are no longer homogeneous. Systems must integrate with systems written in different languages and support new platforms. Web services and Axis combine to provide a great solution to the integration challenge.

CHAPTER 10

Rich Clients with the SWT and JFace

And now for something completely different...

—Monty Python's Flying Circus

UP TO THIS POINT in the book we've focused on the server side and the relatively simple HTML user interfaces. This chapter's aim is to delve into the creation of rich user interfaces in Java with the help of the Open Source community.

The rise of the Internet and the web browser as the universal computing client forced user-interface development and the overall user experience to take a step backwards. Web applications, due to their ease of maintenance in terms of deployment and upgrading, allow you to reach a larger audience. Yet, they deny the user the experience that a full-fledged desktop application can provide. The raw power of today's personal computers is mostly untapped when it comes to browser-based enterprise applications. The browser-based application is to a certain extent a glorified version of the dumb terminal of days gone by. Although Java made its debut with applets, which promised many of the features of rich native applications combined with the ease of maintenance of web applications, the applets' tumultuous evolution has relegated them to a limited functionality— stock tickers and news feeds. This has led many to argue that browser-side Java is effectively dead. The technology wasn't completely to blame because Java on the browser was a casualty of the browser wars and the early problems faced by VM integration in the two leading browsers, Internet Explorer and Netscape Navigator.

Java's client-side technologies have all had their share of criticisms and never conquered the share of the desktop market that many predicted. As with applets, many believe that the rough transition from the Abstract Window Toolkit (AWT) to the early days of Swing, coupled with the overall complexity and paradigm change in UI development introduced by Java (in comparison to the MVC-less world of Visual Basic, Delphi, and other RAD environments) caused Java to lose the battle for the desktop.

In this chapter we introduce the Open Source community's answer to the rich client conundrum in the form of the Eclipse project UI frameworks, namely the Standard Widget Toolkit (SWT) and JFace. This chapter is an introduction by example that sets out to build the administrative interface to the TCMS system. The Eclipse frameworks provide a Java alternative to building robust, responsive, and great-looking desktop applications.

Java on the Desktop

The reality of Java on the desktop is that it hasn't flourished as the community expected. Most discussions put the blame on Sun and the choices made in the AWT and the Swing toolkit implementations.

Abstract Window Toolkit

AWT, by using large chunks of code written in C (referred to as "fat native peers"), relegates work to native implementations of a component. At first the approach seems intelligent but the perils of multiple language implementations and the fact that Sun never opened the native code for the peers implementations made AWT a toolkit that was pretty hard to debug. AWT applications also suffered from the lowest-common-denominator approach, giving them a very inconsistent user experience and a rather primitive look and feel. AWT mitigates OS differences in the C code implementations of a widget, which resulted in a large amount of code that was difficult to diagnose and debug. AWT was light years behind well-established UI toolkits like those provided by OWL, Visual Basic, Delphi, and the plethora of OLE/COM components. Many companies paid dearly by jumping into the AWT world. Nowadays it's very rare to find AWT applications in the wild. AWT has only remained around as a foundational layer to Swing.

Swing

Sun's reaction to AWT's problems was to team up with Netscape's Internet Foundation Classes (IFC) team and come up with a design that would cover all the bases. The Swing toolkit was supposed to put an end to the agony of Java on the desktop. Swing took a completely different approach than AWT. Where AWT relied on peers, Swing's components are pure Java lightweight implementations that use the Java 2D API for rendering. This eradicated the least-common-denominator syndrome and ensured that UIs look consistent from platform to platform. The initial releases, although far better than AWT, lacked in many areas, partly because it was ahead of its time, and partly because it took a purist object-oriented approach to UI development by disregarding the way that most UI developers were building applications. The reality is that creating a UI toolkit is an evolutionary process, and the Java community needed something fast and responsive immediately. Instead it took around five years to get Swing to a state that the generated UIs could compete and blend in with native applications. Throw on top of that, distribution and installation efforts and it's clear to see how the desktop wars were lost.

From the design point of view, as pointed out by Erich Gamma, Swing took an extremely academic, big-design-up-front approach. This approach generated a toolkit that was rather large for a developer to comprehend in a reasonable amount of time. Swing's design is in some people's opinion an excessive use of patterns scenario in which too many layers of indirection are forced onto the developer. We learned this lesson with web applications when it became clear that for some large web applications a strong MVC foundation is indispensable, especially when it comes to maintenance and ease of development. But on the other hand there are also many successful non-MVC applications written in PHP, Perl, or Python. Web developers have choices; Java desktop developers, until recently, did not. Swing gave developers no choice but the MVC way, even for simple applications. At this point in Swing's life, most major problems have been resolved and the increasing computing power on today's PC makes it a viable UI application platform. Yet there's still a sense of lack of acceptance for Swing applications from the general user population. It seems that most Swing applications are used by Java developers. Yet, there are great examples of what it's possible to create with the Swing toolkit such as IDEA's IntelliJ IDE, Borland's JBuilder, and Karsten Lentzsch's JGoodies line of products (http://www.jgoodies.com), some of which have been open sourced with the help of Sun.

We believe that there is room for both Swing and the Eclipse technologies to thrive. As former Delphi developers, we perceive a level of resistance from users when they interact with Swing applications that we don't see when they use Eclipse-based applications. Although the Swing team has made great strides in minimizing the look-and-feel fidelity issues (because Swing draws its own widgets), it's in a constant state of playing catch-up with the different platforms' look and feel, resulting in awkward-looking applications.

The Eclipse User Interface Frameworks

The Eclipse project is described on its website as an "IDE for anything and for nothing in particular." The use of the term IDE in the previous sentence might be a bit misleading because although the composing subsystems of the Eclipse framework have at certain points in their API an IDE-ish flavor to them, the majority of the framework is usable as a general desktop application framework.

The Eclipse project spawned out of the early work of Erich Gamma and the folks at Object Technology International (OTI), which is now an IBM subsidiary. OTI is well known for their work in the areas of development tools (VisualAge) and object languages like Smalltalk and Java.

This chapter deals with using the underlying frameworks created by OTI and IBM to deliver a fast, responsive Java desktop application. Many pages can be written about the controversies surrounding the Eclipse project, its underlying APIs (particularly the SWT), the design choices and the impact that Open Sourcing the code base has created in the community. Instead, you'll focus on building a robust application using Eclipse. For more information on SWT and JFace visit http://www.eclipse.org.

The following are the two main frameworks that you'll learn about:

- **SWT:** A widget set and graphics library that provides a portable graphics API independent of the OS but that relies on the native widgets.

- **JFace:** A model-based UI toolkit that simplifies common UI programming tasks.

Standard Widget Toolkit

SWT is the foundation on which the Eclipse IDE is built upon. SWT delivers the richness and responsiveness of an application build using native widgets, yet it manages to do so in an operating system–independent fashion.

The Eclipse team realized early that creating a cross-platform set of widgets is a daunting task, both in the areas of matching the functionality of mature operating-system widgets and in making the application seamlessly blend with the native applications. SWT takes a hybrid approach between those taken by AWT and Swing. Instead of using "fat native peers," SWT uses a procedural pass-through layer to the OS graphics API. This thin Java Native Interface (JNI) layer enables SWT to control the native widgets. This approach minimizes the amount of native code involved, thereby making debugging SWT a lot easier. SWT also avoids the need for a pluggable look and feel because it adopts and immediately reflects any changes to the underlying OS look and feel.

NOTE Pluggable look and feel is another hotly debated topic. The Eclipse mentality is one of "uniform is better" and we certainly agree with this when it comes to commercial business software. Many other applications can certainly benefit from a pluggable look and feel in the same way that many applications benefit from the use of "skins." If your application needs to support a customizable or personalized look then Swing is the obvious choice.

The SWT approach not only makes the API simpler, but also provides tight integration with hard-to-integrate features such as drag and drop. Drag-and-drop support is another area in which Swing's implementation was plagued for a long time by bugs and inconsistencies. With SWT any improvements in the drag-and-drop behavior of the OS are reflected in your Java applications immediately.

To resolve the least common denominator problem, in SWT widgets that aren't present in a specific platform are emulated using lightweight techniques in the way that it's done in Swing, yet the components are unencumbered by any built-in patterns. A good example is the Tree widget. In Windows, Tree widgets are native components, but in Motif they're emulated. The SWT implementation in Motif contains the Java code to provide the Tree functionality, but in Windows using a Tree widget is simply a matter of calling the correct Windows graphics device interface (GDI) commands. Figure 10-1 shows the three different approaches.

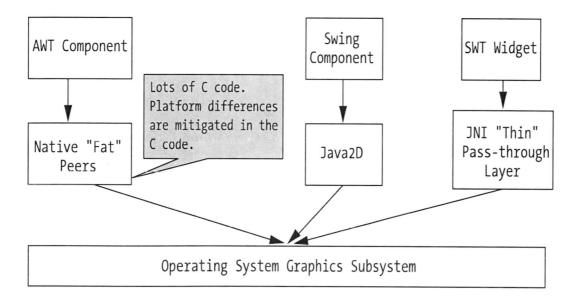

Figure 10-1. Rendering approaches of AWT, SWT, and Swing

The SWT API is the same on all different supported platforms. Behind the scenes SWT uses a factory pattern of sorts to plug the right implementations for a given platform. Not only do SWT applications look like they belong among other native applications, but they also feel like native applications. Figure 10-2 provides a graphical overview of the SWT architecture.

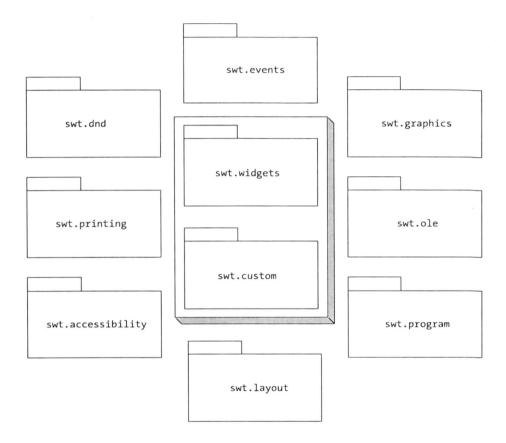

Figure 10-2. SWT packages

At this the time of this writing, SWT has been ported to the following platforms (operating systems and windowing systems): aix/motif, hpux/motif, linux/gtk, linux/motif, linux/qt, macos/carbon, qnx/photon, solaris/motif, win32/win32, and win32-ce/win32. SWT is also a very lightweight API, which makes it ideal for embedded devices as demonstrated by the Windows CE port.

JFace

From the previous description of SWT you should have gotten the impression that it provides a raw widget set. But what about all of the advancements implemented in Swing, such a strong MVC microarchitectures for complex, often-used widgets such as Trees and Tables? To provide a more advanced, model-driven interaction with SWT, the Eclipse team created the JFace toolkit. JFace is a higher-level user interface toolkit that uses the raw SWT widgets to provide model-driven widgets, and to some extent some functionality that isn't available in the Swing libraries such as advanced editors, dialog boxes, and wizards. JFace covers many areas of UI development that developers encounter over and over, and it provides a clean way to accomplish those tasks. JFace depends on SWT, but it doesn't hide SWT widgets. For example JFace viewers, which are model-based content adapters for SWT widgets, provide methods to access the underlying SWT widgets. This duality provides developers with the separation and ability to choose between model-driven UI development and raw widget manipulation.

Figure 10-3 shows a graphical overview of the JFace API.

Some of the packages shown in Figure 10-3 and a short explanation of their functionality are shown here:

- **Window:** The org.eclipse.jface.window package provides window creation and management facilities. Of particular interest is the ApplicationWindow class, which provides a higher-level application window and encapsulates the SWT event loop.

- **Viewers:** The org.eclipse.jface.viewers package provides a framework of Viewers such as TreeViewer and TableViewer, which are model-driven components that make use of SWT widgets and adapt content of a model to the widget.

- **Dialogs:** The org.eclipse.jface.dialogs package provides several commonly used dialog boxes.

- **Actions:** The org.eclipse.jface.actions package provides a UI action framework that's similar to Swing's action framework in order to implement shared behavior between two or more user interface components such as a menu item and toolbar button.

- **Wizards:** The org.eclipse.jface.wizard package provides an advanced framework to create wizards (the familiar dialog boxes that automate repetitive and complex tasks).

- **Resource:** The org.eclipse.jface.resource package provides support for managing resources such as SWT fonts and images.

- **Text:** The org.eclipse.jface.text package and its subpackages provide a framework for creating, manipulating, displaying, and editing text documents.

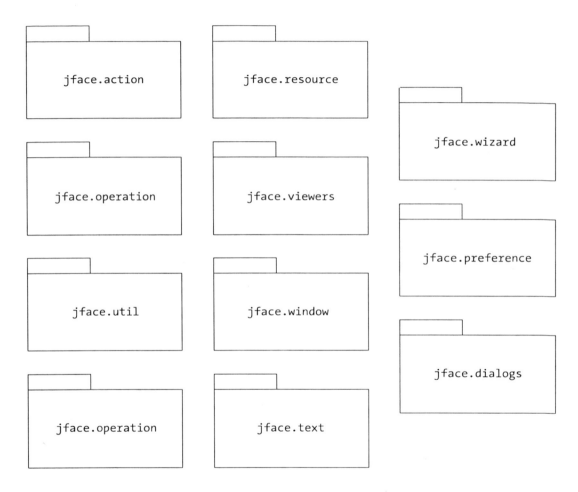

Figure 10-3. JFace packages

SWT Primer

The first step you need to take to start building SWT applications is to get the latest SWT release for your platform. If you've installed the Eclipse IDE on your system, then you already have all the necessary JARs and native libraries. If you don't have Eclipse installed, you can obtain SWT as a separate distribution

(since release 2.1). You can obtain SWT in binary or source form from
http://www.eclipse.org/downloads.

The downloaded file is swt-2.1.1-win32.zip, which is a drop containing the SWT libraries and source code for stand-alone SWT application development. The ZIP file contains a JAR file (swt.jar), a Windows DLL file (or the native library for your chosen platform), a ZIP file with the source code, and an about.html file.

For the following simple examples let's place the contents of the SWT distribution file in a directory named lib and the example Java files in the parent directory of the lib directory. Let's start by looking at the simplest SWT application, which simply shows an empty application window:

```
import org.eclipse.swt.widgets.Display;
import org.eclipse.swt.widgets.Shell;

public class SimplestSWTExample {

    public static void main(String[] args) {
        Display display = new Display();
        Shell shell = new Shell(display);
        shell.setText("Simplest SWT Example");
        shell.pack();
        shell.open();
        while (!shell.isDisposed()) {
            if (!display.readAndDispatch()) {
                display.sleep();
            }
        }
        display.dispose();
    }
}
```

To compile the application use the javac command as usual, and include the swt.jar file in the classpath, as follows:

```
javac -classpath .;lib\swt.jar SimplestSWTExample.java
```

Let's try to run the example using the java command as follows:

```
java -classpath .;lib\swt.jar SimplestSWTExample
```

The console output should produce the following stack trace.

```
Exception in thread "main" java.lang.UnsatisfiedLinkError: no swt-win32-2135 in
java.library.path
        at java.lang.ClassLoader.loadLibrary(Unknown Source)
        at java.lang.Runtime.loadLibrary0(Unknown Source)
        at java.lang.System.loadLibrary(Unknown Source)
        at org.eclipse.swt.internal.Library.loadLibrary(Library.java:108)
        at org.eclipse.swt.internal.win32.OS.<clinit>(OS.java:46)
        at org.eclipse.swt.widgets.Display.internal_new_GC(Display.java:1291)
        at org.eclipse.swt.graphics.Device.init(Device.java:547)
        at org.eclipse.swt.widgets.Display.init(Display.java:1310)
        at org.eclipse.swt.graphics.Device.<init>(Device.java:96)
        at org.eclipse.swt.widgets.Display.<init>(Display.java:291)
        at org.eclipse.swt.widgets.Display.<init>(Display.java:287)
        at SimplestSWTExample.main(SimplestSWTExample.java:10)
```

The error shown is telling you that in order to run the SWT example you need the swt-win32 DLL. Notice that as part of the SWT distribution for Windows you have the swt-win32-VERSION.dll file where VERSION denotes the particular version of the DLL. To make the DLL available to the running JVM use the –Djava.library.path parameter as part of the Java command line as follows (the same applies to other environments such as Linux or Mac OS X):

```
java -classpath .;lib\swt.jar -Djava.library.path=lib  SimplestSWTExample
```

The output should now resemble what's shown in Figure 10-4.

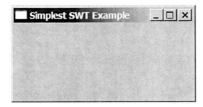

Figure 10-4. A simple SWT example

TIP If you want to eliminate the need for specifying the classpath and java.library.path options in the Java command line you can integrate the SWT JAR and DLL (for Windows) with your Java Runtime Environment (JRE) by copying the JAR files to the JRE's lib/ext directory and the DLL to the JRE's bin directory (the same procedure can be applied to other platforms).

Let's examine the example's code to gain an understanding of how SWT works under the covers. The first object instantiated is of type org.eclipse.swt.widgets.Display, although it's in the SWT Widgets package this class actually isn't a widget but rather a bridge that widgets and other SWT classes use to communicate with the underlying operating system. The Display class extends org.eclipse.swt.graphics.Device (which also has a child class named Printer).

The next class instantiated is the Shell. A SWT Shell is an encapsulation of an operating system's window. Notice that the code sample sets the window title by invoking the setText method on the Shell. The Shell is then told to pack (force the layout of children components) and to open (show) itself.

The next segment of code in the example is at first rather strange for Java developers. If you work with Swing you might be asking yourself why there is a while loop and the end of the example.

```
while (!shell.isDisposed()) {
    if (!display.readAndDispatch()) {
        display.sleep();
    }
}
display.dispose();
```

Actually, the while loop is the event loop or message pump of the application. In AWT or Swing the event loop is actually hidden from the developer. In SWT the Display class is responsible for the event loop; it forwards all OS events affecting the shell or any of its child widgets to the application until the shell is disposed. If you were to leave that code segment out, your application wouldn't be able to respond to any events. This is another example of how the SWT design doesn't hide any of the raw features of the toolkit. This feature, although strange at first, gives developers greater flexibility in their interaction with the underlying OS.

 CAUTION In SWT the UI thread isn't protected or hidden from the developer. In fact, whatever thread creates the Display class becomes the UI thread. This approach facilitates the debugging of threading and timing issues yet it can be confusing to developers accustomed to working with a UI toolkit that hides threading issues from the developer. It's the developers' responsibility to fork a new thread to perform non-UI computationally intensive operations in response to an event. Also, all interaction with the UI must originate from the UI thread, otherwise an org.eclipse.swt.SWTException is thrown.

Working with Widgets

All design issues aside, the essence of any UI toolkit is its available components or widgets. Table 10-1 lists the available SWT widgets and their Swing equivalents.

Table 10-1. SWT Widgets

Widget	Swing Equivalent	Description
Tracker	None	Provides tracking rectangles that provide visual feedback
Menu	JMenu	A container for MenuItems
Button	JButton	A simple button
Label	JLabel	A simpler JLabel with no Image or Border capabilities
ProgressBar	JProgressBar	The traditional progress bar
Sash	JSplitPane	A Sash is actually the Splitter portion, not a container
Scale	JSlider	Selects a value by sliding a knob within a bounded interval
Slider	JSlider, JScrollBar	More like a scrollbar than a Slider
List	JList	A list of strings
Text	JTextField, JPasswordField, JTextArea	A multipurpose text entry field
Combo	JComboBox	A drop-down list for select string values
Group	JPanel	Titled Border

Table 10-1. SWT Widgets (Continued)

Widget	Swing Equivalent	Description
Tree	JTree	The classical tree view interface
Table	JTable	A table of elements
TabFolder	JTabbedPane	A simpler JTabbedPane
ToolBar	JToolBar	A simpler JToolBar
CoolBar	JToolBar	A detachable more configurable toolbar
CLabel	JLabel	A simple label
AnimatedProgress	None	Deprecated instead use ProgressBar with the style SWT.INDETERMINATE
CCombo	JComboBox	A combo box
ViewForm	JPanel	Equivalent to a custom JPanel with three subpanels arrange vertically; used in Eclipse to create a view
SashForm	JSplitPane	A JSplitPane that allows more than two children
CTabFolder	TabFolder	Like TabFolder but with more Style choices
TableTree	None	A combination of a JTree and JTable

In combination with the classes in the JFace packages, the Eclipse UI frameworks provide most of the functionality required to build modern user interfaces. Figure 10-5 provides a graphical representation of the SWT widget and custom packages.

Figure 10-5 shows a partial hierarchy of SWT widgets.

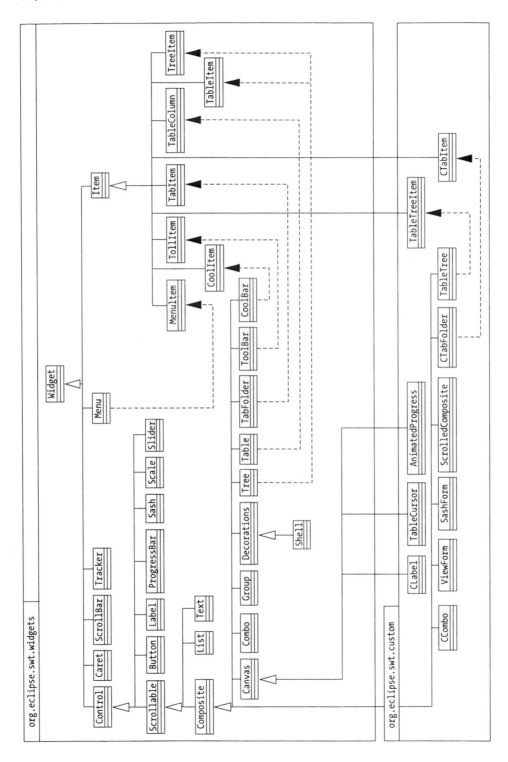

Figure 10-5. SWT widgets

At the top you have the Widget class, which is the top-level class from which all other user interface objects descend. It's analogous to the AWT's Component and the Swing's JComponent. One recurring pattern of usage in SWT is that most new components aren't created by subclassing but by using composition. Furthermore, most SWT classes aren't meant to be extended outside the confines of the SWT implementation. The Widget class also provides a dispose() method that relinquishes any operating-system resources associated with the widget and the widget's children.

Within the Widget class you have the Control class, which represents a windowed user interface class such as Buttons and Labels. Within Control you have Scrollable and down at the bottom of the hierarchy you have Composite and Canvas. These last two classes form the basis for creating your own widgets. Canvas is used when the widget is owner-drawn and Composite is used when you're creating a compound widget.

Probably the most radical difference between working with SWT and working with Swing is how the widgets are constructed. SWT has strict parenting rules for the creation of a widget, that is, you cannot create a widget without a having a parent already created. This is just a natural consequence of the widgets being thin veneers to the native widgets, because the OS resources need to be allocated at construction time. A typical widget constructor takes two arguments: the parent widget and the style bits (which can be constructed by OR-ing together individual integer values). Style bits are a hint to the underlying OS of how the widget should be rendered. The org.eclipse.swt.SWT class contains a large collection of constants that are used for setting the style of a particular widget. Because this is a loosely typed way to set a widget's look and feel, it's important to consult the JavaDoc on a particular widget to learn which styles are applicable because passing an erroneous style wouldn't cause an exception; the styles are simply ignored.

 CAUTION   For certain widgets the style is an idempotent property. That is, a widget style cannot be changed after its creation.

Further examination of Figure 10-5 shows that whole-part widgets such as Trees and Tables contain parts that are descendants of the Item class. For example in the case of a Table, the composing parts are TableColumns and TableItems.

Notice that the Shell class is just a specialization of a Composite (a subclass of Decorations, which provides appearance and behavior for Shell classes). In an SWT application the Shell class is the top-level container that can hold widgets.

The last item to point out is the org.eclipse.swt.custom package, which provides custom widgets that extend in the capabilities of the basic widgets. Also not shown in Figure 10-5 is the Dialog hierarchy, which provides commonly used dialog boxes, including ColorDialog, DirectoryDialog, FileDialog, FontDialog, MessageBox, and PrintDialog.

SWT Layouts

Like AWT and Swing, SWT uses the concept of layouts (or layout managers) to determine the position and size of widgets in a container. An SWT Composite has an associated Layout, and child widgets have associated layout data that enables a layout to make decisions about the size and positioning of a widget. You can find SWT Layouts classes in the org.eclipse.swt.layout package.

Table 10-2 lists the available Layouts in SWT and their equivalent layout in AWT and Swing.

Table 10-2. SWT Layouts

Layout	Description	Swing Equivalent
FillLayout	The default layout; arranges components horizontally on a row or vertically on a column	BoxLayout
RowLayout	Similar to FillLayout but more flexible, allowing multiple rows, fill, wrapping, and custom spacing	FlowLayout
GridLayout	Lays components on a grid; offers many options for fine grained control	GridBagLayout
FormLayout	Relative layout that uses attachments to a container edge or a sibling widget's edge	None
PageBookLayout	Indirectly used with org.eclipse.ui.part.PageBook; not part of SWT or JFace	CardLayout
StackLayout	Stacks components, only top component is visible	CardLayout

SWT Events

The SWT event model is similar to the AWT or Swing event models in that there are listener interfaces for different types of events. Events are handled by implementing one of the listener interfaces and registering the listener implementation with the widget that's producing the event.

The listener registers methods follow the naming convention addXXXListener where XXX is the type of the listener such as Selection, Modify, and so on. All SWT events extend the java.util.EventObject class with information specific to the event.

Untyped Events and Event Handling

Besides having typed methods for all supported types of events, all classes descending from the Widget class have a generic way to add a listener using the method void addListener(int eventType, Listener listener), which adds the listener to the collection of listeners who will be notified when an event of the given type occurs. Also the complement method void removeListener(int eventType, Listener listener) can remove the given listener for a given type of event.

This facility comes in handy when testing event-handling code or if you need to manipulate different types of listeners as a group. For example the following three snippets of code are all equivalent ways to add a selection listener to a Tree widget:

```
// use addListener to add a Listener
tree.addListener(SWT.Selection, new Listener() {
    public void handleEvent(Event arg0) {
        System.out.println("SWT.Selection Event!");
    }
});


// use addSelectionListener and implement the SelectionListener Interface
tree.addSelectionListener(new SelectionListener() {
    public void widgetSelected(SelectionEvent arg0) {
        System.out.println("SWT.Selection Event!");
    }

    public void widgetDefaultSelected(SelectionEvent arg0) {
        System.out.println("SWT.Selection Event!");
    }
});


// use addSelectionListener and override the widgetSelectedMethod of
SelectionAdapter
tree.addSelectionListener(new SelectionAdapter() {
    public void widgetSelected(SelectionEvent arg0) {
        System.out.println("SWT.Selection Event!");
    }
});
```

Equally, for testing purposes only, you could implement a generic event handler by using a case style construct using the integer value of the event type, as the following snipped shows:

```
Listener listener = new Listener() {
    public void handleEvent(Event e) {
        switch (e.type) {
            case SWT.Selection:
                if (e.widget instanceof Table) {
                    // handle Selection event on a Table
                }
                else if (e.widget instanceof Tree) {
                    // handle Selection event on a Tree
                }
                break;
            case SWT.Expand    :
                // handle Expand event
                break;
        }
    }
};
```

You can see that for a large number of widgets and event types this solution can result in a large procedural-looking piece of code. Again, common sense and good programming practices will tell you that a natural progression would be to first try anonymous inner classes by extending an adaptor and alternatively (based on the complexity of the event-handling code) creating a stand-alone event-handling class.

SWT Resources

The next piece of SWT theory you need to explore before moving to the higher level world of JFace is the management of SWT resources. This is an area of great controversy in UI development circles and some clarifications are in order.

In AWT or Swing resource deallocation is handled by the garbage collector, although you can null a resource so that it isn't reachable, which makes it eligible for garbage collection. This is merely a way to provide a hint to the garbage collector. Garbage collection is a good thing when it doesn't get in the way of your user's experience. Garbage-collected languages such as Java tend to foster productivity by removing the burden of programmatically tracking resources. Although garbage-collection algorithms have made great strides most of them aren't fine-tuned for the needs of user interfaces. SWT instead places the burden of deallocating operating-system resources on the programmer. Because SWT objects allocate operating system resources at construction time, a general guideline is that the code that created the resource must dispose of it. This translates to SWT's first rule for resource management:

"If you create it, you dispose it."[1]

As a side effect of SWT's use of the platform's native widgets, SWT resources are bound by the memory allocation and deallocation rules of the operating system. Previously, we mentioned that all SWT widgets are required to have a parent widget at construction time and that the Widget class provides a dispose method. When the dispose method of a Widget class is invoked the disposed methods of all of its children are also invoked, which leads to the second rule of SWT resource management:

"Disposing the parent, disposes of the children."[2]

From the two rules you can see that resources are either disposed explicitly by using the dispose method, which is the case typically with resources like fonts and colors. The disposal of resources like fonts and colors depends on whether they were acquire from the system with the getSystemXXXXX() methods. Even though these resources are usually parented by the display and by rule number two they will be disposed of at the time when the display is disposed. In non-garbage-collected languages, when you ask the OS for a resource you eventually have to give it back. Like Java some of these languages will have an operator similar to the "new" operator in Java, and they also provide a way to "free" the allocated memory for the resource. You know that OS resources are limited, which is why the dispose method in SWT gives you the control to decide when a resource is no longer needed, instead of allowing the garbage collector to decide. Visual controls are typically parented to a Shell class, so for example if you have a shell with a label, a text field, and a button when the shell is disposed of, all of its contained children are, too. These two simple rules will guarantee that your applications are resource conscious, which will translate to a better user experience.

A More Elaborate SWT Example

The essence of using any UI toolkit boils down to knowing how to create UI elements, how to arrange them, and how to wire them together to accomplish a meaningful task in response to a user action. A great source of SWT examples is the SWT Controls application, which is part of the Example Plug-ins distribution, which is available from the Eclipse downloads page. Figure 10-6 shows the ControlExample.java application, which is akin to Swing's SwingSet2 demo. This application provides a good introduction to the available SWT widgets and it will

---

1. "SWT: The Standard Widget Toolkit" by Carolyn MacLeod and Steve Northover (see http://www.eclipse.org/articles/swt-design-2/swt-design-2.html).

2. Ibid.

help you get familiarized with the different styles bits available and the events produced by the different widgets.

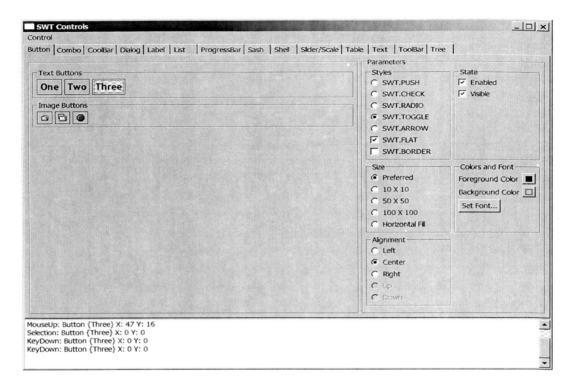

Figure 10-6. SWT controls example

There are two ways to launch the different example applications. As with any other Eclipse plug-in, you can simply unzip the contents of the eclipse-examples-2.1.1.zip file to the location of your Eclipse installation. Once you restart the Eclipse Work Bench from the menu you can select Window ➤ Show View ➤ Other at which point the Show View dialog box will appear, as shown in Figure 10-7.

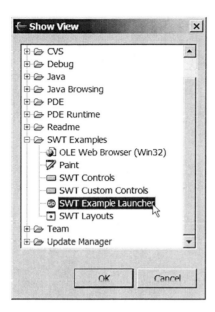

Figure 10-7. Eclipse's Show View dialog box

From the dialog box, select the SWT Example Launcher view, which launches an Eclipse view from which you can choose several example applications, including the SWT controls example that was shown in Figure 10-6.

Of course you don't need Eclipse to run an SWT application, as shown earlier in the chapter. The Eclipse plug-in just makes it easier for you to execute the applications. To launch the controls example application directly from the command line use the following:

```
java -classpath .;swtexamples.jar;c:\swt\swt.jar
    -Djava.library.path=c:\swt
    org.eclipse.swt.examples.controlexample.ControlExample
```

The previous command assumes that the swt.jar and the SWT DLL are in a directory named swt on the drive c:\. Modify accordingly for your platform and the location of the SWT files.

JFace Primer

As mentioned earlier JFace is a collection of helper classes for developing user interface features. One of these helper classes is the ApplicationWindow, which is a high-level Window. The ApplicationWindow class provides support for commonly needed items such as a menu, toolbar, and a status line. Internally, it uses a custom layout to set the menu, toolbar, and the status-line positioning.

Simple JFace Application

Let's start with an empty shell and build on it. The following code snippet will produce the simplest JFace application:

```java
import org.eclipse.jface.window.ApplicationWindow;
import org.eclipse.swt.widgets.Display;
import org.eclipse.swt.widgets.Shell;

/**
 * JFace example
 */
public class MyApplicationWindow extends ApplicationWindow {

    public MyApplicationWindow() {
        this(null);
    }

    public MyApplicationWindow(Shell shell) {
        super(shell);
    }

    public static void main(String[] args) {
        MyApplicationWindow window = new MyApplicationWindow();
        window.setBlockOnOpen(true);
        window.open();
        Display.getCurrent().dispose();
    }
}
```

ApplicationWindow

Notice that ApplicationWindow has a constructor that takes a shell (that is the parent shell). If you pass null to this constructor you're simply stating that the shell that contains this window has no parent shell. To run the application you will need the JAR file jface.jar in addition to the SWT files. JFace isn't available as an individual download. If you install Eclipse, the jface.jar file is located under <eclipse-installation>\plugins\org.eclipse.jface_2.1.1.

 NOTE   Eclipse is able to keep multiple versions of a plug-in in its plug-in repository. In the case of our install we had versions 2.1.0 and 2.1.1 of the JFace plug-in.

To compile the simple JFace application use the following command line:

```
javac -classpath .;lib\swt.jar;lib\jface.jar MyApplicationWindow.java
```

At this point the running application isn't very exciting. The ApplicationWindow class was designed to be subclassed and as such there are a number of protected methods that can be overridden to provide specific functionality to the window. These methods include the following:

- **initializeBounds:** Sets the location and size of the window.

- **configureShell:** Customizes the window's Shell class.

- **createContents:** Returns the contents of the effective client area of the window.

- **createMenuManager:** Returns a new menu manager for the window.

- **createToolBarManager:** Returns a new toolbar manager for the window.

- **createStatusLineManager:** Returns a new status-line manager for the window.

The menu, toolbar, and status line–related methods only configure their respective widgets. In order for them to appear in the window, the class provides corresponding add methods. For example, once you configure the menu using createMenuManager you can add it on the window by using the addMenuBar method.

Let's modify the simple JFace example to experiment with some of the features of ApplicationWindow. Because the menu and toolbar can share actions let's create a couple of Action classes. The first will set the background color of a Composite widget. Let's place it in the client area of the window and the other will handle the closing of the window. Let's use the status line to signal that the widget's color has been changed.

First, let's add the imports necessary to the sample application, as follows:

```
import java.util.Random;
import org.eclipse.jface.action.Action;
import org.eclipse.jface.action.MenuManager;
import org.eclipse.jface.action.ToolBarManager;
import org.eclipse.jface.resource.ImageDescriptor;
import org.eclipse.swt.SWT;
import org.eclipse.swt.graphics.Color;
import org.eclipse.swt.widgets.Composite;
import org.eclipse.swt.widgets.Control;
```

Next you should add a declaration for Composite—it should be placed in the client area of the ApplicationWindow class. Also you're creating two ImageDescriptors, which are lightweight descriptions of an image that you can use to create an image on demand. These will be used by the actions (the images used are 16×16). For the purpose of the example, you can use any two 16×16 images.

```
private Composite _composite;
ImageDescriptor greenImageDesc = ImageDescriptor.createFromFile(
                                MyApplicationWindow.class,
                                "green.gif"
                            );
ImageDescriptor redImageDesc = ImageDescriptor.createFromFile(
                                MyApplicationWindow.class,
                                "red.gif"
                            );
```

JFace Actions

Now, you can implement the actions. One possible way to do so is by using static inner classes. First, there's the ExitAction class. Notice that you set the constructor of the ExitAction to take a parameter of type ApplicationWindow, which is used in the run method to close the given window. Also notice the use of the ImageDescriptor class to assign an image to the action. The ImageDescriptor is a lightweight class that can create an image on demand.

```
private ExitAction _exitAction = new ExitAction(this);

private class ExitAction extends Action {
    ApplicationWindow _window;

    public ExitAction(ApplicationWindow window) {
        _window = window;
        setText("E&xit@Ctrl+X");
        setToolTipText("Exit Application");
        setImageDescriptor(greenImageDesc);
    }

    public void run() {
        _window.close();
    }
}
```

The ChangeColorAction uses an array of five colors (obtained using the Display method getSystemColor and the appropriate SWT integer constant). In the run method of the action you generate a random number in the range 0 to 4 and use it to assign one of the five colors to the background of the Composite that was previously declared. You also set the ApplicationWindow status bar to the String representation of the chosen color. (The Color class toString method returns a String in the form Color {R, G, B} where R, G, and B are the red, green, and blue components of the color.)

```
private ChangeColorAction _changeColorAction = new ChangeColorAction();

private class ChangeColorAction extends Action {
    private Color[] colors;

    public ChangeColorAction() {
        Display d = Display.getDefault();
        setImageDescriptor(redImageDesc);
        setText("Change C&olor@Alt+C");
        setToolTipText("Change Color");

        colors = new Color[] {
        d.getSystemColor(SWT.COLOR_BLACK),
        d.getSystemColor(SWT.COLOR_BLUE),
        d.getSystemColor(SWT.COLOR_RED),
        d.getSystemColor(SWT.COLOR_YELLOW),
        d.getSystemColor(SWT.COLOR_GREEN)};
    }
```

```
        public void run() {
            Random generator = new Random();
            int index = generator.nextInt(4);
            Color color = colors[index];
            _composite.setBackground(color);
            setStatus(color.toString());
        }
    }
```

Configuring the Shell

You can override the configureShell method to modify the appearance of the shell; in this case you'll set the application window title like you did with the first SWT example, as follows:

```
protected void configureShell(Shell shell) {
    super.configureShell(shell);
    shell.setText("JFace Example");
}
```

You can override the initializeBounds methods to set the initial size and location of the window. Notice that to access the shell you make use of the ApplicationWindow's utility method getShell.

```
protected void initializeBounds() {
    getShell().setSize(640, 480);
    getShell().setLocation(0, 0);
}
```

Configuring the Application's Menu

To create a menu you override the createMenuManager method. The MenuManager class is used to add the traditional File menu. Notice that a MenuManager instance is created for each individual submenu. The _changeColorAction and the _exitAction methods are then added to the fileMenu submenu. The submenu MenuManagers are then added to the main MenuManager, which is the return value of the method.

```
protected MenuManager createMenuManager() {
    MenuManager menuManager = new MenuManager();
    MenuManager fileMenu = new MenuManager("&File");
    fileMenu.add(_changeColorAction);
    fileMenu.add(_exitAction);
    menuManager.add(fileMenu);
    return menuManager;
}
```

Configuring the Application's Toolbar

Similar to the Menu construction, the ToolBar method is created by instantiating a ToolBarManager. The Action methods are then added to the ToolBarManager instance, as follows:

```
protected ToolBarManager createToolBarManager(int style) {
    ToolBarManager toolBarManager = new ToolBarManager(style);
    toolBarManager.add(_changeColorAction);
    toolBarManager.add(_exitAction);
    return toolBarManager;
}
```

Enabling UI Elements

To enable the menu, toolbar, and status-line methods, you need to invoke the addMenuBar, addToolBar, and addStatusLine methods and add them to the ApplicationWindow constructor, as follows:

```
public MyApplicationWindow(Shell shell) {
    super(shell);
    addMenuBar();
    addToolBar(SWT.FLAT | SWT.WRAP);
    addStatusLine();
}
```

Creating the Application's Contents

Finally, you override the createContents method, instantiate the Composite that was previously declared (notice that the method takes a Composite as the parent, in this case the parent Composite represents the "client area" of the ApplicationWindow). You create the composite parented on the client's area. The parameter SWT.NONE is one of many integer constants used in the context of appearance-related aspects of widgets, as follows:

```
protected Control createContents(Composite parent) {
    _composite = new Composite(parent, SWT.NONE);
    return _composite;
}
```

The running application should resemble Figure 10-8.

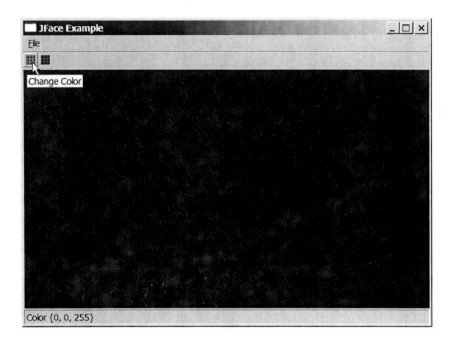

Figure 10-8. JFace application

Case Study: TCMS Admin System

Now that you have an understanding of how SWT and JFace applications are built it's time to apply the knowledge gained to create a robust implementation of a client application that will support some of the administrative functions needed for the TCMS application.

For the sample application you should implement a subset of the Use Cases discovered during the design phase. You'll set out to fulfill use cases 13 to 17 as shown in Table 10-2.

Table 10-2. TCMS Admin Application Use Cases

Use Case ID	Name
UC-13	Browse abstracts
UC-14	Edit abstract
UC-15	Evaluate abstract
UC-16	View news
UC-17	Edit news

Building a Simple Framework for Your Application

The first step in the design of the TCMS Admin application is to find a suitable UI paradigm to work with. For ideas you should look at the Eclipse platform itself and you'll see that an interface similar to the "perspectives" interface of Eclipse will fit the requirements of the TCMS application.

In the Eclipse IDE, perspectives are a combination of editors and views that represent a way to work with a particular aspect of development. For example, there's a Java perspective, a Debug perspective, and a CVS perspective among others. Figure 10-9 shows the Eclipse IDE with the Java perspective active.

The vertical toolbar on the left side of the Eclipse workbench application is referred to as a shortcut bar. Based on the Eclipse UI paradigm we've determine that we need an application window that has a menu, a status Line, a toolbar and a shortcut bar.

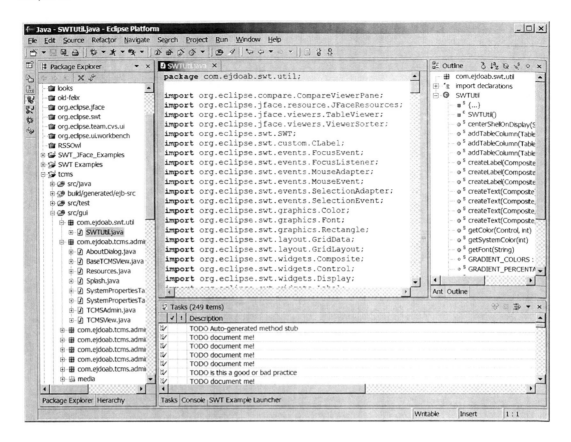

Figure 10-9. Eclipse IDE

To make our work easier we take advantage of the fact that we are working with an open source application and examine the code for the Eclipse Work Bench for ideas. After a quick browse of the source code you should zero in on efforts on the org.eclipse.ui.internal.WorkbenchWindow class. Further examination shows that this class is a subclass of the now familiar JFace application window, which uses a custom layout to accommodate for the shortcut bar. The custom layout, like any other layouts in SWT, extends org.eclipse.swt.widgets.Layout. The layout is a good example of how to build a customized layout for an application. The code for this custom layout is quite extensive so we'll refer you to the book code for further examination. The following code snippet shows the skeleton of the Layout class. Aside from setting the shortcut bar, the code is nearly identical to the one found in the org.eclipse.jface.window.Window class.

```
class TCMSWindowLayout extends Layout {

    protected Point computeSize(Composite composite,
                                int wHint,
                                int hHint,
                                boolean flushCache) {
        // code omitted
    }

    protected void layout(Composite composite, boolean flushCache) {
        // code omitted
    }
}
```

NOTE   We chose not to display the code for the TCMSWindowLayout
because it's fairly long and complex. For those adventurous readers,
you can browse the source for the Window class.

You can set the layout on the TCMSAdmin window in the configureShell
method as shown here:

```
public class TCMSAdmin extends ApplicationWindow {
...

    protected void configureShell(Shell shell) {
        super.configureShell(shell);
        shell.setLayout(new TCMSWindowLayout());
        shell.setText("TCMS Admin");
...
    }
...
}
```

TIP   When building applications with SWT or JFace a great place to
look for inspiration and ideas is the Eclipse Work Bench code itself,
especially because the number of SWT or JFace applications available
as examples is still fairly small.

The About Dialog Box

A typical element of modern UIs is the about box or about dialog box, which is a dialog box that's usually used to display copyright information as well as the application version and system information. For the TCMSAdmin application you'll create a generic about dialog box. The final product is shown in Figures 10-10a and 10-10b.

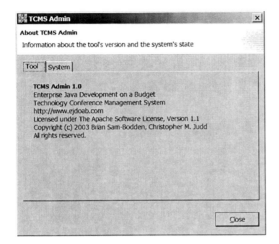 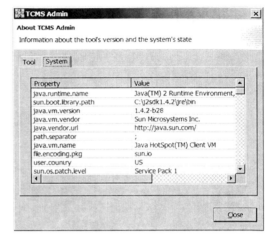

Figures 10-10a and 10-10b. About TCMS dialog box

As you can see, the about dialog box is a simple dialog with a TabFolder that contains two tabs. One tab has text information about the application and the other has a table that displays the system's properties (from java.lang.System.getProperties). The first step is to find a suitable class for the base class for the about dialog box. If you explore the JFace JavaDoc, you'll encounter the org.eclipse.jface.dialogs.TitleAreaDialog class, which is described as a dialog box that has a title area (with an optional image) and a common area for displaying a description or message.

The TitleAreaDialog class provides a createDialogArea method that can be overridden to create the contents of the dialog box. In this method the TabFolder, which is a class that implements the traditional notebook user interface metaphor, is created. One tab contains the _toolPage composite, which will contain a StyleText widget with some text about the application. The other tab will have the _systemPage composite, which will display a JFace TableViewer showing the system properties.

The buildToolPage method creates a composite named Page using a FormLayout. You'll use a FormLayout in order to be able to customize the border between the StyleText field and the TabItem by setting a margin of 20 pixels. The buildToolPage method of the TCMSAdmin window is shown here:

```
StyledText _text;

private Composite buildToolPage(Composite c) {
    Composite page = new Composite(c, SWT.NONE);

    FormLayout formLayout = new FormLayout();
    formLayout.marginHeight = 20;
    formLayout.marginWidth = 20;
    page.setLayout(formLayout);
...
```

Next, the StyleText widget is created and configured. The style is set to SWT.MULTI—so that the text field can handle multiple lines—and SWT.READ_ONLY, so that it cannot be edited, as shown here:

```
_text = new StyledText(page, SWT.MULTI | SWT.READ_ONLY);
_text.setBackground(page.getBackground());
_text.setCaret(null);
_text.setFont(c.getFont());
_text.setCursor(null);
```

To lay out the StyleText widget, you use a FormData object (which works in conjunction with the FormLayout that was previously created). The FormLayout uses FormAttachments, which define how a side of the widget attaches to the parent Composite or to another sibling element. The FormData defines four attachments: top, bottom, left, and right. In the following snippet, you set the StyleText widget to attach itself to the very top (0 percent on the vertical) and to the very bottom (100 percent on the vertical). The second number in the FormAttachment constructor defines an offset in pixels, set to 0. If you recall, previously the margins of the FormLayout were set to 20 pixels. (You could have accomplished the same effect by using the offset values in the FormData.)

```
FormData formData = new FormData();
formData.top = new FormAttachment(0,0);
formData.bottom = new FormAttachment(100,0);
formData.left = new FormAttachment(0,0);
formData.right = new FormAttachment(100,0);
_text.setLayoutData(formData);
```

Next, the StyleWidget is set with the application information text, as shown here:

```
String LINE_SEP = _text.getLineDelimiter();
String title = "TCMS Admin 1.0";
StringBuffer sb = new StringBuffer();
sb.append(title)
  .append(LINE_SEP)
  .append("Enterprise Java Development on a Budget")
  .append(LINE_SEP)
  .append("Technology Conference Management System")
  .append(LINE_SEP)
  .append("http://www.ejdoab.com")
  .append(LINE_SEP)
  .append("Licensed under The Apache Software License, Version 1.1")
  .append(LINE_SEP)
  .append("Copyright (c) 2003 Brian Sam-Bodden, Christopher M. Judd")
  .append(LINE_SEP)
  .append("All rights reserved.");
_text.setText(sb.toString());
```

The StyleText widget is a very versatile component that provides for great control of the displayed text. Let's bold part of the text displayed on the Tool page of the about dialog box. To accomplish this, you use a StyleRange object. You use the StyleRange to select the text represented by the String title (see previous code snippet) and set the fontStyle to SWT.BOLD as shown here:

```
StyleRange styleRange = new StyleRange();
styleRange.start = 0;
styleRange.length = title.length();
styleRange.fontStyle = SWT.BOLD;
_text.setStyleRange(styleRange);

return page;
}
```

With the control page of the about dialog box ready, it's time to move to build the more interesting system page. The system page will contain a table displaying all of the available system properties. To accomplish this, you use a JFace viewer TableViewer.

JFace TableViewer

The JFace TableViewer is a model-based viewer built on top of an SWT Table control. As with other viewers in JFace, the TableViewer has an associated content provider (a class implementing the org.eclipse.jface.viewers.IStructuredContentProvider interface). The content provider is the class that will typically interact with a model to provide the table with data (or for simple cases the model itself can implement the content-provider interface). You can customize the TableViewer further by providing a table label provider, element filters, and element sorters. Figure 10-11 shows the JFace TableViewer and its supporting classes.

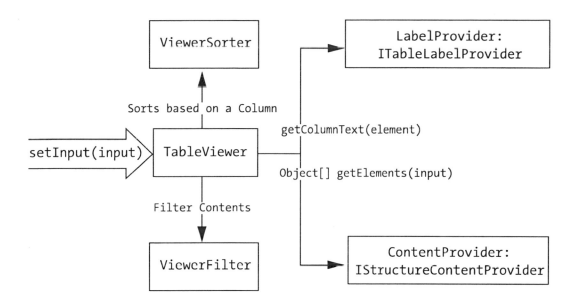

Figure 10-11. JFace TableViewer

As depicted in the figure, the Table viewer uses a ViewerSorted and a ViewerFilter. To retrieve the contents that will be displayed it invokes the getElements method of the ContentProvider, and to retrieve the text for a column header, it invokes the getColumnText method of the LabelProvider.

Table ContentProvider

In the case of the about dialog box, an implementation of an IStructureContentProvider is created that will take an object of type java.util.Properties and return an array of objects containing a name-value pair that will be displayed by the table. For this purpose, a simple class called NameValue was created to encapsulate a name-value pair of Strings.

The loadProperties method takes a Property object and converts its entries into NameValue objects, which are stored in a List object. The content of the list is then returned as an array of objects by the getElements method, as shown here:

```java
public class SystemPropertiesTableContentProvider
    implements IStructuredContentProvider {

    private List properties = new ArrayList();

    public Object[] getElements(Object element) {
        if (element instanceof Properties) {
            loadProperties((Properties)element);
        }
        return properties.toArray();
    }

    public void inputChanged(Viewer viewer, Object oldInput, Object newInput) {
        if (oldInput != null) {
            properties.clear();
        }

        if (newInput != null) {
            Properties newModel = (Properties) newInput;
            loadProperties(newModel);
        }
    }

    public void dispose() {}

    private void loadProperties(Properties props) {
        Iterator i = props.keySet().iterator();

        for (int index = 0, n = props.size(); index < n; index++) {
            String name = (String) i.next();
            String value = props.getProperty(name);
            NameValue nv = new NameValue(name, value);
            properties.add(nv);
        }
    }
}
```

Table LabelProvider

Now that the viewer has a source from which to get its data, you must tell it how to display it. The ITableLabelProvider returns a String value given an element and a column index. The element is of type NameValue and the method must return the name for the first column and the value for the second column, as follows:

```
public String getColumnText(Object element, int column) {
    String result = null;
    if (element instanceof NameValue) {
        NameValue nv = (NameValue)element;
        switch (column) {
            case 0 :
                result = nv.getName();
                break;
            case 1 :
                result = nv.getValue();
                break;
        }
    }
    return result;
}
```

Completing the TableViewer

The buildSystemPage method sets the TableViewer as done previously with the StyleText widget. The TableViewer is created and its content and label providers are set. To further customize the look of the table the getTable method of the Viewer is used to gain access to the table and customize it.

Next, you add two columns to the Viewer's underlying Table. Finally, you add data to the table by invoking the setInput method and passing the Properties object, which is returned by the System.getProperties method, as shown here:

```
private Composite buildSystemPage(Composite c) {
    Composite page = new Composite(c, SWT.NONE);

    FormLayout formLayout = new FormLayout();
    formLayout.marginHeight = 20;
    formLayout.marginWidth = 20;
    page.setLayout(formLayout);

    _tableViewer = new TableViewer(page, SWT.BORDER);
    _tableViewer.setContentProvider(new SystemPropertiesTableContentProvider());
    _tableViewer.setLabelProvider(new SystemPropertiesTableLabelProvider());
```

```
Table table = _tableViewer.getTable();
table.setLinesVisible(true);
table.setHeaderVisible(true);

TableColumn propertyColumn =
    new TableColumn(_tableViewer.getTable(), SWT.LEFT);
propertyColumn.setText("Property");
propertyColumn.setWidth(210);

TableColumn valueColumn = new TableColumn(_tableViewer.getTable(), SWT.LEFT);
propertyColumn.setText("Value");
propertyColumn.setWidth(500);

FormData formData = new FormData();
formData.top = new FormAttachment(0,0);
formData.bottom = new FormAttachment(100,0);
formData.left = new FormAttachment(0,0);
formData.right = new FormAttachment(100,0);
formData.width = 320;
formData.height = 200;

_tableViewer.getTable().setLayoutData(formData);

_tableViewer.setInput(System.getProperties());

return page;
}
```

Finishing the Dialog Box

To finish the dialog box override the following methods provided by TitleAreaDialog:

- **configureShell:** To add a title to the dialog window

- **createContents:** To customize the title and message on the title area of the dialog

- **createButtonsForButtonBar:** To add a Close button to the button bar (instead of the default OK and Cancel buttons)

- **createDialogArea:** To set the TabFolder with the tool and system pages

The source code for the dialog box is shown here:

```
public class AboutDialog extends TitleAreaDialog {
    TabFolder _tabs;
    Composite _toolPage;
    Composite _systemPage;
    StyledText _text;
    TableViewer _tableViewer;

    protected AboutDialog(Shell shell) {
        super(shell);
    }

    protected void configureShell(Shell shell) {
        super.configureShell(shell);
        shell.setText("TCMS Admin");
    }

    protected Control createContents(Composite parent) {
        Control contents = super.createContents(parent);
        setTitle("About TCMS Admin");
        setMessage("Information about the version and the system's state");
        return contents;
    }

    protected Control createDialogArea(Composite parent) {
        Composite outer = (Composite) super.createDialogArea(parent);
        Composite c = new Composite(outer, SWT.NONE);
        c.setLayoutData(new GridData(GridData.FILL_BOTH));
        FormLayout formLayout = new FormLayout();
        formLayout.marginHeight = 10;
        formLayout.marginWidth = 10;
        c.setLayout(formLayout);

        FormData formData = new FormData();
        formData.top = new FormAttachment(0,0);
        formData.bottom = new FormAttachment(100,0);
        formData.left = new FormAttachment(0,0);
        formData.right = new FormAttachment(100,0);

        _tabs = new TabFolder(c, SWT.FLAT);
        _tabs.setLayoutData(formData);
```

```
            TabItem toolTab = new TabItem (_tabs, SWT.NULL);
            toolTab.setText("Tool");
            Composite toolPage = buildToolPage(_tabs);
            toolTab.setControl(toolPage);

            TabItem systemTab = new TabItem(_tabs, SWT.NULL);
            systemTab.setText("System");
            Composite systemPage = buildSystemPage(_tabs);
            systemTab.setControl(systemPage);

            return c;
        }

        protected void createButtonsForButtonBar(Composite parent) {
            // create Close button
            createButton(
                parent,
                IDialogConstants.CLOSE_ID,
                IDialogConstants.CLOSE_LABEL,
                true);
        }

        protected void buttonPressed(int buttonId) {
            super.buttonPressed(buttonId);
            if (IDialogConstants.CLOSE_ID == buttonId) {
                okPressed();
            }
        }

        private Composite buildToolPage(Composite c) {
            ...
        }

        private Composite buildSystemPage(Composite c) {
            ...
        }
    }
```

In the case of the TCMSAdmin application the Action AboutAction method is responsible for launching the about dialog box, as follows:

```
private class AboutAction extends Action {

    public AboutAction() {
        setToolTipText("About this Application");
        setText("&About");
        ...
    }

    public void run() {
        AboutDialog dialog = new AboutDialog(getShell());
        dialog.open();
    }
}
```

Application Preferences

Because the application will need to connect to a J2EE server to retrieve information, and the server can be on the local machine or on a remote location, there's a need to have a flexible way to store the server host address and port that's being used.

A Java programmer's first approach to this would be to use a Java properties file. Yet, when it comes to a rich UI application a properties file isn't enough. You need to find a consistent way for application users to modify application values from the UI.

JFace provides such a facility in the org.eclipse.jface.preference package. This package provides a generic framework to store and retrieve preferences (IPreferenceStore) as well as dialog boxes and individual field editors for specific types of preference values. Field editors are classes used to modify, present, and validate the value of a preference and they are designed to work with a preference store implementation. The following code snippet creates a static inner class (part TCMSAdmin Window) that creates a FieldEditorPreferencePage. To add fields for the two preferences, the createFieldEditors method is overridden and the addField method is invoked.

Notice that you use a StringFieldEditor for the "host" property and an IntegerFieldEditor for the "port" value, as shown here:

```
private static class ServerPreferencesPage extends FieldEditorPreferencePage {
    public ServerPreferencesPage() {
        super("Server", FieldEditorPreferencePage.GRID);
    }

    protected void createFieldEditors() {
        addField(
            new StringFieldEditor(
                "host",
                "&Host:",
                getFieldEditorParent()));
        addField(
            new IntegerFieldEditor(
                "port",
                "&Port:",
                getFieldEditorParent()));
    }
}
```

The Preferences dialog box is launched from an aptly named ShowPreferenceAction class. The preferences need a store backing them; in this implementation you use the simple PreferenceStore implementation, which is backed by a Java properties file. A PreferenceManager is the class that maintains the hierarchy of preference nodes that in turn contain preference pages in which preferences are displayed and edited, as follows:

```
private class ShowPreferencesAction extends Action {
    public ShowPreferencesAction() {
        setToolTipText("Brings up the Application Preferences Dialog");
        setText("&Preferences");
    }

    public void run() {
        PreferenceStore store = getPreferenceStore();

        try {
            store.load();
        } catch (IOException ex) {
            // do nothing
        }
```

```
        PreferenceManager manager = new PreferenceManager();
        PreferencePage serverPage = new ServerPreferencesPage();
        PreferenceNode serverNode = new PreferenceNode("serverNode");
        serverNode.setPage(serverPage);

        manager.addToRoot(serverNode);

        PreferenceDialog dialog = new PreferenceDialog(getShell(), manager);
        dialog.setPreferenceStore(store);

        dialog.open();
    }
}
```

The getPreferenceStore method takes care of initializing the Store and setting any default values, as shown here:

```
public PreferenceStore getPreferenceStore() {
    if (_preferenceStore == null) {
        _preferenceStore = new PreferenceStore("tcms-gui.properties");
        _preferenceStore.setDefault("host", REMOTE_HOST);
        _preferenceStore.setDefault("port", Integer.parseInt(REMOTE_PORT));
    }
    return _preferenceStore;
}
```

The running Preferences dialog box is shown in Figure 10-12.

Accessing the values is a simple matter or getting access to the store and using one of the property accessor methods. The getString method retrieves a value from the preferences store as a String (notice that conversions between datatypes are automatically handled by the framework), as shown here:

```
PreferenceStore store = getPreferenceStore();
String host = store.getString("host");
String port = store.getString("port");
```

When changes to a preference value need to be automatically propagated, you can use a listener of type IPropertyChangeListener to listen to changes on an IPropertyStore implementation.

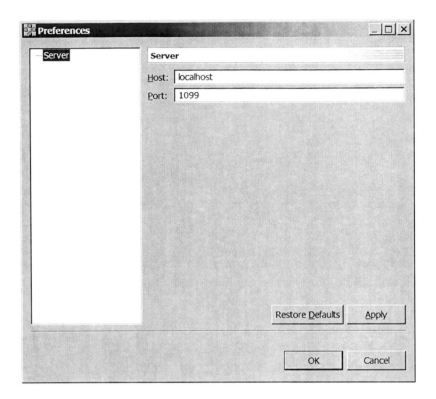

Figure 10-12. Preferences dialog box

Dealing with Resources

As mentioned in the SWT section, the disposal of SWT OS-bounded resources is managed programmatically. This is reflected in SWT's rule about resource management: "If you created it, you dispose of it." Many programmers are taken aback by the outlook of having to manage countless numbers of images and fonts. For this, JFace provides, as part of the org.eclipse.jface.resource package, a set of utility classes to simplify the management of resources.

For the TCMS Admin application you'll be making use of JFace's ImageRegistry class, which is a simple maplike structure that's used to keep a list of named resources. An ImageRegistry can have both Images and ImageDescriptors. Because Images handled by an ImageRegistry are shared, they aren't to be disposed of programmatically. Instead the registry disposes of the images when the application shuts down (actually, this occurs when the Display object used to create the images is disposed of, which is often when the application shuts down, but not necessarily so). Consequently, the resources used by the registry aren't released until the application terminates so it's important to only place images that you use often in the registry. You can manage their images programmatically instead.

For the TCMS application the Resources class was created, which is used to wrap and initialize the contents of an ImageRegistry with the Images contained in a set of directories. To provide Images or ImageDescriptors to the application, you simply retrieve an instance of the ImageRegistry using the static method getImageRegistry and one of the methods get (for Images) or getDescriptor (for ImageDescriptors).

For example, in the code for the Splash screen shown in the Splash Screen section, the following call is used to get the splash image:

```
Resources.getImageRegistry().get("image_splash");
```

Splash Screen

Another commonly needed feature in an application is a splash screen. A splash screen usually consists of a graphic that's shown a few moments before the main window makes its appearance. This is usually required if your application has an initialization period that takes more than a few seconds. It's also customary to use the splash screen to provide the user with feedback on the initialization process.

The following class provides a simple implementation of a splash screen. It uses a graphic and a ProgressBar widget. The increment and scale of the progress bar is configurable and a method to increment the progress bar is provided. For the layout of the ProgressBar a GridLayout is used and an associated GridData object. The GridLayout provides a great amount of flexibility by letting you place widgets in a grid of cells.

```
public class Splash extends Composite {

    ProgressBar _bar;
    Label _label;
    int _increment;

    public Splash(Composite parent, int style) {
        super(parent, style);

        GridLayout layout = new GridLayout();
        layout.numColumns = 1;

        setLayout(layout);
```

```
        _label = new Label(this, SWT.NONE);
        _label.setImage(Resources.getImageRegistry().get("image_splash"));

        GridData gridData = new GridData();
        gridData.horizontalAlignment = GridData.FILL;
        gridData.grabExcessHorizontalSpace = true;

        _bar = new ProgressBar(this, SWT.NONE);
        _bar.setLayoutData(gridData);

        this.pack();
    }
...
    public void increment() {
        _bar.setSelection(_bar.getSelection() + _increment);
    }
}
```

You can invoke the splash screen from an application's main method as shown here. This example also demonstrates an important concept in SWT; namely, how to modify a UI element from a thread other than the UI thread. Similarly to Swing's invokeAndWait(Runnable) and invokeLater(Runnable) methods found in the class SwingUtilities, SWT provides the methods syncExec and asynchExec as part of the Display class. In the following example an artificial delay has been added (approximately 7.5 seconds) to simulate a long-running initialization period:

```
final int loops = 15;

final Shell splashShell = new Shell(SWT.ON_TOP);
final Splash splash = new Splash(splashShell, SWT.NONE);
splash.configureProgressBar(loops, 1);
splashShell.pack();
SWTUtil.centerShellOnDisplay(splashShell, display);

splashShell.open();

display.asyncExec(new Runnable() {
    public void run() {
        for (int i = 0; i < loops; i++) {
            splash.increment();
            try {
                Thread.sleep(500); // half a second
            } catch (Throwable e) {}
        }
```

```
        splashShell.close();
        splashShell.dispose();
    }
});
```

NOTE During the development of the TCMS Admin application a utility class for performing common SWT and JFace operations was created. This class is called SWTUtil.java and consists entirely of static methods. It provides methods for manipulating tables, labels, colors, fonts, and shells among others. This class is available on the online source-code distribution.

The running splash screen is shown in Figure 10-13.

Figure 10-13. TCMS Admin splash screen

Use Case: Abstracts Page

The Abstracts page should enable users to do the following:

- View all abstracts in a Table format

- Edit an abstract's text

- Modify other details about an Abstract

- **Navigator view:** Consisting of a TableViewer that will display the available Abstract pages

- **Text Editor:** Consisting of a StyleText widget that's used to display and edit the Abstract page's text

- **Details Editor:** Consisting of a custom widget that's used to display and edit the values of other Abstract page properties (excluding the Abstract page's text)

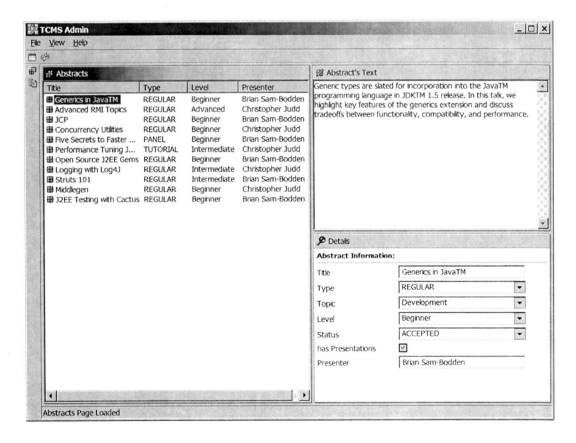

Figure 10-14. Abstracts page

Window Layout

Before jumping into coding the three components of the Abstracts page described previously, you need to create a window that will provide a canvas on which to work. The layout, and look-and-feel requirements for the Abstracts page are as follows:

- All views and editors can be manually resized using splitters.

- All views and editors can be maximized by double-clicking their titles.

- The active view and active editor should display a color gradient on its title bar (this will be demonstrated later in the chapter).

To handle the manual resizing and maximizing you use a Splitter (org.eclipse.compare.Splitter), which is a type of SashForm with support for nesting. A SashForm is a form that can hold multiple children widgets that are separated by splitters. One interesting feature of a Splitter is that maximizing a child component of a Splitter makes the child as large as the topmost enclosing Splitter.

 NOTE   The org.eclipse.compare package is contained in the JAR file compare.jar, which is located in the Eclipse plug-ins repository under the folder org.eclipse.compare_2.1.0. You'll need to add this JAR to your classpath.

The AbstractsPage class is a Composite that contains two such Splitters. The _mainForm Splitter is constructed to lay out its two children horizontally. The child farthest to the left of the _mainForm will be the Navigator view. The child farthest to the right will be the _subForm Splitter, which lays out its children vertically. The top child of the _subForm will be the TextEditor and the bottom child will be the DetailsEditor. The createTableViewForm, createTextEditorForm, and createDetailsForm methods will build the views and editors.

For the individual viewers, you use a CompareViewerPane (org.eclipse.compare.CompareViewerPane), which is a specialized ViewForm (org.eclipse.swt.custom.ViewForm) that adds a Title (CLabel) and a ToolBar. Double-clicking the title bar of a CompareViewer pane maximizes it to the size of the outermost Splitter.

```
public class AbstractsPage extends Composite {
    Splitter _mainForm;
    Splitter _subForm;

    CompareViewerPane _detailsForm;
    Composite _detailsSubForm;

    CompareViewerPane _textForm;
    Composite _textSubForm;

    CompareViewerPane _abstractsTableForm;
    Composite _abstractsTableSubForm;
...
    public AbstractsPage(Composite parent, int style) {
        super(parent, style);
        setLayout(new FillLayout());

        _mainForm = new Splitter(this, SWT.HORIZONTAL);
        createTableViewForm(_mainForm);

        _subForm = new Splitter(_mainForm, SWT.VERTICAL);
        createTextEditorForm(_subForm);
        createDetailsForm(_subForm);
    }
...
}
```

Navigator View

The navigator view uses the TableViewer class. In the TableViewer class example earlier, you'll recall that when you used the TableViewer the dataset was fairly simple to display. In the case of the Abstracts page, you have a more complex situation for which you need to implement a custom data model.

Figure 10-15 shows a sequence diagram of how the AbstractsTableContentProvider uses the AbstractModel to provide content to the TableViewer. Changes to the model are reported to the provider using a simple listener interface, which the provider class implements.

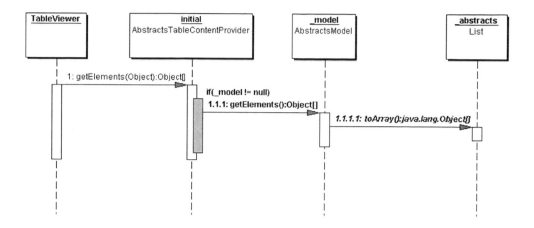

Figure 10-15. TableViewer, Content Provider, and Model

The following code section shows part of the createTableViewForm method.

CompareViewerPane

The CompareViewerPane is constructed using the SashForm as a parent passed as a parameter:

```
...
private void createTableViewForm(SashForm sashForm) {
    _abstractsTableForm = new CompareViewerPane(sashForm, SWT.BORDER);
    _abstractsTableForm.setText("Abstracts");

_abstractsTableForm.setImage(Resources.getImageRegistry().get("icons_abstracts")
);

    _abstractsTableSubForm = new Composite(_abstractsTableForm, SWT.NONE);
    _abstractsTableSubForm.setLayout(new FillLayout());
...
    _abstractsTableForm.setContent(_abstractsTableSubForm);
}
```

TableViewer

The TableViewer is created and, as shown in the previous example, the content and label providers are assigned:

```
TableViewer _tableViewer = null;
_tableViewer = new TableViewer(_abstractsTableSubForm, SWT.BORDER);
_tableViewer.setContentProvider(new AbstractsTableContentProvider());
_tableViewer.setLabelProvider(new AbstractTableLabelProvider());
_tableViewer.getTable().setHeaderVisible(true);
```

To enable the table to be sorted by clicking on a column heading, an AbstractViewerSorter that extends the class org.eclipse.jface.viewers.ViewerSorter is created. During construction the sorted table takes an integer parameter, which determines the criteria used to sort the table (the criteria being the possible column types), as shown here:

```
public class AbstractsViewerSorter extends ViewerSorter {

    public final static int SORT_CRITERIA_TITLE = 0;
    public final static int SORT_CRITERIA_TYPE = 1;
    public final static int SORT_CRITERIA_LEVEL = 2;
    public final static int SORT_CRITERIA_PRESENTER = 3;

    private int _criteria;

    public AbstractsViewerSorter(int criteria) {
        super();
        _criteria = criteria;
    }

    public int compare(Viewer viewer, Object o1, Object o2) {

        ConferenceAbstractDTO dto1 = (ConferenceAbstractDTO) o1;
        ConferenceAbstractDTO dto2 = (ConferenceAbstractDTO) o2;

        switch (_criteria) {
            case SORT_CRITERIA_TITLE :
                return collator.compare(dto1.getTitle(), dto2.getTitle());
            case SORT_CRITERIA_TYPE :
                return collator.compare(dto1.getType(), dto2.getType());
            case SORT_CRITERIA_LEVEL :
                return collator.compare(dto1.getLevel(), dto2.getLevel());
            case SORT_CRITERIA_PRESENTER :
                return collator
                        .compare(dto1.getPresenter(), dto2.getPresenter());
```

```
        default:
            return 0;
        }
    }
...
}
```

Now you can create the columns and assign a sorter to them, as follows:

```
TableColumn typeColumn = new TableColumn(_tableViewer.getTable(), SWT.LEFT);
typeColumn.setText("Type");
typeColumn.setWidth(60);
typeColumn.addSelectionListener(new SelectionAdapter() {
    public void widgetSelected(SelectionEvent e) {
        tableViewer.setSorter(
            new AbstractsViewerSorter(AbstractsViewerSorter.SORT_CRITERIA_TYPE)
        );
    }
});
...
```

SelectionChanged Listener

When the user selects an Abstracts page on the TableViewer, it's expected that the corresponding information for the Abstracts page will be shown on the two editors to the right. To accomplish this, the selection event of the TableViewer need to be detected and the inputs to the editors need to be modified accordingly:

```
StyledText _text;
AbstractsDetailsWidget _details;
...
_tableViewer.addSelectionChangedListener(new ISelectionChangedListener() {

    public void selectionChanged(SelectionChangedEvent event) {
        if (_details.isModified() || _textModified) {
            // prompt to save modifications
            checkToSave(_selected);
        }
        IStructuredSelection selection =
            (IStructuredSelection) event.getSelection();
        _selected = (ConferenceAbstractDTO) selection.getFirstElement();
        _text.removeModifyListener(_textModifiedListener);
```

```
                    if (_selected != null) {
                        _text.setText(_selected.getBody());
                        _text.addModifyListener(_textModifiedListener);
                        _details.setModel(_selected);
                    }
                }
            });
```

Details Editor

The Details Editor is an example of a custom Widget class. In the Details Editor
the "details" about a particular abstract selected in the TableViewer are shown.
As a base class you should choose the ScrolledComposite class
(org.eclipse.swt.custom.ScrolledComposite), which is a Composite that provides
scrollbars and will scroll its contents as needed.

For the Details Editor a combination of widgets is used, including Text,
CCombo, Label, and Button, and they're arranged using a GridLayout.

```
public class AbstractsDetailsWidget extends ScrolledComposite {
    private Text _title;
    private CCombo _type;
    private CCombo _topic;
    private CCombo _level;
    private CCombo _status;
    private Button _presentations;
    private Text _presenter;
    private ConferenceAbstractDTO _model;
    private boolean _modified = false;

    public AbstractsDetailsWidget(Composite parent) {
        super(parent, SWT.H_SCROLL | SWT.V_SCROLL);

        // take as much client area as possible
        setExpandHorizontal(true);
        setExpandVertical(true);

        // internal composite in which to layout the children widgets
        // using a grid layout
        Composite grid = new Composite(this, SWT.NONE);
```

```
// set the background color
grid.setBackground(SWTUtil.getSystemColor(SWT.COLOR_LIST_BACKGROUND));

// create and set the grid layout
GridLayout layout = new GridLayout();
layout.numColumns = 2;
layout.verticalSpacing = 4;
layout.horizontalSpacing = 6;
grid.setLayout(layout);

// add a title label
Label label =
    SWTUtil.createLabel(
        grid,
        "Abstract Information:",
        SWT.WRAP,
        SWT.COLOR_LIST_BACKGROUND);
label.setFont(SWTUtil.getFont(JFaceResources.BANNER_FONT));

// separator
Composite separator = new Composite(grid, SWT.NONE);
separator.setBackground(
    SWTUtil.getColor(separator, SWT.COLOR_TITLE_BACKGROUND_GRADIENT));

GridData separatorGridData = new GridData();
separatorGridData.horizontalSpan = 2;
separatorGridData.horizontalAlignment = GridData.FILL;
separatorGridData.grabExcessHorizontalSpace = true;
separatorGridData.verticalAlignment = GridData.BEGINNING;
separatorGridData.heightHint = 2;
separator.setLayoutData(separatorGridData);

// title field
GridData titleGridData = new GridData();
titleGridData.widthHint = 215;

SWTUtil.createLabel(grid, "Title", SWT.FLAT, SWT.COLOR_LIST_BACKGROUND);
_title = SWTUtil.createText(grid, "", SWT.SINGLE | SWT.BORDER);
_title.setLayoutData(titleGridData);

// type field
GridData typeGridData = new GridData();
typeGridData.widthHint = 200;
```

```
SWTUtil.createLabel(grid, "Type", SWT.FLAT, SWT.COLOR_LIST_BACKGROUND);
_type = new CCombo(grid, SWT.FLAT | SWT.BORDER);
_type.setLayoutData(typeGridData);

// topic field
GridData topicGridData = new GridData();
topicGridData.widthHint = 200;

SWTUtil.createLabel(grid, "Topic", SWT.FLAT, SWT.COLOR_LIST_BACKGROUND);
_topic = new CCombo(grid, SWT.FLAT | SWT.BORDER);

_topic.setLayoutData(topicGridData);

// level field
GridData levelGridData = new GridData();
levelGridData.widthHint = 200;

SWTUtil.createLabel(grid, "Level", SWT.FLAT, SWT.COLOR_LIST_BACKGROUND);
_level = new CCombo(grid, SWT.FLAT | SWT.BORDER);

_level.setLayoutData(levelGridData);

// status field
GridData statusGridData = new GridData();
statusGridData.widthHint = 200;

SWTUtil.createLabel(
    grid,
    "Status",
    SWT.FLAT,
    SWT.COLOR_LIST_BACKGROUND);
_status = new CCombo(grid, SWT.FLAT | SWT.BORDER);

_status.setLayoutData(statusGridData);

// presentations field
SWTUtil.createLabel(
    grid,
    "has Presentations",
    SWT.FLAT,
    SWT.COLOR_LIST_BACKGROUND);
_presentations = new Button(grid, SWT.CHECK | SWT.FLAT);
```

```
_presentations.setBackground(
    SWTUtil.getColor(_presentations, SWT.COLOR_LIST_BACKGROUND));
_presentations.setText("");
_presentations.setSelection(true);
_presentations.setEnabled(false);

// presenter field
GridData presenterGridData = new GridData();
presenterGridData.widthHint = 215;

SWTUtil.createLabel(
    grid,
    "Presenter",
    SWT.FLAT,
    SWT.COLOR_LIST_BACKGROUND);
_presenter - SWTUtil.createText(grid, "");
_presenter.setLayoutData(presenterGridData);

// create and set internal listeners
ModifyListener modifyListener = new ModifyListener() {
    public void modifyText(ModifyEvent e) {
        onTextModified(e);
    }
};

FocusListener focusListener = new FocusListener() {
    public void focusGained(FocusEvent e) {
        onFocusGained(e);
    }

    public void focusLost(FocusEvent e) {
        onFocusLost(e);
    }
};

MouseListener mouseListener = new MouseAdapter() {
    public void mouseDown(MouseEvent event) {
        notifyListeners(SWT.FocusIn, new Event());
        _title.setFocus();
    }
};
```

```
_title.addModifyListener(modifyListener);
_type.addModifyListener(modifyListener);
_topic.addModifyListener(modifyListener);
_level.addModifyListener(modifyListener);
_status.addModifyListener(modifyListener);
_presenter.addModifyListener(modifyListener);

_title.addFocusListener(focusListener);
_type.addFocusListener(focusListener);
_topic.addFocusListener(focusListener);
_level.addFocusListener(focusListener);
_status.addFocusListener(focusListener);
_presenter.addFocusListener(focusListener);

label.addMouseListener(mouseListener);
grid.addMouseListener(mouseListener);

// to ensure that scrollbars show up when needed
Point pt = grid.computeSize(SWT.DEFAULT, SWT.DEFAULT);
setMinWidth(pt.x);
setMinHeight(pt.y);

// add the grid to the widget
setContent(grid);
}
```

ModifyListeners (added to each editable field) are used to trigger a method that sets a modified flag on the editor. If the user selects another abstract from the TableViewer and the modified flag is true for either the TextEditor or the DetailsEditor the checkToSave method is invoked, which brings up the dialog box shown in Figure 10-16.

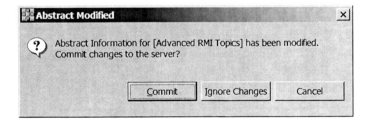

Figure 10-16. Check to Save dialog box

The checkToSave method also illustrates the usage of a JFace MessageDialog.

```
private void checkToSave(ConferenceAbstractDTO selected) {
    MessageDialog dialog =
        new MessageDialog(
            getShell(),
            "Abstract Modified",
            null,
            "Abstract Information for ["
            + selected.getTitle()
            + "] has been modified. Commit changes to the server?",
            MessageDialog.QUESTION,
            new String[] {
                "&Commit",
                "&Ignore Changes",
                IDialogConstants.CANCEL_LABEL
            },
            0
    );

    dialog.open();
    int rc = dialog.getReturnCode();
    switch (rc) {
        case 0 : // save the changes
                ...
            break;
        case 1 : // don't save the changes
            _details.setModified(false);
            _textModified = false;
        case 2 : // cancel
            break;
    }
}
```

Loading Data: Keeping the UI Responsive with Threads

Widgets without meaningful data to display are useless. The TCMS application must be able to communicate with a J2EE server and access the service layer created in Chapter 8 to populate the UI. Because the quality and amount of data in the communications with the J2EE server aren't known, the data you retrieve from the server in a synchronous fashion can result in a UI that appears to be frozen.

The obvious alternative is to run the possibly long process in a separate thread. In the case of the TCMSAdmin application the intent is to prevent the user from interacting with the UI during the data-loading phase, but at the same time informing periodically on the progress of the data-loading operation. This is accomplished by the LoadData class, which implements the IRunnableWithProgress interface, which in turn encapsulates a long-running operation for which the user receives visual feedback. The run method takes an IProgressMonitor, which is the interface used to provide feedback on the status of the operation.

The IProgressMonitor interface provides status notification methods that enable you to programmatically partition a task into a sequence of subtasks and then report on their progress. To mark the beginning of a Task the beginTask method is used. Later, to signal the beginning of a subtask, you use the subTask method. The IProgressMonitor interface also provides the ability to cancel an operation that's in progress programmatically by checking the isCancelled method periodically (in this example you should choose to ignore the cancellation request).

```java
private class LoadData implements IRunnableWithProgress {

    public void run(IProgressMonitor monitor)
        throws InvocationTargetException, InterruptedException {
        monitor.beginTask("Contacting Server", IProgressMonitor.UNKNOWN);
        if (_activeView != null) {
                try {
                    Object[] data = null;
                    String[] topics = null;
                    String[] levels = null;
                    String[] types = null;
                    String[] status = null;

                    if (_serviceFactory == null) {
                        PreferenceStore store = getPreferenceStore();
                        String host = store.getString("host");
                        String port = store.getString("port");
                        _serviceFactory = new ServiceProxyFactory(host, port);
                        monitor.subTask("Obtained Service Proxy Factory");
                    }

                    if (_serviceFactory != null) {
                        _conferenceService = _serviceFactory
                            .getConferencesServices();
                        monitor.subTask("Obtained Conference Service Proxy");
```

```
                    if (_activeView.equals(_abstracts)) {
                        _abstracts.setService(_conferenceService);
                        data = _conferenceService.getAbstractAsArray();
                        monitor.subTask("Retrieved Abstracts List");
                        topics = _conferenceService.getValidTopics();
                        monitor.subTask("Retrieved Topics");
                        levels = _conferenceService.getValidLevels();
                        monitor.subTask("Retrieved Levels");
                        types = _conferenceService.getValidTypes();
                        monitor.subTask("Retrieved Types");
                        status =
                            _conferenceService.getValidAbstractStatus();
                        monitor.subTask("Retrieve Status");

                        _shell
                            .getDisplay()
                            .syncExec(
                                new AbstractsViewUpdater(_abstracts
                                                        ,data
                                                        ,topics
                                                        ,levels
                                                        ,types
                                                        , status)
                            );
                    } else if (_activeView.equals(_news)) {
                        _news.setService(_conferenceService);
                        data = _conferenceService.getNewsAsArray();
                        monitor.subTask("Retrieved News Articles");
                        _shell
                            .getDisplay()
                            .syncExec(new NewsViewUpdater(_news, data));
                    }
                }
                monitor.subTask("Data Loaded");
                monitor.done();
            } catch (RemoteServerException e) {
...

            } catch (DTOCreateException e) {
...

            }
        }
    }
```

The _serviceFactory object is an instance of the ServiceProxyFactory class, which is an abstract factory that's used to retrieve a local proxy to one of the Session Facades developed in Chapter 8. The specific proxy used to retrieve the data is the ConferenceServicesProxy class, which is a proxy to the com.ejdoab.tcms.services.ConferenceServicesBean class. Notice that the use of the syncExec command to update either the Abstracts page or the News page. The runnable classes shown next are what is executed to actually populate the UIs.

```
class AbstractsViewUpdater implements Runnable {
    Object[] _data;
    String[] _topics;
    String[] _levels;
    String[] _types;
    String[] _status;
    AbstractsPage _abstracts;

    public AbstractsViewUpdater(
        AbstractsPage abstracts,
        Object[] data,
        String[] topics,
        String[] levels,
        String[] types,
        String[] status) {
            _abstracts = abstracts;
            _data = data;
            _topics = topics;
            _levels = levels;
            _types = types;
            _status = status;
    }

    public void run() {
        _abstracts.setTopics(_topics);
        _abstracts.setLevels(_levels);
        _abstracts.setTypes(_types);
        _abstracts.setStatus(_status);
        _abstracts.loadData(_data);
    }
}
```

```
class NewsViewUpdater implements Runnable {
    Object[] _data;
    NewsPage _news;

    public NewsViewUpdater(NewsPage news, Object[] data) {
        _news = news;
        _data = data;
    }

    public void run() {
        _news.loadData(_data);
    }
}
}
```

To actually display the progress of the IRunnableWithProgress implemen
tation, you use a ProgressMonitorDialog, which is the typical modal dialog box
that displays progress to the users during a long-running operation. It displays
the typical progress bar and a status message. The following code snippet shows
how you can launch the ProgressMonitorDialog from within an Action:

```
private class RefreshDataAction extends Action {

    public RefreshDataAction() {
        setToolTipText("Refresh the Active Page Data from the Server");
        setText("&Refresh@Alt+R");
        setImageDescriptor(
            Resources.getImageRegistry().getDescriptor("icons_refresh"));
    }

    public void run() {
        ProgressMonitorDialog dialog = new ProgressMonitorDialog(getShell());
        try {
            dialog.run(true, true, new LoadData());
        } catch (InvocationTargetException ex) {
            ...
        } catch (InterruptedException ex) {
            ...
        }
    }
}
```

Figure 10-17 shows the ProgressMonitorDialog that's being controlled by the
IRunnableWithProgress LoadData class.

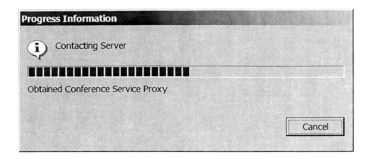

Figure 10-17. The Progress Information dialog box (ProgressMonitorDialog)

Use Case: News Page

The next use case on the UI that you'll work with is the use case for viewing and editing news. The design on the page has a TreeViewer that organizes news articles and items under the date in which they will appear on the web application's News page.

Figure 10-18 shows the final result of the News page.

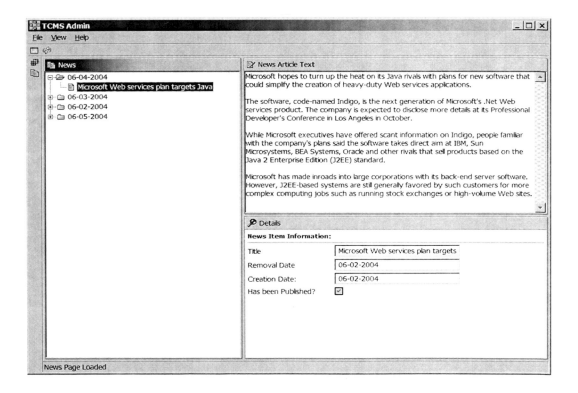

Figure 10-18. The News page

TreeViewer

Another JFace class that's frequently used in applications is the TreeViewer. Like the TableViewer uses the SWT Table widget, the TreeViewer uses an SWT Tree widget for display purposes. Also similar to the TableViewer, the TreeViewer makes use of a content provider (ITreeContentProvider) and a label provider (ILabelProvider).

The News page layout is almost identical to the Abstracts page layout with the exception being that the navigator view contains a TreeViewer instead of a TableViewer. As with the Abstracts page there's a method to create the navigator form as shown here:

```
private void createTreeViewForm(SashForm sashForm) {
    _newsTreeForm = new CompareViewerPane(sashForm, SWT.BORDER);
    _newsTreeForm.setText("News");
    _newsTreeForm.setImage(Resources.getImageRegistry().get("icons_news"));

    _newsTreeSubForm - new Composite(_newsTreeForm, SWT.NONE);
    _newsTreeSubForm.setLayout(new FillLayout());

    _treeViewer = new TreeViewer(_newsTreeSubForm); // create the TreeViewer

    // get the SWT Tree for further customizations
    Tree tree = _treeViewer.getTree();

    // set the content provider
    _treeViewer.setContentProvider(new NewsTreeContentProvider());
    // set the lable provider
    _treeViewer.setLabelProvider(new NewsTreeLabelProvider());

    _newsTreeForm.setContent(_newsTreeSubForm);
...
```

As with the Abstracts page there's a need to detect when the user selects an item on the tree and update the two editors (NewsItemText and NewsItemDetails). For this selection a listener is registered with the TableViewer (implemented as an anonymous inner class) as follows:

...

```
            // handle selection events
        _treeViewer
            .addSelectionChangedListener(new ISelectionChangedListener() {
            public void selectionChanged(SelectionChangedEvent event) {
                IStructuredSelection selection =
                    (IStructuredSelection) event.getSelection();

                Object o = selection.getFirstElement();

                if (o instanceof NewsItemDTO) {
                    if (_details.isModified() || _textModified) {
                        // prompt to save modifications
                        checkToSave(selected);
                    }
                    selected = (NewsItemDTO) o;
                    _text.removeModifyListener(_textModifiedListener);
                    _text.setText(selected.getBody());
                    _text.addModifyListener(_textModifiedListener);
                    _details.setModel(selected);
                }
            }
        });
```

...

Another feature that's commonly added to a TreeViewer is the ability to change the appearance of a Tree node when it's expanded. To accomplish this, you create listeners for two events, SWT.Expand and SWT.Collapse. The following code changes the image associated with the TreeItem based on receiving an expanding or collapsing event. (Notice the use of untyped listeners in this particular case.)

...

```
        // handle tree expansion events
        tree.addListener(SWT.Expand, new Listener() {
            public void handleEvent(Event e) {
                TreeItem item = (TreeItem) e.item;
                item.setImage(
                    Resources.getImageRegistry().get("icons_folder_open"));
            }
        });
```

```
        // handle tree collapsing events
        tree.addListener(SWT.Collapse, new Listener() {
            public void handleEvent(Event e) {
                TreeItem item = (TreeItem) e.item;
                item.setImage(
                    Resources.getImageRegistry().get("icons_folder_close"));
            }
        });
...
```

ContentProvider, LabelProvider, and Data Model

For the News TreeViewer a custom data model was created to organize the data in the hierarchy required. The NewsModel class takes a list of NewsItemsDTO (data transfer objects) and organizes them by their publication date.

 NOTE The NewsModel is an example of a custom data model in an MVC relationship that provides a business representation of the data to be used by the view, which in this case is a TreeViewer. A custom data model provides an intelligent structure for your data when the simple structures provided by the Java Collections API aren't enough.

An important aspect of a UI data model is that it needs to communicate changes to the widgets displaying the model. For the current application there isn't a need for fine-grained notification of changes, therefore a simple listener interface is used (NewsModelListener) with a single method that signals a change in the model (any change, being an addition, deletion, or modification). The NewsModel class is shown here:

```
public class NewsModel {
    private List _newsItems;
    private Map _model = new HashMap();
    private NewsModelListener _listener;

    public NewsModel(Object[] newsItems) {
        super();
        _newsItems = new ArrayList(newsItems.length);
        CollectionUtils.addAll(_newsItems, newsItems);
        createModel();
    }
```

```java
public void add(NewsItemDTO newsItem) {
    Date date = newsItem.getDate();
    String key = Dates.format(date, "MM-dd-yyyy");
    List items = null;
    if (!_model.containsKey(key)) {
        items = new ArrayList();
        _model.put(key, items);
    }
    if (items == null) items = (List)_model.get(key);
    items.add(newsItem);
    fireModelChanged();
}

public void remove(NewsItemDTO newsItem) {
    Date date = newsItem.getDate();
    String key = Dates.format(date, "MM-dd-yyyy");
    List items = (List)_model.get(key);

    if (items != null) {
        items.remove(newsItem);
        fireModelChanged();
    }
}

private void createModel() {
    if (_newsItems != null) {
        // build a list of dates to be used as the key in the map
        Iterator iter = _newsItems.iterator();

        for (int i=0, n = _newsItems.size(); i < n; i++) {
            NewsItemDTO dto = (NewsItemDTO)iter.next();
            Date date = dto.getDate();
            String key = Dates.format(date, "MM-dd-yyyy");
            List items = null;
            if (!_model.containsKey(key)) {
                items = new ArrayList();
                _model.put(key, items);
            }
            if (items == null) {
                items = (List)_model.get(key);
            }
            items.add(dto);
        }
    }
}
```

```java
    public Object[] getChildren(Object object) {
        if (object instanceof String) {
            if (_model.containsKey(object)) {
                List children = (List)_model.get(object);
                return children.toArray();
            }
        }
        return Arrays.EMPTY_OBJECT_ARRAY;
    }

    public Object getParent(Object object) {
        if (object instanceof NewsItemDTO) {
            NewsItemDTO dto = (NewsItemDTO)object;
            return Dates.format(dto.getDate(), "MM-dd-yyyy");
        }
        return null;
    }

    public boolean hasChildren(Object object) {
        if (object instanceof String) {
            if (_model.containsKey(object)) {
                List children = (List)_model.get(object);
                return !children.isEmpty();
            }
        }
        return false;
    }

    protected void fireModelChanged() {
        if (_listener != null) {
            _listener.modelChanged();
        }
    }

    public Object[] getDates() {
        return _model.keySet().toArray();
    }
    ...
}
```

Because the TreeViewer relies on the ContentProvider to get its data, the ContentProvider will use the NewsModel to provide the content. Also, the ContentProvider needs to listen for changes on the model in order to keep the UI up to date. Once the TreeViewer has been set with a Label and a ContentProvider the root element of the tree is set by invoking the setInput method and passing a NewsModel instance. The ContentProvider class NewsTreeContentProvider is shown here:

```
public class NewsTreeContentProvider
    implements ITreeContentProvider, NewsModelListener {

    private NewsModel _model = null;
    private TreeViewer _viewer = null;

    public NewsTreeContentProvider() {}

    public Object[] getChildren(Object object) {
        if (_model != null) {
            return _model.getChildren(object);
        }
        return Arrays.EMPTY_OBJECT_ARRAY;
    }

    public Object getParent(Object object) {
        if (_model != null) {
            return _model.getParent(object);
        }
        return null;
    }

    public boolean hasChildren(Object object) {
        if (_model != null) {
            return _model.hasChildren(object);
        }
        return false;
    }

    public Object[] getElements(Object object) {
        if (object instanceof NewsModel) {
            NewsModel model = (NewsModel)object;
            _model = model;
            return _model.getDates();
        }
        return Arrays.EMPTY_OBJECT_ARRAY;
    }

    public void dispose() {}
```

```
    public void inputChanged(Viewer viewer, Object oldInput, Object newInput) {
        _viewer = (TreeViewer) viewer;

        if (oldInput != null) {
            NewsModel oldModel = (NewsModel)oldInput;
            oldModel.removeChangeListener(this);
        }

        if (newInput != null) {
            NewsModel newModel = (NewsModel)newInput;
            newModel.addChangeListener(this);
        }
    }

    public void modelChanged() {
        _viewer.refresh();
    }
}
```

Finally, the LabelProvider class (NewsTreeLabelProvider) handles the resolution of the text and image for each of the TreeViewer's items. The NewsTreeLabel class is shown here:

```
public class NewsTreeLabelProvider extends LabelProvider {
    public String getText(Object element) {
        if (element instanceof NewsItemDTO) {
            NewsItemDTO dto = (NewsItemDTO)element;
            return dto.getTitle();
        }
        return element.toString();
    }

    public Image getImage(Object element) {
        if (element instanceof NewsItemDTO) {
            return Resources.getImageRegistry().get("icons_news_item");
        }
        return Resources.getImageRegistry().get("icons_folder_close");
    }
}
```

Adding a News Item: JFace Wizards

The last item of functionality to implement is a convenient way for users to add a new news item under a given date. For this you use a JFace wizard. A wizard provides a convenient way to deal with complex or unfamiliar tasks or it streamlines a task by providing a well-defined set of steps that are needed to complete a task. A wizard consists of a series of pages where each page represents a step in the overall process.

The wizard extends the org.eclipse.jface.wizard.Wizard class. To add pages to the wizard, the method addPages is overridden and the addPage method is used to add instances of WizardPage. The Wizard must also provide code to determine if the process can finish (enabling the finish button) by overriding the canFinish method. When the user presses the Finish button, the performFinish method is invoked. The code for the NewsItemWizard class is shown here:

```
public class NewsItemWizard extends Wizard {

    // wizard page instances
    private NewsItemBasicInfoPage basicInfoPage = new NewsItemBasicInfoPage();
    private NewsItemTextPage textPage = new NewsItemTextPage();
    ...
    public NewsItemWizard(NewsModel model, String date) {
        ...
        setWindowTitle("New News Article");
    }

    public void addPages() {
        addPage(basicInfoPage);
        addPage(textPage);
    }

    public boolean performFinish() {
        String title = basicInfoPage.getArticleTitle();
        Date creationDate = basicInfoPage.getCreationDateAsDate();
        String creationDateAsString = basicInfoPage.getCreationDate();
        Date removalDate = basicInfoPage.getRemoveDateAsDate();
        String removalDateAsString = basicInfoPage.getRemoveDate();
        String body = textPage.getArticleBody();
        ...
        return submitted;
    }
}
```

```
    public boolean canFinish() {
        return basicInfoPage.canFlipToNextPage()
            && (StringUtils.isNotEmpty(textPage.getArticleBody()));
    }

    /**
     * Convenience utility method to display the Wizard
     */
    public void showWizard() {
        WizardDialog dialog = new WizardDialog(getShell(), this);
        dialog.open();
    }
    ...
}
```

For the New News Article wizard there are two pages, the NewsItemBasicInfoPage and the NewsItemTextPage. In a WizardPage the createControl method is overridden to create the contents of the Page. To determine if the user can flip to the next page (enable the Next button) the canFlipToNextPage method is overriden.

```
    private class NewsItemBasicInfoPage extends WizardPage implements Listener {
        public NewsItemBasicInfoPage() {
            super("NewsItemBasicInfoPage");
            setTitle("News Article");
            setMessage("Create a New News Article");
        }

        public void createControl(Composite parent) {
            Composite composite = new Composite(parent, SWT.NULL);
            GridLayout layout = new GridLayout();
            layout.numColumns = 2;
            composite.setLayout(layout);

            // title field
            SWTUtil.createLabel(composite, "Article's Title:", SWT.NULL);
            _title = SWTUtil.createText(composite, "", SWT.SINGLE | SWT.BORDER);
            {
                GridData gridData = new GridData(GridData.FILL_HORIZONTAL);
                _title.setLayoutData(gridData);
            }
            ...
```

```
        setControl(composite);
        setDefaults();
        addListeners();
    }
    ...
    public boolean canFlipToNextPage() {
        ...
        return result;
    }
    ...
}
```

Typically the change and modify listeners will be added to the widgets of a WizardPage. You can then implement an untyped listener to validate the current page.

 NOTE   In SWT an untyped event listener refers to an instance of the org.eclipse.swt.widgets.Listener interface that you can add to a widget using the addListener(int eventType, Listener handler) method, which registers the listener to listen to a particular type of event (determined by the integer eventType value). Typically, widgets will also provide a typed listener API that has methods like addSomeEventListener(SomeEventListener handler), which take a specific type of listener.

You can use the setErrorMessage and setMessage methods to display feedback information to the user as the validation takes place. The Eclipse UI guidelines recommend that you validate wizard data in tab order. You can use the setMessage method to display a message when a piece of information is missing, and you can use the setErrorMessage method to signal the user that an input value is incorrect. To refresh the state of the Wizard buttons from within a WizardPage, you can use the updateButtons method:

```
// update the wizard buttons by invoking canFinish and canFlipToNextPage
getWizard().getContainer().updateButtons();
```

Figure 10-19 shows the Wizard dialog box's New News Article page.

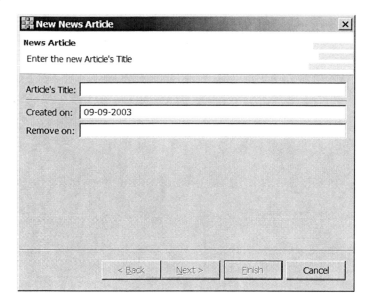

Figure 10-19. New News Article wizard's Basic Info page

Figure 10-20 shows the effect of invoking the setErrorMessage method during the data-validation method.

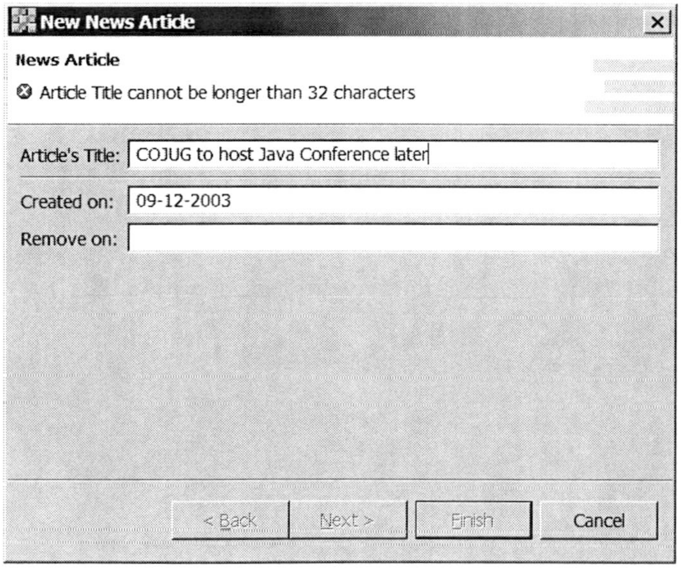

Figure 10-20. Wizard data validation

After the user completes the Basic Info page the next step in the process of adding news items is on the Text page in which users can use the contents of a file as the body of the news item that's being created. In addition, they can type the contents directly into a text field. The text page makes use of the org.eclipse.jface.preference.FileFieldEditor class, which is a convenient class that pairs a single-line text field with a button. When the button is pressed, a native OS File dialog box appears and the selected file will appear on the Text widget, as shown here:

```
_fileFieldEditor = new FileFieldEditor("fileFieldEditor", "File Name:",
Composite);
_fileFieldEditor.setEmptyStringAllowed(false);
```

Figure 10-21 shows the Text Page wizard page after selecting a text file. The filename is then used to load the file contents onto the multiline Text widget, as shown in the Text page.

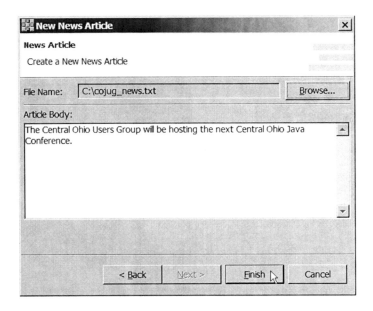

Figure 10-21. New News Article wizard's Text page

Putting It All Together

With the Abstracts page and the News page in place all you need to do is wire them to the main application. The two actions shown here will set the respective pages (tabs) on the PageBook pages.

```
private class ShowAbstractsPageAction extends Action {

    public ShowAbstractsPageAction() {
        setToolTipText("Switch to the Abstract's Page");
        setText("&Abstracts@Alt+A");
        setImageDescriptor(
            Resources.getImageRegistry().getDescriptor("icons_abstracts"));
    }

    public void run() {
        _pages.showPage(_abstracts);
        _activeView = (TCMSView)_abstracts;
        setStatus("Abstracts Page Loaded");
    }
}


private class ShowNewsPageAction extends Action {

    public ShowNewsPageAction() {
        setToolTipText("Switch to the News Page");
        setText("&News@Alt+N");
        setImageDescriptor(
            Resources.getImageRegistry().getDescriptor("icons_news"));
    }

    public void run() {
        _pages.showPage(_news);
        _activeView = (TCMSView)_news;
        setStatus("News Page Loaded");
    }
}
```

Adding a Gradient to the CompareViewerPane

With the core functionality finished now you can invest some time toward making the application look better. One feature commonly found in most modern versions of a graphical operating system is a color gradient on application windows and child windows.

For the TCMSAdmin application a gradient, matching the OS gradient (for those OSs that use gradients) is used. The intended behavior is for a gradient to appear on the navigator view, or on one of the editors for each of the pages in the application based on Focus. For example, if the user clicks the News TreeViewer the title bar will display the gradient. To accomplish this a FocusListener is implemented; in its constructor it takes an instance of a CompareViewerPane.

The method getTopLeft of the CompareViewerPane returns the CLabel that's part of the pane's title. The CLabel (org.eclipse.swt.custom.CLabel) provides a setBackground method that takes an array of Color objects and an integer array of percentages. This method specifies a gradient of colors that will be used as the background of the CLabel, as shown here in the code for the FocusListener:

```
public static class CLabelFocusListener implements FocusListener {
        private CLabel _clabel;

        public CLabelFocusListener(CompareViewerPane cwp) {
            _clabel = (CLabel) cwp.getTopLeft();
        }

        public void focusGained(FocusEvent e) {
            Display display = Display.getDefault();
            _clabel.setForeground(
                display.getSystemColor(SWT.COLOR_TITLE_FOREGROUND));
            _clabel.setBackground(GRADIENT_COLORS, GRADIENT_PERCENTAGES);
        }

        public void focusLost(FocusEvent e) {
            Display display = Display.getDefault();
            _clabel.setForeground(
                display.getSystemColor(SWT.COLOR_INFO_FOREGROUND));
            _clabel.setBackground(null, null);
        }
    }
```

The array of colors and integers are set using SWT constants, which strive to obtain the appropriate colors depending on the platform you're running on.

```
public static Color[] GRADIENT_COLORS;
public static int[] GRADIENT_PERCENTAGES;

private static void initializeColors() {
    // Define active view gradient using same OS title gradient colors.
    Display display = Display.getDefault();
    Color low = display.getSystemColor(SWT.COLOR_TITLE_BACKGROUND);
    Color medium = display.getSystemColor(SWT.COLOR_TITLE_BACKGROUND_GRADIENT);
    Color high = display.getSystemColor(SWT.COLOR_WIDGET_BACKGROUND);
    GRADIENT_COLORS = new Color[] {low, medium, high};
    GRADIENT_PERCENTAGES = new int[] {50, 100};
}
```

Finally, in the code for the Abstracts page and the News page you can assign, to any child components such as the TableViewer for the Abstracts page, the gradient-handler focus listener, which will effectively set the pane's gradient when the user interacts with the TableViewer, as shown here:

```
_abstractsTableForm = new CompareViewerPane(sashForm, SWT.BORDER);
...
CLabelFocusListener gradientHandler = new
CLabelFocusListener(_abstractsTableForm);
...
_tableViewer.getTable().addFocusListener(gradientHandler);
```

Conclusions

In this chapter you learned how to build a commercial-quality GUI application using Java and the Eclipse GUI APIs. SWT and JFace provide a viable alternative to AWT and Swing for certain types of applications. Although SWT and JFace applications are slightly less portable than Swing applications, most modern platforms are currently available. For example, Figure 10-22 shows the TCMS Admin application running under Red Hat Linux.

For experienced Swing developers, SWT and JFace require a fairly flat learning curve. Although it's true that feature by feature Swing is a much more complete toolkit, SWT and JFace provide for most of the needs of modern UI applications. Swing is improving with every new version of the J2SE and we don't expect any one toolkit to reign supreme; they're all just options. Remember in the end it's all about the user. So use whatever will bring you the most return on investment.

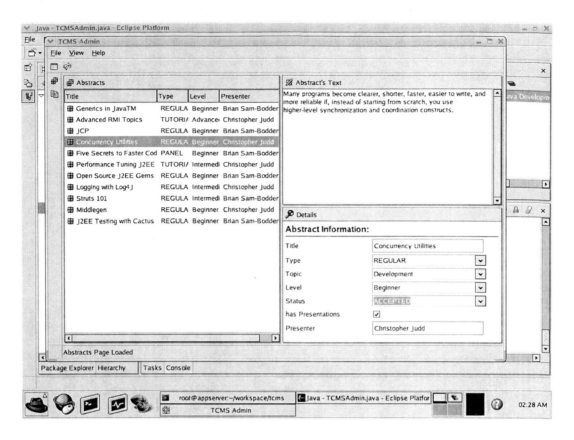

Figure 10-22. The TCMS Admin running under Red Hat Linux

APPENDIX A

Open Source Catalog

TABLE A-1 CONTAINS A LIST of all the Open Source Java projects discussed in *Enterprise Java Development on a Budget: Leveraging Java Open Source Technologies,* and all the projects used by the Technology Conference Management System project. Visit http://www.ejdoab.com for a comprehensive list of valuable Open Source Java projects and discussions.

Table A-1. Open Source Projects

Project	URL	License
Ant	http://ant.apache.org	Apache
Antenna	http://antenna.sourceforge.net	LGPL
ArgoUML	http://argouml.tigris.org	BSD
AspectJ	http://eclipse.org/aspectj/	CPL
Axis	http://xml.apache.org/axis/	Apache
Cactus	http://jakarta.apache.org/cactus/	Apache
Checkstyle	http://checkstyle.sourceforge.net	LGPL
Cocoon	http://cocoon.apache.org	Apache
Commons Collection	http://jakarta.apache.org/commons/	Apache
Commons File Upload	http://jakarta.apache.org/commons/	Apache
Commons IO	http://jakarta.apache.org/commons/	Apache
Commons Lang	http://jakarta.apache.org/commons/	Apache
Commons Logging	http://jakarta.apache.org/commons/	Apache
Commons Validator	http://jakarta.apache.org/commons/	Apache
DbUnit	http://dbunit.sourceforge.net	LGPL

Table A-1. Open Source Projects (Continued)

Project	URL	License
DTDParser	http://www.wutka.com/dtdparser.html	LGPL or Modified Apache
Eclipse	http://www.eclipse.org	CPL
eXML	http://exml.sourceforge.net	Eiffel Forum Freeware
Hibernate	http://www.hibernate.org	LGPL
hsqldb	http://hsqldb.sourceforge.net	Modified Apache
Jalopy	http://jalopy.sourceforge.net	BSD
Java2Html	http://www.java2html.de	GPL or CPL
JavaNCSS	http://www.kclee.com/clemens/java/javancss/	GPL
JBoss	http://www.jboss.org	LGPL
jCVS	http://www.jcvs.org	LGPL
JSTL	http://jakarta.apache.org/taglibs/	Apache
JUnit	http://www.junit.org	CPL
kXML	http://kxml.enhydra.org	Enhydra Public
kSOAP	http://ksoap.enhydra.org	Enhydra Public
Log4j	http://jakarta.apache.org/log4j/	Apache
Maven	http://maven.apache.org	Apache
McKoi SQL Database	http://mckoi.com/database/	GPL
Middlegen	http://boss.bekk.no/boss/middlegen	Modified Apache
NetBeans	http://www.netbeans.org	SPL
OJB	http://db.apache.org/ojb	Apache
OzoneDB	http://www.ozone-db.org	LGPL
Prevayler	http://www.prevayler.org	LGPL
ProGuard	http://proguard.sourceforge.net	GPL and LGPL
RetroGuard	http://www.retrologic.com	LGPL
Struts	http://jakarta.apache.org/struts/	Apache
Turbine	http://jakarta.apache.org/turbine/	Apache

Table A-1. Open Source Projects (Continued)

Project	URL	License
Velocity	http://jakarta.apache.org/velocity/	Apache
WebWork	http://www.opensymphony.com/webwork/	Modified Apache
XDoclet	http://xdoclet.sourceforge.net	Modified Apache
Xindice	http://xml.apache.org/xindice/	Apache

APPENDIX B

CVS Primer

MULTIPLE DEVELOPER projects required a shared source-code repository. Because Open Source projects have many contributors, they definitely require a central repository. Typically these contributors are distributed throughout the world and only connected via the Internet. The de facto standard for Open Source version control is the Concurrent Versions System (CVS). CVS, an Open Source project itself, provides secure multiuser version-control access over networks, including the Internet. This chapter isn't intended to be a comprehensive introduction to CVS and its features, instead the intention is to provide an overview of CVS for the purpose of gaining access to the current source code of Open Source Java projects. A lot of times this is needed because the latest version of the source code is only in CVS, and isn't released in another form. Some well-managed projects release the latest source code every night as ZIP files. An explanation of the CVS architecture and basic commands will be followed by the demonstration of popular Open Source Java CVS clients.

CVS Architecture

Understanding the CVS architecture can provide insight into the CVSROOT environment variable used to connect to CVS servers. The distributed and multiuser nature of CVS makes client/server the ideal model. Similar to the World Wide Web where different types of clients (web browsers) access servers (web servers), you can use different types of CVS clients to access CVS servers (see Figure B-1). Clients can include the command line cvs, WinCVS, jCVS, or IDEs such as Borland JBuilder, Eclipse, and NetBeans. Developers are able to use their CVS client of choice just as web surfers are able to use their web browser of choice.

CVS servers are computers running the CVS server software just like web servers are computers running web-server software such as the Apache web server or Microsoft's IIS. The CVS server is TCP/IP-based and provides access over the Internet from anywhere in the world. The CVS server hosts a Repository. This Repository is a directory on the server machine. Contained within the Repository are multiple modules. Each module is often a separate application or project.

Figure B-1 illustrates the architecture of CVS using the Apache projects as an example. The Apache CVS server is hosted on a computer with the domain name of cvs.apache.org. The CVS Repository is located in the /home/cvspublic directory and separated into more than 50 modules. Figure B-1 only illustrates the two popular modules, Ant and Struts. For the complete list of modules visit `http://cvs.apache.org/viewcvs.cgi/`.

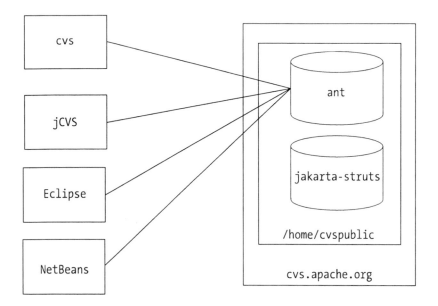

Figure B-1. CVS architecture

 NOTE The authors choose to manage versions of this book using CVS.

Connecting to a CVS Repository requires a properly formatted CVSROOT. The format is as follows:

`:pserver:[[user][:password]@]host[:[port]]/pathToRepository`

The :pserver: indicates that the pserver protocol is being used for the connection. The pserver protocol is used for remote connections via the password authenticating server, and it's the most commonly used way to remotely access a CVS Repository. Another connect type is :ext: for remote shells, which can be useful for running CVS through secure shell (SSH) for secure access to sources over the open Internet. The CVSROOT can optionally contain user and password information. If they aren't provided, the CVS client will prompt you for them. The host is the domain name or IP address of the server. If the CVS server isn't listening on the standard 2401 port, an optional port can be included. The CVSROOT is completed with the directory of the CVS Repository on the server.

In the developer's local workspace, CVS directories are used to keep track of version-controlled files and the Repository. The CVS directory contains the following three files:

- **Entries:** Contains a list of version-controlled files, their version, date, and type.

- **Repository:** Contains the corresponding directory in the Repository.

- **Root:** Contains CVSROOT.

CVS Concepts

CVS attempts to foster collaboration by providing developers access to all files in the Repository. Each developer checks out a copy of the Repository to a local workspace. All changes are made and unit tested in the workspace. When changes are applied to the Repository, the file version is incremented. A version history is maintained.

CVS doesn't require files to be locked in order to change them. It allows multiple developers to work on the same file in their local workspace. When multiple developers make changes to the same file, CVS handles the merging of those files.

CVS Commands

Understanding the basic CVS commands for authentication, checking out, committing, updating, and comparing can make the CVS clients more understandable.

A CVS Repository is a collection of intellectual property that requires restricted access. In the case of Open Source projects, the Repository is available for anyone to view. However, security is used to determine who is authorized to make changes directly to the Repository. The CVS login command is used to authenticate users through username and password verification.

 NOTE CVS authentication doesn't protect files from being viewed during file transfers over the Internet. SSH should be used to protect file transfers in sensitive repositories.

The checkout command maybe the most confusing of all CVS commands because it doesn't have the same meaning as it does in other version-control software (VCS). In CVS, the checkout command is used to get an initial local copy of the module from the CVS Repository Some other VCS software requires files to be locked and refers to this process as "checking out," which causes the confusion.

After the local copy of the source has been modified and unit tested it must be submitted back to the Repository. The commit command is used to apply the local changes or new files to the Repository. The commit command should also be accompanied by a short explanation of the change. The explanation becomes associated with the version change for auditing and communication purposes.

The update command is used to synchronize the local copy with the current version in the Repository. This means that files committed to CVS by other members of the development team will replace the local files. Files that have been modified locally will be noted as modified and may require merging. It's a good idea to update on a daily basis and prior to running a final unit test and commit. Some clients have a query update that identifies the differences between the local copy and the Repository.

CVS provides the diff command to compare files. You can use the diff command to compare local files with those in the Repository. You can also use it to identify differences between versions of the same file.

Open Source Contributing

Open Source repositories typically provide read-only access to developers. To become authorized to commit, a developer must be promoted to committer. The details of the promotion process differ between projects but all projects generally use the same process. Developers create patches and submit them to project-specific mailing lists. Patches are created using the diff command, which compares local changes to the current version in the Repository. Contributors on the mailing list are responsible for applying the patches and committing them. After many successful patch contributions, a developer may be nominated to become a committer. Nominations are put to a vote. There's no need to worry about hanging chads. Voting often occurs through the mailing list. A +1 indicates a vote of support, a –1 is a vote against, and 0 is used to abstain.

CVS Clients

You can use a variety of CVS clients to access CVS repositories. Some clients' sole purpose is to interact with CVS repositories such as the command line and jCVS applications. CVS integration is a popular feature of many IDEs such as Eclipse and NetBeans.

The command line, jCVS, Eclipse, and NetBeans clients will be demonstrated by downloading the source code from the Apache Ant project.

 NOTE   The Apache Ant project contains over 20 MB of source code and may take a while to check out over a small bandwidth.

Command Line

The command line CVS client isn't a Java application but remains a popular means of accessing CVS repositories. The command-line client is also Open Source and it's distributed under the GNU General Public License. Source and binary versions of the command-line client are available from the primary CVS website (`http://www.cvshome.org`).

 NOTE   Most UNIX environments include the command-line version of the CVS client.

Before you can use the command-line client, you must install it. To install it for Windows, first unzip cvs-1.11.4.zip. Next copy cvs-1.11.4.exe to a directory on the system path and rename it to cvs.exe.

The cvs executable operates by passing options and command parameters. The most common option is the –d option, which specifies the CVSROOT. In these examples, the public Apache CVSROOT of :pserver:anoncvs@cvs.apache.org:/home/cvspublic is used.

To download the Apache Ant source code follow these steps:

1. Open a command prompt such as CMD on Windows NT/2000, or bash in Linux.

2. Log in using the login command. cvs will prompt you for a password. Use anoncvs, as follows:

   ```
   cvs -d :pserver:anoncvs@cvs.apache.org:/home/cvspublic login
   ```

3. Check out the Ant module using the checkout command, as follows:

   ```
   cvs -d :pserver:anoncvs@cvs.apache.org:/home/cvspublic checkout ant
   ```

An ant directory will be created that contains subdirectories of source code, documentation, JARs, shell scripts, and more. To build the project just run the build.bat or build.sh scripts (depends on your operating system). To synchronize the local copy with the Repository use the cvs -d :pserver:anoncvs@cvs.apache.org:/home/cvspublic update from the ant directory.

CAUTION It can be risky to use the source code directly from an Open Source project's CVS repository in production. Consider using versions certified as stable releases otherwise it may contain undocumented defects.

jCVS

jCVS is an Open Source and a 100-percent Java swing CVS client. You can download it from http://www.jcvs.org. Aside from the desktop client, jCVS is also available as a web client using servlets.

The jcvsii.jar is an executable JAR that you can launch by double-clicking it in Microsoft Windows, or by executing java -jar jcvsii.jar on the command line. jCVS organizes many of the CVS commands by tabs. For example, to check out a module, use the Checkout tab shown in Figure B-2. Supplying the username, password, module, server, repository, and checkout directory, and pressing the Checkout Module button will create a directory with the name of the module in the checkout directory. Then a copy of the current version of each of the files in the repository will be copied to the new directory.

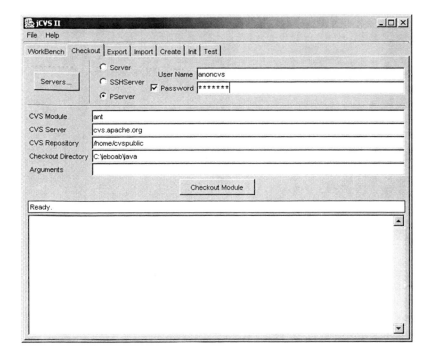

Figure B-2. jCVS Checkout tab

NOTE   To test a connection use the Test tab.

Once a project has been checked out, you can use the WorkBench tab to maintain a reference to the project for easy updates. To add the project to the WorkBench follow these steps (see Figure B-3):

1. Select the Work Bench node.

2. Click the Add New Project button.

3. When the Select Project To Add dialog box appears, locate the Entries file in the CVS directory of the checkout directory.

4. Enter a brief name. Usually the short version of the project name such as ant.

5. Enter a display name such as ant.

6. Optionally, you can provide a description of the project.

7. Click OK.

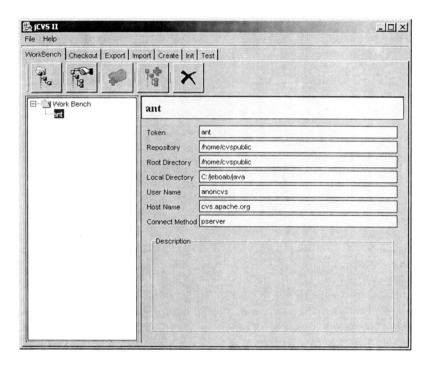

Figure B-3. ant available in the jCVS Work Bench

Accessing the CVS commands, including the update, involves opening the project by either double-clicking the project node or clicking the Open Project button. jCVS provides a project window (see Figure B-4) displaying the files, version, and modified date. The CVS commands are available by right-clicking and opening the context menu. Updating the project with changes in the Repository involves right-clicking the root project node and selecting the Update All Files menu item.

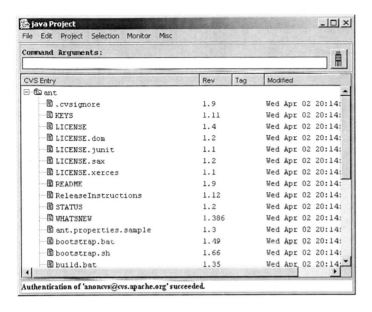

Figure B-4. jCVS project window

 NOTE   Due to a MindBright incompatibility with the new IO in
JDK 1.4, SSHServer connections don't work correctly. If an SSHServer
connection is required, run jCVS under JDK 1.3.

Eclipse

Eclipse is a popular Open Source Java IDE that contains CVS integration. You can
download it from http://www.eclipse.org.

Like many of the Eclipse features, CVS integration is implemented as a view.
To display CVS connections or establish a new connection, select Window ➤
Show View ➤ Other. A dialog box opens. Expand the CVS folder, and choose CVS
Repositories. After you've done this once, it will appear directly in the Show View
window. To establish a CVS connection right-click in the CVS Repositories view
and select New ➤ Repository Location. The Add CVS Repository dialog box
prompts you for the common connection string elements (see Figure B-5).
Clicking the Finish button adds the connection to the CVS Repository list but
doesn't perform a checkout. Unlike many of the other CVS clients, Eclipse provides
direct access to all the modules in the CVS Repository.

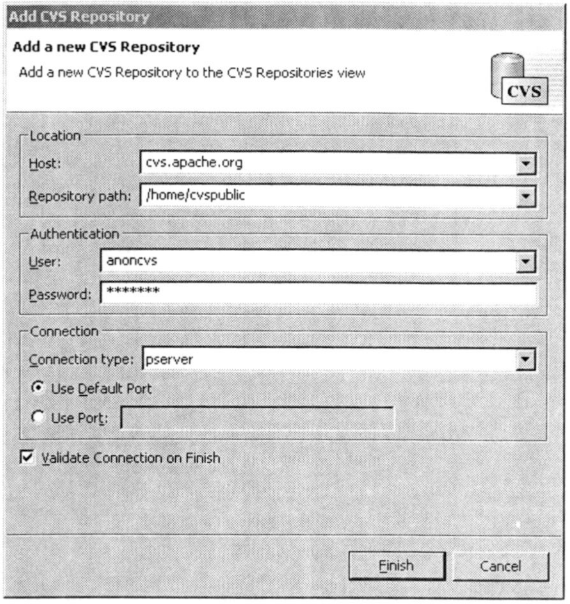

Figure B-5. Eclipse Add CVS Repository dialog box

Expanding the new repository node reveals a Branch, HEAD, and Versions node. You can use the HEAD node to check out and create a new Eclipse project. Expand the HEAD node and locate the desired module from the list of available modules. Right-clicking the desired module reveals the Check Out as Project and the Check Out As options. The Check Out as Project option automatically checks the module out to the Eclipse workspace. If an alternative location is required, use the Check Out As option. Either option will copy the files from the CVS Repository, create a project, and add the project to the navigator.

Once the project is added to the navigator, the CVS commands are available as a submenu on the Team context menu. You can update the project by right-clicking the project and choosing Team ➤ Update.

NetBeans

NetBeans is another popular Open Source Java IDE. NetBeans is available from http://www.netbeans.org.

NetBeans integrates with CVS and other version-control software by mounting the CVS Repository as a virtual file system. To mount a Repository select Versioning ➤ Mount Version Control ➤ CVS from the main menu. NetBeans uses a wizard to configure the connection. The first step in the wizard is to choose a local directory to contain the source code. The second step prompts you for connection string information (see Figure B-6).

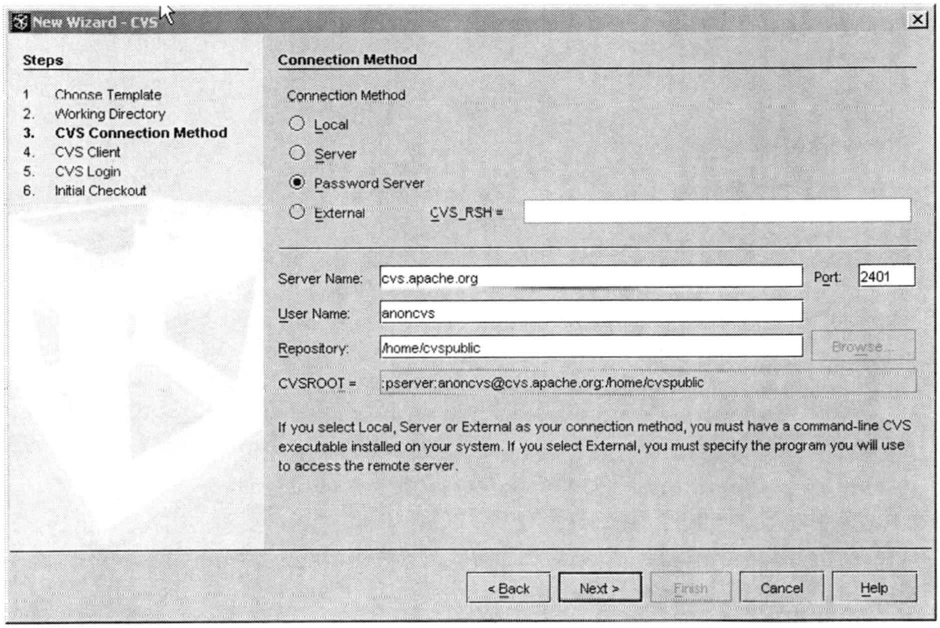

Figure B-6. NetBeans New wizard—CVS

NetBeans provides both a command-line and built-in CVS client. The third step allows you to choose the client interface of choice. The built-in client only works with pserver, which most Open Source CVS servers provide. The fifth step prompts you for a password and includes a login button for checking authentication. If login fails, a message describing the problem will appear under the Password text field. The last step in the wizard asks if an initial checkout should occur. Checking the Check Out a Copy of the Repository Files to Your Working Directory option will copy the contents of the module locally. Checking the box is highly recommended. The checkout command requires some additional information such as the desired module in the CVS Repository, so the Arguments for Checkout Command dialog box will prompt you for the additional information. Enter the desired module name in the Checkout text field (see Figure B-7).

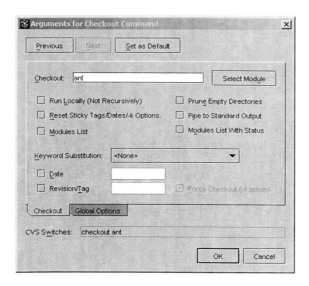

Figure B-6. NetBeans Arguments for Checkout Command dialog box

The CVS commands are available in the CVS submenu by right-clicking and opening the context menu of the mounted file system or the directories and files contained within it. So to update the files with the most current version in the CVS Repository right-click and choose CVS ➤ Update. Some of the CVS commands may have additional arguments. To change the arguments, hold down the Ctrl key while selecting the CVS menu item.

Conclusion

Having access to a project's source code is one of the most compelling reasons for using Open Source. Although most projects provide source bundles in either ZIP or TAR formats, you can gain insight into the project's direction and allow for contribution if you have access to the current source code. If you're familiar with a CVS client, then you know that commands and architecture are necessary for interacting with CVS Repositories.

Further Reading

- ***Open Source Development with CVS* by Karl Fogel:** See
  `http://cvsbook.red-bean.com/cvsbook.html`.

- ***Introduction to CVS* by Jim Blandy:** See `http://www.cvshome.org/docs/`
  `blandy.html`.

- **CVS manual:** See `http://www.cvshome.org/docs/manual/cvs-1.11.10/`
  `cvs.html`.

Index

Symbols

A

W

WAR target, 412, 416–417

web applications

    Ant target responsible for packaging, 416–417

    configuring layout elements, 422–424

    creating common page layouts with Tiles, 417–419

    master layout

        defining, 422, 431

        planning, 419–421

        sample TCMS layout diagram, 419

    setting up with JSTL and Struts, 411–417

web containers

    collocating JBossWeb and EJB, 164–165

    deploying Axis in, 453–456

web pages for unit test results, 135

web services and mobile clients, 449–480

    about SOAP, 449

    Axis

        about, 453

        converting deploy.wsdd to server-config.wsdd, 462–463

        exposing services, 456–463

        JBoss.NET plug-in with, 465

        response from News service's getNews method, 460–462

        setting up and deploying, 453–456

        TCP Monitor, 463

        viewing list of enabled services, 459–460

        web services client for, 463–464

        web services model, 449–450

developing J2ME applications, 465–480

    about J2ME, 465–466

    application size, 467

    JAD files, 466–467

    listing news titles, 470

    midlet classes for MIDP applications, 471–473

    running in emulator, 480

    source code for NewsDisplayable screen, 473–475

    SyncAgent class, 477–480

    unit testing J2ME, 466

    viewing news item details, 470–471, 475–476

web.xml file

    listing installed web-application contexts in JBoss, 413

    mapping, 414

    sample listing of original, 412

    Tag-Library declaration found in, 415

WEB-INF directory, 411–412

WebLogic application server, 166

WebWork, 408

widgets

    customizing text with StyleText, 513–514

    description of SWT, 492–493

    Details Editor example of custom class, 534–538

    hierarchy of, 494–496

    See also SWT

window layout for Abstracts page, 529–530

wizards in JFace, 552–556

WORA (Write Once Run Anywhere) concept, 153–154

WSDD (web services deployment
    descriptor) files, 457, 459–460,
    462–463

WSDL (web service description language)

    function of, 450

    News Service WSDL sample listing,
        450–452

X

XDoclet

    about, 198–199

    annotating ConferenceEJB.java fields,
        206–210

    Ant tasks organized by, 200

    documenting modules for OJB
        distributions, 360

    downloading, 199

    generating

        automatic files and descriptors,
            201–213

        declarations, action mappings, and
            form validation in, 436

    generating OJB mappings with,
        356–357

loading OJB doclets, 357–360

Middlegen reliance on, 222

module tasks

    Hibernate, 389–391

    annotating POJO, 389–391

    documentation for, 389

    XDoclet jar file, 389

    reducing J2EE overhead in, 152

    tags and namespaces, 200–201,
        208–209

Xindice database, 331

XML:DB initiative for XML databases, 331

XML (eXtensible Markup Language)

    generating HTML reports from,
        118–120

    initial organization of TCMS dataset, 146

    native XML databases, 330–331

    News Service WSDL sample listing,
        450–452

    repository_database.xml, 366

    validation framework in Struts, 441

    XML Open Source projects, 11

    See also kXML; struts-config.xml file

Printed in the United States
134449LV00003B/10/P

9 781590 591253